3D Math Primer for Graphics and Game Development

Fletcher Dunn and Ian Parberry

Wordware Publishing, Inc.

Library of Congress Cataloging-in-Publication Data

Dunn, Fletcher.
  3D math primer for graphics and game development / by Fletcher Dunn and Ian Parberry.
    p.   cm.
  ISBN 1-55622-911-9
  1. Computer graphics.   2. Computer games--Programming.   3. Computer science--Mathematics.
  I. Parberry, Ian.   II. Title.
  T385 .D875   2002
  006.6--dc21   2002004615
                                                                              CIP

© 2002, Wordware Publishing, Inc.

An imprint of Jones and Bartlett Publishers

All Rights Reserved

Jones and Bartlett Publishers, LLC
40 Tall Pine Drive
Sudbury, MA 01776
978-443-5000
info@jbpub.com
www.jbpub.com

Printed in the United States of America

ISBN 10: 1-55622-911-9
ISBN 13: 978-1-55622-911-4
10 9 8 7 6 5 4 3 2 1
0205

Contents

Contents

Contents

Acknowledgments

Fletcher would like to thank his high school senior English teacher. She provided constant encouragement and help with proofreading, even though she wasn't really interested in 3D math. She is also his mom. Fletcher would also like to thank his dad for calling him every day to check on the progress of the book or just to talk. Fletcher would like to thank his boss, Mark Randel, for being an excellent teacher, mentor, and role model. Thanks goes to Chris DeSimone and Mario Merino as well, who (unlike Fletcher) actually have artistic ability and helped out with some of the more tricky diagrams in 3D Studio Max. A special thanks to Allen Bogue, Jeff Mills, Jeff Wilkerson, Matt Bogue, Todd Poynter, and Nathan Peugh for their opinions and feedback.

Ian would like to thank his wife for not threatening to cause him physical harm when he took multiple weekends away from his family duties to work on this book. He would like to thank his children for not whining *too* loudly. Also, thanks to the students of his Advanced Game Programming class at the University of North Texas in Spring 2002 for commenting on parts of this book in class. Oh, and thanks to Keith Smiley for the dead sheep.

Both authors would like to extend a very special thanks to Jim and Wes at Wordware for being very patient and providing *multiple* extensions when it was inconvenient for them to do so.

Chapter 1
Introduction

1.1 What is 3D Math?

This book is about 3D math, the study of the mathematics behind the geometry of a 3D world. 3D math is related to computational geometry, which deals with solving geometric problems algorithmically. 3D math and computational geometry have applications in a wide variety of fields that use computers to model or reason about the world in 3D, such as graphics, games, simulation, robotics, virtual reality, and cinematography.

This book covers theory and practice in C++. The "theory" part is an explanation of the relationship between math and geometry in 3D. It also serves as a handy reference for techniques and equations. The "practice" part illustrates how these concepts can be applied in code. The programming language used is C++, but in principle, the theoretical techniques from this book can be applied in any programming language.

This book *is not* just about computer graphics, simulation, or even computational geometry. However, if you plan to study those subjects, you will definitely need the information in this book.

1.2 Why You Should Read This Book

If you want to learn about 3D math in order to program games or graphics, then this book is for you. There are many books out there that promise to teach you how to make a game or put cool pictures up on the screen, so why should you read *this* particular book? This book offers several unique advantages over other books about games or graphics programming:

- **A unique topic**. This book fills a gap that has been left by other books on graphics, linear algebra, simulation, and programming. It is an *introductory* book, meaning we have focused our efforts on providing thorough coverage on fundamental 3D concepts — topics that are normally glossed over in a few quick pages or relegated to an appendix in other publications (because, after all, you already know all this stuff). Our book is definitely the book you should read *first*, before buying that "Write a 3D Video Game in 21 Days" book. This book is not only an introductory book, it is also a reference book — a "toolbox" of equations and techniques that you can browse through on a first reading and then revisit when the need for a specific tool arises.

- **A unique approach**. We take a three-pronged approach to the subject matter: *math*, *geometry*, and *code*. The *math* part is the equations and numbers. This is where most books stop. Of course, the math is important, but to make it powerful, you have to have good intuition about how the math connects with the *geometry*. We will show you not just one but *multiple* ways to relate the numbers with the geometry on a variety of subjects, such as orientation in 3D, matrix multiplication, and quaternions. After the intuition comes the implementation; the *code* part is the practical part. We show real usable code that makes programming 3D math as easy as possible.

- **Unique authors**. Our combined experience brings together academic authority with in-the-trenches practical advice. Fletcher Dunn has six years of professional game programming experience and several titles under his belt on a variety of gaming platforms. He is currently employed as the principal programmer at Terminal Reality and is the lead programmer on *BloodRayne*. Dr. Ian Parberry has 18 years of experience in research and teaching in academia. This is his sixth book, his third on game programming. He is currently a tenured full professor in the Department of Computer Sciences at the University of North Texas. He is nationally known as one of the pioneers of game programming in higher education and has been teaching game programming to undergraduates at the University of North Texas since 1993.

- **Unique pictures**. You cannot learn about a subject like 3D by just reading text or looking at equations. You need pictures, and this book has plenty of them. Flipping through, you will notice that in many sections there is one on almost every page. In other words, we don't just *tell* you something about 3D math, we *show* you. You'll also notice that pictures often appear beside equations or code. Again, this is a result of our unique approach that combines mathematical theory, geometric intuition, and practical implementation.

- **Unique code**. Unlike the code in some other books, the classes in this book are not designed to provide every possible operation you could ever want. They *are* designed to perform specific functions very well and to be easy to understand and difficult to misuse. Because of their simple and focused semantics, you can write a line of code and have it work the *first* time, without twiddling minus signs, swapping sines and cosines, transposing matrices, or otherwise employing "random engineering" until it looks right. Many other books exhibit a common class design flaw of providing *every* possible operation when only a few are actually useful.

- **A unique writing style**. Our style is informal and entertaining, but formal and precise when clarity is important. Our goal is not to amuse you with unrelated anecdotes, but to engage you with interesting examples.

- **A unique web page**. This book does not come with a CD. CDs are expensive and cannot be updated once they are released. Instead, we have created a companion web page, `gamemath.com`. There you will be able to experience interactive demos of some of the concepts that are the hardest to grasp from text and diagrams. You can also download the code (including any bug fixes!) and other useful utilities, find the answers to the exercises, and check out links to other sites concerning 3D math, graphics, and programming.

1.3 What You Should Know Before Reading This Book

The *theory* part of this book assumes a prior knowledge of basic algebra and geometry, such as:

- Manipulating algebraic expressions
- Algebraic laws, such as the associative and distributive laws
- Functions and variables
- Basic 2D Euclidian geometry

In addition, some prior exposure to trigonometry is useful, but not required. A brief review of some key mathematical concepts is included in Appendix A.

For the *practice* part, you need to understand some basics of programming in C++:

- Program flow control constructs
- Functions and parameters
- Object-oriented programming and class design

No specific compiler or target platform is assumed. No "advanced" C++ language features are used. The few language features that you may be unfamiliar with, such as operator overloading and reference arguments, will be explained as they are needed.

1.4 Overview

- **Chapter 1** is the introduction, which you have almost finished reading. Hopefully, it has explained for whom this book is written and why we think you should read the rest of it.
- **Chapter 2** explains the Cartesian coordinate system in 2D and 3D and discusses how the Cartesian coordinate system is used to locate points in space.
- **Chapter 3** discusses examples of coordinate spaces and how they are nested in a hierarchy.
- **Chapter 4** introduces vectors and explains the geometric and mathematical interpretations of vectors.
- **Chapter 5** discusses mathematical operations on vectors and explains the geometric interpretation of each operation.
- **Chapter 6** provides a usable C++ 3D vector class.
- **Chapter 7** introduces matrices from a mathematical and geometric perspective and shows how matrices can be used to perform linear transformations.
- **Chapter 8** discusses different types of linear transformations and their corresponding matrices in detail.
- **Chapter 9** covers a few more interesting and useful properties of matrices.
- **Chapter 10** discusses different techniques for representing orientation and angular displacement in 3D.

- **Chapter 11** provides C++ classes for performing the math from Chapters 7 to 10.
- **Chapter 12** introduces a number of geometric primitives and discusses how to represent and manipulate them mathematically.
- **Chapter 13** presents an assortment of useful tests that can be performed on geometric primitives.
- **Chapter 14** discusses how to store and manipulate triangle meshes and presents a C++ class designed to hold triangle meshes.
- **Chapter 15** is a survey of computer graphics with special emphasis on key mathematical points.
- **Chapter 16** discusses a number of techniques for visibility determination, an important issue in computer graphics.
- **Chapter 17** reminds you to visit our web page and gives some suggestions for further reading.

Chapter 2
The Cartesian Coordinate System

This chapter describes the basic concepts of 3D math. It is divided into three main sections.

- Section 2.1 is about 1D mathematics, the mathematics of counting and measuring. The main concepts introduced are:
  - The math concepts of natural numbers, integers, rational numbers, and real numbers.
  - The relationship between the naturals, integers, rationals and reals on one hand and the programming language concepts of **short**, **int**, **float**, and **double** on the other hand.
  - The First Law of Computer Graphics.
- Section 2.2 introduces 2D Cartesian mathematics, the mathematics of flat surfaces. The main concepts introduced are:
  - The 2D Cartesian plane
  - The origin
  - The *x*- and *y*-axes
  - Orienting the axes in 2D
  - Locating a point in 2D space using Cartesian (*x*,*y*) coordinates
- Section 2.3 extends 2D Cartesian math into 3D. The main concepts introduced are:
  - The *z*-axis
  - The *xy*, *xz*, and *yz* planes
  - Locating a point in 3D space using Cartesian (*x*,*y*,*z*) coordinates
  - Left- and right-handed coordinate systems

3D math is all about measuring locations, distances, and angles precisely and mathematically in 3D space. The most frequently used framework to perform such measurements is called the *Cartesian coordinate system*. Cartesian mathematics was invented by, and named after, a brilliant French philosopher, physicist, physiologist, and mathematician named René Descartes who lived from 1596 to 1650. Descartes is not just famous for inventing Cartesian mathematics, which at the time was a stunning unification of algebra and geometry. He is also well known for taking a pretty good stab at answering the question "How do I know something is true?" This question has kept generations of philosophers happily employed and does not necessarily involve dead sheep (which will disturbingly be a central feature of the next section), unless you really want it to. Descartes rejected the answers proposed by the ancient Greeks, which are *ethos* (roughly, "because I told you so"), *pathos* ("because it would be nice"), and *logos* ("because it makes sense"), and set about figuring it out for himself with a pencil and paper.

2.1   1D Mathematics

You're reading this book because you want to know about 3D mathematics, so you're probably wondering why we're bothering to talk about 1D math. Well, there are a couple of issues about number systems and counting that we would like to clear up before we get to 3D.

Figure 2.1: One dead sheep

Natural numbers, often called *counting numbers*, were invented millennia ago, probably to keep track of dead sheep. The concept of "one sheep" came easily (see Figure 2.1), then "two sheep" and "three sheep," but people very quickly became convinced that this was too much work. They gave up counting at some point and invariably began using "many sheep." Different cultures gave up at different points, depending on their threshold of boredom. Eventually, civilization expanded to the point where we could afford to have people sitting around thinking about numbers instead of doing more survival-oriented tasks, such as killing sheep and eating them. These savvy thinkers immortalized the concept of zero (no sheep), and while they didn't get around to naming *all* of the natural numbers, they figured out various systems whereby we *could* name them if we really wanted to, using digits such as "1", "2", etc. (or if you were Roman, "M", "X", "I," etc.). Mathematics was born.

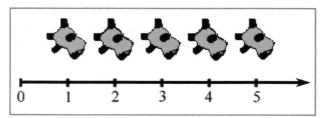

Figure 2.2: A number line for the natural numbers

The habit of lining sheep up in a row so that they can easily be counted leads to the concept of a *number line*, that is, a line with the numbers marked off at regular intervals, as in Figure 2.2. This line can, in principle, go on for as long as we wish, but to avoid boredom we have stopped at five sheep and put on an arrowhead to let you know that the line can continue. Clear thinkers can visualize it going off to infinity, but historical purveyors of dead sheep probably gave this concept little thought, outside of their dreams and fevered imaginings.

At some point in history it was probably realized that you can sometimes, if you are a particularly fast talker, sell a sheep that you don't actually own, thus, simultaneously inventing the important concepts of *debt* and *negative numbers*. Having sold this putative sheep, you would in fact own "negative one" sheep. This would lead to the discovery of *integers*, which consist of the natural numbers and their negative counterparts. The corresponding number line for integers is shown in Figure 2.3.

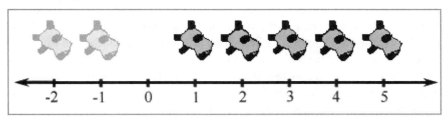

Figure 2.3: A number line for integers (note the ghost sheep for negative numbers)

The concept of poverty probably predated that of debt, leading to a growing number of people who could afford to purchase only half a dead sheep, or perhaps only a quarter. This lead to a burgeoning use of fractional numbers, consisting of one integer divided by another, such as 2/3 or 111/27. Mathematicians called these *rational numbers*, and they fit in the number line in the obvious places between the integers. At some point, people became lazy and invented decimal notation, like writing "3.1415" instead of the longer and more tedious 31415/10000.

After a while, it was noticed that some numbers that appear to turn up in everyday life are not expressible as rational numbers. The classic example is the ratio of the circumference of a circle to its diameter, usually denoted as π (pronounced "pi"). These are the so-called *real numbers*, which include rational numbers and numbers such as π that would, if expressed in decimal form, require an infinite number of decimal places. The mathematics of real numbers is regarded by many to be the most important area of mathematics, and since it is the basis for most forms of engineering, it can be credited with creating much of modern civilization. The cool thing about real numbers is that while rational numbers are countable (that is, placed into one-to-one correspondence with the natural numbers), real numbers are uncountable. The study of natural numbers and integers is called *discrete mathematics*, and the study of real numbers is called *continuous mathematics*.

The truth is, however, that real numbers are nothing more than a polite fiction. They are a relatively harmless delusion, as any reputable physicist will tell you. The universe seems to be not only discrete, but also finite. If there are a finite amount of discrete things in the universe, as currently appears to be the case, then it follows that we can only count to a certain fixed number. Thereafter, we run out of things to count — not only do we run out of dead sheep, but toasters, mechanics, and telephone sanitizers also. It follows that we can describe the universe using only discrete mathematics, and requiring the use of only a finite subset of the natural numbers at that. (Large, yes, but finite.) Somewhere there may be an alien civilization with a level of technology exceeding ours that has never heard of continuous mathematics, the Fundamental Theorem of Calculus, or even the concept of infinity; even if we persist, they will firmly but politely insist on having no truck with π, being perfectly happy to build toasters, bridges, skyscrapers, mass transit, and starships using 3.14159 (or perhaps 3.14159265358979323846426433832795, if they are fastidious) instead.

So why do we use continuous mathematics? It is a useful tool that allows us to do engineering, but the real world is, despite the cognitive dissonance involved in using the term "real," discrete. How does that affect you, the designer of a 3D computer-generated virtual reality? The computer is by its very nature discrete and finite, and you are more likely to run into the consequences of the discreteness and finiteness during its creation that you are likely to in the real world. C++ gives you a variety of different number forms that you can use for counting or measuring in your virtual world. These are the **short**, the **int**, the **float** and the **double**, which can be described as follows (assuming the current PC technology). The **short** is a 16-bit integer that can store 65,536 different values, which means that "many sheep" for a 16-bit computer is 65,537. This sounds like a lot of sheep, but it isn't adequate for measuring distances inside any reasonable kind of virtual reality that take people more than a few minutes to explore. The **int** is a 32-bit integer that can store up to 4,294,967,296 different values, which is probably enough for your purposes. The **float** is a 32-bit value that can store a subset of the rationals — 4,294,967,296 of them, the details not being important here. The **double** is similar, though using 64 bits instead of 32. We will return to this discussion in Section 6.3.1.

The bottom line in choosing to count and measure in your virtual world using **int**s, **float**s, or **double**s is not, as some misguided people would have it, a matter of choosing between discrete **short**s and **int**s versus continuous **float**s and **double**s. It is more a matter of precision. They are all discrete in the end. Older books on computer graphics will advise you to use integers because floating-point hardware is slower than integer hardware, but this is no longer the case. So which should you choose? At this point, it is probably best to introduce you to the First Law of Computer Graphics and leave you to think about it:

The First Law of Computer Graphics: If it looks right, it *is* right.

We will be doing a large amount of trigonometry in this book. Trigonometry involves real numbers, such as π, and real-valued functions, such as sine and cosine (which we'll get to later). Real numbers are a convenient fiction, so we will continue to use them. How do you know this is true? You know because, Descartes notwithstanding, we told you so, because it would be nice, and because it makes sense.

2.2 2D Cartesian Mathematics

You have probably used 2D Cartesian coordinate systems even if you have never heard the term *Cartesian* before. *Cartesian* is mostly just a fancy word for rectangular. If you have ever looked at the floor plans of a house, used a street map, seen a football game, or played chess, you have been exposed to 2D Cartesian coordinate space.

2.2.1 An Example: The Hypothetical City of Cartesia

Let's imagine a fictional city named Cartesia. When the Cartesia city planners were laying out the streets, they were very particular, as illustrated in the map of Cartesia in Figure 2.4.

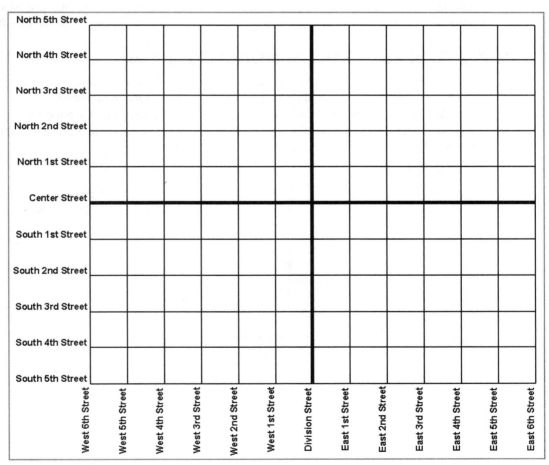

Figure 2.4: Map of the hypothetical city of Cartesia

As you can see from the map, Center Street runs east-west through the middle of town. All other east-west streets (parallel to Center Street) are named based on whether they are north or south of Center Street and how far away they are from Center Street. Examples of streets which run east-west are North 3rd Street and South 15th Street.

The other streets in Cartesia run north-south. Division Street runs north-south through the middle of town. All other north-south streets (parallel to Division Street) are named based on whether they are east or west of Division street, and how far away they are from Division Street. So we have streets such as East 5th Street and West 22nd Street.

The naming convention used by the city planners of Cartesia may not be creative, but it certainly is practical. Even without looking at the map, it is easy to find the doughnut shop at North 4th and West 2nd. It's also easy to determine how far you will have to drive when traveling from one place to another. For example, to go from that doughnut shop at North 4th and West 2nd to the police station at South 3rd and Division, you would travel seven blocks south and two blocks east.

2.2.2 Arbitrary 2D Coordinate Spaces

Before Cartesia was built, there was nothing but a large flat area of land. The city planners arbitrarily decided where the center of town would be, which direction to make the roads run, how far apart to space the roads, etc. Much like the Cartesia city planners laid down the city streets, we can establish a 2D Cartesian coordinate system anywhere we want — on a piece of paper, a chessboard, a chalkboard, a slab of concrete, or a football field.

Figure 2.5 shows a diagram of a 2D Cartesian coordinate system.

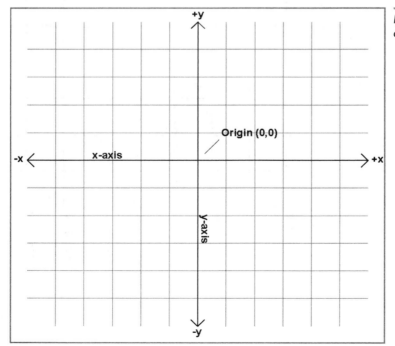

Figure 2.5: A 2D Cartesian coordinate space

As illustrated in Figure 2.5, a 2D Cartesian coordinate space is defined by two pieces of information:

■ Every 2D Cartesian coordinate space has a special location, called the *origin*, which is the "center" of the coordinate system. The origin is analogous to the center of the city in Cartesia.

■ Every 2D Cartesian coordinate space has two straight lines that pass through the origin. Each line is known as an *axis* and extends infinitely in two opposite directions. The two axes are perpendicular to each other. (Actually, they don't *have* to be, but most of the coordinate systems we will look at will have perpendicular axes.) The two axes are analogous to Center and Division streets in Cartesia. The grid lines in the diagram are analogous to the other streets in Cartesia.

At this point, it is important to highlight a few significant differences between Cartesia and an abstract mathematical 2D space:

■ The city of Cartesia has official city limits. Land outside of the city limits is not considered part of Cartesia. A 2D coordinate space, however, extends infinitely. Even though we usually only concern ourselves with a small area within the plane defined by the coordinate space, this plane, in theory, is boundless. In addition, the roads in Cartesia only go a certain distance (perhaps to the city limits), and then they stop. Our axes and grid lines, on the other hand, each extend potentially infinitely in two directions.

■ In Cartesia, the roads have thickness. Lines in an abstract coordinate space have location and (possibly infinite) length, but no real thickness.

■ In Cartesia, you can only drive on the roads. In an abstract coordinate space, *every* point in the plane of the coordinate space is part of the coordinate space, not just the area on the "roads." The grid lines are only drawn for reference.

In Figure 2.5, the horizontal axis is called the x-axis, with positive x pointing to the right. The vertical axis is the y-axis, with positive y pointing up. This is the customary orientation for the axes in a diagram. Note that "horizontal" and "vertical" are terms that are inappropriate for many 2D spaces that arise in practice. For example, imagine the coordinate space on top of a desk — both axes are "horizontal," and neither axis is really "vertical."

The city planners of Cartesia could have made Center Street run north-south instead of east-west. Or they could have placed it at a completely arbitrary angle. (For example, Long Island, New York is reminiscent of Cartesia, where for convenience the streets numbered "1st Street," "2nd Street," etc., run across the island and the avenues numbered "1st Avenue," "2nd Avenue," etc., run along its long axis. The geographic orientation of the long axis of the island is an arbitrary freak of nature.) In the same way, we are free to place our axes in any way that is convenient to us. We must also decide for each axis which direction we consider to be positive. For example, when working with images on a computer screen, it is customary to use the coordinate system shown in Figure 2.6. Notice that the origin is in the upper left-hand corner, $+x$ points to the right, and $+y$ points *down* rather than up.

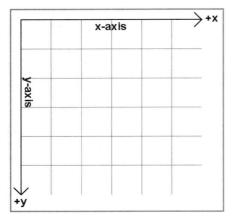

Figure 2.6: Screen coordinate space

Unfortunately, when Cartesia was being laid out, the only mapmakers were in the neighboring town of Dyslexia. The minor-level functionary who sent the contract out to bid neglected to take into account that the dyslexic mapmaker was equally likely to draw his maps with north pointing up, down, left, or right; although he always drew the east-west line at right angles to the north-south line, he often got east and west backward. When his boss realized that the job had gone to the lowest bidder, who happened to live in Dyslexia, many hours were spent in committee meetings trying to figure out what to do. The paperwork had been done, the purchase order had been issued, and bureaucracies being what they are, it would be too expensive and time-consuming to cancel the order. Still, nobody had any idea what the mapmaker would deliver. A committee was hastily formed.

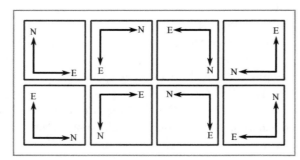

Figure 2.7: Possible map axis orientations in 2D

The committee quickly decided that there were only eight possible orientations that the mapmaker could deliver, shown in Figure 2.7. In the best of all possible worlds, he would deliver a map oriented as shown in the top-left rectangle, with north pointing to the top of the page and east to the right, which is what people usually expect. A subcommittee decided to name this the *normal orientation*.

After the meeting had lasted a few hours and tempers were beginning to fray, it was decided that the other three variants shown in the top row of Figure 2.7 were probably acceptable too, because they could be transformed to the normal orientation by placing a pin in the center of the page and rotating the map around the pin. (You can do this too by placing this book flat on a table and turning it.) Many hours were wasted by tired functionaries putting pins into various places in the maps shown in the second row of Figure 2.7, but no matter how fast they twirled them, they couldn't seem to transform them to the normal orientation. It wasn't until everybody important had given up and gone home that a tired intern, assigned to clean up the used coffee cups, noticed that the maps in the second row could be transformed into the normal orientation by holding them up against a light and viewing them from the back. (You can do this too by holding Figure 2.7 up to the light and viewing it from the back. You'll have to turn it too of course.) The writing was backward too, but it was decided that if Leonardo da Vinci (1452-1519) could handle backward writing in the 15th century, then the citizens of Cartesia, though by no means his intellectual equivalent (probably due to daytime TV), could probably handle it in the 21st century also.

In summary, no matter what orientation we choose for the *x* and *y* axes, we can always rotate the coordinate space around so that +*x* points to our right, and +*y* points up. For our example of screen-space coordinates, imagine turning upside down and looking at the screen from behind the monitor. In any case, these rotations do not distort the original shape of the coordinate system (even though we may be looking at it upside down or reversed). So in one particular sense, all 2D coordinate systems are "equal." Later, we will discover the surprising fact that this is not the case in 3D.

2.2.3 Specifying Locations in 2D Using Cartesian Coordinates

A coordinate space is a framework for specifying location precisely and mathematically. To define the location of a point in a Cartesian coordinate space, we use Cartesian *coordinates*. In 2D, two numbers are used to specify a location. (The fact that we use two numbers to describe the location of a point is the reason it's called *two*-dimensional space. In 3D, we will use three numbers.) These two numbers are named *x* and *y*. Analogous to the street names in Cartesia, each number specifies which side of the origin the point is on, and how far away the point is from the origin in a given direction. More precisely, each number is the *signed distance* (that is, positive in one direction and negative in the other) to one of the axes, measured along a line parallel to the other axis. This may sound complicated, but it's really very simple. Figure 2.8 shows how points are located in 2D Cartesian space.

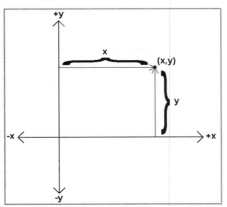

Figure 2.8: How to locate a point using 2D Cartesian coordinates

As shown in Figure 2.8, the x coordinate designates the signed distance from the point to the y-axis, measured along a line parallel to the x-axis. Likewise, the y coordinate designates the signed distance from the point to the x-axis, measured along a line parallel to the y-axis. By "signed distance," we mean that distance in one direction is considered positive, and distance in the opposite direction is considered negative.

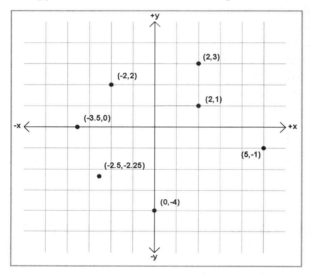

Figure 2.9: Example points labeled with 2D Cartesian coordinates

The standard notation that is used when writing a pair of coordinates is to surround the numbers in parentheses, with the x value listed first, like (x, y). Figure 2.9 shows several points and their Cartesian coordinates. Notice that the points to the left of the y-axis have negative x values, while those to the right of the y-axis have positive x values. Likewise, points with positive y are located above the x-axis, and points with negative y are below the x-axis. Also notice that *any* point can be specified, not just the points at grid line intersections. You should study this figure until you are sure that you understand the pattern.

2.3 From 2D to 3D

Now that we understand how Cartesian space works in 2D, let's leave the flat 2D world and begin to think about 3D space. It might seem at first that 3D space is only 50 percent more complicated than 2D. After all, it's just *one* more dimension, and we already had *two*. Unfortunately, this is not the case. For a variety of reasons, 3D space is *more* than incrementally more difficult for humans to visualize and describe than 2D space. (One possible reason for this difficulty could be that our physical world is 3D, while illustrations in books and on computer screens are 2D.) It is frequently the case that a problem that is "easy" to solve in 2D is much more difficult or even undefined in 3D. Still, many concepts in 2D do extend directly into 3D, and we will frequently use 2D to establish an understanding of a problem and develop a solution, and then extend that solution into 3D.

2.3.1 Extra Dimension, Extra Axis

In 3D, we require three axes to establish a coordinate system. The first two axes are called the x-axis and y-axis, just as in 2D. (However, it is not accurate to say that these are the *same* as the 2D axes. We will discuss this more later.) We call the third axis (predictably) the z-axis. Usually, we set things up so that all axes are mutually perpendicular. That is, each one is perpendicular to the others. Figure 2.10 shows an example of a 3D coordinate space:

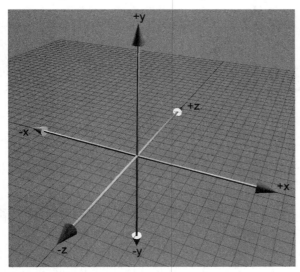

Figure 2.10: A 3D Cartesian coordinate space

As discussed in Section 2.2.2, it is customary in 2D for +x to point to the right and +y to point up. (Sometimes +y may point down, but in either case, the x-axis is horizontal and the y-axis is vertical.) These are fairly standard conventions. However, in 3D, the conventions for arrangement of the axes in diagrams and the assignment of the axes onto physical dimensions (left, right, up, down, forward, back) are not very standardized. Different authors and fields of study have different conventions. In Section 2.3.4 we will discuss the conventions used in this book.

As mentioned earlier, it is not entirely appropriate to say that the x-axis and y-axis in 3D are the "same" as the x-axis and y-axis in 2D. In 3D, any pair of axes defines a plane that contains the two axes and is perpendicular to the third axis. (For example, the plane containing the x- and y-axes is the xy plane, which is perpendicular to the z-axis. Likewise, the xz plane is perpendicular to the y-axis, and the yz plane is perpendicular to the x-axis.) We can consider any of these planes a 2D Cartesian coordinate space in its own right. For example, if we assign +x, +y, and +z to point right, up, and forward, respectively, then the 2D coordinate space of the "ground" is the xz plane.

2.3.2 Specifying Locations in 3D

In 3D, points are specified using three numbers, x, y, and z, which give the signed distance to the yz, xz, and xy planes, respectively. This distance is measured along a line parallel to the axis. For example, the x-value is the signed distance to the yz plane, measured along a line parallel to the *x*-axis. Don't let this precise definition of how points in 3D are located confuse you. It is a straight-forward extension of the process for 2D, as shown in Figure 2.11:

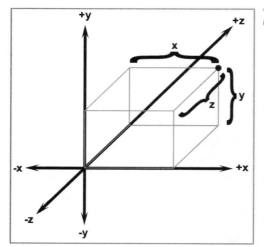

Figure 2.11: Locating points in 3D

2.3.3 Left-handed vs. Right-handed Coordinate Spaces

As we discussed in Section 2.2.2, all 2D coordinate systems are "equal" in the sense that for any two 2D coordinate spaces A and B, we can rotate coordinate space A so that +*x* and +*y* point in the same direction as they do in coordinate space B. (We are assuming perpendicular axes.) Let's examine this idea in more detail.

Figure 2.5 shows the "standard" 2D coordinate space. Notice that the difference between this coordinate space and "screen" coordinate space shown in Figure 2.6 is that the *y*-axis points in opposite directions. However, imagine rotating Figure 2.6 clockwise 180° so that +*y* points up and +*x* points to the left. Now rotate it by "turning the page" and viewing the diagram from behind. Notice that now the axes are oriented in the "standard" directions like in Figure 2.5. No matter how many times we flip an axis, we can always find a way to rotate things back into the standard orientation.

Let's see how this idea extends into 3D. Examine Figure 2.10 once more. Notice that +*z* points into the page. Does it have to be this way? What if we made +*z* point out of the page? This is certainly allowed, so let's flip the *z*-axis.

Now can we rotate the coordinate system around so that things line up with the original coordinate system? As it turns out, we cannot. We can rotate things to line up *two* axes at a time, but the third axis always points in the wrong direction! (If you have trouble visualizing this, don't worry. In a moment we will illustrate this principle in more concrete terms.)

All 3D coordinate spaces are *not* equal; some pairs of coordinate systems cannot be rotated to line up with each other. There are exactly two distinct types of 3D coordinate spaces: *left-handed* coordinate spaces and *right-handed* coordinate spaces. If two coordinate spaces have the same handedness, then they can be rotated such that the axes are aligned. If they are of opposite handedness, then this is not possible.

What exactly do "left-handed" and "right-handed" mean? First, let's look at a simple and intuitive way to identify the handedness of a particular coordinate system. The easiest and most illustrative way to identify the handedness of a particular coordinate system is to use, well, your hands! With your left hand, make an "L" with your thumb and index finger. (You may have to put the book down….) Your thumb should be pointing to your right, and your index finger should be pointing up. Now extend your third finger so it points directly forward. (This may require some dexterity — don't do this in public or you may offend someone!) You have just formed a left-handed coordinate system. Your thumb, index finger, and third finger point in the +*x*, +*y*, and +*z* directions, respectively. This is shown in Figure 2.12.

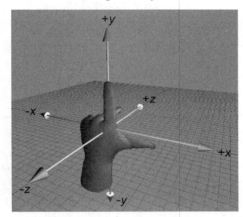

Figure 2.12: Left-handed coordinate space

Now perform the same experiment with your right hand. Notice that your index finger still points up, and your third finger points forward. However, with your right hand, your thumb will point to the *left*. This is a right-handed coordinate system. Again, your thumb, index finger, and third finger point in the +*x*, +*y*, and +*z* directions, respectively. A right-handed coordinate system is shown in Figure 2.13.

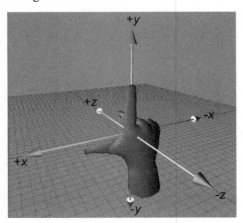

Figure 2.13: Right-handed coordinate space

Try as you might, you cannot rotate your hands into a position so that all three fingers simultaneously point the same direction on both hands. (Bending your fingers is not allowed....)

When looking toward the origin from...	Clockwise rotation in a left-handed coordinate space rotates...	Clockwise rotation in a right-handed coordinate space rotates...
+x	+y toward +z +z toward –y –y toward –z –z toward +y	+y toward –z –z toward –y –y toward +z +z toward +y
+y	+x toward –z –z toward –x –x toward +z +z toward +x	+x toward +z +z toward –x –x toward –z –z toward +x
+z	+x toward +y +y toward –x –x toward –y –y toward +x	+x toward –y –y toward –x –x toward +y +y toward +x

Figure 2.14: Comparison of left- and right-handed coordinate systems

Now that we have discussed the intuitive definition of left- and right-handed coordinate systems, let's discuss a more technical one based on clockwise rotation. Study the table shown in Figure 2.14. To understand how to read this table, examine the first row. Imagine that you are looking at the origin from the positive end of the x-axis. (You are facing the –x direction.) Now imagine rotating the y- and z-axes clockwise about the x-axis. In a left-handed coordinate system, the positive end of the y-axis rotates toward the positive end of the z-axis and the positive end of the z-axis rotates toward the negative end of the y-axis, etc. This situation is illustrated in Figure 2.15.

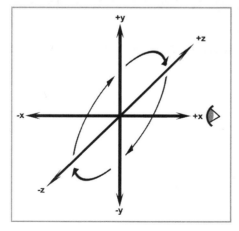

Figure 2.15: Viewing a left-handed coordinate space from the positive end of the x-axis

In a right-handed coordinate system, the opposite occurs: the positive end of the *y*-axis rotates toward the negative end of the *z*-axis, etc. The difference lies in which directions are considered "positive." We are performing the same rotation in both cases.

Any left-handed coordinate system can be transformed into a right-handed coordinate system, or vice versa. The easiest way to do this is by swapping the positive and negative ends of one axis. Notice that if we flip *two* axes, it is the same as rotating the coordinate space 180° about the third axis, which does not change the handedness of the coordinate space.

Both left-handed and right-handed coordinate systems are perfectly valid, and despite what you might read in other books, neither is "better" than the other. People in various fields of study certainly have preferences for one or the other depending on their backgrounds. For example, traditional computer graphics literature typically uses left-handed coordinate systems, whereas the more math-oriented linear algebra people tend to prefer right-handed coordinate systems. Of course, these are gross generalizations, so always check to see what coordinate system is being used. The bottom line, however, is that it's just a matter of a negative sign in the *z* coordinate. So, appealing to the First Law of Computer Graphics in Section 2.1, if you apply a tool, technique, or resource from another book, web page, or article and it doesn't look right, try flipping the sign on the *z* axis.

2.3.4 Some Important Conventions Used in This Book

When designing a 3D virtual world, there are several design decisions that we have to make beforehand, such as left-handed or right-handed coordinate system, which direction is +y, etc. The mapmakers from Dyslexia had to choose from among eight different ways to assign the axes in 2D (see Figure 2.7). In 3D, we have a total of 48 different combinations to choose from. Twenty-four of these combinations are left-handed, and 24 are right-handed.

Different situations can call for different conventions in the sense that certain things can be easier if you adopt the right ones. Usually, however, it is not a major deal as long as you establish the conventions early in your design process and stick to them. All of the basic principles discussed in this book are applicable, regardless of the conventions used. For the most part, all of the equations and techniques given are applicable regardless of convention as well. However, in some cases there are some slight, but critical, differences in application dealing with left-handed versus right-handed coordinate spaces. When those differences arise, they will be pointed out.

In this book, we use a left-handed coordinate system. +*x*, +*y*, and +*z* point right, up, and forward, respectively. This is illustrated in Figure 2.16.

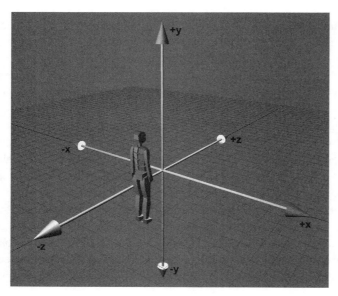

Figure 2.16: The left-handed coordinate system conventions used in this book

In situations where "right" and "forward" are not appropriate terms (for example, when we discuss the world coordinate space), we will assign +*x* to "east" and +*z* to "north."

2.4 Exercises

1. Give the coordinates of the following points:

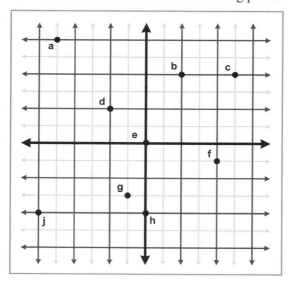

Figure 2.17

2. List the 48 different possible ways that the 3D axes may be assigned to the directions "north," "east," and "up." Identify which of these combinations are left-handed and which are right-handed.

3. In the popular modeling program 3D Studio Max, the default orientation of the axes is for $+x$ to point right, $+y$ to point forward, and $+z$ to point up. Is this a left- or right-handed coordinate space?

Chapter 3

Multiple Coordinate Spaces

This chapter introduces the idea of multiple coordinate systems. It is divided into five main sections.

- Section 3.1 justifies the need for multiple coordinate systems.
- Section 3.2 introduces some common coordinate systems. The main concepts introduced are:
    - World space
    - Object space
    - Camera space
    - Inertial space
- Section 3.3 discusses nested coordinate spaces, commonly used for animating hierarchically segmented objects in 3D space.
- Section 3.4 describes how to specify one coordinate system in terms of another.
- Section 3.5 describes coordinate space transformations. The main concepts are:
    - Transforming between object space and inertial space
    - Transforming between inertial space and world space

In Chapter 2, we discussed how we can establish a coordinate space anywhere we want simply by picking a point to be the origin and deciding on the directions we want the axes to be oriented. We usually don't make these decisions arbitrarily; we form coordinate spaces for specific reasons (one might say "different spaces for different cases"). This chapter gives some examples of common coordinate spaces that are used for graphics and games. We will then discuss how coordinate spaces are nested within other coordinate spaces.

3.1 Why Multiple Coordinate Spaces?

Why do we need more than one coordinate space? After all, any *one* 3D coordinate system extends infinitely and thus contains all points in space. So we could just pick a coordinate space, declare it to be the "world" coordinate space, and all points could be located using this coordinate space. Wouldn't that be easier? In practice, the answer to this is "no." Most people find it more convenient to use different coordinate spaces in different situations.

The reason multiple coordinate spaces are used is that certain pieces of information are only known in the context of a particular reference frame. It is true that, theoretically, all points could be expressed using a single "world" coordinate system. However, for a certain point **a**, we may not know the coordinates of **a** in the "world" coordinate system. However, we may be able to express **a** using some *other* coordinate system. For example, the residents of Cartesia (see Section 2.2.1) use a map of their city with the origin centered, quite sensibly, at the center of town and the axes directed along the cardinal points of the compass. The residents of Dyslexia use a map of their city with the coordinates centered at an arbitrary point and the axes running in some arbitrary direction that probably seemed like a good idea at the time. The citizens of both cities are quite happy with their respective maps, but the State Transportation Engineer assigned the task of running up a budget for the first highway between Cartesia and Dyslexia needs a map showing the details of both cities, which introduces a third coordinate system that is superior to *him*, though not necessarily to anybody else. The major points on both maps need to be translated from the local coordinates of the respective city to the new coordinate system to make the new map.

The concept of multiple coordinate systems has historical precedent. While Aristotle (384-322 BCE), in his books *On the Heavens* and *Physics*, proposed a *geocentric* universe with the Earth at the origin, Aristarchus (ca. 310-230 BCE) proposed a *heliocentric* universe with the Sun at the origin. So we can see that more than two millennia ago the choice of coordinate system was already a hot topic for discussion. The issue wasn't settled for another couple of millennia until Nicholas Copernicus (1473-1543) observed in his book *De Revolutionibus Orbium Coelestium* ("On the Revolutions of the Celestial Orbs") that the orbits of the planets can be explained more simply in a heliocentric universe without all the mucking about with wheels within wheels in a geocentric universe. Of course, not everybody could appreciate the math, which is what got Galileo Galilei (1520-1591) in so much trouble during the Inquisition, since the church had reasons of its own (having little if anything to do with math) for believing in a geocentric universe.

In *Sand-Reckoner,* Archimedes (d. 212 BCE), perhaps motivated by some of the concepts introduced in Section 2.1, developed a notation for writing down very large numbers, numbers much larger than anybody had ever counted to at that time. Instead of choosing to count dead sheep as in Section 2.1, he chose to count the number of grains of sand that it would take to fill the universe. (He estimated that it would take 8×10^{63} grains of sand, but he did not, however, address the question of where we would get the sand from.) In order to make the numbers larger, he chose Aristarchus' revolutionary new heliocentric universe rather than the geocentric universe generally accepted at the time. In a heliocentric universe, the Earth orbits the Sun, in which case the fact that the stars show no parallax means that they must be much farther away than Aristotle could ever have imagined. To make his life more difficult, Archimedes deliberately chose the coordinate system that would produce larger numbers. We will use the direct opposite of his approach. In creating our virtual universe inside the computer, we will choose coordinate systems that make our lives *easier*, not *harder*.

In today's enlightened times, we are accustomed to hearing in the media about *cultural relativism*, which promotes the idea that it is incorrect to consider one culture or belief system or national agenda to be superior to another. It's not too great a leap of the imagination to extend this to what we might call "transformational relativism," that no place, orientation, or coordinate system can be considered superior to others. In a certain sense, that's true, but to paraphrase George Orwell in *Animal Farm*, "All coordinate systems are considered equal, but some are more equal than others." Let's look at some examples of common coordinate systems that you will meet in 3D graphics.

3.2 Some Useful Coordinate Spaces

Different coordinate spaces are needed because some information is only meaningful in a particular context.

3.2.1 World Space

One of the authors of this book wrote in Lewisville, Texas (near Dallas and Fort Worth). More precisely, his location is:

- Latitude: 33° 01' North
- Longitude: 96° 59' West

The other author wrote in Denton, Texas, at:

- Latitude: 33° 11' North
- Longitude: 97° 07' West

These values express our "absolute" position in the world. You don't need to know where Denton, Lewisville, Texas, or even the United States is to use this information because the position is absolute. (The astute reader will note that these coordinates are not Cartesian coordinates, but rather, they are *polar* coordinates. That is not significant for this discussion — we live in a flat 2D world wrapped around a sphere, a concept that supposedly eluded most people until Christopher Columbus verified it experimentally.) The origin, or (0,0) point in the world, was decided for historical reasons to be located on the equator at the same longitude as the Royal Observatory in the town of Greenwich, England.

The *world coordinate system* is a special coordinate system that establishes the "global" reference frame for all other coordinate systems to be specified. In other words, we can express the position of other coordinate spaces in terms of the world coordinate space, but we cannot express the world coordinate space in terms of any larger, outer coordinate space.

In a non-technical sense, the world coordinate system establishes the "largest" coordinate system that we care about, so the world coordinate system need not actually be the whole world. For example, if we wanted to render a view of Cartesia, for all practical purposes Cartesia would be "the world," since we wouldn't care where Cartesia is located (or even if it exists at all). In different situations, your world coordinate space will define a different "world." In Section 4.3.1 we will discuss how "absolute position" is technically undefined. In this book, we will use the term "absolute" to mean "absolute with respect to the largest coordinate space we care about." In other words, "absolute" to us will mean "expressed in the world coordinate space."

The world coordinate space is also known for obvious reasons as the *global* or *universal* coordinate space.

Some examples of questions that are typically asked in world space include questions about initial conditions and the environment, such as:

- What is the position and orientation of each object?
- What is the position and orientation of the camera?
- What is the terrain like in each position in the world? (For example, hills, mountains, buildings, lakes.)
- How does each object get from where it is to where it wants to be? (Motion planning for nonplayer characters.)

3.2.2 Object Space

Object space is the coordinate space associated with a particular object. Every object has its own independent object space. When an object moves or changes orientation, the object coordinate space associated with that object is carried along with it, so it moves or changes orientation too. For example, we all carry our own personal coordinate system around with us. If we were to ask you to "take one step forward," we are giving you an instruction in your object space. (Please forgive us for referring to you as an object.) We have no idea which way you will move in absolute terms. Some of you will move north, some south, and others in different directions. Concepts such as "forward," "back," "left," and "right" are meaningful in object coordinate space. When someone gives you driving directions, sometimes you are told to "turn left" and other times you are told to "go east." "Turn left" is a concept that is expressed in object space, and "east" is expressed in world space.

Locations can be specified in object space as well as directions. For example, if I asked you where the muffler on your car was located, you wouldn't tell me "in Chicago," even if you lived in Chicago. I'm asking where it is *within your car*. In other words, I want you to express the location of your muffler in the object space of your car.

In certain contexts, object space is also known as *modeling space*, since the coordinates for the vertices of a model are expressed in modeling space. It is also known as *body space*.

Some examples of questions that can be asked in object space are:

- Is there another object near me that I need to interact with? (Do I need to kill it?)
- In what direction is it? Is it in front of me? Slightly to my left? To my right? (So I can shoot at it or run in the opposite direction.)

3.2.3 Camera Space

Camera space is the coordinate space associated with an observer. Camera space is similar to screen space except that camera space is a 3D space, whereas screen space is a 2D space. Camera space can be considered a special object space, where the "object" that defines the coordinate space is the camera defining the viewpoint for the scene. In camera space, the camera is at the origin with $+x$ pointing to the right, $+z$ pointing forward (into the screen, or the direction the camera is facing), and $+y$ pointing "up" (not "up" with respect to the world, but "up" with respect to the top of the camera). Figure 3.1 shows a diagram of camera space.

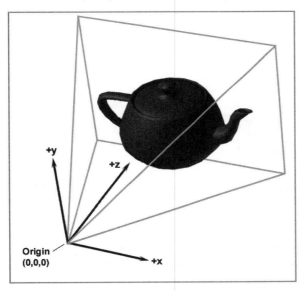

Figure 3.1: Camera space

Note that other books may use different conventions for the orientation of the axes in camera space. In particular, many graphics books that use a right-handed coordinate system point $-z$ into the screen, with $+z$ coming out of the screen toward the viewer.

Typical questions asked in camera space include queries about what is to be drawn on the screen (graphics questions), such as:

- Is a given point in 3D space in front of the camera?
- Is a given point in 3D space on screen, or is it off to the left, right, top, or bottom edges of the camera frustum? (The *frustum* is the pyramid of space that can be seen by the camera.)
- Is an object completely on screen, partially on screen, or completely off screen?
- Which of the two objects is in front of the other? (This is called *occlusion* information.)

Notice that the answers to these questions are critical if we wish to render anything. In Section 15.3 we will learn how 3D camera space is related to 2D screen space through a process known as *projection*.

3.2.4 Inertial Space

Sometimes the right terminology is the key to unlocking a better understanding of a subject. In an attempt to simplify the transformations between world and object space, we will use a new coordinate space called the *inertial* coordinate space, which is in a certain sense "halfway" between object space and world space. The origin of inertial space is the same as the origin of the *object* space, and the axes of inertial space are parallel with the axes of *world* space. Figure 3.2 illustrates this principle in 2D. (Notice that we have chosen to consider the point between the robot's feet as the origin of the robot's object space, rather than the robot's center of mass.)

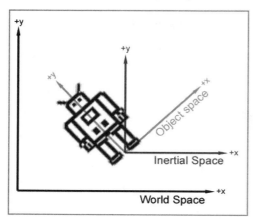

Figure 3.2: Object, inertial, and world spaces

Why is inertial space interesting? To transform a point between object space and inertial space requires only *rotation*, and to transform a point between inertial space and world space requires only a change of location, or a *translation*. Thinking about these two things independently is easier than trying to cope with both of them. This is shown in Figures 3.3 to 3.5. Figure 3.3 shows the axes of the robot's object space in black. Clearly, the robot thinks that her *y*-axis points from her feet to her head and that her *x*-axis points to her left. The robot's inertial space is obtained from her object space by rotating her object axes about their origin until the axes are parallel with the world axes (Figure 3.4). Finally, inertial space can be transformed to world space by moving the origin of inertial space to the origin of world space (Figure 3.5). We will return to this concept in Section 3.5.

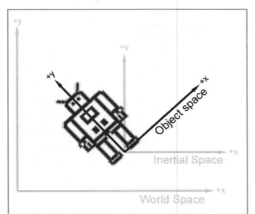

Figure 3.3: The robot's object space

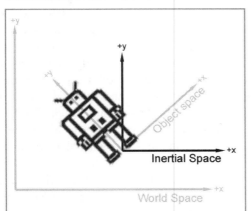

Figure 3.4: The robot's inertial space

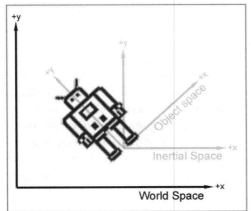

Figure 3.5: The world space

3.3 Nested Coordinate Spaces

Each object in your 3D virtual universe has its own coordinate space — its own origin and its axes. Its origin could be located at its center of mass, for example. Its axes specify which direction it considers to be "up," "right," and "forward," relative to its origin. A 3D model created by an artist for your virtual world will have its origin and axes decided by the artist, and the points that make up the polygon mesh will be relative to the object space defined by this origin and axes. For example, the center of a sheep could be placed at (0,0,0), the tip of its snout at (0,0,1000), the tip if its tail at (0,0,−1200), and the tip of its right ear at (100,200,800). These are the locations of these parts in sheep space.

The position and orientation of an object at any point in time needs to be specified in world coordinates so that we can compute the interactions between nearby objects. To be precise, we must specify the location and orientation of the object's axes in world coordinates. To specify the city of Cartesia's position (see Section 2.2.1) in world space, we could state that the origin is at latitude $q°$ and longitude $p°$ and that the positive x-axis points east and the positive y-axis points north. To locate the sheep in your virtual world, it is sufficient to specify the location of its origin and the orientation of its axes in world space. The world location of the tip of its snout, for example, can be worked out from the relative position of its snout to the world coordinates of its origin. If the sheep is not actually being drawn, we can save effort by keeping track of only the location and orientation of its object space in world space. It becomes necessary to compute the world coordinates of its snout, tail, and right ear only at certain times, like when it moves into view of the camera.

Since the object space moves around in world space, it is convenient to view the world space as a "parent" space and the object space as a "child" space. It is also convenient to break objects into subobjects and to animate them independently. For example, as the sheep walks, its head swings back and forth and its ears flap up and down. In the coordinate space of the sheep's head, the ears appear to be flapping up and down; since the motion is in the y-axis only, it is relatively easy to understand and animate. In the sheep's coordinate space, its head is swinging from side to side along the sheep's x-axis, which is again relatively easy to understand. Now suppose that the sheep is moving along the world's z-axis. Each of the three actions — ears flapping, head swinging, and sheep moving forward — involves a single axis and is easy to understand and draw in isolation from the others. The motion of the tip of the sheep's right ear, however, traces a complicated path through the world coordinate space, truly a nightmare for a programmer to compute from scratch. By breaking the sheep into a hierarchically organized sequence of objects with nested coordinate spaces, the motion can be computed in separate components and combined with relative ease using linear algebra tools, such as matrices and vectors, as we will see in later chapters.

It's convenient to think of the sheep's coordinate space moving relative to world space, the sheep's head coordinate space moving relative to the sheep's space, and the sheep's ear space moving relative to the sheep's head space. Thus, we view the head space as a child of the sheep space and the ear space as a child of the head space. Object space can be divided into many different subspaces at many different levels, depending on the complexity of the object being animated.

We can say that the child coordinate space is *nested* in the parent coordinate space. This parent-child relationship between coordinate spaces defines a hierarchy, or tree, of coordinate spaces. The world coordinate space is the root of this tree. The nested coordinate space tree can change dynamically during the lifetime of your virtual world. For example, the sheep's fleece can be sheared and taken away from the sheep. Thus, the fleece coordinate space goes from being a child of the sheep body's coordinate space to being a child of the world space. The hierarchy of nested coordinate spaces is dynamic and can be arranged in a manner that is most convenient for the information that is important to us.

3.4 Specifying Coordinate Spaces

At this point, the reader may ask a very important question: exactly *how* do we specify a coordinate space relative to another coordinate space?

Recall from Section 2.2.2 that a coordinate system is defined by its *origin* and *axes*. The *origin* defines the *position* of the coordinate space. The *axes* describe the *orientation* of the coordinate space. (In addition, the axes can describe other information, such as scale and skew. For the moment, we will assume that the axes are perpendicular and the units used by the axes are the same as the units used by the parent coordinate space.) If we can find a way to describe the origin and the axes, then we have documented the coordinate space.

Specifying the position of the coordinate space is straightforward. All we have to do is describe the location of the origin. Of course, we express this point using the parent coordinate space, not the local child space. The origin, by definition, is always (0,0,0) if we express it using the child coordinate space.

Specifying the orientation, and the other information that can be described by the axes, in 3D is a far more complicated matter, and we will defer the details to Chapter 10.

3.5 Coordinate Space Transformations

Suppose that in our virtual world a robot is attempting to pick up a herring sandwich. We know the position of the sandwich and the position of the robot in world coordinates. To pick up the sandwich, the robot must be able to answer some basic questions in its own coordinate space, such as, "Which way should I turn to face the sandwich?" "How far away is the sandwich?" "Which way do I move my herring sandwich scoop to get in position to pick up the sandwich?"

Suppose that we wish to render an image of the robot picking up the sandwich, and the scene is illuminated by a light mounted in the center of the robot's chest. We know the position of the light within the robot's object space, but in order to properly light the scene, we must know the position of the light in world space.

These two problems are different aspects of the same basic problem — we know how to express a point in one coordinate space, and we need to express that point in some other coordinate space. The technical term for this computation is a *coordinate space transformation*. We need to *transform* the position from world space to object space (in the example of the sandwich) or from object space to world space (in the example of the light). Notice that neither the sandwich nor the light really *move*. We are just expressing their locations in a different coordinate space.

In Section 3.2.4, we learned that we can transform between object and world space by using inertial space as an intermediary. We can transform between object space and inertial space by rotation, and we can transform between inertial space and world space by translation.

Suppose we are attempting to transform the center point of the light from the robot's object space into world space. We know where the light is located in the robot's object space — the large rectangle at the center of its chest. We can see in Figure 3.6 that it is located on the object's y-axis in the positive direction, so its x coordinate is 0. To be specific, let's say the light is at location $(0,100)$ in object space. Instead of thinking about how to transform the point from object space into world space, however, we are going to think about how to transform object axes into world axes. This will in fact give us a general transformation that we can apply to any point, not just the light.

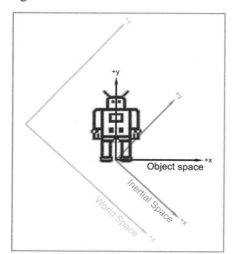

Figure 3.6: The robot in object space

We first rotate to transform the object space axes into inertial axes. We can visualize the transformation by imagining the object coordinate space rotating to line up the object axes with the inertial axes. If we rotate the object space axes in Figure 3.6 clockwise 45°, we get the inertial space axes in Figure 3.7. Note that on the axes of inertial space, the light is now in the positive y direction and the negative x direction, so the location of the light in inertial space would be something like $(-300,600)$.

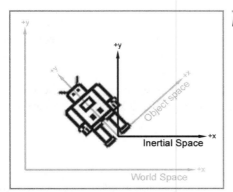

Figure 3.7: The robot in inertial space

Second, we translate to transform the axes from inertial to world space. We can visualize the transformation by imagining the origin moving from the origin of the inertial coordinate space in Figure 3.7 down and to the left to line up with the world origin. Notice that the light is now in the positive direction on both of the world axes, and so it is at (1200,1000) in world space.

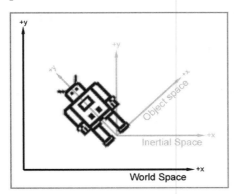

Figure 3.8: The robot in world space

To summarize the example, in order to transform the axes from inertial space to world space:

1. The object axes are transformed to inertial axes by rotating them clockwise 45°.
2. The inertial axes are transformed to world axes by moving them down and to the left.
3. Therefore, the object axes are transformed to world axes by rotating them clockwise 45° and then moving them down and to the left.

From the perspective of a point on the object, like the light in the large rectangle on the robot's chest, the opposite happens:

1. The point is transformed from (0,100) in the object space to (−300,600) in inertial space by rotating it *counterclockwise* 45°.
2. The point is transformed from (−300,600) in inertial space to (1200,1000) in world space by moving *up and right*.
3. Therefore, a point is transformed from object space to world space by rotating it *counterclockwise* 45° and then moving it *up and right*.

Why are the rotation and translation for a point in the opposite direction than they were for the axes? It's like driving around in a car. For example, if you move forward, the world seems to move backward. If you turn left, the world appears to move right. The world does the opposite of what you do.

The beauty of this method is that by first thinking about what happens to the axes, we come up with a transformation that can be applied to any point. We'll talk about this more in Section 8.1.

3.6 Exercises

1. Draw a nested space hierarchy tree for the sheep described in Section 3.3, assuming that its head, ears, upper legs, lower legs, and body move independently.

2. Suppose our object axes are transformed to world axes by rotating them counterclockwise around the y-axis by 42° and then translating six units along the z-axis and 12 units along the x-axis. Describe this transformation from the perspective of a point on the object.

3. Which coordinate space is the most appropriate in which to ask the following questions? (Object, inertial, camera, or world)

    a. Is my computer in front of me or behind me?

    b. Is the book east or west of me?

    c. How do I get from one room to another?

    d. Can I see my computer?

Chapter 4

Vectors

This chapter introduces the concept of vectors. It is divided into three main sections.

- Section 4.1 covers some of the basic mathematical properties of vectors. The main concepts are:
  - ◆ Vector
  - ◆ Scalar
  - ◆ Vector dimension
  - ◆ Row vs. column vectors
- Section 4.2 discusses how vectors may be interpreted geometrically. The main concepts are:
  - ◆ How to draw a vector
  - ◆ Position and displacement
  - ◆ How to express a vector as an array of numbers
  - ◆ How to express a vector as a series of displacements
- Section 4.3 discusses the often confusing relationship between points and vectors. The main concepts are:
  - ◆ Relative position
  - ◆ Displacement vs. position

Vectors are the formal mathematical entities we use to do 2D and 3D math. The word *vector* has two distinct, but related, meanings. One meaning is primarily abstract and mathematical, while the other meaning is geometric. Many books will focus on one interpretation or the other. However, in order to be proficient with 3D math, we will need to understand both interpretations of vectors and how the two interpretations are related.

4.1 Vector — A Mathematical Definition

To mathematicians, a *vector* is a list of numbers. Programmers will recognize the synonymous term *array*. Mathematically, a vector is simply an *array* of numbers. If this abstract definition of a vector doesn't inspire you, don't worry. Like many mathematical subjects, we must first introduce some terminology and notation before we can get to the "fun stuff."

4.1.1 Vectors vs. Scalars

Mathematicians distinguish between vector and *scalar* (pronounced SKAY-lur) quantities. *Scalar* is the technical term for an ordinary number. We use this term specifically when we wish to emphasize that a particular quantity is *not* a vector quantity. For example, as we will discuss shortly, "velocity" and "displacement" are vector quantities, while "speed" and "distance" are scalar quantities.

4.1.2 Vector Dimension

The *dimension* of a vector tells how many numbers the vector contains. Vectors may be of any positive dimension, including one. In fact, a scalar can be considered a 1D vector. In this book, we will primarily be interested in 2D, 3D, and (later) 4D vectors.

4.1.3 Notation

When writing a vector, mathematicians surround the list of numbers with square brackets. For example: [1, 2, 3]. When we write a vector inline in a paragraph, we usually put commas between the numbers. When we write it out in an equation, the commas are often omitted. In either case, a vector written horizontally is called a *row* vector. Vectors are also frequently written vertically:

$$\begin{bmatrix} 1 \\ 2 \\ 3 \end{bmatrix}$$

A vector written vertically is a *column* vector. In this book, we will use both notations. For now, the distinction between row and column vectors won't matter. However, in Section 7.1.8 we will discuss why, in certain circumstances, the distinction is critical.

When we wish to refer to the individual components in a vector, we use subscript notation. In math literature, integer indices are used to access the elements. For example, $\mathbf{v}_1$ refers to the first element in $\mathbf{v}$. However, since we are specifically interested in 2D, 3D, and 4D vectors, rather than vectors of arbitrary dimension n, we will rarely use this notation. Instead, we will use x and y to refer to the elements in a 2D vector, x, y, and z to refer to elements in a 3D vector, and x, y, z, and w to refer to elements in a 4D vector. Equation 4.1 illustrates both notations:

Equation 4.1:
Vector subscript
notation

$$\mathbf{a} = \begin{bmatrix} 1 \\ 2 \end{bmatrix} \qquad \begin{aligned} \mathbf{a}_1 &= \mathbf{a}_x = 1 \\ \mathbf{a}_2 &= \mathbf{a}_y = 2 \end{aligned}$$

$$\mathbf{b} = \begin{bmatrix} 3 \\ 4 \\ 5 \end{bmatrix} \qquad \begin{aligned} \mathbf{b}_1 &= \mathbf{b}_x = 3 \\ \mathbf{b}_2 &= \mathbf{b}_y = 4 \\ \mathbf{b}_3 &= \mathbf{b}_z = 5 \end{aligned}$$

$$\mathbf{c} = \begin{bmatrix} 6 \\ 7 \\ 8 \\ 9 \end{bmatrix} \qquad \begin{aligned} \mathbf{c}_1 &= \mathbf{c}_x = 6 \\ \mathbf{c}_2 &= \mathbf{c}_y = 7 \\ \mathbf{c}_3 &= \mathbf{c}_z = 8 \\ \mathbf{c}_4 &= \mathbf{c}_w = 9 \end{aligned}$$

Notice that the components of a 4D vector are not in alphabetical order. The fourth value is *w*.

4.2 Vector — A Geometric Definition

Now that we have discussed what a vector is mathematically, let's look at a more geometric interpretation of vectors. Geometrically speaking, a *vector* is a directed line segment that has *magnitude* and *direction*.

■   The *magnitude* of a vector is the length of the vector. A vector may have any nonnegative length.

■   The *direction* of a vector describes which way the vector is pointing in space. Note that *direction* is not exactly the same as *orientation*, a distinction we will re-examine in Section 10.1.

4.2.1 What Does a Vector Look Like?

Figure 4.1 shows an illustration of a vector in 2D:

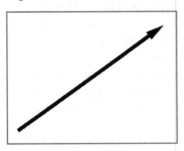

Figure 4.1: A 2D vector

It looks like an arrow, right? This is the standard way to represent a vector graphically since the two defining characteristics of a vector are captured, its magnitude and direction.

We will sometimes refer to the *head* and *tail* of a vector. As shown in Figure 4.2, the head is the end of the vector with the arrow on it (where the vector "ends"), and the tail is the other end (where the vector "starts"):

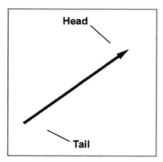

Figure 4.2: A vector has a head and a tail

4.2.2 Position vs. Displacement

Where is this vector? Actually, that is not an appropriate question. Vectors do not have *position*, only magnitude and direction. This may sound impossible, but many quantities we deal with on a daily basis have magnitude and direction, but no position. For example:

■ **Displacement:** *"Take three steps forward."* This sentence seems to be all about positions, but the actual quantity used in the sentence is a relative displacement and does not have an absolute position. This relative displacement consists of a magnitude (three steps) and a direction (forward), so it could be represented using a vector.

■ **Velocity:** *"I am traveling northeast at 50 MPH."* This sentence describes a quantity that has magnitude (50 MPH) and direction (northeast), but no position. The concept of "northeast at 50 MPH" can be represented using a vector.

Notice that *displacement* and *velocity* are technically different from the terms *distance* and *speed*. *Displacement* and *velocity* are vector quantities and entail a direction, whereas *distance* and *speed* are scalar quantities and do not specify a direction.

Because vectors are used to express displacements and relative differences between things, they can describe relative positions: "My house is 3 blocks east of here." However, you should not think of vectors as having absolute positions. (More on relative vs. absolute position in Section 4.3.1.) To help enforce this, when you imagine a vector, picture an arrow. Remember that the length and direction of this arrow is significant, but not the position.

Since vectors do not have a position, we can represent them on a diagram anywhere we choose, provided that the length and direction of the vector are represented correctly. We will often use this to our advantage by "sliding" the vector around into a meaningful location on a diagram.

4.2.3 Specifying Vectors

The numbers in a vector measure *signed displacements* in each dimension. For example, in 2D, we list the displacement parallel to both the *x*-axis and the *y*-axis:

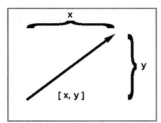

Figure 4.3: Vectors are specified by giving the signed displacement in each dimension

Figure 4.4 shows several 2D vectors and their values:

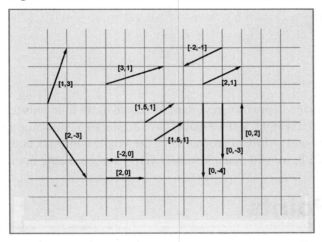

Figure 4.4: Examples of 2D vectors and their values

Notice that a vector's position on the diagram is irrelevant. (The axes are conspicuously absent to enforce this policy, although we do assume the standard convention of $+x$ pointing to the right and $+y$ pointing up.) For example, there are two vectors shown in Figure 4.4 with the value $[1.5, 1]$, but they are not in the same place on the diagram.

3D vectors are a simple extension of 2D vectors. A 3D vector contains three numbers which measure the signed displacements in the x, y, and z directions, just as you'd expect.

4.2.4 Vectors as a Sequence of Displacements

One helpful way to think about the displacement described by a vector is to break the vector into its axially aligned components. When these axially aligned displacements are combined, they cumulatively define the displacement defined by the vector as a whole.

For example, the 3D vector $[1, -3, 4]$ represents a single displacement, but we can visualize this displacement as moving one unit to the right, three units down, and then four units forward. (Assume our convention that $+x$, $+y$, and $+z$ point right, up, and forward, respectively. Also note that we do not "turn" between steps, so "forward" is always parallel to $+z$.) This is illustrated in Figure 4.5 on the following page.

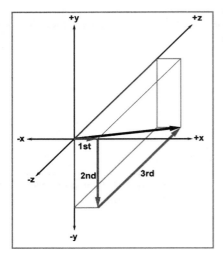

Figure 4.5: Interpreting a vector as a sequence of displacements

The order in which we perform the steps is not important. We could move four units forward, three units down, and then one unit to the right, and we would have displaced by the same total amount. The different orderings correspond to different routes along the axially aligned bounding box containing the vector. In Section 5.8, we will mathematically verify this geometric intuition.

4.3 Vectors vs. Points

Recall that a "point" has a location, but no real size or thickness. In this chapter, we have learned how a "vector" has magnitude and direction, but no position. So "points" and "vectors" have different purposes, conceptually. A "point" specifies a position, and a "vector" specifies a displacement.

Examine Figure 4.6 below, which compares an illustration from Chapter 2 (Figure 2.8) showing how 2D points are located, with a figure from earlier in this chapter (Figure 4.3) showing how 2D vectors are specified. It seems that there is a strong relationship between points and vectors. In this section, we'll examine this important relationship.

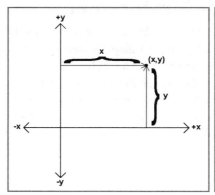 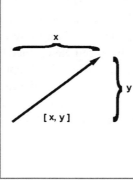

Figure 4.6: Locating points vs. specifying vectors

4.3.1 Relative Position

In Section 4.2.2, we discussed the fact that vectors can describe *relative* positions because they can describe displacements. The idea of a relative position is fairly straightforward: the position of something is specified by describing where it is in relation to some other known location.

This begs the question, where are these "known" locations? What is an "absolute" position? It is surprising to realize that there is no such thing! Every attempt to describe a position requires that we describe it relative to something else. Any description of a position is meaningful only in the context of some (typically "larger") reference frame. We have already touched on this subject in Chapter 3 when we discussed nested coordinate spaces.

Theoretically, we could establish a reference frame encompassing everything in existence and select a point to be the "origin" of this space, and thus defining the "absolute" coordinate space. (This is assuming we could somehow overcome the effects of relativity, such as the curvature of space. In fact, one important implication of the Theory of Relativity is that it is impossible to establish an absolute reference frame.) However, even if such an absolute coordinate space were possible, it would not be practical. Luckily for us, absolute positions in the universe aren't important. Do you know *your* precise position in the universe right now?

4.3.2 The Relationship Between Points and Vectors

Vectors are used to describe displacements, and therefore, they can describe relative positions. Points are used to specify positions. We have just established in Section 4.3.1 that *any* method of specifying a position will be relative. Therefore, we must conclude that points are relative. They are relative to the origin of the coordinate system used to specify their coordinates. This leads us to the relationship between points and vectors.

Figure 4.7 illustrates how the point (x, y) is related to the vector $[x, y]$, given arbitrary values for x and y.

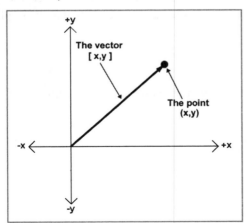

Figure 4.7: The relationship between points and vectors

As you can see, if we start at the origin and move by the amount specified by the vector $[x, y]$, we will end up at the location described by the point (x, y). Another way to say this is that the vector $[x, y]$ gives the displacement from the origin to the point (x, y).

While this seems obvious, it is important to understand that points and vectors are conceptually distinct, but mathematically equivalent. This confusion between "points" and "vectors" can be a stumbling block for beginners, but it needn't be a problem for you. When you think of a location, think of a point and visualize a dot. When you think of a displacement, think of a vector and visualize an arrow.

In many cases, displacements are from the origin, and so the distinction between points and vectors will be a fine one. However, we will often deal with quantities that are *not* relative to the origin, or any other point for that matter. In these cases it will be important to visualize these quantities as an arrow rather than a point.

The math we will develop in the following chapters operates on "vectors" rather than "points." Keep in mind that any point can be represented as a vector from the origin.

4.4 Exercises

1. Let:

$$\mathbf{a} = \begin{bmatrix} -3 & 8 \end{bmatrix}, \mathbf{b} = \begin{bmatrix} 4 \\ 0 \\ 5 \end{bmatrix}, \mathbf{c} = \begin{bmatrix} 16 \\ -1 \\ 4 \\ 6 \end{bmatrix}$$

   a. Identify $\mathbf{a}$, $\mathbf{b}$, and $\mathbf{c}$ as row or column vectors, and give the dimension of each vector.

   b. Compute $\mathbf{b}_y + \mathbf{c}_w + \mathbf{a}_x + \mathbf{b}_z$.

2. Identity the quantities in each of the following sentences as scalar or vector. For vector quantities, give the magnitude and direction. (Note: some directions may be implicit.)

   a. How much do you weigh?

   b. Do you have any idea how fast you were going?

   c. It's two blocks north of here.

   d. We're cruising from Los Angeles to New York at 600mph, at an altitude of 33,000ft.

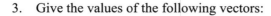

3. Give the values of the following vectors:

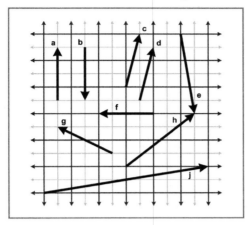

4. Identify the following statements as true or false. If the statement is false, explain why.

    a. The size of a vector in a diagram doesn't matter. We just need to draw it in the right place.

    b. The displacement expressed by a vector can be visualized as a sequence of axially aligned displacements.

    c. These axially aligned displacements from the previous question must occur in the proper order.

    d. The vector [x, y] gives the displacement from the point (x, y) to the origin.

Chapter 5

Operations on Vectors

This chapter is about operations on vectors. It is divided into twelve main sections.

- Section 5.1 discusses the difference between the information found in a linear algebra textbook and the information applicable for geometrical operations.
- Section 5.2 discusses some notational conventions we will use in this book to make the data type of variables clear.
- Section 5.3 introduces a special vector known as the zero vector and discusses some of its important properties.
- Section 5.4 defines vector negation.
- Section 5.5 describes how to compute the magnitude of a vector.
- Section 5.6 describes how a scalar may be multiplied by a vector.
- Section 5.7 introduces normalized vectors and explains how to normalize a vector.
- Section 5.8 explains how to add and subtract two vectors and gives several important applications of this operation.
- Section 5.9 presents the distance formula and explains why it works.
- Section 5.10 discusses the first type of vector product, the dot product.
- Section 5.11 discusses a second type of vector product, the cross product.
- Section 5.12 presents a list of vector algebra identities.

In Chapter 4, we discussed what vectors are geometrically and mentioned that the term *vector* has a precise definition in mathematics. This chapter describes in detail the mathematical operations we perform on vectors. For each operation, we will first define the mathematical rules for performing the operation and then describe the geometric interpretations of the operation.

5.1 Linear Algebra vs. What We Need

The branch of mathematics that deals primarily with vectors is called *linear algebra*. As mentioned in Section 4.1, a vector is nothing more than an array of numbers in linear algebra. This highly generalized abstraction allows us to explore a large set of mathematical problems. For example, in linear algebra, vectors and matrices of dimension n are used to solve a system of n linear equations for n unknowns. This is a very interesting and useful study, but it is not of primary interest to our investigation of 3D math.

For 3D math, we are primarily concerned with the geometric interpretations of vectors and vector operations. The level of generality employed by linear algebra textbooks precludes decent coverage on the geometric interpretations. For example, a linear algebra textbook can teach you the precise rules for multiplying a vector by a matrix. These rules are important, but, in this book, we will also discuss several ways to interpret the numbers inside a 3×3 matrix geometrically and *why* multiplying a vector by a matrix can perform a coordinate space transformation. (We'll do this in Section 7.2.)

Since our focus is geometric, we will omit many details of linear algebra that do not further our understanding of 2D or 3D geometry. While we will often discuss properties or operations for vectors of an arbitrary dimension n, we will usually focus on 2D, 3D, and (later) 4D vectors and matrices.

5.2 Typeface Conventions

As you know, *variables* are placeholder symbols used to stand for unknown quantities. In 3D math, we work with scalar, vector, and (later) matrix quantities, so it is important that we make it clear what type of data is represented by a particular variable. In this book, we use different fonts for variables of different types:

- *Scalar variables* will be represented by lowercase Roman or Greek letters in italics: $a, b, x, y, z, \theta, \lambda$.
- *Vector variables* of any dimension will be represented by lowercase letters in boldface: **a**, **b**, **u**, **v**, **q**, **r**.
- *Matrix variables* will be represented using uppercase letters in boldface: **A**, **B**, **M**, **R**.

Note that other authors use different conventions. One common convention, used frequently when writing vectors by hand, is to draw a half-arrow over the vector, like this: $\vec{a}$

5.3 The Zero Vector

For any set, the *additive identity* of the set is the element x, such that for all y in the set, $y+x=y$. (The typeface used here is not intended to limit the discussion to the set of scalars. We are talking about elements in any set.)

For the set of vectors of a particular dimension, the additive identity element is the so-called "zero vector" of that dimension, which has zeros in every position. We denote a zero vector of any dimension using a boldface zero, as shown below:

$$\mathbf{0} = \begin{bmatrix} 0 \\ 0 \\ \vdots \\ 0 \end{bmatrix}$$

For example, the 3D zero vector is [0, 0, 0].

The zero vector is special because it is the only vector with a magnitude of zero. For any other magnitude, there are an infinite number of vectors of that magnitude, and they form a circle, as shown below in Figure 5.1. The zero vector is also unique because it is the only vector that does not have a direction.

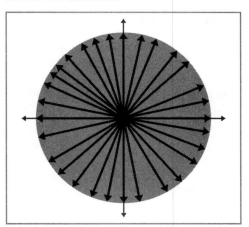

Figure 5.1: For any positive magnitude, there are an infinite number of vectors with that magnitude.

Although we will graphically depict the zero vector using a point, it is not entirely accurate to think of the zero vector as a "point," in the sense that it does not define a location. Instead, think of the zero vector as a way to express the concept of "no displacement," much as the scalar zero stands for the concept of "no quantity."

5.4 Negating a Vector

For any set, the *additive inverse* of x, denoted by $-x$, is the element that yields the additive identity of that set (zero) when added to x. Put simply: $x + (-x) = 0$. (Again, despite the typeface used for the variables, we are talking about sets in general.) In other words, elements in the set can be negated.

The negation operation can be applied to vectors. Every vector $\mathbf{v}$ has an additive inverse $-\mathbf{v}$ of the same dimension as $\mathbf{v}$, such that $\mathbf{v} + (-\mathbf{v}) = \mathbf{0}$. (We will learn how to add vectors in Section 5.8.)

5.4.1 Official Linear Algebra Rules

To negate a vector of any dimension, we simply negate each component of the vector. Stated formally:

Equation 5.1:
Negating a
vector

$$-\begin{bmatrix} a_1 \\ a_2 \\ \vdots \\ a_{n-1} \\ a_n \end{bmatrix} = \begin{bmatrix} -a_1 \\ -a_2 \\ \vdots \\ -a_{n-1} \\ -a_n \end{bmatrix}$$

Applying this to the specific cases of 2D, 3D, and 4D vectors, we have:

Equation 5.2:
Negating 2D,
3D, and 4D
vectors

$$-\begin{bmatrix} x & y \end{bmatrix} = \begin{bmatrix} -x & -y \end{bmatrix}$$
$$-\begin{bmatrix} x & y & z \end{bmatrix} = \begin{bmatrix} -x & -y & -z \end{bmatrix}$$
$$-\begin{bmatrix} x & y & z & w \end{bmatrix} = \begin{bmatrix} -x & -y & -z & -w \end{bmatrix}$$

A few examples:

$$-\begin{bmatrix} 4 & -5 \end{bmatrix} = \begin{bmatrix} -4 & 5 \end{bmatrix}$$
$$-\begin{bmatrix} -1 & 0 & \sqrt{3} \end{bmatrix} = \begin{bmatrix} 1 & 0 & -\sqrt{3} \end{bmatrix}$$
$$-\begin{bmatrix} 1.34 & -3/4 & -5 & 10 \end{bmatrix} = \begin{bmatrix} -1.34 & 3/4 & 5 & -10 \end{bmatrix}$$

5.4.2 Geometric Interpretation

Negating a vector results in a vector of the same magnitude but opposite direction. Figure 5.2 illustrates this:

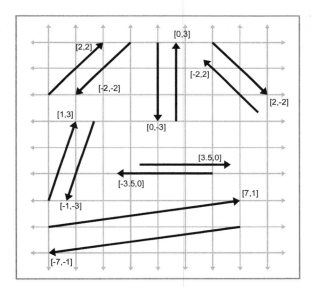

Figure 5.2: Examples of vectors and their negatives

Remember, the position at which a vector is drawn on a diagram is irrelevant. Only the magnitude and direction are important.

5.5 Vector Magnitude (Length)

As we have discussed before, vectors have magnitude and direction. However, you might have noticed that neither the magnitude nor the direction is expressed explicitly in the vector! For example, the magnitude of the 2D vector [3, 4] is neither 3 nor 4; it's 5. Since the magnitude of the vector is not expressed explicitly, we must compute it. The magnitude of a vector is also known as the *length* or *norm* of the vector.

5.5.1 Official Linear Algebra Rules

In linear algebra, the magnitude of a vector is denoted using double vertical bars surrounding the vector. This is similar to the single vertical bar notation used for the "absolute value" operation for scalars. This notation and the equation for computing the magnitude of a vector of arbitrary dimension *n* are shown below:

Equation 5.3:
Vector
magnitude

$$\|\mathbf{v}\| = \sqrt{\mathbf{v}_1{}^2 + \mathbf{v}_2{}^2 + \cdots + \mathbf{v}_{n-1}{}^2 + \mathbf{v}_n{}^2}$$

$$\|\mathbf{v}\| = \sqrt{\sum_{i=1}^{n} \mathbf{v}_i{}^2}$$

Thus, the magnitude of a vector is the square root of the sum of the squares of the components of the vector. This sounds complicated, but the magnitude equations for 2D and 3D vectors are actually very simple:

Equation 5.4: Vector magnitude for 2D and 3D vectors

$$\|\mathbf{v}\| = \sqrt{\mathbf{v}_x{}^2 + \mathbf{v}_y{}^2} \quad \text{(for a 2D vector } \mathbf{v})$$

$$\|\mathbf{v}\| = \sqrt{\mathbf{v}_x{}^2 + \mathbf{v}_y{}^2 + \mathbf{v}_z{}^2} \quad \text{(for a 3D vector } \mathbf{v})$$

The magnitude of a vector is a nonnegative scalar quantity. Here's an example of how to compute the magnitude of a 3D vector:

$$
\begin{aligned}
\left\| \begin{bmatrix} 5 & -4 & 7 \end{bmatrix} \right\| &= \sqrt{5^2 + (-4)^2 + 7^2} \\
&= \sqrt{25 + 16 + 49} \\
&= \sqrt{90} \\
&= 3\sqrt{10} \\
&\approx 9.4868
\end{aligned}
$$

 Note: Some books use a single bar notation to indicate vector magnitude, like this: $|\mathbf{v}|$.

5.5.2 Geometric Interpretation

Let's try to get a better understanding of why Equation 5.4 works. For any vector $\mathbf{v}$ in 2D, we can form a right triangle with $\mathbf{v}$ as the hypotenuse:

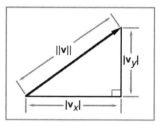

Figure 5.3: Geometric interpretation of the magnitude equation

Notice that the lengths of the legs are the absolute values of the components $\mathbf{v}_x$ and $\mathbf{v}_y$. The components of the vector may be negative, since they are *signed* displacements, but the *length* is always positive.

The Pythagorean theorem states that for any right triangle, the square of the length of the hypotenuse is equal to the sum of the squares of the lengths of the other two sides. When this theorem is applied to Figure 5.3, we have:

$$\|\mathbf{v}\|^2 = |\mathbf{v}_x|^2 + |\mathbf{v}_y|^2$$

Since $|x|^2 = x^2$, we can omit the absolute value symbols:

$$\|\mathbf{v}\|^2 = \mathbf{v}_x{}^2 + \mathbf{v}_y{}^2$$

After taking the square root of both sides and simplifying, we get:

$$\sqrt{\|\mathbf{v}\|^2} = \sqrt{\mathbf{v}_x{}^2 + \mathbf{v}_y{}^2}$$
$$\|\mathbf{v}\| = \sqrt{\mathbf{v}_x{}^2 + \mathbf{v}_y{}^2}$$

which is the same as Equation 5.4. The proof of the magnitude equation in 3D is only slightly more complicated.

5.6 Vector Multiplication by a Scalar

Although we cannot add a vector and a scalar, we can multiply a vector and a scalar. The result is a vector that is parallel with the original vector, except with a different length and possibly opposite direction.

5.6.1 Official Linear Algebra Rules

Vector-times-scalar multiplication is straightforward; we simply multiply each component of the vector by the scalar. The scalar and vector may be given in either order, but we almost always write the scalar on the left. Stated formally:

Equation 5.5:
Multiplying a
vector by a
scalar

$$k \begin{bmatrix} a_1 \\ a_2 \\ \vdots \\ a_{n-1} \\ a_n \end{bmatrix} = \begin{bmatrix} a_1 \\ a_2 \\ \vdots \\ a_{n-1} \\ a_n \end{bmatrix} k = \begin{bmatrix} ka_1 \\ ka_2 \\ \vdots \\ ka_{n-1} \\ ka_n \end{bmatrix}$$

This rule when applied to 3D vectors as an example:

Equation 5.6:
Multiplying a
3D vector by
a scalar

$$k \begin{bmatrix} x \\ y \\ z \end{bmatrix} = \begin{bmatrix} x \\ y \\ z \end{bmatrix} k = \begin{bmatrix} kx \\ ky \\ kz \end{bmatrix}$$

A vector may also be divided by a nonzero scalar. This is equivalent to multiplying by the reciprocal of the scalar:

Equation 5.7:
Dividing a 3D
vector by a
scalar

$$\frac{\mathbf{v}}{k} = \left(\frac{1}{k} \right) \mathbf{v} = \begin{bmatrix} \mathbf{v}_x/k \\ \mathbf{v}_y/k \\ \mathbf{v}_z/k \end{bmatrix} \qquad \text{for 3D vector } \mathbf{v} \text{ and nonzero scalar } k.$$

Some examples:

$$2\begin{bmatrix} 1 & 2 & 3 \end{bmatrix} = \begin{bmatrix} 2 & 4 & 6 \end{bmatrix}$$
$$-3\begin{bmatrix} -5 & 0 & 0.4 \end{bmatrix} = \begin{bmatrix} 15 & 0 & -1.2 \end{bmatrix}$$
$$\begin{bmatrix} 4.7 & -6 & 8 \end{bmatrix}/2 = \begin{bmatrix} 2.35 & -3 & 4 \end{bmatrix}$$

A few notes:

- When we multiply a vector and a scalar, we do not use a multiplication symbol. The multiplication is signified by placing the two quantities side by side (usually with the vector on the right).
- Scalar-times-vector multiplication and division both occur before any addition and subtraction. For example, $3\mathbf{a}+\mathbf{b}$ is the same as $(3\mathbf{a})+\mathbf{b}$, not $3(\mathbf{a}+\mathbf{b})$.
- A scalar may not be divided by a vector, and a vector may not be divided by another vector.
- Vector negation can be viewed as the special case of multiplying a vector by the scalar -1.

5.6.2 Geometric Interpretation

Geometrically, multiplying a vector by a scalar k has the effect of scaling the length by a factor of $|k|$. For example, to double the length of a vector, we would multiply the vector by 2. If $k < 0$, then the direction of the vector is flipped. Figure 5.4 illustrates a vector multiplied by several different scalars.

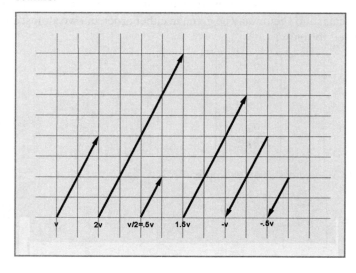

Figure 5.4: A 2D vector multiplied by various scalars

5.7 Normalized Vectors

For many vector quantities, we are concerned with direction and not magnitude. For example, "which way am I facing?" In these cases, it is often convenient to use *unit vectors*. A unit vector is a vector that has a magnitude of 1. Unit vectors are also known as *normalized* vectors or simply *normals*.

5.7.1 Official Linear Algebra Rules

For any nonzero vector $\mathbf{v}$, we can compute a unit vector $\mathbf{v}_{norm}$ that points in the same direction as $\mathbf{v}$. This process is known as "normalizing" the vector. To normalize a vector, we divide the vector by its magnitude:

Equation 5.8:
Normalizing
a vector

$$\mathbf{v}_{norm} = \frac{\mathbf{v}}{\|\mathbf{v}\|}, \mathbf{v} \neq \mathbf{0}$$

For example, to normalize the 2D vector [12, -5]:

$$\frac{\begin{bmatrix} 12 & -5 \end{bmatrix}}{\left\| \begin{bmatrix} 12 & -5 \end{bmatrix} \right\|} = \frac{\begin{bmatrix} 12 & -5 \end{bmatrix}}{\sqrt{12^2 + (-5)^2}}$$

$$= \frac{\begin{bmatrix} 12 & -5 \end{bmatrix}}{\sqrt{169}}$$

$$= \frac{\begin{bmatrix} 12 & -5 \end{bmatrix}}{13}$$

$$= \begin{bmatrix} \frac{12}{13} & \frac{-5}{13} \end{bmatrix}$$

$$\approx \begin{bmatrix} 0.923 & -0.385 \end{bmatrix}$$

The zero vector cannot be normalized. Mathematically, this is not allowed, since it would result in division by zero. Geometrically, it makes sense because the zero vector does not define a direction.

5.7.2 Geometric Interpretation

In 2D, if we draw a unit vector with the tail at the origin, the head of the vector will touch a unit circle centered at the origin. (A unit circle has a radius of 1.) In 3D, unit vectors touch the surface of a unit sphere. Figure 5.5 shows several vectors in 2D in gray and their normalized counterparts in black:

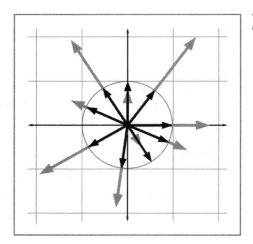

Figure 5.5: Normalizing vectors in 2D

5.8 Vector Addition and Subtraction

We can add and subtract two vectors, provided they are of the same dimension. The result is a vector quantity of the same dimension as the vector operands. We use the same notation for vector addition and subtraction that is used for addition and subtraction of scalars.

5.8.1 Official Linear Algebra Rules

The linear algebra rules for vector addition are simple: to add two vectors, we add the corresponding components:

Equation 5.9:
Adding two
vectors

$$
\begin{bmatrix} a_1 \\ a_2 \\ \vdots \\ a_{n-1} \\ a_n \end{bmatrix}
+
\begin{bmatrix} b_1 \\ b_2 \\ \vdots \\ b_{n-1} \\ b_n \end{bmatrix}
=
\begin{bmatrix} a_1 + b_1 \\ a_2 + b_2 \\ \vdots \\ a_{n-1} + b_{n-1} \\ a_n + b_n \end{bmatrix}
$$

Subtraction can be interpreted as adding the negative, so $\mathbf{a} - \mathbf{b} = \mathbf{a} + (-\mathbf{b})$:

Equation 5.10:
Subtracting two
vectors

$$
\begin{bmatrix} a_1 \\ a_2 \\ \vdots \\ a_{n-1} \\ a_n \end{bmatrix}
-
\begin{bmatrix} b_1 \\ b_2 \\ \vdots \\ b_{n-1} \\ b_n \end{bmatrix}
=
\begin{bmatrix} a_1 \\ a_2 \\ \vdots \\ a_{n-1} \\ a_n \end{bmatrix}
+
\left(-
\begin{bmatrix} b_1 \\ b_2 \\ \vdots \\ b_{n-1} \\ b_n \end{bmatrix}
\right)
=
\begin{bmatrix} a_1 - b_1 \\ a_2 - b_2 \\ \vdots \\ a_{n-1} - b_{n-1} \\ a_n - b_n \end{bmatrix}
$$

For example:

$$\mathbf{a} = \begin{bmatrix} 1 \\ 2 \\ 3 \end{bmatrix}, \mathbf{b} = \begin{bmatrix} 4 \\ 5 \\ 6 \end{bmatrix}, \mathbf{c} = \begin{bmatrix} 7 \\ -3 \\ 0 \end{bmatrix}$$

$$\mathbf{a} + \mathbf{b} = \begin{bmatrix} 1 \\ 2 \\ 3 \end{bmatrix} + \begin{bmatrix} 4 \\ 5 \\ 6 \end{bmatrix} = \begin{bmatrix} 1+4 \\ 2+5 \\ 3+6 \end{bmatrix} = \begin{bmatrix} 5 \\ 7 \\ 9 \end{bmatrix}$$

$$\mathbf{a} - \mathbf{b} = \begin{bmatrix} 1 \\ 2 \\ 3 \end{bmatrix} - \begin{bmatrix} 4 \\ 5 \\ 6 \end{bmatrix} = \begin{bmatrix} 1-4 \\ 2-5 \\ 3-6 \end{bmatrix} = \begin{bmatrix} -3 \\ -3 \\ -3 \end{bmatrix}$$

$$\mathbf{b} + \mathbf{c} - \mathbf{a} = \begin{bmatrix} 4 \\ 5 \\ 6 \end{bmatrix} + \begin{bmatrix} 7 \\ -3 \\ 0 \end{bmatrix} - \begin{bmatrix} 1 \\ 2 \\ 3 \end{bmatrix} = \begin{bmatrix} 4+7-1 \\ 5+(-3)-2 \\ 6+0-3 \end{bmatrix} = \begin{bmatrix} 10 \\ 0 \\ 3 \end{bmatrix}$$

A few notes:

■ A vector cannot be added or subtracted with a scalar or a vector of a different dimension.

■ Just as with scalar addition and subtraction, vector addition is commutative, but vector subtraction is not. ($\mathbf{a}+\mathbf{b} = \mathbf{b}+\mathbf{a}$ is always true, but $\mathbf{a}-\mathbf{b} = -(\mathbf{b}-\mathbf{a})$, so $\mathbf{a}-\mathbf{b} = \mathbf{b}-\mathbf{a}$ is only true if $\mathbf{a} = \mathbf{b}$.)

5.8.2 Geometric Interpretation

We can add vectors **a** and **b** geometrically by positioning the vectors so that the head of **a** touches the tail of **b**, and then draw a vector from the tail of **a** to the head of **b**. This is known as the "triangle rule" of vector addition. We can also subtract vectors in a similar fashion. Examine Figure 5.6:

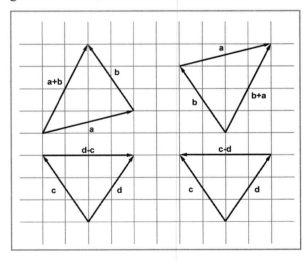

Figure 5.6: 2D vector addition and subtraction using the triangle rule

The previous figure provides geometric evidence that vector addition is commutative, but vector subtraction is not. Notice that the vector labeled **a**+**b** is identical to the vector labeled **b**+**a**, but the vectors **d**–**c** and **c**–**d** point in opposite directions because **d**–**c** = –(**c**–**d**).

The triangle rule can be extended to more than two vectors. For example:

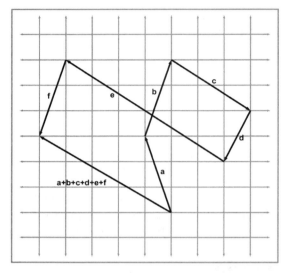

Figure 5.7: Extending the triangle rule to more than two vectors

Armed with the triangle rule, we can now verify something mathematically that we stated geometrically in Section 4.2.4: a vector can be interpreted as a sequence of axially aligned displacements. Figure 5.8 is a reproduction of Figure 4.5, which shows how the vector [1, –3, 4] may be interpreted as a displacement of one unit to the right, three units down, and then four units forward:

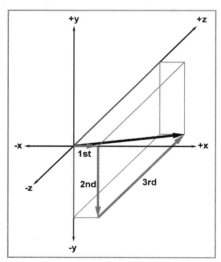

Figure 5.8: Interpreting a vector as a sequence of displacements

We can interpret Figure 5.8 mathematically using vector addition:

$$\begin{bmatrix} 1 \\ -3 \\ 4 \end{bmatrix} = \begin{bmatrix} 1 \\ 0 \\ 0 \end{bmatrix} + \begin{bmatrix} 0 \\ -3 \\ 0 \end{bmatrix} + \begin{bmatrix} 0 \\ 0 \\ 4 \end{bmatrix}$$

This seems obvious, but it is a very powerful concept. We will use a similar technique in Section 7.2.1 to transform vectors from one coordinate space to another.

5.8.3 Vector from One Point to Another

It is very common that we will need to compute the displacement from one point to another. In this case, we can use the triangle rule and vector subtraction. Figure 5.9 shows how the displacement vector from **a** to **b** can be computed by subtracting **a** from **b**:

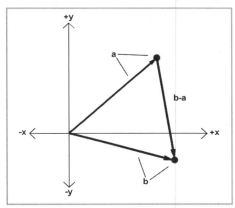

*Figure 5.9: Using 2D vector subtraction to compute the vector from point **a** to point **b***

As the diagram above shows, to compute the vector from **a** to **b,** we interpret the points **a** and **b** as vectors from the origin, and then use the triangle rule. In fact, vectors are defined in some texts as the subtraction of two points.

Notice that the vector subtraction **b**–**a** yields a vector *from* **a** to **b**. It doesn't make any sense to simply find the vector "between two points," since the language in this sentence does not specify a direction. We must always form a vector that goes *from* one point *to* another point.

5.9   **The Distance Formula**

We are now prepared to introduce one of the most important formulas in computational geometry — the distance formula. This formula is used to compute the distance between two points.

First, let's define distance as the length of the line segment between the two points. Since a vector is a directed line segment, it makes sense geometrically that the distance between the two points would be equal to the length of a vector from one point to the other. Let's derive the distance formula in 3D. First, we will compute the vector **d** from **a** to **b**. We learned how to do this in Section 5.8.3. In 3D:

$$d = b - a = \begin{bmatrix} b_x - a_x \\ b_y - a_y \\ b_z - a_z \end{bmatrix}$$

The distance between a and b is equal to the length of the vector d, which we learned how to compute in Section 5.5.

$$\text{distance}(a, b) = \|d\| = \sqrt{d_x^2 + d_y^2 + d_z^2}$$

Substituting for d, we get:

Equation 5.11:
The 3D distance formula
$$\text{distance}(a, b) = \|b - a\| = \sqrt{(b_x - a_x)^2 + (b_y - a_y)^2 + (b_z - a_z)^2}$$

Thus, we have derived the distance formula in 3D. The 2D equation is even more simple:

Equation 5.12:
The 2D distance formula
$$\text{distance}(a, b) = \|b - a\| = \sqrt{(b_x - a_x)^2 + (b_y - a_y)^2}$$

Let's look at an example in 2D:

$$\begin{aligned}
\text{distance}\left(\begin{bmatrix} 5 & 0 \end{bmatrix}, \begin{bmatrix} -1 & 8 \end{bmatrix}\right) &= \sqrt{(-1-5)^2 + (8-0)^2} \\
&= \sqrt{(-6)^2 + 8^2} \\
&= \sqrt{36 + 64} \\
&= \sqrt{100} \\
&= 10
\end{aligned}$$

Notice that it does not matter which point is a and which point is b. If we define d to be the vector from b to a instead of from a to b, we will derive a slightly different, but mathematically equivalent, equation.

5.10 Vector Dot Product

In Section 5.6 we learned that we can multiply a vector by a scalar. We can also multiply two vectors together. There are two types of vector products. The first vector product we will discuss is the *dot product* (also known as the *inner product*).

5.10.1 Official Linear Algebra Rules

The name "dot product" comes from the dot symbol used in the notation: $a \cdot b$. Just like scalar-times-vector multiplication, vector dot product is performed before addition and subtraction. However, while we usually omit the multiplication symbol when multiplying two scalars or a scalar and a vector, we do not omit the dot symbol when performing a vector dot product.

The dot product of two vectors is the sum of the products of corresponding components. This results in a scalar:

Equation 5.13:
Vector dot
product

$$\begin{bmatrix} a_1 \\ a_2 \\ \vdots \\ a_{n-1} \\ a_n \end{bmatrix} \cdot \begin{bmatrix} b_1 \\ b_2 \\ \vdots \\ b_{n-1} \\ b_n \end{bmatrix} = \mathbf{a}_1\mathbf{b}_1 + \mathbf{a}_2\mathbf{b}_2 + \cdots + \mathbf{a}_{n-1}\mathbf{b}_{n-1} + \mathbf{a}_n\mathbf{b}_n$$

This can be expressed succinctly using summation notation:

Equation 5.14:
Vector dot
product
expressed using
summation
notation

$$\mathbf{a} \cdot \mathbf{b} = \sum_{i=1}^{n} \mathbf{a}_i\mathbf{b}_i$$

Apply these rules to the 2D and 3D cases:

Equation 5.15:
2D and 3D dot
product

$\mathbf{a} \cdot \mathbf{b} = \mathbf{a}_x\mathbf{b}_x + \mathbf{a}_y\mathbf{b}_y$ **a** and **b** are 2D vectors

$\mathbf{a} \cdot \mathbf{b} = \mathbf{a}_x\mathbf{b}_x + \mathbf{a}_y\mathbf{b}_y + \mathbf{a}_z\mathbf{b}_z$ **a** and **b** are 3D vectors

It is obvious from inspection of the equations that vector dot product is commutative: **a·b** = **b·a**. More vector algebra laws concerning the dot product will be given in Section 5.12.

Examples of the dot product in 2D and 3D:

$$\begin{bmatrix} 4 & 6 \end{bmatrix} \cdot \begin{bmatrix} -3 & 7 \end{bmatrix} = (4)(-3) + (6)(7) = 30$$

$$\begin{bmatrix} 3 \\ -2 \\ 7 \end{bmatrix} \cdot \begin{bmatrix} 0 \\ 4 \\ -1 \end{bmatrix} = (3)(0) + (-2)(4) + (7)(-1) = -15$$

5.10.2 Geometric Interpretation

Generally speaking, the dot product in any dimension tells how "similar" two vectors are; the larger the dot product, the more similar the two vectors. Geometrically, we can be more precise. Examine Figure 5.10:

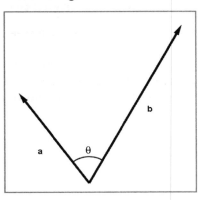

Figure 5.10: The dot product is related to the angle between two vectors

The dot product is equal to the product of the magnitudes of the vectors and the cosine of the angle between the vectors:

Equation 5.16:
Geometric
interpretation of
the vector dot
product

$$\mathbf{a} \cdot \mathbf{b} = \|\mathbf{a}\|\|\mathbf{b}\| \cos \theta$$

(Remember that in 3D, the angle between two vectors is measured in the plane that contains both vectors.)

Solving for θ:

Equation 5.17:
Computing the
angle between
two vectors
using the dot
product

$$\theta = \operatorname{acos} \left(\frac{\mathbf{a} \cdot \mathbf{b}}{\|\mathbf{a}\|\|\mathbf{b}\|} \right)$$

We can avoid the division in Equation 5.17 if we know that $\mathbf{a}$ and $\mathbf{b}$ are unit vectors. In this case, the denominator of the above equation is trivially 1, and we are left with:

Equation 5.18:
Computing the
angle between
two unit vectors

$\theta = \operatorname{acos} (\mathbf{a} \cdot \mathbf{b})$, $\mathbf{a}$ and $\mathbf{b}$ are unit vectors

If we do not need the exact value of θ, and only a classification of the relative orientation of $\mathbf{a}$ and $\mathbf{b}$, then we only need the *sign* of the dot product:

a·b	θ	Angle is	a and b are
> 0	$0° \leq \theta < 90°$	acute	pointing in basically the same direction
0	$\theta = 90°$	right	perpendicular
< 0	$90° < \theta \leq 180°$	obtuse	pointing in basically opposite directions

Figure 5.11: The sign of the dot product gives a rough classification of the angle between two vectors

Since the magnitude of the vectors does not affect the sign of the dot product, the above table applies regardless of the magnitudes of $\mathbf{a}$ and $\mathbf{b}$. However, notice that if either $\mathbf{a}$ or $\mathbf{b}$ is the zero vector, then $\mathbf{a} \cdot \mathbf{b}$ will always equal zero. Thus, the dot product interprets the zero vector as being perpendicular to every other vector.

5.10.3 Projecting One Vector onto Another

Given two vectors $\mathbf{v}$ and $\mathbf{n}$, it is possible to separate $\mathbf{v}$ into two values, $\mathbf{v}_{\parallel}$ and $\mathbf{v}_{\perp}$. They are parallel and perpendicular to $\mathbf{n}$, respectively, such that $\mathbf{v} = \mathbf{v}_{\parallel} + \mathbf{v}_{\perp}$. We sometimes refer to parallel portion $\mathbf{v}_{\parallel}$ as the result of *projecting* $\mathbf{v}$ onto $\mathbf{n}$.

We compute the projection by using the dot product. Figure 5.12 below illustrates the geometry involved:

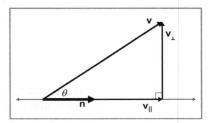

Figure 5.12: Projecting one vector onto another

Let's solve for $\mathbf{v}_{\parallel}$. First, we can see that $\mathbf{v}_{\parallel}$ is parallel to $\mathbf{n}$, and so it can be expressed as:

$$\mathbf{v}_{\parallel} = \mathbf{n}\frac{\|\mathbf{v}_{\parallel}\|}{\|\mathbf{n}\|}$$

So, if we can solve for just the magnitude of $\mathbf{v}_{\parallel}$, we can then compute the vector value. Luckily, we can do this easily using elementary trigonometry:

$$\cos\theta = \frac{\|\mathbf{v}_{\parallel}\|}{\|\mathbf{v}\|}$$

$$\cos\theta\|\mathbf{v}\| = \|\mathbf{v}_{\parallel}\|$$

Substitute $\|\mathbf{v}_{\parallel}\|$ into our original equation and apply the geometric interpretation of the dot product from Equation 5.16:

Equation 5.19: Projecting one vector onto another

$$\begin{aligned} \mathbf{v}_{\parallel} &= \mathbf{n}\frac{\|\mathbf{v}\|\cos\theta}{\|\mathbf{n}\|} \\ &= \mathbf{n}\frac{\|\mathbf{v}\|\|\mathbf{n}\|\cos\theta}{\|\mathbf{n}\|^2} \\ &= \mathbf{n}\frac{\mathbf{v}\cdot\mathbf{n}}{\|\mathbf{n}\|^2} \end{aligned}$$

Of course, if $\mathbf{n}$ is a unit vector, then the division is unnecessary.

Once we know $\mathbf{v}_{\parallel}$, we can easily solve for $\mathbf{v}_{\perp}$:

$$\begin{aligned} \mathbf{v}_{\perp} + \mathbf{v}_{\parallel} &= \|v\| \\ \mathbf{v}_{\perp} &= \|\mathbf{v}\| - \mathbf{v}_{\parallel} \\ &= \|\mathbf{v}\| - \mathbf{n}\frac{\mathbf{v}\cdot\mathbf{n}}{\|\mathbf{n}\|^2} \end{aligned}$$

In the rest of this book, we will make use of these equations several times to separate a vector into components that are parallel and perpendicular to another vector.

5.11 Vector Cross Product

The other vector product, known as the *cross product* or *outer product*, applies to 3D vectors only. Unlike the dot product, which yields a scalar and is commutative, the vector cross product yields a 3D vector and is not commutative.

5.11.1 Official Linear Algebra Rules

Like the dot product, the term "cross product" comes from the symbol used in the notation: $\mathbf{a} \times \mathbf{b}$. We always write the cross symbol, rather than omitting it like we do with scalar multiplication. The equation for the cross product is given by:

Equation 5.20:
Cross product

$$\begin{bmatrix} x_1 \\ y_1 \\ z_1 \end{bmatrix} \times \begin{bmatrix} x_2 \\ y_2 \\ z_2 \end{bmatrix} = \begin{bmatrix} y_1 z_2 - z_1 y_2 \\ z_1 x_2 - x_1 z_2 \\ x_1 y_2 - y_1 x_2 \end{bmatrix}$$

An example:

$$\begin{bmatrix} 1 \\ 3 \\ 4 \end{bmatrix} \times \begin{bmatrix} 2 \\ -5 \\ 8 \end{bmatrix} = \begin{bmatrix} (3)(8) - (-4)(-5) \\ (-4)(2) - (1)(8) \\ (1)(-5) - (3)(2) \end{bmatrix} = \begin{bmatrix} 4 \\ -16 \\ 10 \end{bmatrix}$$

The cross product enjoys the same level of operator precedence as the dot product; multiplication occurs before addition and subtraction. When dot product and cross product are used together, the cross product takes precedence: $\mathbf{a} \cdot \mathbf{b} \times \mathbf{c} = \mathbf{a} \cdot (\mathbf{b} \times \mathbf{c})$. Because the dot product returns a scalar, $(\mathbf{a} \cdot \mathbf{b}) \times \mathbf{c}$ is undefined since you cannot take the cross product of a scalar and a vector. The operation $\mathbf{a} \cdot \mathbf{b} \times \mathbf{c}$ is known as the *triple product*. We will learn some special properties of this computation in Section 9.1.

As was mentioned earlier, the vector cross product is not commutative. In fact, it is anticommutative: $\mathbf{a} \times \mathbf{b} = -(\mathbf{b} \times \mathbf{a})$. Cross product is not associative, either. In general, $(\mathbf{a} \times \mathbf{b}) \times \mathbf{c} \neq \mathbf{a} \times (\mathbf{b} \times \mathbf{c})$. More vector algebra laws concerning the cross product will be given in Section 5.12.

5.11.2 Geometric Interpretation

The cross product yields a vector that is perpendicular to the original two vectors, as illustrated in Figure 5.13:

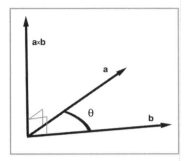

Figure 5.13: Vector cross product

In this diagram, vectors **a** and **b** are laying in a flat plane with the vector labeled **a**×**b** pointing straight up out of the plane, perpendicular to **a** and **b**.

The length of **a**×**b** is equal to the product of the magnitudes of **a** and **b** and the sine of the angle between **a** and **b**:

Equation 5.21:
The magnitude
of the cross
product is
related to the
sine of the angle
between the
vectors

$$\|\mathbf{a} \times \mathbf{b}\| = \|\mathbf{a}\|\|\mathbf{b}\| \sin \theta$$

As it turns out, this is also equal to the area of the parallelogram formed on two sides by **a** and **b**. Let's see if we can't verify why this is true. Examine Figure 5.14 below:

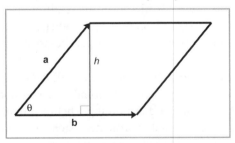

Figure 5.14: The cross product and the area of a parallelogram

We know from classical geometry that the area of the parallelogram is bh, the product of the base and the height. We can verify that this is true by "clipping" off a triangle from one end and moving it to the other end, forming a rectangle, as shown in the following illustration:

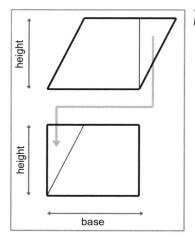

Figure 5.15: Area of a parallelogram

The area of a rectangle is given by its length and width. In this case, the area is the product bh. Since the area of the rectangle is equal to the area of the parallelogram, the area of the parallelogram must also be bh.

Back to Figure 5.14. Let a and b be the lengths of **a** and **b**, respectively. Note that $\sin \theta = h/a$:

$$
\begin{aligned}
A &= bh \\
&= b(a \sin \theta) \\
&= \|\mathbf{a}\|\|\mathbf{b}\| \sin \theta \\
&= \|\mathbf{a} \times \mathbf{b}\|
\end{aligned}
$$

If either **a** or **b** is parallel, or if **a** or **b** is the zero vector, then **a**×**b** = **0**. The cross product interprets the zero vector as being parallel to every other vector. Notice that this is different from the dot product, which interprets the zero vector as being *perpendicular* to every other vector. (Of course, it is ill-defined to describe the zero vector as being perpendicular or parallel to any vector, since the zero vector has no direction.)

We have stated that **a**×**b** is perpendicular to **a** and **b**. But there are two directions that are perpendicular to **a** and **b**. Which of these two directions does **a**×**b** point? We can determine the direction of **a**×**b** by placing the tail of **b** at the head of **a** and examining whether we make a clockwise or counterclockwise turn from **a** to **b**. In a left-handed coordinate system, **a**×**b** points toward you if the vectors **a** and **b** make a clockwise turn from your viewpoint. It points away from you if **a** and **b** make a counterclockwise turn. In a right-handed coordinate system, the exact opposite occurs. If **a** and **b** make a counterclockwise turn, **a**×**b** points toward you, and if **a** and **b** make a clockwise turn, **a**×**b** points away from you.

The following figures show clockwise and counterclockwise turns:

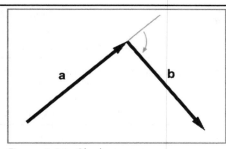

Figure 5.16: Clockwise turn

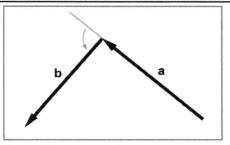

Figure 5.17: Counterclockwise turn

In a left-handed coordinate system, $\mathbf{a}{\times}\mathbf{b}$ (not shown) points toward you. In a right-handed coordinate system, $\mathbf{a}{\times}\mathbf{b}$ points away from you.

In a left-handed coordinate system, $\mathbf{a}{\times}\mathbf{b}$ (not shown) points away from you. In a right-handed coordinate system, $\mathbf{a}{\times}\mathbf{b}$ points toward from you.

Notice that to make the clockwise or counterclockwise determination, we must align the head of **a** with the tail of **b**. Compare this to Figure 5.13, where the tails are aligned. The tail-to-tail alignment shown in Figure 5.13 is the correct way to position the vectors to measure the angle between them. However, to judge clockwise or counterclockwise turns, the vectors should be aligned head-to-tail, as shown above.

One of the most important uses of the cross product is to create a vector that is perpendicular to a plane (see Section 12.5), triangle (Section 12.6), or polygon (Section 12.7).

5.12 Linear Algebra Identities

Figure 5.18 lists some useful vector identities. Many of these identities are obvious, but they are listed here just for the sake of completeness. All of these identities can be derived from the definitions given in earlier sections.

Identity	Comments
$\mathbf{a} + \mathbf{b} = \mathbf{b} + \mathbf{a}$	Commutative property of vector addition.
$\mathbf{a} - \mathbf{b} = \mathbf{a} + (-\mathbf{b})$	Definition of vector subtraction.
$(\mathbf{a} + \mathbf{b}) + \mathbf{c} = \mathbf{a} + (\mathbf{b} + \mathbf{c})$	Associative property of vector addition.
$s(t\mathbf{a}) = (st)\mathbf{a}$	Associative property of scalar multiplication.
$k(\mathbf{a} + \mathbf{b}) = k\mathbf{a} + k\mathbf{b}$	Scalar multiplication distributes over vector addition.
$\|k\mathbf{a}\| = |k|\|\mathbf{a}\|$	Multiplying a vector by a scalar scales the magnitude by a factor equal to the absolute value of the scalar.

Identity	Comments
$\|\mathbf{a}\| \geq 0$	The magnitude of a vector is nonnegative.
$\|\mathbf{a}\|^2 + \|\mathbf{b}\|^2 = \|\mathbf{a} + \mathbf{b}\|^2$	The Pythagorean theorem applied to vector addition.
$\|\mathbf{a}\| + \|\mathbf{b}\| \geq \|\mathbf{a} + \mathbf{b}\|$	Triangle rule of vector addition. (No side can be longer than the sum of the lengths of the other two sides.)
$\mathbf{a} \cdot \mathbf{b} = \mathbf{b} \cdot \mathbf{a}$	Commutative property of dot product.
$\|\mathbf{a}\| = \sqrt{\mathbf{a} \cdot \mathbf{a}}$	Vector magnitude defined using dot product.
$k(\mathbf{a} \cdot \mathbf{b}) = (k\mathbf{a}) \cdot \mathbf{b} = \mathbf{a} \cdot (k\mathbf{b})$	Associative property of scalar multiplication with dot product.
$\mathbf{a} \cdot (\mathbf{b} + \mathbf{c}) = \mathbf{a} \cdot \mathbf{b} + \mathbf{a} \cdot \mathbf{c}$	Dot product distributes over vector addition and subtraction.
$\mathbf{a} \times \mathbf{a} = \mathbf{0}$	The cross product of any vector with itself is the zero vector. (Because any vector is parallel with itself.)
$\mathbf{a} \times \mathbf{b} = -(\mathbf{b} \times \mathbf{a})$	Cross product is anti-commutative.
$\mathbf{a} \times \mathbf{b} = (-\mathbf{a}) \times (-\mathbf{b})$	Negating both operands to the cross product results in the same vector.
$k(\mathbf{a} \times \mathbf{b}) = (k\mathbf{a}) \times \mathbf{b} = \mathbf{a} \times (k\mathbf{b})$	Associative property of scalar multiplication with cross product.
$\mathbf{a} \times (\mathbf{b} + \mathbf{c}) = \mathbf{a} \times \mathbf{b} + \mathbf{a} \times \mathbf{c}$	Cross product distributes over vector addition and subtraction.
$\mathbf{a} \cdot (\mathbf{a} \times \mathbf{b}) = 0$	The dot product of any vector with the cross product of that vector and another vector is zero. (The cross product produces a perpendicular vector, and the dot product of perpendicular vectors is zero.)

Figure 5.18: Table of vector algebra identities

5.13 Exercises

1. Evaluate the following vector expressions:

   a. $-\begin{bmatrix} 3 & 7 \end{bmatrix}$

   b. $\left\| \begin{bmatrix} -12 & 5 \end{bmatrix} \right\|$

   c. $\left\| \begin{bmatrix} 8 & -3 & 1/2 \end{bmatrix} \right\|$

   d. $3\begin{bmatrix} 4 & -7 & 0 \end{bmatrix}$

   e. $\begin{bmatrix} 4 & 5 \end{bmatrix}/2$

2. Normalize the following vectors:

   a. $\begin{bmatrix} 12 & 5 \end{bmatrix}$

   b. $\begin{bmatrix} 8 & -3 & 1/2 \end{bmatrix}$

3. Evaluate the following vector expressions:

   a. $\begin{bmatrix} 3 \\ 10 \\ 7 \end{bmatrix} - \begin{bmatrix} 8 \\ -7 \\ 4 \end{bmatrix}$

   b. $3\begin{bmatrix} a \\ b \\ c \end{bmatrix} - 4\begin{bmatrix} 2 \\ 10 \\ -6 \end{bmatrix}$

4. Compute the distance between the following pairs of points:

   a. $\begin{bmatrix} 3 \\ 10 \\ 7 \end{bmatrix}, \begin{bmatrix} 8 \\ -7 \\ 4 \end{bmatrix}$

   b. $\begin{bmatrix} 10 \\ 6 \end{bmatrix}, \begin{bmatrix} -14 \\ 30 \end{bmatrix}$

5. Evaluate the following vector expressions:

   a. $\begin{bmatrix} 2 \\ 6 \end{bmatrix} \cdot -38$

   b. $3\begin{bmatrix} -2 \\ 0 \\ 4 \end{bmatrix} \cdot \left(\begin{bmatrix} 8 \\ -2 \\ 3/2 \end{bmatrix} + \begin{bmatrix} 0 \\ 9 \\ 7 \end{bmatrix} \right)$

6. Compute the angle between the vectors [1, 2] and [–6, 3].

7. Given the two vectors

   $$\mathbf{v} = \begin{bmatrix} 4 \\ 3 \\ -1 \end{bmatrix}, \mathbf{n} = \begin{bmatrix} \frac{\sqrt{2}}{2} \\ \frac{\sqrt{2}}{2} \\ 0 \end{bmatrix}$$

   separate **v** into components that are perpendicular and parallel to **n**. (**n** is a unit vector.)

8. Compute the value of

$$\begin{bmatrix} 3 \\ 10 \\ 7 \end{bmatrix} \times \begin{bmatrix} 8 \\ -7 \\ 4 \end{bmatrix}$$

9. A man is boarding a plane. The airline has a rule that no carry-on item may be more than two feet long, two feet wide, or two feet tall. The man has a very valuable sword that is three feet long. He is able to carry the sword on board with him. How is he able to do this? What is the longest possible item that he could carry on?

10. Verify Figure 5.7 on page 56 mathematically.

11. Is the coordinate system used in Figure 5.13 on page 63 a left-handed or right-handed coordinate system?

12. Assume that Texas is flat. A minute of latitude is approximately 1.15 miles in length. At the authors' latitude (see Section 3.2.1), a minute of longitude is approximately 0.97 miles in length. There are 60 minutes in one degree of latitude or longitude. How far apart are the authors?

Chapter 6

A Simple 3D Vector Class

This chapter puts theory into practice with a simple C++ vector class, `Vector3`. It is divided into three main sections.

- Section 6.1 discusses the operations we want to implement in `Vector3`.
- Section 6.2 contains the complete code listing for `Vector3`.
- Section 6.3 discusses some of the design decisions embodied in class `Vector3` (and all of the other C++ classes in this book).

The preceding chapters have focused on the theory of 3D math. In this chapter, we'll turn for the first time to the practice of 3D math by introducing a C++ class to represent a 3D vector.

6.1 Class Interface

Good class design always begins with the question, "What operations do I want to perform using this class, and what values do I want to perform them on?" In other words, "What do I want this class to *do?*" We know that we will use this class to store the *x*, *y*, and *z* values for a 3D vector. We also know we will need some basic operations, such as the ability to:

- Access the individual components of the vector (*x*, *y*, and *z*).
- Assign one vector to another.
- Compare two vectors for equality.

From Chapter 5 we know that we will need to perform the following vector operations:

- Set a vector to the zero vector.
- Negate a vector.
- Compute the magnitude of a vector.
- Multiply or divide a vector by a scalar.
- Normalize a vector.

- Add or subtract two vectors.
- Compute the distance between two points (expressed as vectors).
- Compute the dot product of two vectors.
- Compute the cross product of two vectors.

6.2 Class Vector3 Definition

Below is the complete listing for Vector3.h, which contains the definition of class Vector3:

Listing 6.1: Vector3.h

```
/////////////////////////////////////////////////////////////////////////
//
// class Vector3 — a simple 3D vector class
//
/////////////////////////////////////////////////////////////////////////

class Vector3 {
public:

// Public representation: Not many options here.

    float x,y,z;

// Constructors

    // Default constructor leaves vector in
    // an indeterminate state

    Vector3() {}

    // Copy constructor

    Vector3(const Vector3 &a) : x(a.x), y(a.y), z(a.z) {}

    // Construct given three values

    Vector3(float nx, float ny, float nz) : x(nx), y(ny), z(nz) {}

// Standard object maintenance

    // Assignment. We adhere to C convention and
    // return reference to the lvalue

    Vector3 &operator =(const Vector3 &a) {
        x = a.x; y = a.y; z = a.z;
        return *this;
    }

    // Check for equality

    bool operator ==(const Vector3 &a) const {
        return x==a.x && y==a.y && z==a.z;
    }
```

```
    bool operator !=(const Vector3 &a) const {
        return x!=a.x || y!=a.y || z!=a.z;
    }


// Vector operations

    // Set the vector to zero

    void zero() { x = y = z = 0.0f; }

    // Unary minus returns the negative of the vector

    Vector3 operator –() const { return Vector3(–x,–y,–z); }

    // Binary + and – add and subtract vectors

    Vector3 operator +(const Vector3 &a) const {
        return Vector3(x + a.x, y + a.y, z + a.z);
    }

    Vector3 operator –(const Vector3 &a) const {
        return Vector3(x – a.x, y – a.y, z – a.z);
    }

    // Multiplication and division by scalar

    Vector3 operator *(float a) const {
        return Vector3(x*a, y*a, z*a);
    }

    Vector3 operator /(float a) const {
        float oneOverA = 1.0f / a; // NOTE: no check for divide by zero here
        return Vector3(x*oneOverA, y*oneOverA, z*oneOverA);
    }

    // Combined assignment operators to conform to
    // C notation convention

    Vector3 &operator +=(const Vector3 &a) {
        x += a.x; y += a.y; z += a.z;
        return *this;
    }

    Vector3 &operator –=(const Vector3 &a) {
        x –= a.x; y –= a.y; z –= a.z;
        return *this;
    }

    Vector3 &operator *=(float a) {
        x *= a; y *= a; z *= a;
        return *this;
    }

    Vector3 &operator /=(float a) {
        float oneOverA = 1.0f / a;
        x *= oneOverA; y *= oneOverA; z *= oneOverA;
        return *this;
    }
```

```
        // Normalize the vector

        void   normalize() {
                float magSq = x*x + y*y + z*z;
                if (magSq > 0.0f) { // check for divide-by-zero
                        float oneOverMag = 1.0f / sqrt(magSq);
                        x *= oneOverMag;
                        y *= oneOverMag;
                        z *= oneOverMag;
                }
        }

        // Vector dot product. We overload the standard
        // multiplication symbol to do this

        float operator *(const Vector3 &a) const {
                return x*a.x + y*a.y + z*a.z;
        }
};

//////////////////////////////////////////////////////////////////////////
//
// Nonmember functions
//
//////////////////////////////////////////////////////////////////////////

// Compute the magnitude of a vector

inline float vectorMag(const Vector3 &a) {
        return sqrt(a.x*a.x + a.y*a.y + a.z*a.z);
}

// Compute the cross product of two vectors

inline Vector3 crossProduct(const Vector3 &a, const Vector3 &b) {
        return Vector3(
                a.y*b.z — a.z*b.y,
                a.z*b.x — a.x*b.z,
                a.x*b.y — a.y*b.x
        );
}

// Scalar on the left multiplication, for symmetry

inline Vector3 operator *(float k, const Vector3 &v) {
        return Vector3(k*v.x, k*v.y, k*v.z);
}

// Compute the distance between two points

inline float distance(const Vector3 &a, const Vector3 &b) {
        float dx = a.x — b.x;
        float dy = a.y — b.y;
        float dz = a.z — b.z;
        return sqrt(dx*dx + dy*dy + dz*dz);
}

//////////////////////////////////////////////////////////////////////////
//
// Global variables
```

```
//
/////////////////////////////////////////////////////////////////////////

// We provide a global zero vector constant

extern const Vector3 kZeroVector;
```

6.3   Design Decisions

Every person who writes code does it slightly different. In this section, we will discuss a number of design choices reflected in all of the code in this book, using class `Vector3` as an example. We will also comment on some techniques or options that are *not* reflected in class `Vector3`, that we have seen in code on the Internet or tried ourselves and found to be a bad idea. There is no one "right" way to write a vector class, but we will offer some advice from our experience.

6.3.1 Floats vs. Doubles

The first major choice that must be made is whether to use floats or doubles in your vector class. We have chosen to use floats. There are circumstances in which the extra precision provided by doubles is necessary. For example, if your world is very large, say bigger than 200 miles or so, and you still need precision down to the inch, then the 24 bits of mantissa in a 32-bit float is not quite enough. If your world is less than a mile, a 32-bit float is probably quite sufficient, since 24 bits of mantissa is precise to about the nearest $1/250^{th}$ of an inch. If you don't need double precision, you can make substantial savings in memory, and possibly performance, by using floats.

6.3.2 Operator Overloading

C++ allows *overloaded operators*. This means that you can define the operation that is performed when an operator such as "+" is used with objects of your class. You define the behavior in a function, which is invoked when the operator is used. Aside from the syntax, which seems unusual if you have not seen it before, an overloaded operator is just like any other function. Overloaded operators can be member or nonmember functions, they accept parameters, and they can be expanded inline.

Because vectors are mathematical entities, it makes sense to overload operators to make their use in code more closely resemble their use on paper. We overload the following operators:

- Vector multiplication and division by a scalar.
- Vector negation.
- Vector addition and subtraction.
- Vector dot product.

6.3.3 Provide Only the Most Important Operations

It is tempting to add too much to your classes. It is especially tempting to overload too many operators. After all, you're going to use this thing everywhere, right? Why not make it do everything you could want? Before you have used a vector class extensively, you don't really know what operations you need on a large scale. But in our opinion (and one of us is a professional game programmer with over a decade of experience), the operations provided in Listing 6.1 are probably what you will use in 99% of your code.

One group of operations that is commonly added, but should be avoided, is shorthand for working with scalars. For example, you may think it would be really handy to have a constructor that accepts a scalar k and sets all three components to k. But, by creating a nifty little shortcut for this seldom used operation, you have created all sorts of possibilities for accidental conversions from scalar to vector. It's not straightforward. It could cause confusion and programmer error, so it's best to avoid it.

Another common technique is to overload the array operator (`operator []`) or conversion to `float*`. This is done so that the components may be accessed by integer index. For a vector class to use with geometric problems, we access the elements by name (x, y, and z), rather than by index. However, it may be your preference to be able to access the elements by index. In this case, you should either make an explicit function or overload the array operator (`operator []`), rather than providing `operator float*`. The array operator can check for array bounds errors, and it does not introduce the possibility of accidental conversions.

You can imagine all sorts of other operations that could be added, such as extracting the largest or smallest component of the vector, etc. Our advice is to wait to add any function to your vector class until you actually use them in three different places in the code.

6.3.4 Don't Overload Too Many Operators

Especially avoid overloading too many operators, unless it is *extremely* obvious what the operation does. Otherwise, use a function. As a general programming rule, *tedium is preferred over ambiguity*. In other words, preventing accidental errors is more important than saving a few keystrokes.

In particular, avoid the temptation to overload the following commonly overloaded operations:

■ **Cross product.** Cross product is used frequently, but not as frequently as dot product, which is the first reason that dot product has the overloaded `operator*` and cross product does not. The other reason is that "*" looks more like a dot than a cross. Since cross product is used so frequently (and this operator overloading thing is so neat!), it is tempting to overload some *other* operator for cross product. Particularly, the "%" operator is appealing, since "%" has the correct operator precedence and looks somewhat like a cross. No C operator, other than "*", signifies "multiplication," and no operator uses the cross symbol, so there really is no appropriate operator to use. An overloaded operator is not going to be that much more "elegant" than a function call for cross product. However, the overloaded operator will very likely be less clear than a function call, especially to another programmer who doesn't really see the resemblance between "%" and "×".

■ **Component-wise multiplication or (worse) division**. If you really want to have this operation (and our experience is that it is seldom used), then use a nonmember function. Overloaded operators for these operations are confusing.

■ **Relational operators**. The tests for equality and inequality are well defined. Either two vectors are identical, or they are not identical. The other relational operators, however, are not well defined. What does it mean for one vector to be "less than" another? We advise against attempting to define some "meaningful" behavior, which you will most likely only end up using in one or two places. (One common "meaningful" behavior is the so-called *lexographic* sort, which can be useful for some implementations of computational geometry algorithms. Even in this case, it's probably best to have a separate function.)

■ **Vector magnitude**. Again, using an operator for vector magnitude is not straightforward and should be avoided.

6.3.5 Use Const Member Functions

Use const member functions as much as possible. If you are unfamiliar with the motivation for const member functions, it's a way for a function to promise to the caller that, "I won't modify the object." The compiler enforces this promise. This can be a great way to make sure that your code has no unanticipated side effects. That is, things aren't getting modified without you knowing.

6.3.6 Use Const Reference Arguments

In addition to const member functions, all of the functions that accept vectors accept a constant reference (const&) to a vector. Passing an argument by value to a function involves a constructor call. Passing a const reference allows us to conceptually pass arguments by value, but actually they are passed by reference (address) and without any constructor calls for speed. In addition, if the function is not inline, passing a vector by value on the stack requires more space (and thus more time to push the argument on the stack) than passing by reference.

When we pass a vector variable to a function that accepts a const reference, the address of the argument is passed directly, just as if we had passed the argument using a pointer. When we pass a vector expression to a function that accepts a const reference, the compiler generates code to evaluate the vector expression into a temporary variable, and then passes the address of the temporary to the function. So we get the best of both worlds. Conceptually, we get pass-by-value, so we can pass vector expressions to functions, letting the compiler do the tedious job of creating temporary variables. Under the hood, the function actually uses pass-by-reference, which is faster.

6.3.7 Member vs. Nonmember Functions

Another design decision reflected in the code is the decision to make certain functions nonmember functions, as opposed to member functions. A member function is declared in the class definition and is invoked as a member of the class, with an implicit `this` pointer as one parameter. (For example, the `zero()` function is a member function.) A nonmember function is an ordinary function that does not have an implicit `this` pointer. (For example, the `vectorMag()` function.) Many operations can be coded using either a member function or a nonmember function that accepts a single vector argument. We prefer the nonmember style for most such functions. When an operation needs to be applied to a vector expression (as opposed to just a vector variable), the nonmember style looks better. For example:

Listing 6.2: Member vs. nonmember function semantics

```
class Vector3 {
public:
        ...

        // member function to compute the magnitude

        float mag() const;
};

// Nonmember version:

float vectorMag(const Vector3 &a);

...

void    foo() {
        Vector3 a,b;
        float m;

        // If computing the length of a vector
        // variable, both forms look fine:

        m = a.mag();
        m = vectorMag(a);

        // But when we have a vector expression,
        // the member function style looks awkward:

        m = (a + b).mag();

        // The nonmember version is much easier to read:

        m = vectorMag(a + b);
}
```

We use the nonmember function style for:

■ Magnitude

■ Cross product

■ Distance

The only member functions declared (other than the overloaded operators, which do not suffer from this "weird syntax" problem) are `zero()` and `normalize()`. It is not useful to call these functions on vector expressions, so the "weird syntax" problem will not occur.

6.3.8 No Default Initialization

The default constructor does not perform any initialization. If you declare a variable of type `Vector3`, you must initialize it. This is the same as the C intrinsic types, such as `int` and `float`. The vector class allocates no resources but can be used in many speed-critical places, so our preference is to not perform default initialization. It may be your preference to have the default constructor provide some sort of initialization, the most obvious choice being to zero the vector.

6.3.9 Don't Use Virtual Functions

We do not use virtual functions in our vector class. There are multiple reasons for this. First, the ability to "customize" the vector operations is not very useful. Dot product is dot product — it will always be the same thing.

Second, `Vector3` is a speed-critical class. The compiler's optimizer would not be able to generate inline expansion of member functions in many cases if virtual functions were used.

Third, using virtual functions necessitates the hidden pointer to the virtual function table. This pointer must be initialized any time a vector is declared, and it adds 25% to the class size. It is common to store large arrays of vectors, and all that space for the v-table pointers is inordinately wasteful in many cases.

Virtual functions just aren't a good fit for a vector class.

6.3.10 Don't Use Information Hiding

Information hiding is the practice of declaring member variables in the private or protected section, allowing access to those members only through *accessor functions*. The idea is that implementation details should be hidden from the users of a class, and the use of the class is restricted to a limited set of well-defined operations, which are exported by public member functions. Direct member variable access often works contrary to this end.

For example, the user of a string class should not need to know how the string class works internally or be allowed to manipulate internal members directly. The string operations, such as assignment, concatenation, substring extraction, etc., should be exported through a set of well-defined public member functions.

The use of accessor functions also allows the class designed to maintain *invariants*, or relationships between member variables which we assume to always be true. (For example, we may store the length of the string in a member variable for immediate access. In this case, the invariant is that our length variable contains the correct length of the string. When the string changes, we must update the length member to maintain the invariant.) Changes to private member variables can only happen in the member functions of the class. So if a bug violates an invariant, there are a limited number of functions that need to be checked for the bug.

In most cases, information hiding is a wise decision. However, for a vector class, information hiding is not appropriate. The representation of a 3D vector is obvious; you store three numbers: *x*, *y*, and *z*. Functions such as `getX()` and `setX()` only clutter the code. In addition, there are no invariants we need to maintain. Any three numbers could be stored in a vector, so what would we check for in our accessor functions? Nothing is gained by information hiding, but simplicity and efficiency suffer.

In our vector class, all member functions and variables will be public.

6.3.11 Global Zero Vector Constant

We declare a global zero vector constant, which we call `kZeroVector`. This is handy for passing a zero vector to a function instead of creating a zero vector on the fly every time with the constructor call `Vector3(0.0f,0.0f,0.0f)`.

6.3.12 No "point3" Class

We will use the vector class to store 3D "points," such as the vertices of a triangle mesh, instead of using, as some people do, a special `Point3` class. Section 4.3 established that points and vectors are mathematically equivalent. So certainly there is not a strict *need* for a point class. The argument for having a separate class for points is that points and vectors are conceptually distinct. This is a somewhat valid argument. However, there is often a fine line between a "point" and a "vector." (See Section 4.3.2.) Our experience is that any benefits of the conceptual distinction provided by a separate `Point3` class are vastly outweighed by the problems it creates.

For example, let's say we have a function that rotates a point or vector about the *y*-axis by a certain amount. (We will learn how to use matrices to do this in Section 8.2.2.) This operation is the same mathematically for points and vectors. However, if we decide to use two different classes for points and vectors, we are faced with two options:

- We write two versions of our function, one that accepts a `Vector3` argument and another that accepts a `Point3` argument.
- We make our function accept type `Vector3` and convert arguments of type `Point3` whenever they are passed to the function. (Or the other way around.)

Both of these scenarios are bad, but let's examine the second option in more detail. The conversion between `Vector3` and `Point3` that takes place can either happen explicitly or implicitly. Let's say we make the conversion explicit. This means we will be casting between vectors and points everywhere. (If you don't believe us, try it.) If the conversion happens implicitly (i.e., we define a constructor or a conversion operator), then we can freely assign between points and vectors, and the benefit of having two distinct classes is largely lost.

There are probably C++ contortions that can be done to avoid many problems like this. The point is, we are bending over backward just so we can have a `Point3` class. It just isn't worth it.

Use the same class to store "points" and "vectors." Whether you actually name your class "point" or "vector" is up to you.

6.3.13 A Word on Optimization

If you have seen vector classes elsewhere, this vector class may seem very simple in comparison. Many vector classes on the Internet and other sources are much more complicated, usually for the sake of "optimization." There are two reasons to keep our vector class as simple as possible:

- First, this book is intended to teach you how to program 3D math. All unnecessary complexities were removed so that there would be as few impediments to your understanding as possible.

- Second, and more importantly, we have not been convinced that such so-called "optimizations" actually increase execution performance significantly.

Let's elaborate just a bit more on this second point. A famous programming rule of thumb states, "95% of the time is spent in 5% of the code." In other words, to speed up execution, you must find the bottleneck and optimize it. Another famous quote related to optimization is, "Premature optimization is the root of all evil." Optimizing code that isn't the bottleneck complicates the code without appreciable benefit.

In the video game industry, performance is critical, and there are frequently times when vector processing can be an execution bottleneck. In these cases, optimization is necessary and extremely effective. However, almost invariably the way to get the biggest performance boost is to perform the operations using a special platform-specific processing unit. Unfortunately, idiosyncrasies of the vector processing unit (such as alignment restrictions or lack of a dot product operation) frequently make it impossible to design the vector class to take advantage of the vector processing unit in all situations. A large part of optimizing vector math code is to completely rearrange the code in order to exploit superscalar architecture, or perform an entire batch of operations in parallel on a separate processor. No amount of tweaking of the vector class can accomplish these high-level optimizations. Even when optimizing some vector math in an inner loop, hand-tuned assembly on sequences of vector operations will be much faster than the fastest compiler-generated code could possibly be, no matter how well the vector class is "optimized."

These observations have caused us to divide vector math code (and code in general) into two categories. The first category contains the majority of code. Not much time is actually spent in this code, and therefore, optimization will not provide huge performance gains. The second category is the minority of code in which optimization is actually effective and often necessary. Rearranging the data structures or writing hand-tuned assembly is almost always significantly faster than compiler-generated code, no matter how well organized the vector class. (Notice that the above discussion applies to low-level optimization at the assembly instruction level and does not necessarily apply to higher-level optimizations, such as using better algorithms.)

The bottom line: if you're seriously concerned about speed, optimizing your vector class will only speed up code that should be written in assembly. Also, it won't make it as fast as the assembly would be. It will speed up the code elsewhere, but, unfortunately, not much time is spent in that code, so the gains will be relatively small. In our opinion, such small gains are not worth the added complexities to the vector class.

At the same time, "optimizing" a vector class usually results in considerable complications to the design of the vector class. This extra complexity can take its toll on compile times, your sanity, and (depending on how the optimizations were written) the aesthetic quality of code written using the vector class.

There are two specific optimizations that we should comment on in more detail. The first is fixed-point math, and the second is returning references to temporary variables.

Back in "the old days" (a few years ago), floating-point math was considerably slower than integer math on consumer systems. Most notably, floating-point multiplication was slow. Programmers used fixed-point math in order to circumvent this problem. If you are unfamiliar with fixed-point math, the basic idea behind the technique is that a number is stored with a fixed number of fractional bits. For example, there might be eight fractional bits, which would mean a number would be stored times 256. So the number 3.25 would be stored as 3.25×256 = 832. Except in a few special cases, fixed-point math is an optimization technique of the past. Today's processors not only can perform floating math in the same number of cycles as integer math, but they have dedicated vector processors to perform floating-point *vector* math. Use floating-point math in your vector class.

In our vector class, many of the vector operations (such as addition, subtraction, and multiplication by a scalar) have been coded to return an actual object of type Vector3. Depending on the compiler, this can be implemented in a variety of different ways. At the very least, returning a class object always results in at least one constructor call (according to the C++ standard). We have tried to code our functions with the constructor call in the actual return statement so that the compiler doesn't generate any "extra" constructor calls. Unfortunately, it is true that returning a class object *can* have performance implications.

However, beware of a special optimization "trick" that is often used to avoid these constructor calls. The basic idea is to maintain a pool of temporary class objects. Instead of returning an actual class object, the result of the function is computed into a temporary object, and then a reference to this temporary is returned. It usually looks something like this:

```cpp
// Maintain a pool of temporary objects

int         nextTemp;
Vector3     tempList[256];

// Get a pointer to the next temporary object

inline Vector3      *nextTempVector() {

    // Advance pointer and loop it

    nextTemp = (nextTemp + 1) & 255;

    // Return pointer to the slot

    return &tempList[nextTemp];
}

// Now rather than returning an actual class object,
// we can return a reference to a temporary. For example,
// the addition operator could be implemented like this:

const Vector3 &operator +(const Vector3 &a, const Vector3 &b) {

    // Snag a temp.

    Vector3 *result = nextTempVector();

    // Compute the result.
```

```
        result->x = a.x + b.x;
        result->y = a.y + b.y;
        result->z = a.z + b.z;

        // Return reference. No constructor calls!

        return *result;
}

// Now we can add and subtract vectors using the same
// natural syntax, just as before. Vector expressions
// with multiple additions and subtractions work, provided
// that no more than 256 temporaries are used in the same
// expression. (A very reasonable restriction.)

Vector3     a, b;
Vector3     c = a + b;
```

At first glance, this appears to be a great idea. The overhead of maintaining the index variable is usually less than the compiler's overhead of copy constructors and returning temporary objects. Overall, performance is increased (slightly).

There's just one problem. Our simple system of using a looping index variable assumes a great deal about the lifetime of temporary objects. In other words, we assume that when we create a temporary object, we won't need that object again by the time 256 more temporaries have been created. For simple vector expressions, this is usually not a problem. The problem comes when we pass these references into functions. A temporary passed into a function should not expire before the completion of the function. For example:

```
// A set of vertices of a triangle mesh

void   bias(
       const Vector3 inputList[],
       int n,
       const Vector3 &offset,
       Vector3 outputList[]
) {
       for (int i = 0 ; i < n ; ++i) {
              outputList[i] = intputList[i] + offset;
       }
}

// Elsewhere in the code...

void   foo() {

       const int n = 512;
       Vector3     *before = new Vector3[n];
       Vector3     *after = new Vector3[n];

       // … (Compute the bounding box into min and max)

       Vector3     min, max;

       // Let's recenter the model about its centroid
```

```
        // YIKES! But this doesn't work because our temporary
        // (min + max) / 2.0f gets trampled inside the function!

        bias(before, n, (min + max) / 2.0f, after);

        // ...
}
```

Of course, this example is a bit contrived in order to illustrate the problem in as few lines of code as possible, but certainly the problem does arise in practice. No matter how big we make our pool, we are in danger of having a bug, since even the most simple function may result in millions of temporary objects being created. The basic problem is that evaluation of the lifespan of a temporary must be done at *compile time* (by the compiler), not at run time.

Bottom line: keep your classes simple. In the very few cases where the overhead of constructor calls and the like is a significant problem, write the code in hand-tuned C++ or assembly. Also, you can write your function to accept a pointer where the return value should be placed, rather than actually returning a class object. However, don't complicate 100% of the code in order to optimize 2% of it.

Chapter 7

Introduction to Matrices

This chapter introduces the theory and application of matrices. It is divided into two main sections.

- Section 7.1 discusses some of the basic properties and operations of matrices strictly from a mathematical perspective. (More matrix operations are discussed in Chapter 9.)
- Section 7.2 explains how to interpret these properties and operations geometrically.

Matrices are of fundamental importance in 3D math, where they are primarily used to describe the relationship between two coordinate spaces. They do this by defining a computation to transform vectors from one coordinate space to another.

7.1 Matrix — A Mathematical Definition

In linear algebra, a matrix is a rectangular grid of numbers arranged into *rows* and *columns*. Recalling our earlier definition of vector as a one-dimensional array of numbers, a matrix may likewise be defined as a *two-dimensional array* of numbers. (The *two* in "two-dimensional array" comes from the fact that there are rows and columns, and it should not be confused with 2D vectors or matrices.) A vector is an array of scalars, and a matrix is an array of vectors.

7.1.1 Matrix Dimensions and Notation

Just as we defined the dimension of a vector by counting how many numbers it contained, we will define the size of a matrix by counting how many rows and columns it contains. An $r \times c$ matrix (read "r by c") has r rows and c columns. Here is an example of a 4×3 matrix:

$$\begin{bmatrix} 4 & 0 & 12 \\ -5 & \sqrt{4} & 3 \\ 12 & -4/3 & -1 \\ 1/2 & 18 & 0 \end{bmatrix}$$

This 4×3 matrix illustrates the standard notation for writing matrices. We arrange the numbers in a grid, surrounded by square brackets. Note that other authors surround the grid of numbers with parentheses rather than brackets. Other authors use straight vertical lines. We will reserve this notation for an entirely separate concept related to matrices, the *determinant* of a matrix. (We will discuss determinants in Section 9.1.)

As we mentioned in Section 5.2, we will represent a matrix variable with uppercase letters in boldface, for example: **M**, **A**, **R**. When we wish to refer to the individual elements within a matrix, we use subscript notation, usually with the corresponding lowercase letter in italics. This is shown below for a 3×3 matrix:

$$\mathbf{M} = \begin{bmatrix} m_{11} & m_{12} & m_{13} \\ m_{21} & m_{22} & m_{23} \\ m_{31} & m_{32} & m_{33} \end{bmatrix}$$

m_{ij} denotes the element in **M** at row i and column j. Matrices use 1-based indices, so the first row and column are numbered one. For example, m_{12} (read "*m* one two," not "*m* twelve") is the element in the first row, second column. Notice that this is different from the C programming language, which uses 0-based array indices. A matrix does not have a column 0 or row 0. This difference in indexing can cause some confusion if using actual C arrays to define matrices. (This is one reason we won't use arrays to define matrices in our code.)

7.1.2 Square Matrices

Matrices with the same number of rows as columns are called *square* matrices and are of particular importance. In this book, we will be interested in 2×2, 3×3, and 4×4 matrices.

The *diagonal elements* of a square matrix are those elements where the row and column index are the same. For example, the diagonal elements of the 3×3 matrix **M** are m_{11}, m_{22}, and m_{33}. The other elements are *non-diagonal* elements. The diagonal elements form the *diagonal* of the matrix:

$$\begin{bmatrix} m_{11} & m_{12} & m_{13} \\ m_{21} & m_{22} & m_{23} \\ m_{31} & m_{32} & m_{33} \end{bmatrix}$$

If all non-diagonal elements in a matrix are zero, then the matrix is a *diagonal matrix*. For example:

$$\begin{bmatrix} 3 & 0 & 0 & 0 \\ 0 & 1 & 0 & 0 \\ 0 & 0 & -5 & 0 \\ 0 & 0 & 0 & 2 \end{bmatrix}$$

A special diagonal matrix is the *identity matrix*. The identity matrix of dimension n, denoted $\mathbf{I}_n$, is the $n \times n$ matrix with 1's on the diagonal and 0's elsewhere. For example, the 3×3 identity matrix is:

Equation 7.1:
The 3D identity matrix

$$\mathbf{I}_3 = \begin{bmatrix} 1 & 0 & 0 \\ 0 & 1 & 0 \\ 0 & 0 & 1 \end{bmatrix}$$

Often, the context will make the dimension of the identity matrix used in a particular situation clear. In these cases, we will omit the subscript and simply refer to the identity matrix as $\mathbf{I}$.

The identity matrix is special because it is the *multiplicative identity element* for matrices. (We will learn about matrix multiplication in Section 7.1.6.) The basic idea is that if you multiply a matrix by the identity matrix, you get the original matrix. So, in some ways, the identity matrix is for matrices what the number 1 is for scalars.

7.1.3 Vectors as Matrices

Matrices may have any positive number of rows and columns, including one. We have already encountered matrices with one row or one column: vectors! A vector of dimension n can be viewed either as a $1 \times n$ matrix or as an $n \times 1$ matrix. A $1 \times n$ matrix is known as a *row vector*, and an $n \times 1$ matrix is known as a *column vector*. Row vectors are written horizontally, and column vectors are written vertically:

$$\begin{bmatrix} 1 & 2 & 3 \end{bmatrix} \quad \begin{bmatrix} 4 \\ 5 \\ 6 \end{bmatrix}$$

Until now, we have used the two notations interchangeably. Indeed, geometrically they are identical, and in most cases the distinction is not important. However, for reasons that will soon become apparent, when we use vectors with matrices, we must be very clear about whether our vector is a row or column vector.

7.1.4 Transposition

Consider a matrix $\mathbf{M}$ with dimensions $r \times c$. The *transpose* of $\mathbf{M}$ (denoted $\mathbf{M}^T$) is the $c \times r$ matrix where the columns are formed from the rows of $\mathbf{M}$. In other words, $\mathbf{M}^T_{ij} = \mathbf{M}_{ji}$. This "flips" the matrix diagonally. Equation 7.2 gives two examples of transposing matrices:

Equation 7.2:
Transposing matrices

$$\begin{bmatrix} 1 & 2 & 3 \\ 4 & 5 & 6 \\ 7 & 8 & 9 \\ 10 & 11 & 12 \end{bmatrix}^T = \begin{bmatrix} 1 & 4 & 7 & 10 \\ 2 & 5 & 8 & 11 \\ 3 & 6 & 9 & 12 \end{bmatrix} \qquad \begin{bmatrix} a & b & c \\ d & e & f \\ g & h & i \end{bmatrix}^T = \begin{bmatrix} a & d & g \\ b & e & h \\ c & f & i \end{bmatrix}$$

For vectors, transposition turns row vectors into column vectors and vice versa:

Equation 7.3:
Transposing
converts
between row
and column
vectors

$$\begin{bmatrix} x & y & z \end{bmatrix}^T = \begin{bmatrix} x \\ y \\ z \end{bmatrix} \qquad \begin{bmatrix} x \\ y \\ z \end{bmatrix}^T = \begin{bmatrix} x & y & z \end{bmatrix}$$

Transposition notation is often used to write column vectors inline in a paragraph, like this: $[1, 2, 3]^T$.

There are two fairly obvious, but significant, observations concerning matrix transposition:

- $(\mathbf{M}^T)^T = \mathbf{M}$ for a matrix $\mathbf{M}$ of any dimension. In other words, if we transpose a matrix, and then transpose it again, we get the original matrix. This rule also applies to vectors.
- $\mathbf{D}^T = \mathbf{D}$ for any diagonal matrix $\mathbf{D}$, including the identity matrix $\mathbf{I}$.

7.1.5 Multiplying a Matrix with a Scalar

A matrix $\mathbf{M}$ may be multiplied with a scalar k, resulting in a matrix of the same dimension as $\mathbf{M}$. We denote matrix multiplication with a scalar by placing the scalar and the matrix side by side, usually with the scalar on the left. No multiplication symbol is necessary. The multiplication takes place in the straightforward fashion; each element in the resulting matrix $k\mathbf{M}$ is the product of k and the corresponding element in $\mathbf{M}$. For example:

Equation 7.4:
Multiplying a
4×3 matrix
by a scalar

$$k\mathbf{M} = k \begin{bmatrix} m_{11} & m_{12} & m_{13} \\ m_{21} & m_{22} & m_{23} \\ m_{31} & m_{32} & m_{33} \\ m_{41} & m_{42} & m_{43} \end{bmatrix} = \begin{bmatrix} km_{11} & km_{12} & km_{13} \\ km_{21} & km_{22} & km_{23} \\ km_{31} & km_{32} & km_{33} \\ km_{41} & km_{42} & km_{43} \end{bmatrix}$$

7.1.6 Multiplying Two Matrices

In certain situations, we can take the product of two matrices. The rules that govern when matrix multiplication is allowed, and how the result is computed, may at first seem bizarre. An $r \times n$ matrix $\mathbf{A}$ may be multiplied by an $n \times c$ matrix $\mathbf{B}$. The result, denoted $\mathbf{AB}$, is an $r \times c$ matrix.

For example, assume that $\mathbf{A}$ is a 4×2 matrix, and $\mathbf{B}$ is a 2×5 matrix. Then $\mathbf{AB}$ is a 4×5 matrix:

$$\underset{\substack{r \times n \\ 4 \times 2}}{\mathbf{A} \begin{bmatrix} ? & ? \\ ? & ? \\ ? & ? \\ ? & ? \end{bmatrix}} \underset{\substack{n \times c \\ 2 \times 5}}{\mathbf{B} \begin{bmatrix} ? & ? & ? & ? & ? \\ ? & ? & ? & ? & ? \end{bmatrix}} = \underset{\substack{r \times c \\ 4 \times 5}}{\mathbf{AB} \begin{bmatrix} ? & ? & ? & ? & ? \\ ? & ? & ? & ? & ? \\ ? & ? & ? & ? & ? \\ ? & ? & ? & ? & ? \end{bmatrix}}$$

must match

columns in result

rows in result

If the number of columns in **A** does not match the number of rows in **B**, then the multiplication **AB** is undefined.

Matrix multiplication is computed as follows: let the matrix **C** be the $r{\times}c$ product **AB** of the $r{\times}n$ matrix **A** with the $n{\times}c$ matrix **B**. Then each element c_{ij} is equal to the vector dot product of row i of **A** with column j of **B**. More formally:

$$c_{ij} = \sum_{k=1}^{n} a_{ik} b_{kj}$$

(See Appendix A if you don't know what the symbol that looks like a "Z" means.)

This sounds complicated, but there is a simple pattern. For each element c_{ij} in the result, locate row i in **A** and column j in **B**. Multiply the corresponding elements of the row and column, and sum the products. (This is equivalent to the dot product of row i in **A** with column j in **B**.) c_{ij} is equal to this sum.

Let's look at an example. Below we show how to compute c_{24}:

$$
\begin{bmatrix}
c_{11} & c_{12} & c_{13} & c_{14} & c_{15} \\
c_{21} & c_{22} & c_{23} & c_{24} & c_{25} \\
c_{31} & c_{32} & c_{33} & c_{34} & c_{35} \\
c_{41} & c_{42} & c_{43} & c_{44} & c_{45}
\end{bmatrix}
=
\begin{bmatrix}
a_{11} & a_{12} \\
a_{21} & a_{22} \\
a_{31} & a_{32} \\
a_{41} & a_{42}
\end{bmatrix}
\begin{bmatrix}
b_{11} & b_{12} & b_{13} & b_{14} & b_{15} \\
b_{21} & b_{22} & b_{23} & b_{24} & b_{25}
\end{bmatrix}
$$

$$c_{24} = a_{21} b_{14} + a_{22} b_{24}$$

The element in the second row and fourth column of **C** is equal to the dot product of the second row of **A** with the fourth column of **B**.

Another way to help remember the pattern is to write **B** above **C**, as shown below. This aligns the proper row from **A** with a column from **B** for each element in the result **C**:

$$
\begin{bmatrix}
b_{11} & b_{12} & b_{13} & b_{14} & b_{15} \\
b_{21} & b_{22} & b_{23} & b_{24} & b_{25}
\end{bmatrix}
$$

$$
\begin{bmatrix}
a_{11} & a_{12} \\
a_{21} & a_{22} \\
a_{31} & a_{32} \\
a_{41} & a_{42}
\end{bmatrix}
\begin{bmatrix}
c_{11} & c_{12} & c_{13} & c_{14} & c_{15} \\
c_{21} & c_{22} & c_{23} & c_{24} & c_{25} \\
c_{31} & c_{32} & c_{33} & c_{34} & c_{35} \\
c_{41} & c_{42} & c_{43} & c_{44} & c_{45}
\end{bmatrix}
$$

$$c_{43} = a_{41} b_{13} + a_{42} b_{23}$$

For geometric applications, we will be particularly interested in multiplying square matrices — the $2{\times}2$ and $3{\times}3$ cases are especially important to us. Equation 7.5 gives the complete equation for $2{\times}2$ matrix multiplication:

Equation 7.5:
2×2 matrix
multiplication

$$\mathbf{AB} = \begin{bmatrix} a_{11} & a_{12} \\ a_{21} & a_{22} \end{bmatrix} \begin{bmatrix} b_{11} & b_{12} \\ b_{21} & b_{22} \end{bmatrix}$$

$$= \begin{bmatrix} a_{11}b_{11} + a_{12}b_{21} & a_{11}b_{12} + a_{12}b_{22} \\ a_{21}b_{11} + a_{22}b_{21} & a_{21}b_{12} + a_{22}b_{22} \end{bmatrix}$$

Let's look at a 2×2 example with some real numbers:

$$\mathbf{A} = \begin{bmatrix} -3 & 0 \\ 5 & 1/2 \end{bmatrix}, \mathbf{B} = \begin{bmatrix} -7 & 2 \\ 4 & 6 \end{bmatrix}$$

$$\mathbf{AB} = \begin{bmatrix} -3 & 0 \\ 5 & 1/2 \end{bmatrix} \begin{bmatrix} -7 & 2 \\ 4 & 6 \end{bmatrix}$$

$$= \begin{bmatrix} (-3)(-7) + (0)(4) & (-3)(2) + (0)(6) \\ (5)(-7) + (1/2)(4) & (5)(2) + (1/2)(6) \end{bmatrix}$$

$$= \begin{bmatrix} 21 & -6 \\ -33 & 13 \end{bmatrix}$$

Now for the 3×3 case:

Equation 7.6:
3×3 matrix
multiplication

$$\mathbf{AB} = \begin{bmatrix} a_{11} & a_{12} & a_{13} \\ a_{21} & a_{22} & a_{23} \\ a_{31} & a_{32} & a_{33} \end{bmatrix} \begin{bmatrix} b_{11} & b_{12} & b_{13} \\ b_{21} & b_{22} & b_{23} \\ b_{31} & b_{32} & b_{33} \end{bmatrix}$$

$$= \begin{bmatrix} a_{11}b_{11} + a_{12}b_{21} + a_{13}b_{31} & a_{11}b_{12} + a_{12}b_{22} + a_{13}b_{32} & a_{11}b_{13} + a_{12}b_{23} + a_{13}b_{33} \\ a_{21}b_{11} + a_{22}b_{21} + a_{23}b_{31} & a_{21}b_{12} + a_{22}b_{22} + a_{23}b_{32} & a_{21}b_{13} + a_{22}b_{23} + a_{23}b_{33} \\ a_{31}b_{11} + a_{32}b_{21} + a_{33}b_{31} & a_{31}b_{12} + a_{32}b_{22} + a_{33}b_{32} & a_{31}b_{13} + a_{32}b_{23} + a_{33}b_{33} \end{bmatrix}$$

And a 3×3 example with some real numbers:

$$\mathbf{A} = \begin{bmatrix} 1 & -5 & 3 \\ 0 & -2 & 6 \\ 7 & 2 & -4 \end{bmatrix}, \mathbf{B} = \begin{bmatrix} -8 & 6 & 1 \\ 7 & 0 & -3 \\ 2 & 4 & 5 \end{bmatrix}$$

$$\mathbf{AB} = \begin{bmatrix} 1 & -5 & 3 \\ 0 & -2 & 6 \\ 7 & 2 & -4 \end{bmatrix} \begin{bmatrix} -8 & 6 & 1 \\ 7 & 0 & -3 \\ 2 & 4 & 5 \end{bmatrix}$$

$$= \begin{bmatrix} (1)(-8) + (-5)(7) + (3)(2) & (1)(6) + (-5)(0) + (3)(4) & (1)(1) + (-5)(-3) + (3)(5) \\ (0)(-8) + (-2)(7) + (6)(2) & (0)(6) + (-2)(0) + (6)(4) & (0)(1) + (-2)(-3) + (6)(5) \\ (7)(-8) + (2)(7) + (-4)(2) & (7)(6) + (2)(0) + (-4)(4) & (7)(1) + (2)(-3) + (-4)(5) \end{bmatrix}$$

$$= \begin{bmatrix} -37 & 18 & 31 \\ -2 & 24 & 36 \\ -50 & 26 & -19 \end{bmatrix}$$

Beginning in Section 9.4, we will also use 4×4 matrices.

A few interesting notes concerning matrix multiplication:

■ Multiplying any matrix **M** by a square matrix **S** on either side results in a matrix of the same size as **M**, provided that the sizes of the matrices are such that the multiplication is allowed. If **S** is the identity matrix **I**, then the result is the original matrix **M**:

$$\mathbf{MI} = \mathbf{IM} = \mathbf{M}$$

(That's the reason it's called the *identity* matrix!)

- Matrix multiplication is *not* commutative:
  $$\mathbf{AB} \neq \mathbf{BA}$$

- Matrix multiplication is associative:
  $$(\mathbf{AB})\mathbf{C} = \mathbf{A}(\mathbf{BC})$$

  (Assuming that the sizes of **A**, **B**, and **C** are such that multiplication is allowed, note that if $(\mathbf{AB})\mathbf{C}$ is defined, then $\mathbf{A}(\mathbf{BC})$ is always defined as well.) The associativity of matrix multiplication extends to multiple matrices. For example:

  $$\mathbf{ABCDEF} = ((((\mathbf{AB})\mathbf{C})\mathbf{D})\mathbf{E})\mathbf{F} = \mathbf{A}((((\mathbf{BC})\mathbf{D})\mathbf{E})\mathbf{F}) = (\mathbf{AB})(\mathbf{CD})(\mathbf{EF})$$

  It is interesting to note that although all parenthesizations compute the correct result, some groupings require fewer scalar multiplications than others. The problem of finding the parenthesization that minimizes the number of scalar multiplications is known as the *matrix chain* problem.

- Matrix multiplication also associates with multiplication by a scalar or a vector:
  $$(k\mathbf{A})\mathbf{B} = k(\mathbf{AB}) = \mathbf{A}(k\mathbf{B}) \quad (\mathbf{vA})\mathbf{B} = \mathbf{v}(\mathbf{AB})$$

- Transposing the product of two matrices is the same as taking the product of their transposes in reverse order:
  $$(\mathbf{AB})^T = \mathbf{B}^T\mathbf{A}^T$$

  This can be extended to more than two matrices:

  $$(\mathbf{M}_1\mathbf{M}_2 \cdots \mathbf{M}_{n-1}\mathbf{M}_n)^T = \mathbf{M}_n{}^T\mathbf{M}_{n-1}{}^T \cdots \mathbf{M}_2{}^T\mathbf{M}_1{}^T$$

7.1.7 Multiplying a Vector and a Matrix

Since a vector can be considered a matrix with one row or one column, we can multiply a vector and a matrix using the rules discussed in the previous section. It becomes very important whether we are using row or column vectors. Below we show how 3D row and column vectors may be pre- or post-multiplied by a 3×3 matrix:

Equation 7.7:
Multiplying 3D row and column vectors with a 3×3 matrix

$$\begin{bmatrix} x & y & z \end{bmatrix} \begin{bmatrix} m_{11} & m_{12} & m_{13} \\ m_{21} & m_{22} & m_{23} \\ m_{31} & m_{32} & m_{33} \end{bmatrix} = \begin{bmatrix} xm_{11} + ym_{21} + zm_{31} & xm_{12} + ym_{22} + zm_{32} & xm_{13} + ym_{23} + zm_{33} \end{bmatrix}$$

$$\begin{bmatrix} m_{11} & m_{12} & m_{13} \\ m_{21} & m_{22} & m_{23} \\ m_{31} & m_{32} & m_{33} \end{bmatrix} \begin{bmatrix} x \\ y \\ z \end{bmatrix} = \begin{bmatrix} xm_{11} + ym_{12} + zm_{13} \\ xm_{21} + ym_{22} + zm_{23} \\ xm_{31} + ym_{32} + zm_{33} \end{bmatrix}$$

$$\begin{bmatrix} m_{11} & m_{12} & m_{13} \\ m_{21} & m_{22} & m_{23} \\ m_{31} & m_{32} & m_{33} \end{bmatrix} \begin{bmatrix} x & y & z \end{bmatrix} = (undefined)$$

$$\begin{bmatrix} x \\ y \\ z \end{bmatrix} \begin{bmatrix} m_{11} & m_{12} & m_{13} \\ m_{21} & m_{22} & m_{23} \\ m_{31} & m_{32} & m_{33} \end{bmatrix} = (undefined)$$

As you can see, when we multiply a row vector on the left by a matrix on the right, the result is a row vector. When we multiply a matrix on the left by a column vector on the right, the result is a column vector. The other two combinations are not allowed; you cannot multiply a matrix on the left by a row vector on the right, nor can you multiply a column vector on the left by a matrix on the right.

There are three interesting observations concerning vector-times-matrix multiplication:

■ Each element in the resulting vector is the dot product of the original vector with a single row or column from the matrix.

■ Each element in the matrix determines how much "weight" a particular element in the input vector contributes to an element in the output vector. For example, m_{11} controls how much of the input x value goes toward the output x value.

■ Vector-times-matrix multiplication distributes over vector addition. That is, for vectors **v** and **w** and matrices **M**:

$$(\mathbf{v} + \mathbf{w})\mathbf{M} = \mathbf{v}\mathbf{M} + \mathbf{w}\mathbf{M}$$

7.1.8 Row vs. Column Vectors

In this section, we will explain why the distinction between row and column vectors is significant and give our rationale for preferring row vectors. In Equation 7.7, when we multiply a row vector on the left with a matrix on the right, we get the row vector:

$$\begin{bmatrix} xm_{11} + ym_{21} + zm_{31} & xm_{12} + ym_{22} + zm_{32} & xm_{13} + ym_{23} + zm_{33} \end{bmatrix}$$

Compare that with the result when a column vector on the right is multiplied by a matrix on the left:

$$\begin{bmatrix} xm_{11} + ym_{12} + zm_{13} \\ xm_{21} + ym_{22} + zm_{23} \\ xm_{31} + ym_{32} + zm_{33} \end{bmatrix}$$

Disregarding the fact that one is a row vector and the other is a column vector, the values for the components of the vector are *not* the same! This is why the distinction between row and column vectors is so important.

In this book, we will use column vectors *only* when the distinction between row and column vectors is not important. If the distinction is at all relevant (for example, if vectors are used in conjunction with matrices), then we will use row vectors.

There are several reasons for using row vectors instead of column vectors:

■ Row vectors format nicely when they are used inline in a paragraph. For example, the row vector [1, 2, 3] fits nicely in this sentence. But notice how the column vector
$$\begin{bmatrix} 4 \\ 5 \\ 6 \end{bmatrix}$$

causes formatting problems. The same sorts of problems occur in source code as well. Some authors use transposed row vectors to write column vectors inline in their text, like $[4, 5, 6]^T$. Using row vectors from the beginning avoids all this weirdness.

■ More importantly, when we discuss how matrix multiplication can be used to perform coordinate space transformations, it will be convenient for the vector to be on the left and the matrix on the right. In this way, the transformation will read like a sentence. This is especially important when more than one transformation takes place. For example, if we wish to transform a vector **v** by the matrices **A**, **B**, and **C**, in that order, we write **vABC**. Notice that the matrices are listed in order of transformation from left to right. If column vectors are used, then the matrix is on the left, and the transformations will occur in order from right to left. In this case, we would write **CBAv**. We will discuss concatenation of multiple transformation matrices in detail in Section 8.7.

■ DirectX uses row vectors.

The arguments in favor of column vectors are:

■ Column vectors usually format nicer in equations. (Examine Equation 7.7 on page 89.)

■ Linear algebra textbooks typically use column vectors.

■ Several famous computer graphics "bibles" use column vectors. (For example, [8], [17].)

■ OpenGL uses column vectors.

Different authors use different conventions. When you use someone else's equation or source code, be very careful that you know whether they are using row or column vectors. If a book uses column vectors, its equations for matrices will be transposed compared to the equations we present in this book. In addition, when column vectors are used, vectors are pre-multiplied by a matrix, as opposed to the convention chosen in this book, to multiply row vectors by a matrix on the right. This causes the order of multiplication to be reversed between the two styles when multiple matrices and vectors are multiplied together. For example, the multiplication **vABC** is valid only with row vectors. The corresponding multiplication would be written **CBAv** if column vectors were used.

Transposition-type mistakes like this can be a common source of frustration when programming 3D math. Luckily, the C++ matrix classes we will present in Chapter 11 are designed so that direct access to the individual matrix elements is seldom needed. Thus, the frequency of these types of errors is minimized.

7.2 Matrix — A Geometric Interpretation

In general, a square matrix can describe any *linear transformation*. In Section 8.8.1, we will provide a complete definition of linear transformation. For now, it will suffice to say that a linear transformation preserves straight and parallel lines, and there is no translation — the origin does not move. While a linear transformation preserves straight lines, other properties of the geometry, such as lengths, angles, areas, and volumes, are possibly altered by the transformation. In a non-technical sense, a linear transformation may "stretch" the coordinate space, but it doesn't "curve" or "warp" it. This is a very useful set of transformations:

- Rotation
- Scale
- Orthographic projection
- Reflection
- Shearing

Chapter 8 discusses each of these transformations in detail. For now, we will attempt to gain some understanding of the relationship between a particular matrix and the transform it represents.

7.2.1 How Does a Matrix Transform Vectors?

In Section 4.2.4, we discussed how a vector may be interpreted geometrically as a sequence of axially-aligned displacements. For example, the vector $[1, -3, 4]$ can be interpreted as a displacement of $[1, 0, 0]$, followed by a displacement of $[0, -3, 0]$, followed by a displacement of $[0, 0, 4]$. Section 5.8.2 described how this sequence of displacements can be interpreted as a sum of vectors according to the triangle rule:

$$\begin{bmatrix} 1 \\ -3 \\ 4 \end{bmatrix} = \begin{bmatrix} 1 \\ 0 \\ 0 \end{bmatrix} + \begin{bmatrix} 0 \\ -3 \\ 0 \end{bmatrix} + \begin{bmatrix} 0 \\ 0 \\ 4 \end{bmatrix}$$

In general, for any vector $\mathbf{v}$, we can write $\mathbf{v}$ in "expanded" form:

$$\mathbf{v} = \begin{bmatrix} x \\ y \\ z \end{bmatrix} = \begin{bmatrix} x \\ 0 \\ 0 \end{bmatrix} + \begin{bmatrix} 0 \\ y \\ 0 \end{bmatrix} + \begin{bmatrix} 0 \\ 0 \\ z \end{bmatrix}$$

Let's rewrite this expression in a slightly different form:

$$\mathbf{v} = \begin{bmatrix} x \\ y \\ z \end{bmatrix} = x \begin{bmatrix} 1 \\ 0 \\ 0 \end{bmatrix} + y \begin{bmatrix} 0 \\ 1 \\ 0 \end{bmatrix} + z \begin{bmatrix} 0 \\ 0 \\ 1 \end{bmatrix}$$

Notice that the unit vectors on the right-hand side are x-, y-, and z-axes. We have just expressed mathematically a concept we established in Section 4.2.3: each coordinate of a vector specifies the signed displacement parallel to corresponding axes.

Let's rewrite the sum one more time. This time, we will define the vectors $\mathbf{p}$, $\mathbf{q}$, and $\mathbf{r}$ to be unit vectors pointing in the $+x$, $+y$, and $+z$, directions, respectively:

Equation 7.8:
Expressing a
vector as a
linear
combination of
basis vectors
$$\mathbf{v} = x\mathbf{p} + y\mathbf{q} + z\mathbf{r}$$

Now we have expressed the vector **v** as a linear combination of the vectors **p**, **q**, and **r**. The vectors **p**, **q**, and **r** are known as *basis vectors*. We are accustomed to using the cardinal axes as basis vectors, but, in fact, a coordinate space may be defined using *any* three vectors, provided the three vectors are *linearly independent* (which basically means that they don't lie in a plane). If we construct a 3×3 matrix **M** using **p**, **q**, and **r** as the rows of the matrix, we get:

Equation 7.9:
Interpreting a
matrix as a set
of basis vectors

$$\mathbf{M} = \begin{bmatrix} \mathbf{p} \\ \mathbf{q} \\ \mathbf{r} \end{bmatrix} = \begin{bmatrix} \mathbf{p}_x & \mathbf{p}_y & \mathbf{p}_z \\ \mathbf{q}_x & \mathbf{q}_y & \mathbf{q}_z \\ \mathbf{r}_x & \mathbf{r}_y & \mathbf{r}_z \end{bmatrix}$$

Multiplying a vector by this matrix, we get:

$$\begin{bmatrix} x & y & z \end{bmatrix} \begin{bmatrix} \mathbf{p}_x & \mathbf{p}_y & \mathbf{p}_z \\ \mathbf{q}_x & \mathbf{q}_y & \mathbf{q}_z \\ \mathbf{r}_x & \mathbf{r}_y & \mathbf{r}_z \end{bmatrix} = \begin{bmatrix} x\mathbf{p}_x + y\mathbf{q}_x + z\mathbf{r}_x & x\mathbf{p}_y + y\mathbf{q}_y + z\mathbf{r}_y & x\mathbf{p}_z + y\mathbf{q}_z + z\mathbf{r}_z \end{bmatrix}$$
$$= x\mathbf{p} + y\mathbf{q} + z\mathbf{r}$$

This is the same as our original equation for computing **v** after transformation. We have discovered the key idea that:

> If we interpret the rows of a matrix as the basis vectors of a coordinate space, then multiplication by the matrix performs a coordinate space transformation. If **aM=b**, we say that **M** transformed **a** to **b**.

From this point forward, the terms *transformation* and *multiplication* will be largely synonymous.

The bottom line is that there's nothing especially magical about matrices. They simply provide a compact way to represent the mathematical operations required to perform a coordinate space transformation. Furthermore, using linear algebra to manipulate matrices is a convenient way to take simple transformations and derive more complicated transformations. We will investigate this idea in Section 8.7.

7.2.2 What Does a Matrix Look Like?

"Unfortunately, no one can be told what the matrix is — you have to see it for yourself." This is not only a line from a great movie, it's true for linear algebra matrices as well. Until you develop an ability to visualize a matrix, it is just nine numbers in a box. We have stated that a matrix represents a coordinate space transformation. So when we visualize the matrix, we are visualizing the transformation, the new coordinate system. But what does this transformation look like? What is the relationship between a particular 3D transformation (i.e., rotation, shearing, etc.) and those nine numbers inside a 3×3 matrix? How can we construct a matrix to perform a given transform (other than by copying the equations blindly out of a book)?

To begin to answer these questions, let's examine what happens when the basis vectors [1, 0, 0], [0, 1, 0], and [0, 0, 1] are multiplied by an arbitrary matrix **M**:

$$\begin{bmatrix} 1 & 0 & 0 \end{bmatrix} \begin{bmatrix} m_{11} & m_{12} & m_{13} \\ m_{21} & m_{22} & m_{23} \\ m_{31} & m_{32} & m_{33} \end{bmatrix} = \begin{bmatrix} m_{11} & m_{12} & m_{13} \end{bmatrix}$$

$$\begin{bmatrix} 0 & 1 & 0 \end{bmatrix} \begin{bmatrix} m_{11} & m_{12} & m_{13} \\ m_{21} & m_{22} & m_{23} \\ m_{31} & m_{32} & m_{33} \end{bmatrix} = \begin{bmatrix} m_{21} & m_{22} & m_{23} \end{bmatrix}$$

$$\begin{bmatrix} 0 & 0 & 1 \end{bmatrix} \begin{bmatrix} m_{11} & m_{12} & m_{13} \\ m_{21} & m_{22} & m_{23} \\ m_{31} & m_{32} & m_{33} \end{bmatrix} = \begin{bmatrix} m_{31} & m_{32} & m_{33} \end{bmatrix}$$

As you can see, when we multiply the basis vector [1, 0, 0] by $\mathbf{M}$, the resulting vector is the first row of $\mathbf{M}$. Similar statements can be made regarding the other two rows. This is a critical observation:

> Each row of a matrix can be interpreted as a basis vector after transformation.

This is the same basic idea that we discovered in the previous section, only we have come at it from a slightly different angle. This very powerful concept has two important implications:

- First, we have a simple way to take any matrix and visualize what sort of transformation the matrix represents. Later in this section we will give examples of how to do this in 2D and 3D.

- Second, we have the ability to make the reverse construction — given a desired transformation (i.e. rotation, scale, etc.). We can derive a matrix which represents that transformation. All we have to do is figure out what the transformation does to basis vectors and fill in those transformed basis vectors into the rows of a matrix. This trick is used extensively in Chapter 8, where we will discuss the fundamental transformations and show how to construct matrices to perform those transformations.

Let's look at a couple of examples. First we will examine a 2D example to get ourselves warmed up and then a full-fledged 3D example. Examine the following 2×2 matrix:

$$\mathbf{M} = \begin{bmatrix} 2 & 1 \\ -1 & 2 \end{bmatrix}$$

What sort of transformation does this matrix represent? First, let's extract the basis vectors $\mathbf{p}$ and $\mathbf{q}$ from the rows of the matrix:

$$\mathbf{p} = \begin{bmatrix} 2 & 1 \end{bmatrix}$$
$$\mathbf{q} = \begin{bmatrix} -1 & 2 \end{bmatrix}$$

Figure 7.1 shows these vectors in the Cartesian plane, along with the "original" basis vectors (the x-axis and y-axis), for reference:

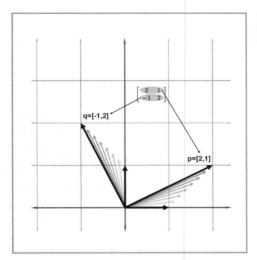

Figure 7.1: Visualizing the row vectors of a 2D transform matrix

As Figure 7.1 illustrates, the +*x* basis vector is transformed into the vector labeled **p** above, and the *y* basis vector is transformed into the vector labeled **q**. So one way to visualize a matrix in 2D is to visualize the "L" formed by the row vectors. In this example, we can easily see that part of the transformation represented by **M** is a counterclockwise rotation of about 26°.

Of course, *all* vectors are affected by a linear transformation, not just the basis vectors. While we can get a very good idea what this transformation looks like from the "L," we can gain further insight on the effect the transformation has on the rest of the vectors by completing the 2D parallelogram formed by the basis vectors:

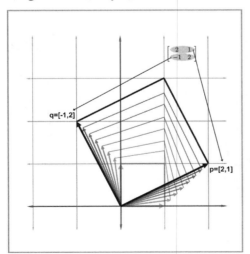

Figure 7.2: The 2D parallelogram formed by the rows of a matrix

This parallelogram is also known as a "skew box." Drawing an object inside the box can also help:

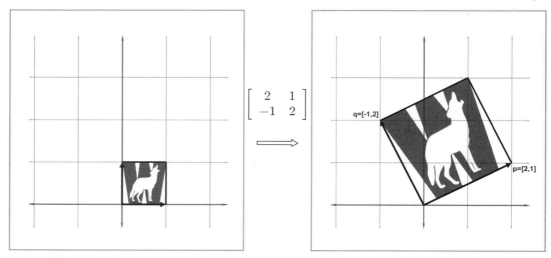

$$\begin{bmatrix} 2 & 1 \\ -1 & 2 \end{bmatrix}$$

Figure 7.3: Drawing an object inside the box helps visualize the transformation

It is clear that our example matrix **M** not only rotates the coordinate space, it also scales it.

We can extend the techniques we used to visualize 2D transformations into 3D. In 2D, we had two basis vectors that formed an "L." In 3D, we have three basis vectors, and they form a "tripod." First, let's show an object before transformation. Figure 7.4 shows a teapot, a unit cube, and the basis vectors in the "identity" position:

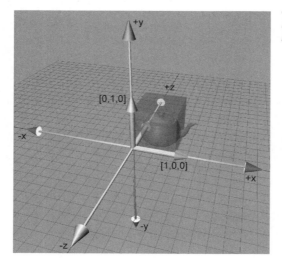

Figure 7.4: Teapot, unit cube, and basis vectors before transformation

(In order to avoid cluttering up the diagram, we have not labeled the +*z* basis vector [0,0,1], which is partially obscured by the teapot and cube.)

Now consider the 3D transformation matrix below:

$$\begin{bmatrix} 0.707 & -0.707 & 0 \\ 1.250 & 1.250 & 0 \\ 0 & 0 & 1 \end{bmatrix}$$

Extracting the basis vectors from the rows of the matrix, we can visualize the transformation represented by this matrix. The transformed basis vectors, cube, and teapot are shown below:

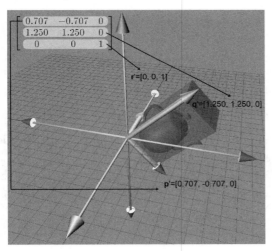

Figure 7.5: Teapot, unit cube, and basis vectors after transformation

As you can see, the transformation consists of a clockwise rotation about the *z*-axis by about 45° and a non-uniform scale that makes the teapot "taller" than it was originally. Notice that the +*z* basis vector was unaltered by the transformation because the third row of the matrix is [0,0,1].

7.2.3 Summary

Before we move on, let's review the key concepts of Section 7.2:

- The rows of a square matrix can be interpreted as the basis vectors of a coordinate space.
- To transform a vector from the original coordinate space to the new coordinate space, we multiply the vector by the matrix.
- The transformation from the original coordinate space to the coordinate space defined by these basis vectors is a linear transformation. A linear transformation preserves straight lines, and parallel lines remain parallel. However, angles, lengths, areas, and volumes may be altered after transformation.
- Multiplying the zero vector by any square matrix results in the zero vector. Therefore, the linear transformation represented by a square matrix has the same origin as the original coordinate space. The transformation does not contain translation.

■ We can visualize a matrix by visualizing the basis vectors of the coordinate space after transformation. These basis vectors form an "L" in 2D and a tripod in 3D. Using a box or auxiliary object also helps in visualization.

7.3 **Exercises**

1. Use the following matrices:

$$A = \begin{bmatrix} 13 & 4 & -8 \\ 12 & 0 & 6 \\ -3 & -1 & 5 \\ 10 & -2 & 5 \end{bmatrix} \quad B = \begin{bmatrix} k_x & 0 \\ 0 & k_y \end{bmatrix} \quad C = \begin{bmatrix} 15 & 8 \\ -7 & 3 \end{bmatrix}$$

$$D = \begin{bmatrix} 0 & 1 & 3 \end{bmatrix} \quad E = \begin{bmatrix} a & g \\ b & h \\ c & i \\ d & j \\ f & k \end{bmatrix} \quad F = \begin{bmatrix} x \\ y \\ z \\ w \end{bmatrix}$$

   a. For each matrix **A** through **F** above, give the dimensions of the matrix and identify the matrix as square and/or diagonal.

   b. Determine if the following matrix multiplications are allowed, and if so, give the dimensions of the resulting matrix.
   - DA
   - AD
   - BC
   - AF
   - E^TB
   - DFA

   c. Compute the following transpositions:
   - A^T
   - E^T
   - B^T

2. Compute the following products:

   a. $\begin{bmatrix} 1 & -2 \\ 5 & 0 \end{bmatrix} \begin{bmatrix} -3 & 7 \\ 4 & 1/3 \end{bmatrix}$

   b.
   $\begin{bmatrix} 3 & -1 & 4 \end{bmatrix} \begin{bmatrix} -2 & 0 & 3 \\ 5 & 7 & -6 \\ 1 & -4 & 2 \end{bmatrix}$

3. Manipulate the following matrix product to remove the parentheses:

$$\left((\mathbf{AB})^T (\mathbf{CDE})^T\right)^T$$

4. What type of transformation is represented by the following 2D matrix?

$$\begin{bmatrix} 0 & -1 \\ 1 & 0 \end{bmatrix}$$

Chapter 8

Matrices and Linear Transformations

This chapter discusses the implementation of linear transformations using matrices. It is divided into eight sections.

- Section 8.1 describes the relationship between transforming an object and transforming the coordinate space used to describe the object.

- Sections 8.2 through 8.6 describe the primitive linear transformations of rotation, scaling, orthographic projection, reflection, and shearing, respectively. For each transformation, examples and equations are given in 2D and 3D.

- Section 8.7 shows how a sequence of primitive transformations may be combined using matrix multiplication to form a more complicated transformation.

- Section 8.8 discusses various interesting categories of transformations, including linear, affine, invertible, angle-preserving, orthogonal, and rigid body transforms.

In Chapter 7, we investigated some of the basic mathematical properties of matrices. We also developed a geometric understanding of matrices and their relationship to coordinate space transformations in general. This chapter discusses this relationship between matrices and linear transformations in more detail.

To be more specific, this chapter is concerned with expressing linear transformations in 3D using 3×3 matrices. Linear transformations were introduced in Section 7.2. Recall that one important property of *linear* transformations is that they do not contain translation. A transformation that contains translation is known as an *affine* transformation. Affine transformations in 3D cannot be implemented using 3×3 matrices. We will see a formal definition of affine transformations in Section 8.8.2, and we will learn how to use 4×4 matrices to represent affine transformations in Section 9.4.3.

8.1 Transforming an Object vs. Transforming the Coordinate Space

Before we can talk about transformations, we must be very precise about exactly *what* we are transforming. We talked briefly about the relationship between transforming objects and transforming coordinate spaces in Section 3.5. Let's take a closer look now.

Consider the 2D example of "rotating an *object* clockwise 20°." When *transforming an object*, we mean that we are transforming the points of the object. These points move to a new position, and we use the same coordinate system to express the location of the points before and after transformation. Figure 8.1 illustrates this graphically.

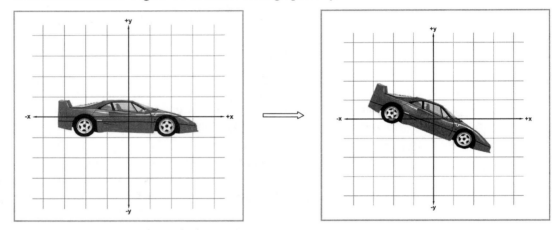

Figure 8.1: Rotating an object clockwise 20°

Compare that with the concept of *transforming the coordinate space*. When we rotate the coordinate space, the points of the object do not actually move; we are just expressing their location using a different coordinate space, as illustrated in Figure 8.2.

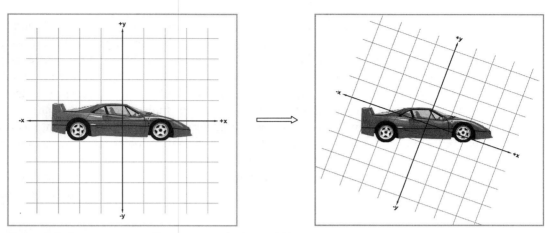

Figure 8.2: Rotating a coordinate space clockwise 20°

In a few minutes, we will show how the two types of transformations are, in a sense, equivalent. For now, let's discuss the conceptual merits of each.

The utility of transforming the object is fairly obvious. For example, in order to render the car, it will be necessary to transform the points from the object space of the car into world space, and then into camera space.

But why would we ever transform the coordinate space? Looking at Figure 8.3, it doesn't seem like there are many interesting things that we can accomplish by rotating the coordinate space into this awkward position. However, by examining Figure 8.3, we see how rotating the coordinate space can be put to good use.

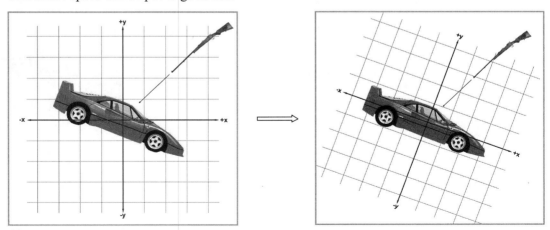

Figure 8.3: A useful example of rotating a coordinate space

In this figure, we have introduced a rifle that is firing a bullet at the car. As indicated by the coordinate space on the left, we would normally begin by knowing about the gun and the trajectory of the bullet in world space. Now, imagine transforming the coordinate space in line with the car's object space while keeping the car, the gun, and the trajectory of the bullet still. Now we know the position of the gun and the trajectory of the bullet in the object space of the car, and we could perform intersection tests to see if and where the bullet would hit the car.

Of course, we could just as easily have transformed the points of the car into world space and performed the test in world space, but that would be much slower since the car is probably modeled using many vertices and triangles, and there is only one gun. For now, don't worry about the details of actually performing the transformations; that's what the remainder of this chapter is for. Just remember that we can transform an object, or we can transform a coordinate space. Sometimes one or the other is more appropriate.

It is useful for us to maintain a conceptual distinction and to think about transforming the object in some cases and transforming the coordinate space in other cases. However, the two operations are actually equivalent. Transforming an object by a certain amount is equivalent to transforming the coordinate space by the *opposite* amount.

For example, let's take the diagram from the right-hand side of Figure 8.2, which shows the coordinate space rotated clockwise 20°. We will rotate the entire diagram (the coordinate space *and* the car) so that the coordinate space is back to the "standard" orientation on the page. Since we are rotating the entire diagram, we are merely looking at things from a different perspective, and we are not changing the relationship between the car and the coordinate space.

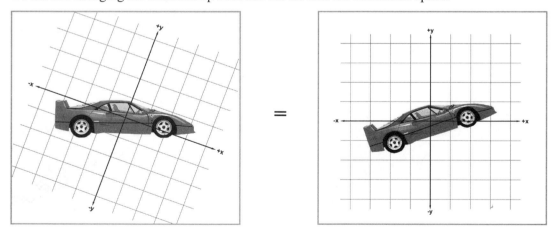

Figure 8.4: Rotating the coordinate space is the same as rotating the object by the opposite amount

Notice that this is the same as if we had started with the original diagram and rotated the car counterclockwise 20°. So rotating the coordinate space clockwise 20° is the same as rotating the object counterclockwise 20°. In general, transforming the geometry of an object is equivalent to transforming the coordinate space used to describe the geometry of the object by the exact *opposite* amount.

When multiple transformations are involved, we perform the transformations in the opposite order. For example, if we rotate the object clockwise 20° and then scale it by 200%, this is equivalent to scaling the coordinate space by 50% and then rotating the coordinate space counterclockwise 20°. We will discuss how to combine multiple transformations in Section 8.7.

The following sections present equations for constructing matrices to perform various transformations. These discussions will assume the perspective that the object is being transformed and the coordinate space remains stationary. Remember that we can always transform the coordinate space by transforming the object by the opposite amount.

8.2 Rotation

We have already seen general examples of rotation matrices. Now let's develop a more rigorous definition.

8.2.1 Rotation in 2D

In 2D, we are restricted to rotation about a point. Since we are not considering translation at the moment, we will restrict our discussion even further to rotation about the origin. A 2D rotation about the origin has only one parameter, the angle θ, which defines the amount of rotation. Counterclockwise rotation is usually (but not always) considered positive, and clockwise rotation is considered negative. Figure 8.5 shows how the basis vectors **p** and **q** are rotated about the origin, resulting in the new basis vectors **p'** and **q'**:

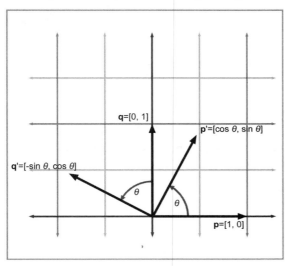

Figure 8.5: Rotation about the origin in 2D

Now that we know the values of the basis vectors after rotation, we can build our matrix:

Equation 8.1:
2D rotation
matrix

$$\mathbf{R}(\theta) = \begin{bmatrix} \mathbf{p}' \\ \mathbf{q}' \end{bmatrix} = \begin{bmatrix} \cos\theta & \sin\theta \\ -\sin\theta & \cos\theta \end{bmatrix}$$

8.2.2 3D Rotation about Cardinal Axes

In 3D, rotation occurs about an axis rather than a point. (In this case, the term *axis* refers to a line about which something rotates, and it does not necessarily have to be one of the cardinal *x*, *y*, or *z* axes.) Again, since we are not considering translation, we will limit the discussion to rotation about an axis that passes through the origin.

When we rotate about an axis by an amout θ, we need to know which way is considered "positive" and which way is considered "negative." The standard way to do this in a left-handed coordinate system (like the coordinate system used in this book) is called the *left-hand rule*. First, we must define which way our axis points. Of course, the axis of rotation is theoretically infinite in length, but we still consider it having a positive and negative end, just like the standard cardinal axes that define our coordinate space. The left-hand rule works like this: put your left hand in the "thumbs up" position, with your thumb pointing toward the positive end of the axis of rotation. Positive rotation about the axis of rotation is in the direction that your fingers are curled. This is illustrated below:

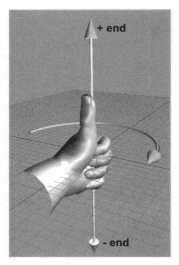

Figure 8.6: The left-hand rule defines positive rotation in a left-handed coordinate system

If you are using a right-handed coordinate system, then a similar rule applies, using your right hand instead of your left:

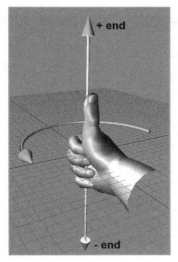

Figure 8.7: The right-hand rule defines positive rotation in a right-handed coordinate system

Figure 8.8 shows an alternative definition of positive rotation:

Viewed from	Left-handed coordinate system		Right-handed coordinate system	
	Positive rotation	Negative rotation	Positive rotation	Negative rotation
The negative end of the axis, looking toward the positive end of the axis	Counter-clockwise	Clockwise	Clockwise	Counter-clockwise
The positive end of the axis, looking toward the negative end of the axis	Clockwise	Counter-clockwise	Counter-clockwise	Clockwise

Figure 8.8: Positive and negative rotation about an axis

The most common type of rotation we will perform is a simple rotation about one of the cardinal axes. Let's start with rotation about the *x*-axis, shown in Figure 8.9:

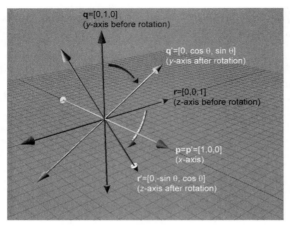

After constructing a matrix from the rotated basis vectors, we have:

Equation 8.2:
3D matrix to
rotate about
the x-axis

$$\mathbf{R}_x(\theta) = \begin{bmatrix} \mathbf{p}' \\ \mathbf{q}' \\ \mathbf{r}' \end{bmatrix} = \begin{bmatrix} 1 & 0 & 0 \\ 0 & \cos\theta & \sin\theta \\ 0 & -\sin\theta & \cos\theta \end{bmatrix}$$

Rotation about the *y*-axis is similar:

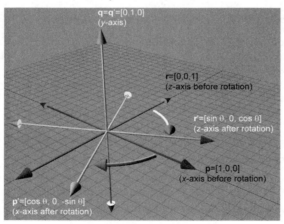

The matrix to rotate about the *y*-axis:

Equation 8.3:
3D matrix to
rotate about
the y-axis

$$\mathbf{R}_y(\theta) = \begin{bmatrix} \mathbf{p}' \\ \mathbf{q}' \\ \mathbf{r}' \end{bmatrix} = \begin{bmatrix} \cos\theta & 0 & -\sin\theta \\ 0 & 1 & 0 \\ \sin\theta & 0 & \cos\theta \end{bmatrix}$$

Finally, rotating about the z-axis:

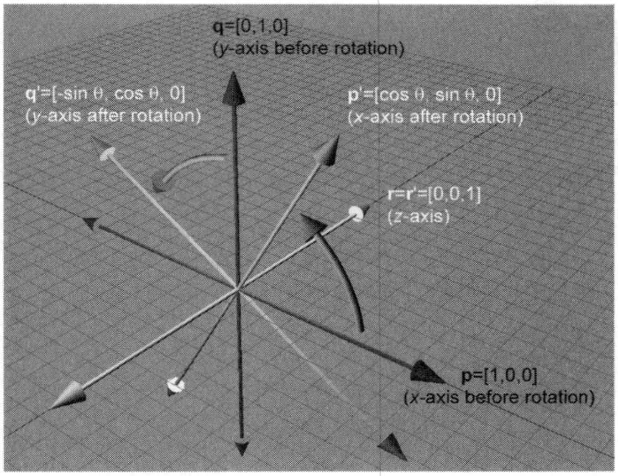

Figure 8.11: Rotating about the z-axis in 3D

Equation 8.4:
3D matrix to
rotate about
the z-axis

$$\mathbf{R}_z(\theta) = \left[\begin{array}{c} \mathbf{p}' \\ \mathbf{q}' \\ \mathbf{r}' \end{array} \right] = \left[\begin{array}{ccc} \cos\theta & \sin\theta & 0 \\ -\sin\theta & \cos\theta & 0 \\ 0 & 0 & 1 \end{array} \right]$$

8.2.3 3D Rotation about an Arbitrary Axis

We can also rotate about an arbitrary axis in 3D, provided of course that the axis passes through the origin, since we are not considering translation at the moment. This is more complicated and less common than rotating about a cardinal axis. The axis will be defined by a unit vector $\mathbf{n}$. As before, we will define θ to be the amount of rotation about the axis.

Let's derive a matrix to rotate about $\mathbf{n}$ by the angle θ. In other words, we wish to derive the matrix $\mathbf{R}(\mathbf{n}, \theta)$ such that

$$\mathbf{vR}(\mathbf{n}, \theta) = \mathbf{v}'$$

where $\mathbf{v}'$ is the vector $\mathbf{v}$ after rotating about $\mathbf{n}$. Let us first see if we can express $\mathbf{v}'$ in terms of $\mathbf{v}$, $\mathbf{n}$, and θ. The basic idea is to solve the problem in the plane perpendicular to $\mathbf{n}$, which is a much simpler 2D problem. To do this, we will separate $\mathbf{v}$ into two values, $\mathbf{v}_{\parallel}$ and $\mathbf{v}_{\perp}$, which are parallel and perpendicular to $\mathbf{n}$, respectively, such that $\mathbf{v} = \mathbf{v}_{\parallel} + \mathbf{v}_{\perp}$. (We learned the math for this in Section 5.10.3.) Since $\mathbf{v}_{\parallel}$ is parallel to $\mathbf{n}$, it will not be affected by the rotation about $\mathbf{n}$. So if we can rotate $\mathbf{v}_{\perp}$ about $\mathbf{n}$ to compute $\mathbf{v}'_{\perp}$, then we can compute $\mathbf{v}' = \mathbf{v}_{\parallel} + \mathbf{v}'_{\perp}$. To compute $\mathbf{v}'_{\perp}$, we will construct the vectors $\mathbf{v}_{\parallel}$, $\mathbf{v}_{\perp}$, and an intermediate vector $\mathbf{w}$, according to Figure 8.12.

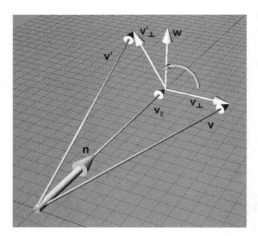

Figure 8.12: Rotating a vector about an arbitrary axis

The diagram above illustrates the following vectors:

- $\mathbf{v}_\parallel$ is the portion of $\mathbf{v}$ that is parallel to $\mathbf{n}$. Another way to say this is that $\mathbf{v}_\parallel$ is the value of $\mathbf{v}$ *projected onto* $\mathbf{n}$. This can be computed by $(\mathbf{v\cdot n})\mathbf{n}$.

- $\mathbf{v}_\perp$ is the portion of $\mathbf{v}$ that is perpendicular to $\mathbf{n}$. Since $\mathbf{v} = \mathbf{v}_\parallel + \mathbf{v}_\perp$, $\mathbf{v}_\perp$ can be computed by $\mathbf{v} - \mathbf{v}_\parallel$. $\mathbf{v}_\perp$ is the result of projecting $\mathbf{v}$ onto the plane perpendicular to $\mathbf{n}$.

- $\mathbf{w}$ is a vector that is mutually perpendicular to $\mathbf{v}_\parallel$ and $\mathbf{v}_\perp$, and it has the same length as $\mathbf{v}_\perp$. $\mathbf{w}$ and $\mathbf{v}_\perp$ lie in the plane perpendicular to $\mathbf{n}$. $\mathbf{w}$ is the result of rotating $\mathbf{v}_\perp$ about $\mathbf{n}$ by $90°$. $\mathbf{w}$ can be computed by $\mathbf{n}\times\mathbf{v}_\perp$.

Now we can see that the portion of $\mathbf{v'}$ perpendicular to $\mathbf{n}$ is given by:

$$\mathbf{v}'_\perp = \cos\theta\mathbf{v}_\perp + \sin\theta\mathbf{w}$$

Substituting for $\mathbf{v}_\perp$ and $\mathbf{w}$:

$$
\begin{aligned}
\mathbf{v}_\parallel &= (\mathbf{v} \cdot \mathbf{n})\,\mathbf{n} \\
\mathbf{v}_\perp &= \mathbf{v} - \mathbf{v}_\parallel \\
&= \mathbf{v} - (\mathbf{v} \cdot \mathbf{n})\,\mathbf{n} \\
\mathbf{w} &= \mathbf{n} \times \mathbf{v}_\perp \\
&= \mathbf{n} \times (\mathbf{v} - \mathbf{v}_\parallel) \\
&= \mathbf{n} \times \mathbf{v} - \mathbf{n} \times \mathbf{v}_\parallel \\
&= \mathbf{n} \times \mathbf{v} - \mathbf{0} \\
&= \mathbf{n} \times \mathbf{v} \\
\mathbf{v}'_\perp &= \cos\theta\mathbf{v}_\perp + \sin\theta\mathbf{w} \\
&= \cos\theta\,(\mathbf{v} - (\mathbf{v} \cdot \mathbf{n})\,\mathbf{n}) + \sin\theta\,(\mathbf{n} \times \mathbf{v})
\end{aligned}
$$

Substituting for **v'**, we have:

$$\begin{aligned}
\mathbf{v}' &= \mathbf{v}'_\perp + \mathbf{v}_\parallel \\
&= \cos\theta\,(\mathbf{v} - (\mathbf{v}\cdot\mathbf{n})\,\mathbf{n}) + \sin\theta\,(\mathbf{n}\times\mathbf{v}) + (\mathbf{v}\cdot\mathbf{n})\,\mathbf{n}
\end{aligned}$$

Now that we have expressed **v'** in terms of **v**, **n**, and θ, we can compute what the basis vectors are after transformation and construct our matrix. We'll work through the first basis vector:

$$\mathbf{p} = \begin{bmatrix} 1 & 0 & 0 \end{bmatrix}$$

$$\mathbf{p}' = \cos\theta\,(\mathbf{p} - (\mathbf{p}\cdot\mathbf{n})\,\mathbf{n}) + \sin\theta\,(\mathbf{n}\times\mathbf{p}) + (\mathbf{p}\cdot\mathbf{n})\,\mathbf{n}$$

$$= \cos\theta \left(\begin{bmatrix} 1 \\ 0 \\ 0 \end{bmatrix} - \left(\begin{bmatrix} 1 \\ 0 \\ 0 \end{bmatrix} \cdot \begin{bmatrix} \mathbf{n}_x \\ \mathbf{n}_y \\ \mathbf{n}_z \end{bmatrix} \right) \begin{bmatrix} \mathbf{n}_x \\ \mathbf{n}_y \\ \mathbf{n}_z \end{bmatrix} \right) + \sin\theta \left(\begin{bmatrix} \mathbf{n}_x \\ \mathbf{n}_y \\ \mathbf{n}_z \end{bmatrix} \times \begin{bmatrix} 1 \\ 0 \\ 0 \end{bmatrix} \right) + \left(\begin{bmatrix} 1 \\ 0 \\ 0 \end{bmatrix} \cdot \begin{bmatrix} \mathbf{n}_x \\ \mathbf{n}_y \\ \mathbf{n}_z \end{bmatrix} \right) \begin{bmatrix} \mathbf{n}_x \\ \mathbf{n}_y \\ \mathbf{n}_z \end{bmatrix}$$

$$= \cos\theta \left(\begin{bmatrix} 1 \\ 0 \\ 0 \end{bmatrix} - \mathbf{n}_x \begin{bmatrix} \mathbf{n}_x \\ \mathbf{n}_y \\ \mathbf{n}_z \end{bmatrix} \right) + \sin\theta \begin{bmatrix} 0 \\ \mathbf{n}_z \\ -\mathbf{n}_y \end{bmatrix} + \mathbf{n}_x \begin{bmatrix} \mathbf{n}_x \\ \mathbf{n}_y \\ \mathbf{n}_z \end{bmatrix}$$

$$= \cos\theta \begin{bmatrix} 1 - \mathbf{n}_x{}^2 \\ -\mathbf{n}_x\mathbf{n}_y \\ -\mathbf{n}_x\mathbf{n}_z \end{bmatrix} + \sin\theta \begin{bmatrix} 0 \\ \mathbf{n}_z \\ -\mathbf{n}_y \end{bmatrix} + \begin{bmatrix} \mathbf{n}_x{}^2 \\ \mathbf{n}_x\mathbf{n}_y \\ \mathbf{n}_x\mathbf{n}_z \end{bmatrix}$$

$$= \begin{bmatrix} \cos\theta - \mathbf{n}_x{}^2\cos\theta \\ -\mathbf{n}_x\mathbf{n}_y\cos\theta \\ -\mathbf{n}_x\mathbf{n}_z\cos\theta \end{bmatrix} + \begin{bmatrix} 0 \\ \mathbf{n}_z\sin\theta \\ -\mathbf{n}_y\sin\theta \end{bmatrix} + \begin{bmatrix} \mathbf{n}_x{}^2 \\ \mathbf{n}_x\mathbf{n}_y \\ \mathbf{n}_x\mathbf{n}_z \end{bmatrix}$$

$$= \begin{bmatrix} \cos\theta - \cos\theta\mathbf{n}_x{}^2 + \mathbf{n}_x{}^2 \\ -\mathbf{n}_x\mathbf{n}_y\cos\theta + \mathbf{n}_z\sin\theta + \mathbf{n}_x\mathbf{n}_y \\ -\mathbf{n}_x\mathbf{n}_z\cos\theta - \mathbf{n}_y\sin\theta + \mathbf{n}_x\mathbf{n}_z \end{bmatrix}$$

$$= \begin{bmatrix} \mathbf{n}_x{}^2\,(1 - \cos\theta) + \cos\theta \\ \mathbf{n}_x\mathbf{n}_y\,(1 - \cos\theta) + \mathbf{n}_z\sin\theta \\ \mathbf{n}_x\mathbf{n}_z\,(1 - \cos\theta) - \mathbf{n}_y\sin\theta \end{bmatrix}$$

The derivation of the other two basis vectors is similar and produces the following results:

$$\mathbf{q} = \begin{bmatrix} 0 & 1 & 0 \end{bmatrix} \qquad\qquad \mathbf{r} = \begin{bmatrix} 0 & 0 & 1 \end{bmatrix}$$

$$\mathbf{q}' = \begin{bmatrix} \mathbf{n}_x\mathbf{n}_y\,(1 - \cos\theta) - \mathbf{n}_z\sin\theta \\ \mathbf{n}_y{}^2\,(1 - \cos\theta) + \cos\theta \\ \mathbf{n}_y\mathbf{n}_z\,(1 - \cos\theta) + \mathbf{n}_x\sin\theta \end{bmatrix} \qquad \mathbf{r}' = \begin{bmatrix} \mathbf{n}_x\mathbf{n}_z\,(1 - \cos\theta) + \mathbf{n}_y\sin\theta \\ \mathbf{n}_y\mathbf{n}_z\,(1 - \cos\theta) - \mathbf{n}_x\sin\theta \\ \mathbf{n}_z{}^2\,(1 - \cos\theta) + \cos\theta \end{bmatrix}$$

 Note: We used column vectors above strictly so that the equations would format nicely.

Constructing the matrix from these basis vectors:

Equation 8.5:
3D matrix to
rotate about an
arbitrary axis

$$\mathbf{R}(\mathbf{n},\theta) = \begin{bmatrix} \mathbf{p}' \\ \mathbf{q}' \\ \mathbf{r}' \end{bmatrix} = \begin{bmatrix} \mathbf{n}_x{}^2\,(1 - \cos\theta) + \cos\theta & \mathbf{n}_x\mathbf{n}_y\,(1 - \cos\theta) + \mathbf{n}_z\sin\theta & \mathbf{n}_x\mathbf{n}_z\,(1 - \cos\theta) - \mathbf{n}_y\sin\theta \\ \mathbf{n}_x\mathbf{n}_y\,(1 - \cos\theta) - \mathbf{n}_z\sin\theta & \mathbf{n}_y{}^2\,(1 - \cos\theta) + \cos\theta & \mathbf{n}_y\mathbf{n}_z\,(1 - \cos\theta) + \mathbf{n}_x\sin\theta \\ \mathbf{n}_x\mathbf{n}_z\,(1 - \cos\theta) + \mathbf{n}_y\sin\theta & \mathbf{n}_y\mathbf{n}_z\,(1 - \cos\theta) - \mathbf{n}_x\sin\theta & \mathbf{n}_z{}^2\,(1 - \cos\theta) + \cos\theta \end{bmatrix}$$

8.3 Scale

We can scale an object to make it proportionally bigger or smaller by a factor of k. If we apply the same scale the same in every direction, "dilating" the object about the origin, we are performing a *uniform* scale. Uniform scale preserves angles and proportions. Lengths increase or decrease uniformly by a factor of k, areas by a factor of k^2, and volumes (in 3D) by a factor of k^3.

If we wish to "stretch" or "squash" the object, we can apply different scale factors in different directions, resulting in *non-uniform* scale. Non-uniform scale does not preserve angles. Lengths, areas, and volumes are adjusted by a factor that varies according to the orientation relative to the direction of scale.

If $|k| < 1$, then the object gets "shorter" in that direction. If $|k| > 1$, then the object gets "longer." If $k = 0$, then we have an *orthographic projection*. We will discuss orthographic projection in Section 8.4. If $k < 0$, then we have a *reflection*. Reflections are covered in Section 8.5. For the remainder of this section, we will assume that $k > 0$.

Applying non-uniform scale has an effect very similar to shearing (see Section 8.6). In fact, it is impossible to distinguish between shearing and non-uniform scale.

8.3.1 Scaling along Cardinal Axes

The simplest way to perform scale is to apply a separate scale factor along each cardinal axis. The scale is applied about the perpendicular axis (in 2D) or plane (in 3D). If the scale factors for all axes are equal, then the scale is uniform; otherwise, it is non-uniform.

In 2D, we have two scale factors, k_x and k_y. Figure 8.13 shows an object with various scale values for k_x and k_y.

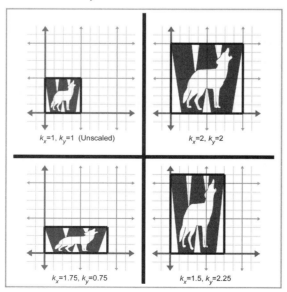

Figure 8.13: Scaling a 2D object with various factors for k_x and k_y

$k_x=1, k_y=1$ (Unscaled)

$k_x=2, k_y=2$

$k_x=1.75, k_y=0.75$

$k_x=1.5, k_y=2.25$

As is intuitively obvious, the basis vectors **p** and **q** are independently affected by the corresponding scale factors:

$$\begin{array}{ccccccc}
\mathbf{p}' & = & k_x\mathbf{p} & = & k_x\begin{bmatrix} 1 & 0 \end{bmatrix} & = & \begin{bmatrix} k_x & 0 \\ 0 & k_y \end{bmatrix} \\
\mathbf{q}' & = & k_y\mathbf{q} & = & k_y\begin{bmatrix} 0 & 1 \end{bmatrix} & = &
\end{array}$$

Constructing the matrix from the basis vectors:

Equation 8.6:
2D matrix to
scale on
cardinal axes
$$\mathbf{S}(k_x, k_y) = \begin{bmatrix} \mathbf{p}' \\ \mathbf{q}' \end{bmatrix} = \begin{bmatrix} k_x & 0 \\ 0 & k_y \end{bmatrix}$$

For 3D, we add a third scale factor k_z, and the 3D scale matrix is then given by:

Equation 8.7:
3D matrix to
scale on
cardinal axes
$$\mathbf{S}(k_x, k_y, k_z) = \begin{bmatrix} k_x & 0 & 0 \\ 0 & k_y & 0 \\ 0 & 0 & k_z \end{bmatrix}$$

8.3.2 Scale in an Arbitrary Direction

We can apply scale independent of the coordinate system used by scaling in an arbitrary direction. We will define **n** to be the unit vector parallel to the direction of scale, and k will be the scale factor to be applied about the line (in 2D) or plane (in 3D) that passes through the origin and is perpendicular to **n**.

Let's derive an expression that, given an arbitrary vector **v**, computes **v'** in terms of **v**, **n**, and k. To do this, we will separate **v** into two values, $\mathbf{v}_\parallel$ and $\mathbf{v}_\perp$, which are parallel and perpendicular to **n**, respectively, such that $\mathbf{v} = \mathbf{v}_\parallel + \mathbf{v}_\perp$. $\mathbf{v}_\parallel$ is the projection of **v** onto **n**. From Section 5.10.3, we know that $\mathbf{v}_\parallel$ is given by $(\mathbf{v}\cdot\mathbf{n})\mathbf{n}$. Since $\mathbf{v}_\perp$ is perpendicular to **n**, it will not be affected by the scale operation. Thus, $\mathbf{v}'=\mathbf{v}'_\parallel + \mathbf{v}_\perp$, and all we are left with is to compute the value of $\mathbf{v}'_\parallel$. Since $\mathbf{v}_\parallel$ is parallel to the direction of scale, $\mathbf{v}'_\parallel$ is trivially given by $k\mathbf{v}_\parallel$. This is shown below in Figure 8.14:

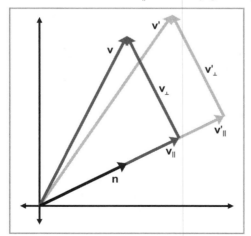

Figure 8.14: Scaling a vector along an arbitrary direction

Summarizing the known vectors and substituting, we have:

$$\mathbf{v} = \mathbf{v}_\parallel + \mathbf{v}_\perp$$
$$\mathbf{v}_\parallel = (\mathbf{v} \cdot \mathbf{n}) \, \mathbf{n}$$
$$\mathbf{v}'_\perp = \mathbf{v}_\perp$$
$$= \mathbf{v} - \mathbf{v}_\parallel$$
$$= \mathbf{v} - (\mathbf{v} \cdot \mathbf{n}) \, \mathbf{n}$$
$$\mathbf{v}'_\parallel = k \mathbf{v}_\parallel$$
$$= k \, (\mathbf{v} \cdot \mathbf{n}) \, \mathbf{n}$$
$$\mathbf{v}' = \mathbf{v}'_\perp + \mathbf{v}'_\parallel$$
$$= \mathbf{v} - (\mathbf{v} \cdot \mathbf{n}) \, \mathbf{n} + k \, (\mathbf{v} \cdot \mathbf{n}) \, \mathbf{n}$$
$$= \mathbf{v} + (k - 1) \, (\mathbf{v} \cdot \mathbf{n}) \, \mathbf{n}$$

Now that we know how to scale an arbitrary vector, we can compute the value of the basis vectors after scaling. We'll work through the first basis vector in 2D. The other basis vector is derived in a similar manner, and so we merely present the results. (Note that column vectors are used in the equations below strictly to make the equations format nicely.)

$$\mathbf{p} = \begin{bmatrix} 1 & 0 \end{bmatrix}$$
$$\mathbf{p}' = \mathbf{p} + (k - 1) \, (\mathbf{p} \cdot \mathbf{n}) \, \mathbf{n}$$
$$= \begin{bmatrix} 1 \\ 0 \end{bmatrix} + (k - 1) \left(\begin{bmatrix} 1 \\ 0 \end{bmatrix} \cdot \begin{bmatrix} \mathbf{n}_x \\ \mathbf{n}_y \end{bmatrix} \right) \begin{bmatrix} \mathbf{n}_x \\ \mathbf{n}_y \end{bmatrix}$$
$$= \begin{bmatrix} 1 \\ 0 \end{bmatrix} + (k - 1) \, \mathbf{n}_x \begin{bmatrix} \mathbf{n}_x \\ \mathbf{n}_y \end{bmatrix}$$
$$= \begin{bmatrix} 1 \\ 0 \end{bmatrix} + \begin{bmatrix} (k - 1) \, \mathbf{n}_x{}^2 \\ (k - 1) \, \mathbf{n}_x \mathbf{n}_y \end{bmatrix}$$
$$= \begin{bmatrix} 1 + (k - 1) \, \mathbf{n}_x{}^2 \\ (k - 1) \, \mathbf{n}_x \mathbf{n}_y \end{bmatrix}$$
$$\mathbf{q} = \begin{bmatrix} 0 & 1 \end{bmatrix}$$
$$\mathbf{q}' = \begin{bmatrix} (k - 1) \, \mathbf{n}_x \mathbf{n}_y \\ 1 + (k - 1) \, \mathbf{n}_y{}^2 \end{bmatrix}$$

Forming a matrix from the basis vectors, we arrive at the 2D matrix to scale by a factor of k in an arbitrary direction specified by the unit vector $\mathbf{n}$:

Equation 8.8:
2D matrix to
scale in an
arbitrary
direction

$$\mathbf{S}(\mathbf{n}, k) = \begin{bmatrix} \mathbf{p}' \\ \mathbf{q}' \end{bmatrix} \begin{bmatrix} 1 + (k - 1) \, \mathbf{n}_x{}^2 & (k - 1) \, \mathbf{n}_x \mathbf{n}_y \\ (k - 1) \, \mathbf{n}_x \mathbf{n}_y & 1 + (k - 1) \, \mathbf{n}_y{}^2 \end{bmatrix}$$

In 3D, the basis vectors are computed by:

$$\mathbf{p} = \begin{bmatrix} 1 & 0 & 0 \end{bmatrix}$$

$$\mathbf{p}' = \mathbf{p} + (k-1)(\mathbf{p} \cdot \mathbf{n})\mathbf{n}$$

$$= \begin{bmatrix} 1 \\ 0 \\ 0 \end{bmatrix} + (k-1)\left(\begin{bmatrix} 1 \\ 0 \\ 0 \end{bmatrix} \cdot \begin{bmatrix} \mathbf{n}_x \\ \mathbf{n}_y \\ \mathbf{n}_z \end{bmatrix}\right)\begin{bmatrix} \mathbf{n}_x \\ \mathbf{n}_y \\ \mathbf{n}_z \end{bmatrix}$$

$$= \begin{bmatrix} 1 \\ 0 \\ 0 \end{bmatrix} + (k-1)\mathbf{n}_x\begin{bmatrix} \mathbf{n}_x \\ \mathbf{n}_y \\ \mathbf{n}_z \end{bmatrix}$$

$$= \begin{bmatrix} 1 \\ 0 \\ 0 \end{bmatrix} + \begin{bmatrix} (k-1)\mathbf{n}_x{}^2 \\ (k-1)\mathbf{n}_x\mathbf{n}_y \\ (k-1)\mathbf{n}_x\mathbf{n}_z \end{bmatrix}$$

$$= \begin{bmatrix} 1 + (k-1)\mathbf{n}_x{}^2 \\ (k-1)\mathbf{n}_x\mathbf{n}_y \\ (k-1)\mathbf{n}_x\mathbf{n}_z \end{bmatrix}$$

$$\mathbf{q} = \begin{bmatrix} 0 & 1 & 0 \end{bmatrix}$$

$$\mathbf{q}' = \begin{bmatrix} (k-1)\mathbf{n}_x\mathbf{n}_y \\ 1 + (k-1)\mathbf{n}_y{}^2 \\ (k-1)\mathbf{n}_y\mathbf{n}_z \end{bmatrix}$$

$$\mathbf{r} = \begin{bmatrix} 0 & 0 & 1 \end{bmatrix}$$

$$\mathbf{r}' = \begin{bmatrix} (k-1)\mathbf{n}_x\mathbf{n}_z \\ (k-1)\mathbf{n}_y\mathbf{n}_z \\ 1 + (k-1)\mathbf{n}_z{}^2 \end{bmatrix}$$

The 3D matrix to scale by a factor of k in an arbitrary direction specified by the unit vector $\mathbf{n}$ is:

Equation 8.9:
3D matrix to
scale in an
arbitrary
direction

$$\mathbf{S}(\mathbf{n}, k) = \begin{bmatrix} \mathbf{p}' \\ \mathbf{q}' \\ \mathbf{r}' \end{bmatrix}\begin{bmatrix} 1 + (k-1)\mathbf{n}_x{}^2 & (k-1)\mathbf{n}_x\mathbf{n}_y & (k-1)\mathbf{n}_x\mathbf{n}_z \\ (k-1)\mathbf{n}_x\mathbf{n}_y & 1 + (k-1)\mathbf{n}_y{}^2 & (k-1)\mathbf{n}_y\mathbf{n}_z \\ (k-1)\mathbf{n}_x\mathbf{n}_z & (k-1)\mathbf{n}_y\mathbf{n}_z & 1 + (k-1)\mathbf{n}_z{}^2 \end{bmatrix}$$

8.4 Orthographic Projection

In general, the term *projection* refers to any dimension-reducing operation. As we mentioned in Section 8.3, one way we can achieve projection is to use a scale factor of zero in a direction. In this case, all the points are flattened, or *projected*, onto the perpendicular axis (in 2D) or plane (in 3D). This type of projection is an *orthographic* projection, also known as a *parallel* projection, since the lines from the original points to their projected counterparts are parallel. We will learn about another type of projection, perspective projection, in Section 9.4.4.

8.4.1 Projecting onto a Cardinal Axis or Plane

The simplest type of projection occurs when we project onto a cardinal axis (in 2D) or plane (in 3D). This is illustrated in Figure 8.15:

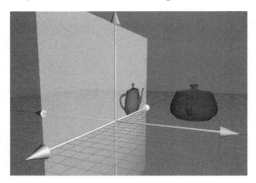

Figure 8.15: Projecting a 3D object onto a cardinal plane

Projection onto a cardinal axis or plane most frequently occurs not by actual transformation, but by simply discarding one of the dimensions while assigning the data into a variable of lesser dimension. For example, we may turn a 3D object into a 2D object by discarding the z components of the points and copying only x and y.

However, we can also project onto a cardinal axis or plane by using a scale value of zero on the perpendicular axis. For completeness, we will present the matrices for these transformations:

Equation 8.10:
2D matrix to project onto the *x*-axis

$$\mathbf{P}_x = \mathbf{S}\left(\begin{bmatrix} 0 & 1 \end{bmatrix}, 0\right) = \begin{bmatrix} 1 & 0 \\ 0 & 0 \end{bmatrix}$$

Equation 8.11:
2D matrix to project onto the *y*-axis

$$\mathbf{P}_y = \mathbf{S}\left(\begin{bmatrix} 1 & 0 \end{bmatrix}, 0\right) = \begin{bmatrix} 0 & 0 \\ 0 & 1 \end{bmatrix}$$

Equation 8.12:
3D matrix to project onto the *xy*-plane

$$\mathbf{P}_{xy} = \mathbf{S}\left(\begin{bmatrix} 0 & 0 & 1 \end{bmatrix}, 0\right) = \begin{bmatrix} 1 & 0 & 0 \\ 0 & 1 & 0 \\ 0 & 0 & 0 \end{bmatrix}$$

Equation 8.13:
3D matrix to project onto the *xz*-plane

$$\mathbf{P}_{xz} = \mathbf{S}\left(\begin{bmatrix} 0 & 1 & 0 \end{bmatrix}, 0\right) = \begin{bmatrix} 1 & 0 & 0 \\ 0 & 0 & 0 \\ 0 & 0 & 1 \end{bmatrix}$$

Equation 8.14:
3D matrix to project onto the *yz*-plane

$$\mathbf{P}_{yz} = \mathbf{S}\left(\begin{bmatrix} 1 & 0 & 0 \end{bmatrix}, 0\right) = \begin{bmatrix} 0 & 0 & 0 \\ 0 & 1 & 0 \\ 0 & 0 & 1 \end{bmatrix}$$

8.4.2 Projecting onto an Arbitrary Line or Plane

We can also project onto any arbitrary line (in 2D) or plane (in 3D). As always, since we are not considering translation, the line or plane must pass through the origin. The projection will be defined by a unit vector $\mathbf{n}$ that is perpendicular to the line or plane.

We can derive the matrix to project in an arbitrary direction by applying a zero scale factor along this direction, using the equations we developed in 8.3.2. In 2D:

Equation 8.15:
2D matrix to
project onto an
arbitrary line

$$
\begin{aligned}
\mathbf{P}(\mathbf{n}) &= \mathbf{S}(\mathbf{n}, 0) \\
&= \begin{bmatrix} 1 + (0-1)\,\mathbf{n}_x{}^2 & (0-1)\,\mathbf{n}_x\mathbf{n}_y \\ (0-1)\,\mathbf{n}_x\mathbf{n}_y & 1 + (0-1)\,\mathbf{n}_y{}^2 \end{bmatrix} \\
&= \begin{bmatrix} 1 - \mathbf{n}_x{}^2 & -\mathbf{n}_x\mathbf{n}_y \\ -\mathbf{n}_x\mathbf{n}_y & 1 - \mathbf{n}_y{}^2 \end{bmatrix}
\end{aligned}
$$

Remember that $\mathbf{n}$ is *perpendicular* to the line onto which we are projecting, not parallel to it. In 3D, we project onto the plane perpendicular to $\mathbf{n}$:

Equation 8.16:
3D matrix to
project onto an
arbitrary plane

$$
\begin{aligned}
\mathbf{P}(\mathbf{n}) &= \mathbf{S}(\mathbf{n}, 0) \\
&= \begin{bmatrix} 1 + (0-1)\,\mathbf{n}_x{}^2 & (0-1)\,\mathbf{n}_x\mathbf{n}_y & (0-1)\,\mathbf{n}_x\mathbf{n}_z \\ (0-1)\,\mathbf{n}_x\mathbf{n}_y & 1 + (0-1)\,\mathbf{n}_y{}^2 & (0-1)\,\mathbf{n}_y\mathbf{n}_z \\ (0-1)\,\mathbf{n}_x\mathbf{n}_z & (0-1)\,\mathbf{n}_y\mathbf{n}_z & 1 + (0-1)\,\mathbf{n}_z{}^2 \end{bmatrix} \\
&= \begin{bmatrix} 1 - \mathbf{n}_x{}^2 & -\mathbf{n}_x\mathbf{n}_y & -\mathbf{n}_x\mathbf{n}_z \\ -\mathbf{n}_x\mathbf{n}_y & 1 - \mathbf{n}_y{}^2 & -\mathbf{n}_y\mathbf{n}_z \\ -\mathbf{n}_x\mathbf{n}_z & -\mathbf{n}_y\mathbf{n}_z & 1 - \mathbf{n}_z{}^2 \end{bmatrix}
\end{aligned}
$$

8.5 Reflection

Reflection (also called *mirroring*) is a transformation that "flips" the object about a line (in 2D) or a plane (in 3D). Figure 8.16 shows the result of reflecting an object.

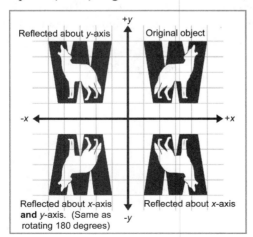

Reflected about y-axis — Original object

-x — +x

Reflected about x-axis and y-axis. (Same as rotating 180 degrees) — Reflected about x-axis

Figure 8.16: Reflecting an object about an axis in 2D

Reflection can be accomplished easily by applying a scale factor of –1. Let $\mathbf{n}$ be a 2D unit vector. Then the following matrix performs a reflection about the axis of reflection that passes through the origin and is perpendicular to $\mathbf{n}$:

Equation 8.17:
2D matrix to reflect about an arbitrary axis

$$
\begin{aligned}
\mathbf{R(n)} &= \mathbf{S(n, -1)} \\
&= \begin{bmatrix} 1 + (-1-1)\,\mathbf{n}_x{}^2 & (-1-1)\,\mathbf{n}_x\mathbf{n}_y \\ (-1-1)\,\mathbf{n}_x\mathbf{n}_y & 1 + (-1-1)\,\mathbf{n}_y{}^2 \end{bmatrix} \\
&= \begin{bmatrix} 1 - 2\mathbf{n}_x{}^2 & -2\mathbf{n}_x\mathbf{n}_y \\ -2\mathbf{n}_x\mathbf{n}_y & 1 - 2\mathbf{n}_y{}^2 \end{bmatrix}
\end{aligned}
$$

In 3D, we have a reflecting plane instead of an axis. The following matrix reflects about a plane through the origin perpendicular to the unit vector $\mathbf{n}$:

Equation 8.18:
3D matrix to reflect about an arbitrary plane

$$
\begin{aligned}
\mathbf{R(n)} &= \mathbf{S(n, -1)} \\
&= \begin{bmatrix} 1 + (-1-1)\,\mathbf{n}_x{}^2 & (-1-1)\,\mathbf{n}_x\mathbf{n}_y & (-1-1)\,\mathbf{n}_x\mathbf{n}_z \\ (-1-1)\,\mathbf{n}_x\mathbf{n}_y & 1 + (-1-1)\,\mathbf{n}_y{}^2 & (-1-1)\,\mathbf{n}_y\mathbf{n}_z \\ (-1-1)\,\mathbf{n}_x\mathbf{n}_z & (-1-1)\,\mathbf{n}_y\mathbf{n}_z & 1 + (-1-1)\,\mathbf{n}_z{}^2 \end{bmatrix} \\
&= \begin{bmatrix} 1 - 2\mathbf{n}_x{}^2 & -2\mathbf{n}_x\mathbf{n}_y & -2\mathbf{n}_x\mathbf{n}_z \\ -2\mathbf{n}_x\mathbf{n}_y & 1 - 2\mathbf{n}_y{}^2 & -2\mathbf{n}_y\mathbf{n}_z \\ -2\mathbf{n}_x\mathbf{n}_z & -2\mathbf{n}_y\mathbf{n}_z & 1 - 2\mathbf{n}_z{}^2 \end{bmatrix}
\end{aligned}
$$

Notice that an object can only be "reflected" once. If we reflect it again (even about a different axis or plane), then the object is flipped back to "right side out," and it is the same as if we had rotated the object from its initial position.

8.6 Shearing

Shearing is a transformation that "skews" the coordinate space, stretching it non-uniformly. Angles are not preserved; however, surprisingly, areas and volumes are. The basic idea is to add a multiple of one coordinate to the other. For example, in 2D, we might take a multiple of y and add it to x, so that $x' = x + sy$. This is shown in Figure 8.17:

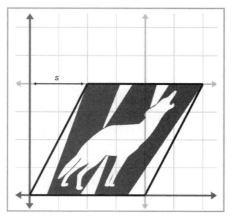

Figure 8.17: Shearing in 2D

The matrix that performs this shear is:

$$\mathbf{H}_x(s) = \begin{bmatrix} 1 & 0 \\ s & 1 \end{bmatrix}$$

The notation $\mathbf{H}_x$ denotes that the x coordinate is sheared by the other coordinate, y. The parameter s controls the amount and direction of the shearing. The other 2D shear matrix, $\mathbf{H}_y$ is given below:

$$\mathbf{H}_y(s) = \begin{bmatrix} 1 & s \\ 0 & 1 \end{bmatrix}$$

In 3D, we can take one coordinate and add different multiples of that coordinate to the other two coordinates. The notation $\mathbf{H}_{xy}$ indicates that the x and y coordinates are shifted by the other coordinate, z. These matrices are given below:

Equation 8.19:
3D shear
matrices

$$\mathbf{H}_{xy}(s,t) = \begin{bmatrix} 1 & 0 & 0 \\ 0 & 1 & 0 \\ s & t & 1 \end{bmatrix}$$

$$\mathbf{H}_{xz}(s,t) = \begin{bmatrix} 1 & 0 & 0 \\ s & 1 & t \\ 0 & 0 & 1 \end{bmatrix}$$

$$\mathbf{H}_{yz}(s,t) = \begin{bmatrix} 1 & s & t \\ 0 & 1 & 0 \\ 0 & 0 & 1 \end{bmatrix}$$

Shearing is a seldom-used transform. It is also known as a *skew* transform. Combining shearing and scaling (uniform or non-uniform) creates a transformation that is indistinguishable from a transformation containing rotation and non-uniform scale.

8.7 Combining Transformations

In this section we show how to take a sequence of transformation matrices and combine (or "concatenate") them into one single transformation matrix. This new matrix will represent the cumulative result of applying all of the original transformations in order.

One very common example of this is in rendering. Imagine there is an object at an arbitrary position and orientation in the world. We wish to render this object given a camera in any position and orientation. To do this, we must take the vertices of the object (assuming we are rendering some sort of triangle mesh) and transform them from object space into world space, and then from world space into camera space. The math involved is summarized below:

$$\begin{aligned} \mathbf{p}_{world} &= \mathbf{p}_{object}\mathbf{M}_{object \to world} \\ \mathbf{p}_{camera} &= \mathbf{p}_{world}\mathbf{M}_{world \to camera} \\ &= (\mathbf{p}_{object}\mathbf{M}_{object \to world})\mathbf{M}_{world \to camera} \end{aligned}$$

From Section 7.1.6 we know that matrix multiplication is associative, and so we can compute one matrix to transform directly from object to camera space:

$$\mathbf{p}_{camera} = (\mathbf{p}_{object}\mathbf{M}_{object \to world})\mathbf{M}_{world \to camera}$$
$$= \mathbf{p}_{object}(\mathbf{M}_{object \to world}\mathbf{M}_{world \to camera})$$

Thus, we can concatenate the matrices outside the loop and have only one matrix multiplication inside the loop (remember there are many vertices):

$$\mathbf{M}_{object \to camera} = \mathbf{M}_{object \to world}\mathbf{M}_{world \to camera}$$
$$\mathbf{p}_{camera} = \mathbf{p}_{object}\mathbf{M}_{object \to camera}$$

So we see that matrix concatenation works from an algebraic perspective using the associative property of matrix multiplication. Let's see if we can't get a more geometric interpretation of what's going on. Recall our breakthrough discovery from Section 7.2 that the rows of a matrix contain the basis vectors after transformation. This is true even in the case of multiple transformations. Notice that in the matrix product $\mathbf{AB}$, each resulting row is the product of the corresponding row from $\mathbf{A}$ times the matrix $\mathbf{B}$. In other words, let the row vectors $\mathbf{a}_1$, $\mathbf{a}_2$, and $\mathbf{a}_3$ stand for the rows of $\mathbf{A}$. Then matrix multiplication can alternatively be written like this:

$$\mathbf{A} = \begin{bmatrix} \mathbf{a}_1 \\ \mathbf{a}_2 \\ \mathbf{a}_3 \end{bmatrix}$$

$$\mathbf{AB} = \begin{bmatrix} \mathbf{a}_1 \\ \mathbf{a}_2 \\ \mathbf{a}_3 \end{bmatrix} \mathbf{B}$$

$$= \begin{bmatrix} \mathbf{a}_1\mathbf{B} \\ \mathbf{a}_2\mathbf{B} \\ \mathbf{a}_3\mathbf{B} \end{bmatrix}$$

This makes it explicitly clear that the rows of the product of $\mathbf{AB}$ are actually the result of transforming the basis vectors in $\mathbf{A}$ by $\mathbf{B}$.

8.8 Classes of Transformations

We can classify transformations using several criteria. In this section, we will discuss classes of transformations. For each class, we will describe the properties of the transformations that belong to that class and specify which of the primitive transformations from Sections 8.2 through 8.6 belong to that class.

The classes of transformations are not mutually exclusive, nor do they necessarily follow an "order" or "hierarchy" with each one more or less restrictive than the next.

When we discuss transformations in general, we may make use of the synonymous terms *mapping* or *function*. In the most general sense, a *mapping* is simply a rule that takes an input and produces an output. We denote that a mapping $\mathbf{F}$ maps $\mathbf{a}$ to $\mathbf{b}$ by writing $\mathbf{F}(\mathbf{a}) = \mathbf{b}$ (read "$\mathbf{F}$ of $\mathbf{a}$

equals **b**"). Of course, we will be primarily interested in mappings that can be expressed using matrix multiplication, but it is important to note that other mappings are possible.

8.8.1 Linear Transformations

We met linear functions informally in Section 7.2. Mathematically, a mapping $\mathbf{F}(\mathbf{a})$ is *linear* if
$$\mathbf{F}(\mathbf{a} + \mathbf{b}) = \mathbf{F}(\mathbf{a}) + \mathbf{F}(\mathbf{b})$$

and

$$\mathbf{F}(k\mathbf{a}) = k\mathbf{F}(\mathbf{a})$$

This is a fancy way of stating that the mapping **F** is linear if it preserves the basic operations of addition and multiplication by a scalar. If we add two vectors and then perform the transformation, we get the same result as if we perform the transformation on the two vectors individually and then add the transformed vectors. Likewise, if we scale a vector and then transform it, we should get the same resulting vector as when we transform the vector and then scale it.

There are two important implications of this definition of linear transformation:

■ The mapping $\mathbf{F}(\mathbf{a}) = \mathbf{a}\mathbf{M}$, where **M** is any square matrix, is a linear transformation because

$$
\begin{aligned}
\mathbf{F}(\mathbf{a} + \mathbf{b}) &= (\mathbf{a} + \mathbf{b})\mathbf{M} \\
&= \mathbf{a}\mathbf{M} + \mathbf{b}\mathbf{M} \\
&= \mathbf{F}(\mathbf{a}) + \mathbf{F}(\mathbf{b})
\end{aligned}
$$

and

$$
\begin{aligned}
\mathbf{F}(k\mathbf{a}) &= (k\mathbf{a})\mathbf{M} \\
&= k(\mathbf{a}\mathbf{M}) \\
&= k\mathbf{F}(\mathbf{a})
\end{aligned}
$$

■ Any linear transformation will transform the zero vector into the zero vector. (If $\mathbf{F}(\mathbf{0}) = \mathbf{a}$, $\mathbf{a} \neq \mathbf{0}$, then **F** cannot be a linear mapping, since $\mathbf{F}(k\mathbf{0}) = \mathbf{a}$ and therefore $\mathbf{F}(k\mathbf{0}) \neq k\mathbf{F}(\mathbf{0})$.) Because of this, linear transformations do not contain translation.

Since all of the transformations we discussed in Sections 8.2 through 8.6 can be expressed using matrix multiplication, they are all linear transformations.

In some literature, a linear transformation is defined as one in which parallel lines remain parallel after transformation. This is almost completely accurate, with one slight exception: projection. (When a line is projected and becomes a single point, can we consider that point parallel to anything?) Excluding this one technicality, the intuition is correct. A linear transformation may "stretch" things, but straight lines are not "warped" and parallel lines remain parallel.

8.8.2 Affine Transformations

An *affine* transformation is a linear transformation followed by translation. Thus, the set of affine transformations is a superset of the set of linear transformations. Any linear transformation is an affine translation, but not all affine transformations are linear transformations.

Since all of the transformations we discussed in this chapter are linear transformations, they are also all affine transformations.

The class of affine transformations is the most general class of transformations that we will consider. Any transformation of the form $\mathbf{v'} = \mathbf{vM} + \mathbf{b}$ is an affine transformation.

8.8.3 Invertible Transformations

A transformation is *invertible* if there exists an opposite transformation that "undoes" the original transformation. In other words, a mapping $\mathbf{F(a)}$ is invertible if there exists a mapping $\mathbf{F}^{-1}$, such that $\mathbf{F}^{-1}(\mathbf{F(a)}) = \mathbf{a}$ for all $\mathbf{a}$.

There are non-affine invertible transformations, but we will not consider them for the moment. For now we'll concentrate on determining if an affine transformation is invertible. An affine transformation is a linear transformation followed by a translation. Obviously, we can always "undo" the translation portion by simply translating by the opposite amount. So the question becomes whether or not the linear transformation is invertible.

Intuitively, we know that all of the transformations other than projection can be "undone." When an object is projected, we effectively discard one dimension worth of information, and this information cannot be recovered. Thus, all of the primitive transformations other than projection are invertible.

Since any linear transformation can be expressed as multiplication by a matrix, finding the inverse of a linear transformation is equivalent to finding the inverse of a matrix. We will discuss how to do this in Section 9.2. If the matrix is *singular* (it has no inverse), then the transformation is *non-invertible*. The determinant of an invertible matrix is nonzero.

8.8.4 Angle-preserving Transformations

A transformation is *angle-preserving* if the angle between two vectors is not altered in either magnitude or direction after transformation. Only translation, rotation, and uniform scale are angle-preserving transformations. An angle-preserving matrix preserves proportions. We do not consider reflection an angle-preserving transformation because even though the *amount* of angle between two vectors is the same after transformation, the *direction* of angle may be inverted. All angle-preserving transformations are affine and invertible.

8.8.5 Orthogonal Transformations

Orthogonal is a term that is used to describe a matrix with certain properties. We will defer a complete discussion of orthogonal matrices until Section 9.3, but the basic idea is that the axes remain perpendicular, and no scale is applied. Orthogonal transformations are interesting because it is easy to compute their inverse.

Translation, rotation, and reflection are the only orthogonal transformations. Lengths, angles, areas, and volumes are all preserved (although in saying this we must be careful of our precise definition of angle, area, and volume, since reflection is an orthogonal transformation).

As we will learn in Chapter 9, the determinant of an orthogonal matrix is ± 1.

All orthogonal transformations are affine and invertible.

8.8.6 Rigid Body Transformations

A *rigid body* transformation is one that changes the location and orientation of an object but not its shape. All angles, lengths, areas, and volumes are preserved. Translation and rotation are the only rigid body transformations. Reflection is not considered a rigid body transformation.

Rigid body transformations are also known as *proper* transformations. All rigid body transformations are orthogonal, angle-preserving, invertible, and affine.

The determinant of any rotation matrix is 1.

8.8.7 Summary of Types of Transformations

The following table summarizes the relationship between the various classes and types of transformations. In this table, a "yes" means that the transformation in that row *always* has the property associated with that column. The absence of a "yes" does not mean "never," but rather, "not always."

Transform	Linear	Affine	Invertible	Angle preserving	Orthogonal	Rigid Body	Lengths preserved	Areas/ volumes preserved	Determinant
Linear transformations	Y	Y							
Affine transformations		Y							
Invertible transformations			Y						$\neq 0$
Angle-preserving transformations		Y	Y	Y					
Orthogonal transformations		Y	Y		Y				± 1
Rigid body transformations		Y	Y	Y	Y	Y	Y	Y	
Translation		Y	Y	Y	Y	Y	Y	Y	
Rotation[1]	Y	Y	Y	Y	Y	Y	Y	Y	1
Uniform scale[2]	Y	Y	Y	Y					K^n [3]
Non-uniform scale[2]	Y	Y	Y						
Orthographic projection[4]	Y	Y							0

Transform	Linear	Affine	Invertible	Angle preserving	Orthogonal	Rigid Body	Lengths preserved	Areas/ volumes preserved	Determinant
Reflection[5]	Y	Y	Y		Y		Y	Y[6]	−1
Shearing	Y	Y	Y					Y[7]	1

Notes:
1 About the origin in 2D or an axis passing through the origin in 3D.
2 About the origin, using positive scale factors.
3 The determinant is the square of the scale factor in 2D and the cube of the scale factor in 3D.
4 Onto a line (2D) or plane (3D) that passes through the origin.
5 About a line (2D) or plane (3D) that passes through the origin.
6 Not considering "negative" area or volume.
7 Surprisingly!

8.9 Exercises

1. Construct a matrix to rotate −22° about the x-axis.

2. Construct a matrix to rotate 30° about the y-axis.

3. Construct a matrix that transforms a vector from inertial space to object space. From the "identity orientation," the object rotated 30° around its y-axis and then −22° about its x-axis.

4. Express the object's z-axis using inertial coordinates.

5. Construct a matrix to rotate 164° about the z-axis.

6. Construct a matrix to rotate −5° about the axis [99, −99, 99].

7. Construct a matrix that doubles the height, width, and length of an object.

8. Construct a matrix to scale by a factor of 5 about the plane through the origin perpendicular to the vector [99, −99, 99].

9. Construct a matrix to orthographically project onto the plane through the origin perpendicular to the vector [99, −99, 99].

10. Construct a matrix to reflect orthographically about the plane through the origin perpendicular to the vector [99, −99, 99]. Construct the reflection matrix which mirrors about the plane through the origin perpendicular to the vector [−99, 99, −99].

11. Does the matrix below express a linear transformation? Affine?
$$\begin{bmatrix} 34 & 1.7 & \pi \\ \sqrt{2} & 0 & 18 \\ 4 & -9 & -1.3 \end{bmatrix}$$

Chapter 9

More on Matrices

This chapter extends our discussion of matrices from Chapters 7 and 8. It is divided into four sections.

- Section 9.1 covers the determinant of a matrix.
- Section 9.2 covers the inverse of a matrix.
- Section 9.3 discusses orthogonal matrices.
- Section 9.4 introduces 4×4 homogenous matrices for affine transformations in 3D.

Chapter 7 presented a few of the most important properties and operations of matrices and discussed how matrices are related to geometric transformations in general. In Chapter 8 we discussed this relationship in detail. In this chapter, we complete our detailed coverage of matrices by discussing some additional interesting and useful matrix operations.

9.1 Determinant of a Matrix

For every square matrix, there is a special scalar called the *determinant* of the matrix. The determinant has many useful properties in linear algebra, and it also has interesting geometric interpretations.

9.1.1 Official Linear Algebra Rules

The determinant of a square matrix $\mathbf{M}$ is denoted $|\mathbf{M}|$ or "det $\mathbf{M}$." The determinant of a non-square matrix is undefined. The definition of the determinant of a matrix of arbitrary size $n \times n$ is fairly complicated, so we will first discuss the 2×2 and 3×3 cases.

The determinant of a 2×2 matrix is given by:

Equation 9.1: Determinant of a 2×2 matrix

$$|\mathbf{M}| = \begin{vmatrix} m_{11} & m_{12} \\ m_{21} & m_{22} \end{vmatrix} = m_{11}m_{22} - m_{12}m_{21}$$

Notice that when we write the determinant of a matrix, we place vertical lines surrounding the grid of numbers, omitting the square brackets.

Equation 9.1 can be easier to remember with the following diagram. Simply multiply entries along the diagonal and back-diagonal, and then subtract the back-diagonal term from the diagonal term.

$$+ \diagdown \quad \diagup -$$
$$\begin{matrix} m_{11} & m_{12} \\ m_{21} & m_{22} \end{matrix}$$

A few examples:

$$\begin{vmatrix} 2 & 1 \\ -1 & 2 \end{vmatrix} = (2)(2) - (1)(-1) = 4 + 1 = 5$$

$$\begin{vmatrix} -3 & 4 \\ 2 & 5 \end{vmatrix} = (-3)(5) - (4)(2) = -15 - 8 = -23$$

$$\begin{vmatrix} a & b \\ c & d \end{vmatrix} = ad - bc$$

The determinant of a 3×3 matrix is given by:

Equation 9.2:
Determinant of
a 3×3 matrix

$$\begin{vmatrix} m_{11} & m_{12} & m_{13} \\ m_{21} & m_{22} & m_{23} \\ m_{31} & m_{32} & m_{33} \end{vmatrix} = \begin{aligned} & m_{11}m_{22}m_{33} + m_{12}m_{23}m_{31} + m_{13}m_{21}m_{32} \\ & - m_{13}m_{22}m_{31} - m_{12}m_{21}m_{33} - m_{11}m_{23}m_{32} \end{aligned}$$

$$= m_{11}(m_{22}m_{33} - m_{23}m_{32}) + m_{12}(m_{23}m_{31} - m_{21}m_{33}) + m_{13}(m_{21}m_{32} - m_{22}m_{31})$$

A similar diagram can be used to memorize this formula. We write two copies of the matrix **M** side by side and once again multiply entries along the diagonals and back-diagonals. This time, add the diagonal terms and subtract the back-diagonal terms.

$$+ \quad + \quad + \qquad - \quad - \quad -$$
$$\begin{matrix} m_{11} & m_{12} & m_{13} & m_{11} & m_{12} & m_{13} \\ m_{21} & m_{22} & m_{23} & m_{21} & m_{22} & m_{23} \\ m_{31} & m_{32} & m_{33} & m_{31} & m_{32} & m_{33} \end{matrix}$$

An example:

$$\begin{vmatrix} 3 & -2 & 0 \\ 1 & 4 & -3 \\ -1 & 0 & 2 \end{vmatrix} = (3)\left((4)(2) - (-3)(0)\right) + (-2)\left((-3)(-1) - (1)(2)\right) + (0)\left((1)(0) - (4)(-1)\right)$$

$$= 24 + (-2) + 0$$

$$= 22$$

If we interpret the rows of a 3×3 matrix as three vectors, then the determinant of the matrix is equivalent to the so-called "triple product" of the three vectors:

$$\begin{vmatrix} \mathbf{a}_x & \mathbf{a}_y & \mathbf{a}_z \\ \mathbf{b}_x & \mathbf{b}_y & \mathbf{b}_z \\ \mathbf{c}_x & \mathbf{c}_y & \mathbf{c}_z \end{vmatrix} = \mathbf{a}_x\mathbf{b}_y\mathbf{c}_z + \mathbf{a}_y\mathbf{b}_z\mathbf{c}_x + \mathbf{a}_z\mathbf{b}_x\mathbf{c}_y - \mathbf{a}_z\mathbf{b}_y\mathbf{c}_x - \mathbf{a}_y\mathbf{b}_x\mathbf{c}_z - \mathbf{a}_x\mathbf{b}_z\mathbf{c}_y$$
$$= (\mathbf{a}_y\mathbf{b}_z - \mathbf{a}_z\mathbf{b}_y)\,\mathbf{c}_x + (\mathbf{a}_z\mathbf{b}_x - \mathbf{a}_x\mathbf{b}_z)\,\mathbf{c}_y + (\mathbf{a}_x\mathbf{b}_y - \mathbf{a}_y\mathbf{b}_x)\,\mathbf{c}_z$$
$$= (\mathbf{a} \times \mathbf{b}) \cdot \mathbf{c}$$

Assume **M** is a matrix with r rows and c columns. Let $\mathbf{M}^{\{ij\}}$ denote the matrix obtained by deleting row i and column j from **M**. This matrix will obviously have $r-1$ rows and $c-1$ columns. The submatrix $\mathbf{M}^{\{ij\}}$ is known as a *minor* of **M**. Consider the 3×3 matrix **M**:

$$\mathbf{M} = \begin{bmatrix} -4 & -3 & 3 \\ 0 & 2 & -2 \\ 1 & 4 & -1 \end{bmatrix}$$

The minor $\mathbf{M}^{\{12\}}$ is the 2×2 matrix that is the result of deleting the first row and second column from **M**:

$$\begin{bmatrix} -4 & -3 & 3 \\ 0 & 2 & -2 \\ 1 & 4 & -1 \end{bmatrix} \implies \mathbf{M}^{\{12\}} = \begin{bmatrix} 0 & -2 \\ 1 & -1 \end{bmatrix}$$

The *cofactor* of a square matrix **M** at a given row and column is the signed determinant of the corresponding minor of **M**:

Equation 9.3:
Matrix cofactor $c_{ij} = (-1)^{i+j}\left|\mathbf{M}^{\{ij\}}\right|$

As shown above, we will use the notation c_{ij} to denote the cofactor of **M** in row i, column j. Notice that a minor is a matrix quantity, while a cofactor is a scalar quantity. The $(-1)^{(i+j)}$ term in the computation of the cofactor has the effect of negating every other cofactor in a checkerboard pattern:

$$\begin{bmatrix} + & - & + \\ - & + & - \\ + & - & + \end{bmatrix}$$

We will use minors and cofactors in the next section to compute determinants of an arbitrary dimension n and again in Section 9.2.1 to compute the inverse of a matrix.

There are several equivalent definitions that exist for the determinant of a matrix of arbitrary dimension n. The definition we will now consider expresses a determinant in terms of its cofactors. (This definition is recursive, since a cofactor itself is a determinant of a submatrix.)

First, we arbitrarily select a row or column from the matrix. For each element in the row or column, we multiply this element by the corresponding cofactor. Summing these products yields the determinant of the matrix. For example, arbitrarily selecting row i, the determinant can be computed by:

Equation 9.4:
Computing an
$n \times n$
determinant
using cofactors

$$|\mathbf{M}| = \sum_{j=1}^{n} m_{ij}c_{ij} = \sum_{j=1}^{n} m_{ij}(-1)^{i+j}\left|\mathbf{M}^{\{ij\}}\right|$$

As an example, let's rewrite the equation for a 3×3 determinant:

$$
\begin{vmatrix}
m_{11} & m_{12} & m_{13} & m_{14} \\
m_{21} & m_{22} & m_{23} & m_{24} \\
m_{31} & m_{32} & m_{33} & m_{34} \\
m_{41} & m_{42} & m_{43} & m_{44}
\end{vmatrix}
= m_{11}\begin{vmatrix} m_{22} & m_{23} & m_{24} \\ m_{32} & m_{33} & m_{34} \\ m_{42} & m_{43} & m_{44} \end{vmatrix}
- m_{12}\begin{vmatrix} m_{21} & m_{23} & m_{24} \\ m_{31} & m_{33} & m_{34} \\ m_{41} & m_{43} & m_{44} \end{vmatrix}
$$

$$
+ m_{13}\begin{vmatrix} m_{21} & m_{22} & m_{24} \\ m_{31} & m_{32} & m_{34} \\ m_{41} & m_{42} & m_{44} \end{vmatrix}
- m_{14}\begin{vmatrix} m_{21} & m_{22} & m_{23} \\ m_{31} & m_{32} & m_{33} \\ m_{41} & m_{42} & m_{43} \end{vmatrix}
$$

Now, let's derive the 4×4 matrix determinant:

$$
\begin{aligned}
& m_{11}\left(m_{22}(m_{33}m_{44} - m_{34}m_{43}) + m_{23}(m_{34}m_{42} - m_{32}m_{44}) + m_{24}(m_{32}m_{43} - m_{33}m_{42})\right) \\
& - m_{12}\left(m_{21}(m_{33}m_{44} - m_{34}m_{43}) + m_{23}(m_{34}m_{41} - m_{31}m_{44}) + m_{24}(m_{31}m_{43} - m_{33}m_{41})\right) \\
& + m_{13}\left(m_{21}(m_{32}m_{44} - m_{34}m_{42}) + m_{22}(m_{34}m_{41} - m_{31}m_{44}) + m_{24}(m_{31}m_{42} - m_{32}m_{41})\right) \\
& - m_{14}\left(m_{21}(m_{32}m_{43} - m_{33}m_{42}) + m_{22}(m_{33}m_{41} - m_{31}m_{43}) + m_{23}(m_{31}m_{42} - m_{32}m_{41})\right)
\end{aligned}
$$

Expanding the cofactors we have:

Equation 9.5:
Determinant of
a 4×4 matrix

$$
\begin{aligned}
& m_{11}\left(m_{22}(m_{33}m_{44} - m_{34}m_{43}) - m_{32}(m_{23}m_{44} + m_{24}m_{43}) + m_{42}(m_{23}m_{34} - m_{24}m_{33})\right) \\
& - m_{21}\left(m_{12}(m_{33}m_{44} - m_{34}m_{43}) - m_{32}(m_{13}m_{44} + m_{14}m_{43}) + m_{42}(m_{13}m_{34} - m_{14}m_{33})\right) \\
& + m_{31}\left(m_{12}(m_{23}m_{44} - m_{24}m_{43}) - m_{22}(m_{13}m_{44} + m_{14}m_{43}) + m_{42}(m_{13}m_{24} - m_{14}m_{23})\right) \\
& - m_{41}\left(+m_{12}(m_{23}m_{34} - m_{24}m_{33}) - m_{22}(m_{13}m_{34} + m_{14}m_{33}) + m_{32}(m_{13}m_{24} - m_{14}m_{23})\right)
\end{aligned}
$$

As you can imagine, the complexity of equations for determinants of higher degree grows exponentially. Luckily, we can perform an operation known as "pivoting," which does not affect the value of the determinant but causes a particular row or column to be filled with zeros, except for a single element (the "pivot" element). Then only one cofactor has to be evaluated. A complete discussion of pivoting is outside the scope of this book.

Some important characteristics concerning determinants are:

■ The determinant of a matrix product is equal to the product of the determinants:
$|\mathbf{AB}| = |\mathbf{A}||\mathbf{B}|$

This extends to more than two matrices:
$|\mathbf{M}_1\mathbf{M}_2 \cdots \mathbf{M}_{n-1}\mathbf{M}_n| = |\mathbf{M}_1||\mathbf{M}_2| \cdots |\mathbf{M}_{n-1}||\mathbf{M}_n|$

■ The determinant of the transpose of a matrix is equal to the original determinant:
$|\mathbf{M}^T| = |\mathbf{M}|$

■ If any row or column in a matrix contains all zeros, then the determinant of that matrix is zero.

- Exchanging any pair of rows (or pair of columns) negates the determinant.
- Adding any nonzero multiple of a row/column to another row/column does not change the value of the determinant.

9.1.2 Geometric Interpretation

The determinant of a matrix has an interesting geometric interpretation. In 2D, the determinant is equal to the signed area of the parallelogram, or *skew box*, that has the basis vectors as two sides (see Figure 9.1). (We discussed how we can use skew boxes to visualize coordinate space transformations in Section 7.2.2.) By *signed area*, we mean that the area is negative if the skew box is "flipped" relative to its original orientation.

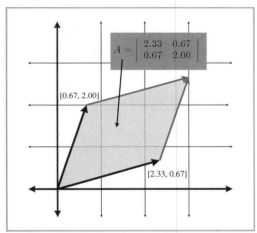

Figure 9.1: The determinant in 2D is the signed area of the skew box formed by the transformed basis vectors

In 3D, the determinant is the signed area of the *parallelepiped* that has the transformed basis vectors as three edges. The determinant will be negative in 3D if the object is turned "inside out" as a result of the transformation.

The determinant is related to the change in size that results from transforming by the matrix. The absolute value of the determinant is related to the change in area (in 2D) or volume (in 3D) that will occur as a result of transforming an object by the matrix, and the sign of the determinant indicates whether any reflection or projection is contained in the matrix.

The determinant of the matrix can also be used to help classify the type of transformation represented by a matrix. If the determinant of a matrix is zero, then the matrix contains a projection. If the determinant of a matrix is negative, then reflection is contained in the matrix. See Section 8.8 for more about different classes of transformations.

9.2 Inverse of a Matrix

Another important operation that only applies to square matrices is the *inverse* of a matrix.

9.2.1 Official Linear Algebra Rules

The inverse of a square matrix $\mathbf{M}$, denoted $\mathbf{M}^{-1}$, is the matrix such that when we multiply $\mathbf{M}$ by $\mathbf{M}^{-1}$ on either side, the result is the identity matrix. In other words:

Equation 9.6:
Matrix inverse

$$\mathbf{M}(\mathbf{M}^{-1}) = \mathbf{M}^{-1}\mathbf{M}^{-1} = \mathbf{I}$$

Not all matrices have an inverse. An obvious example is a matrix with a row or column filled with zeros. No matter what you multiply this matrix by, you will end up with a matrix full of zeros. If a matrix has an inverse, it is said to be *invertible* or *non-singular*. A matrix that does not have an inverse is said to be *non-invertible* or *singular*. The determinant of a singular matrix is zero and the determinant of a non-singular matrix is nonzero, so checking the magnitude of the determinant is a good test for invertibility. Also, for any invertible matrix $\mathbf{M}$, the vector equality $\mathbf{vM} = \mathbf{0}$ is true only when $\mathbf{v} = \mathbf{0}$.

The *classical adjoint* of $\mathbf{M}$, denoted "adj $\mathbf{M}$," is defined to be the transpose of the matrix of cofactors. Let's look at an example. Take the 3×3 matrix $\mathbf{M}$ given earlier:

$$\mathbf{M} = \begin{bmatrix} -4 & -3 & 3 \\ 0 & 2 & -2 \\ 1 & 4 & -1 \end{bmatrix}$$

Computing the cofactors of $\mathbf{M}$:

$$c_{11} = +\begin{vmatrix} 2 & -2 \\ 4 & -1 \end{vmatrix} = 6 \quad c_{12} = -\begin{vmatrix} 0 & -2 \\ 1 & -1 \end{vmatrix} = -2 \quad c_{13} = +\begin{vmatrix} 0 & 2 \\ 1 & 4 \end{vmatrix} = -2$$

$$c_{21} = -\begin{vmatrix} -3 & 3 \\ 4 & -1 \end{vmatrix} = 9 \quad c_{22} = +\begin{vmatrix} -4 & 3 \\ 1 & -1 \end{vmatrix} = 1 \quad c_{23} = -\begin{vmatrix} -4 & -3 \\ 1 & 4 \end{vmatrix} = 13$$

$$c_{31} = +\begin{vmatrix} -3 & 3 \\ 2 & -2 \end{vmatrix} = 0 \quad c_{32} = -\begin{vmatrix} -4 & 3 \\ 0 & -2 \end{vmatrix} = -8 \quad c_{33} = +\begin{vmatrix} -4 & -3 \\ 0 & 2 \end{vmatrix} = -8$$

The classical adjoint of $\mathbf{A}$ is the transpose of the matrix of cofactors:

$$\text{adj } \mathbf{M} = \begin{bmatrix} c_{11} & c_{12} & c_{13} \\ c_{21} & c_{22} & c_{23} \\ c_{31} & c_{32} & c_{33} \end{bmatrix}^T = \begin{bmatrix} 6 & -2 & -2 \\ 9 & 1 & 13 \\ 0 & -8 & -8 \end{bmatrix}^T = \begin{bmatrix} 6 & 9 & 0 \\ -2 & 1 & -8 \\ -2 & 13 & -8 \end{bmatrix}$$

Once we have the classical adjoint, we can compute the inverse of the matrix by dividing by the determinant (which, incidentally, goes a long way toward explaining why matrices with zero determinants are not invertible). In other words:

Equation 9.7:
The inverse of a
matrix can be
computed as the
classical adjoint
divided by the
determinant

$$\mathbf{M}^{-1} = \frac{\text{adj } \mathbf{M}}{|\mathbf{M}|}$$

For example, to find the inverse of the matrix from above, we have:

$$
\begin{aligned}
\mathbf{M}^{-1} &= \frac{\text{adj } \mathbf{M}}{|\mathbf{M}|} \\
&= \frac{\begin{bmatrix} 6 & 9 & 0 \\ -2 & 1 & -8 \\ -2 & 13 & -8 \end{bmatrix}}{-24} \\
&= \begin{bmatrix} -1/4 & -3/8 & 0 \\ 1/12 & -1/24 & 1/3 \\ 1/12 & -13/24 & 1/3 \end{bmatrix}
\end{aligned}
$$

There are other techniques that can be used to compute the inverse of a matrix, such as Gaussian elimination. Many linear algebra textbooks incorrectly assert that such techniques are better suited for implementation on a computer because they require fewer arithmetic operations. This may be true for large matrices or matrices with a structure that may be exploited. However, for arbitrary matrices of smaller order, like the ones we work with in geometric applications, the classical adjoint method is likely to be faster. The reason is that the classical adjoint method provides for a branchless implementation, which is likely to be faster on today's superscalar architecture and dedicated vector processors.

Now for a few important properties concerning matrix inverses:

■ The inverse of the inverse of a matrix is the original matrix:

$$(\mathbf{M}^{-1})^{-1} = \mathbf{M}$$

Of course, this assumes that **M** is non-singular.

■ The identity matrix is its own inverse:

$$\mathbf{I}^{-1} = \mathbf{I}$$

■ The inverse of the transpose of a matrix is the transpose of the inverse of the matrix:

$$(\mathbf{M}^T)^{-1} = (\mathbf{M}^{-1})^T$$

■ The inverse of a matrix product is equal to the product of the inverses of the matrices taken in reverse order:

$$(\mathbf{AB})^{-1} = \mathbf{B}^{-1}\mathbf{A}^{-1}$$

This extends to more than two matrices:

$$(\mathbf{M}_1 \mathbf{M}_2 \cdots \mathbf{M}_{n-1} \mathbf{M}_n)^{-1} = \mathbf{M}_n^{-1} \mathbf{M}_{n-1}^{-1} \cdots \mathbf{M}_2^{-1} \mathbf{M}_1^{-1}$$

9.2.2 Geometric Interpretation

The inverse of a matrix is useful geometrically because it allows us to compute the "reverse" or "opposite" of a transformation — a transformation that "undoes" another transformation if they are performed in sequence. So, if we take a vector, transform it by a matrix $\mathbf{M}$, and then transform it by the inverse $\mathbf{M}^{-1}$ of $\mathbf{M}$, then we will get the original vector back. We can easily verify this algebraically:

$$\begin{aligned} (\mathbf{v}\mathbf{M})\mathbf{M}^{-1} &= \mathbf{v}(\mathbf{M}\mathbf{M}^{-1}) \\ &= \mathbf{v}\mathbf{I} \\ &= \mathbf{v} \end{aligned}$$

9.3 Orthogonal Matrices

In this section, we will investigate a special class of square matrices known as *orthogonal* matrices.

9.3.1 Official Linear Algebra Rules

A square matrix $\mathbf{M}$ is orthogonal if and only if the product of the matrix and its transpose is the identity matrix:

Equation 9.8:
Definition of
orthogonal
matrix

$$\mathbf{M} \text{ is orthogonal} \quad \Longleftrightarrow \quad \mathbf{M}\mathbf{M}^T = \mathbf{I}$$

Recall from Section 9.2 that, by definition, a matrix times its inverse is the identity matrix:
$$\mathbf{M}\mathbf{M}^{-1} = \mathbf{I}$$
Thus, if a matrix is orthogonal, the transpose and the inverse are equal:

$$\mathbf{M} \text{ is orthogonal} \quad \Longleftrightarrow \quad \mathbf{M}^T = \mathbf{M}^{-1}$$

This is extremely powerful information, since the inverse of a matrix is often needed, and orthogonal matrices arise so frequently in practice in 3D graphics. For example, it was mentioned in Section 8.8.5 that rotation and reflection matrices are orthogonal. If we know that our matrix is orthogonal, we can essentially avoid computing the inverse, which is a relatively costly computation.

9.3.2 Geometric Interpretation

Orthogonal matrices are interesting to us primarily since their inverse is trivial to compute. But how do we know if a matrix is orthogonal in order to exploit its structure?

In many cases, we may have information about the way the matrix was constructed and, therefore, know *a priori* that the matrix contains only rotation and/or reflection. This is a very common situation and will be the case when we write the C++ class `RotationMatrix` in Section 11.4.

What if we don't know anything in advance about the matrix? In other words, how can we tell if an arbitrary matrix $\mathbf{M}$ is orthogonal? In order to do this, let's look at the definition of an orthogonal matrix given above, using a 3×3 matrix as an example. Assume $\mathbf{M}$ is a 3×3 matrix. Then by definition, $\mathbf{M}$ is orthogonal if and only if $\mathbf{MM}^T=\mathbf{I}$. Let's see what this means exactly:

$$\mathbf{MM}^T = \mathbf{I}$$

$$\begin{bmatrix} m_{11} & m_{12} & m_{13} \\ m_{21} & m_{22} & m_{23} \\ m_{31} & m_{32} & m_{33} \end{bmatrix} \begin{bmatrix} m_{11} & m_{21} & m_{31} \\ m_{12} & m_{22} & m_{32} \\ m_{13} & m_{23} & m_{33} \end{bmatrix} = \begin{bmatrix} 1 & 0 & 0 \\ 0 & 1 & 0 \\ 0 & 0 & 1 \end{bmatrix}$$

This gives us nine equations, all of which must be true in order for $\mathbf{M}$ to be orthogonal:

$$m_{11}m_{11} + m_{12}m_{12} + m_{13}m_{13} = 1$$
$$m_{11}m_{21} + m_{12}m_{22} + m_{13}m_{23} = 0$$
$$m_{11}m_{31} + m_{12}m_{32} + m_{13}m_{33} = 0$$
$$m_{21}m_{11} + m_{22}m_{12} + m_{23}m_{13} = 0$$
$$m_{21}m_{21} + m_{22}m_{22} + m_{23}m_{23} = 1$$
$$m_{21}m_{31} + m_{22}m_{32} + m_{23}m_{33} = 0$$
$$m_{31}m_{11} + m_{32}m_{12} + m_{33}m_{13} = 0$$
$$m_{31}m_{21} + m_{32}m_{22} + m_{33}m_{23} = 0$$
$$m_{31}m_{31} + m_{32}m_{32} + m_{33}m_{33} = 1$$

Let the vectors $\mathbf{r}_1$, $\mathbf{r}_2$, and $\mathbf{r}_3$ stand for the rows of $\mathbf{M}$:

$$\mathbf{r}_1 = \begin{bmatrix} m_{11} & m_{12} & m_{13} \end{bmatrix}$$
$$\mathbf{r}_2 = \begin{bmatrix} m_{21} & m_{22} & m_{23} \end{bmatrix}$$
$$\mathbf{r}_3 = \begin{bmatrix} m_{31} & m_{32} & m_{33} \end{bmatrix}$$
$$\mathbf{M} = \begin{bmatrix} \mathbf{r}_1 \\ \mathbf{r}_2 \\ \mathbf{r}_3 \end{bmatrix}$$

Now we can rewrite the nine equations more compactly:

$$\mathbf{r}_1 \cdot \mathbf{r}_1 = 1 \qquad \mathbf{r}_1 \cdot \mathbf{r}_2 = 0 \qquad \mathbf{r}_1 \cdot \mathbf{r}_3 = 0$$
$$\mathbf{r}_2 \cdot \mathbf{r}_1 = 0 \qquad \mathbf{r}_2 \cdot \mathbf{r}_2 = 1 \qquad \mathbf{r}_2 \cdot \mathbf{r}_3 = 0$$
$$\mathbf{r}_3 \cdot \mathbf{r}_1 = 0 \qquad \mathbf{r}_3 \cdot \mathbf{r}_2 = 0 \qquad \mathbf{r}_3 \cdot \mathbf{r}_3 = 1$$

Now we can make some interpretations:

- First, the dot product of a vector with itself is one if and only if the vector is a unit vector. Therefore, the first, fourth, and ninth equations will only be true when r_1, r_2, and r_3 are unit vectors.

- Second, recall from Section 5.10.2 that the dot product of two vectors is zero if and only if they are perpendicular. Therefore, the other equations are true when r_1, r_2, and r_3 are mutually perpendicular.

So, for a matrix to be orthogonal, the following must be true:

- Each row of the matrix must be a unit vector.

- The rows of the matrix must be mutually perpendicular.

Similar statements can be made regarding the *columns* of the matrix. This is made obvious by noting that if $\mathbf{M}$ is orthogonal, then $\mathbf{M}^T$ is orthogonal as well.

When computing a matrix inverse, we will usually only take advantage of orthogonality *if we know in advance* that a matrix is orthogonal. If we don't know in advance, it's usually a waste of time to check. In the best of all possible worlds, checking for orthogonality to find that the matrix is indeed orthogonal and then transposing may take as much time as going ahead and inverting the hard way anyway. Also, if the matrix turns out to not be orthogonal, then checking was *definitely* a waste of time.

There is one important note on terminology that can be slightly confusing. In linear algebra, a set of vectors is considered an *orthogonal basis* if they are mutually perpendicular. It is not required that they have unit length. If they do have unit length, they are an *orthonormal basis*. Thus, the rows/columns of an *orthogonal matrix* are orthonormal basis vectors. However, constructing a matrix from a set of orthogonal basis vectors does not necessarily result in an orthogonal matrix (unless the basis vectors are also orthonormal).

9.3.3 Orthogonalizing a Matrix

Sometimes we encounter a matrix that is slightly out of orthogonality. We may have acquired bad data from an external source, or we may have accumulated floating-point error (which is called "matrix creep"). In these situations, we would like to *orthogonalize* the matrix, resulting in a matrix that has mutually perpendicular unit vector axes and is (hopefully) as close to the original matrix as possible.

The standard algorithm for constructing a set of orthogonal basis vectors (the rows of a matrix) is known as *Gram-Schmidt* orthogonalization. The basic idea is to go through the rows of the matrix in order. For each row vector, we subtract off the portion of that vector that is parallel to the proceeding rows, which must result in a perpendicular vector.

Let's look at the 3×3 case as an example. As before, let r_1, r_2, and r_3 stand for the rows of a 3×3 matrix $\mathbf{M}$. Then an orthogonal set of row vectors, r'_1, r'_2, and r'_3, can be computed according to the following algorithm:

Equation 9.9:
Gram-Schmidt
orthogonaliza-
tion of 3D basis
vectors

$$\mathbf{r}'_1 \Leftarrow \mathbf{r}_1$$

$$\mathbf{r}'_2 \Leftarrow \mathbf{r}_2 - \frac{\mathbf{r}_2 \cdot \mathbf{r}'_1}{\mathbf{r}'_1 \cdot \mathbf{r}'_1}\mathbf{r}'_1$$

$$\mathbf{r}'_3 \Leftarrow \mathbf{r}_3 - \frac{\mathbf{r}_3 \cdot \mathbf{r}'_1}{\mathbf{r}'_1 \cdot \mathbf{r}'_1}\mathbf{r}'_1 - \frac{\mathbf{r}_3 \cdot \mathbf{r}'_2}{\mathbf{r}'_2 \cdot \mathbf{r}'_2}\mathbf{r}'_2$$

The vectors $\mathbf{r}'_1$, $\mathbf{r}'_2$, and $\mathbf{r}'_3$ are now mutually perpendicular, and so they are an orthogonal basis. However, they may not necessarily be unit vectors. We need an orthonormal basis to form an orthogonal matrix, and so we must normalize the vectors. (Again, the terminology can be confusing. Please see the note at the end of the previous section.) Notice that if we normalize the vectors as we go, rather than in a second pass, then we can avoid all of the divisions.

The Gram-Schmidt algorithm is biased, depending on the order in which the basis vectors are listed. As an obvious example, $\mathbf{r}_1$ never changes. A variation on the algorithm that is not biased toward any particular axis is to not attempt to completely orthogonalize the entire matrix in one pass. We select some small fraction k, and instead of subtracting off *all* of the projection, we only subtract off k of it. We also subtract the projection on the *original* axis, not the adjusted one. In this way, the order in which we perform the operations does not matter and we have no dimensional bias. This algorithm is summarized below:

$$\mathbf{r}'_1 \Leftarrow \mathbf{r}_1 - k\frac{\mathbf{r}_1 \cdot \mathbf{r}_2}{\mathbf{r}_2 \cdot \mathbf{r}_2}\mathbf{r}_2 - k\frac{\mathbf{r}_1 \cdot \mathbf{r}_3}{\mathbf{r}_3 \cdot \mathbf{r}_3}\mathbf{r}_3$$

$$\mathbf{r}'_2 \Leftarrow \mathbf{r}_2 - k\frac{\mathbf{r}_2 \cdot \mathbf{r}_1}{\mathbf{r}_1 \cdot \mathbf{r}_1}\mathbf{r}_1 - k\frac{\mathbf{r}_2 \cdot \mathbf{r}_3}{\mathbf{r}_3 \cdot \mathbf{r}_3}\mathbf{r}_3$$

$$\mathbf{r}'_3 \Leftarrow \mathbf{r}_3 - k\frac{\mathbf{r}_3 \cdot \mathbf{r}_1}{\mathbf{r}_1 \cdot \mathbf{r}_1}\mathbf{r}_1 - k\frac{\mathbf{r}_3 \cdot \mathbf{r}_2}{\mathbf{r}_2 \cdot \mathbf{r}_2}\mathbf{r}_2$$

One iteration of this algorithm results in a set of basis vectors that are slightly *more* orthogonal that the original vectors, but perhaps not completely orthogonal. By repeating this procedure multiple times, we can eventually converge on an orthogonal basis. Selecting an appropriately small value for k (say, ¼) and iterating a sufficient number of times (say, ten) gets us fairly close. Then, we can use the standard Gram-Schmidt algorithm to guarantee a perfectly orthogonal basis.

9.4 4×4 Homogenous Matrices

Up until now, we have used only 2D and 3D vectors. In this section, we will introduce 4D vectors and the so-called "homogenous" coordinate. There is nothing mysterious or magical about 4D vectors and matrices (and no, the fourth coordinate in this case isn't "time"). As we will see, 4D vectors and 4×4 matrices are nothing more than a notational convenience for what are simple 3D operations.

9.4.1 4D Homogenous Space

As was mentioned in Section 4.1.3, 4D vectors have four components, with the first three components being the standard x, y, and z components. The fourth component in a 4D vector is w (because they ran out of letters in the alphabet!) and is sometimes referred to as the *homogenous* coordinate.

To understand how the standard physical 3D space is extended into 4D, let's first examine homogenous coordinates in 2D, which are of the form (x, y, w). Imagine the standard 2D plane existing in 3D at the plane $w = 1$. So the physical 2D point (x, y) is represented in homogenous space $(x, y, 1)$. For all points that are *not* in the plane $w = 1$, we can compute the corresponding 2D point by projecting the point onto the plane $w = 1$ and dividing by w. So the homogenous coordinate (x, y, w) is mapped to the physical 2D point $(x/w, y/w)$. This is shown in Figure 9.2.

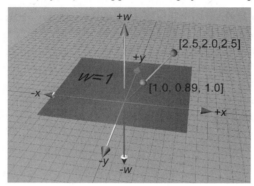

Figure 9.2: Projecting homogenous coordinates onto the plane $w = 1$ in 2D

Thus, for any given physical 2D point (x, y), there are an infinite number of corresponding points in homogenous space. All of them are of the form (kx, ky, k), provided that $k \neq 0$. These points form a line through the homogenous origin.

When $w = 0$ the division is undefined and there is no corresponding physical point in 2D space. However, we can interpret a 2D homogenous point of the form $(x, y, 0)$ as a "point at infinity," which defines a direction rather than a location. There is more on this in the next section.

The same basic idea applies to 4D coordinates. The physical 3D points can be thought of as living in the "plane" in 4D at $w = 1$. A 4D point is of the form (x, y, z, w), and we project a 4D point onto this "plane" to yield the corresponding physical 3D point $(x/w, y/w, z/w)$. When $w = 0$ the 4D point represents a "point at infinity," which defines a direction rather than a location.

Homogenous coordinates and projection by division by w are interesting, but why on earth would we want to use 4D space? There are two primary reasons for using 4D vectors and 4×4 matrices. The first reason, which we will discuss in the next section, is actually nothing more than a notational convenience.

9.4.2 4×4 Translation Matrices

Recall from Section 8.8.1 that a 3×3 transformation matrix represents a *linear transformation* that does not contain translation. Due to the nature of matrix multiplication, the zero vector is always transformed into the zero vector, and, therefore, any transformation that can be represented by a matrix multiplication cannot contain translation. This is unfortunate, since matrix multiplication and inversion are very convenient tools for composing complicated transformations out of simple ones and manipulating nested coordinate space relationships. It would be nice if we could find a way to somehow extend the standard 3×3 transformation matrix to be able to handle transformations with translation. 4×4 matrices provide a mathematical "kludge" which allows us to do this.

Assume for the moment that w is always one. Thus, the standard 3D vector $[x, y, z]$ will always be represented in 4D as $[x, y, z, 1]$. Any 3×3 transformation matrix can be represented in 4D as shown below:

$$\begin{bmatrix} m_{11} & m_{12} & m_{13} \\ m_{21} & m_{22} & m_{23} \\ m_{31} & m_{32} & m_{33} \end{bmatrix} \implies \begin{bmatrix} m_{11} & m_{12} & m_{13} & 0 \\ m_{21} & m_{22} & m_{23} & 0 \\ m_{31} & m_{32} & m_{33} & 0 \\ 0 & 0 & 0 & 1 \end{bmatrix}$$

When we multiply a 4D vector of the form $[x, y, z, 1]$ by a matrix of the form shown above, we get the same result as the standard 3×3 case, only the result in this case is a 4D vector with $w = 1$:

$$\begin{bmatrix} x & y & z \end{bmatrix} \begin{bmatrix} m_{11} & m_{12} & m_{13} \\ m_{21} & m_{22} & m_{23} \\ m_{31} & m_{32} & m_{33} \end{bmatrix}$$

$$= \begin{bmatrix} xm_{11} + ym_{21} + zm_{31} & xm_{12} + ym_{22} + zm_{32} & xm_{13} + ym_{23} + zm_{33} \end{bmatrix}$$

$$\begin{bmatrix} x & y & z & 1 \end{bmatrix} \begin{bmatrix} m_{11} & m_{12} & m_{13} & 0 \\ m_{21} & m_{22} & m_{23} & 0 \\ m_{31} & m_{32} & m_{33} & 0 \\ 0 & 0 & 0 & 1 \end{bmatrix}$$

$$= \begin{bmatrix} xm_{11} + ym_{21} + zm_{31} & xm_{12} + ym_{22} + zm_{32} & xm_{13} + ym_{23} + zm_{33} & 1 \end{bmatrix}$$

Now for the interesting part. In 4D, we can also express translation as a matrix multiplication, something we were unable to do in 3D:

Equation 9.10: Using a 4×4 matrix to perform translation in 3D

$$\begin{bmatrix} x & y & z & 1 \end{bmatrix} \begin{bmatrix} 1 & 0 & 0 & 0 \\ 0 & 1 & 0 & 0 \\ 0 & 0 & 1 & 0 \\ \Delta x & \Delta y & \Delta z & 1 \end{bmatrix} = \begin{bmatrix} x + \Delta x & y + \Delta y & z + \Delta z & 1 \end{bmatrix}$$

It is important to understand that matrix multiplication is still a *linear transformation*, even in 4D. Matrix multiplication cannot represent "translation" in 4D, and the 4D zero vector will always be transformed back into the 4D zero vector. The reason this trick works to translate points in 3D is that we are actually *shearing* 4D space. (Compare Equation 9.10 with the shear matrices from

Section 8.6.) The "plane" in 4D that corresponds to physical 3D space does not pass through the origin in 4D. Thus, when we shear 4D space, we are able to translate in 3D.

Let's examine what happens when we perform a transformation without translation followed by a transformation with only translation. Let $\mathbf{R}$ be a rotation matrix. (In fact, $\mathbf{R}$ could possibly contain other 3D linear transformations, but for now, let's assume $\mathbf{R}$ only contains rotation.) Let $\mathbf{T}$ be a translation matrix of the form in Equation 9.10.

$$\mathbf{R} = \begin{bmatrix} r_{11} & r_{12} & r_{13} & 0 \\ r_{21} & r_{22} & r_{23} & 0 \\ r_{31} & r_{32} & r_{33} & 0 \\ 0 & 0 & 0 & 1 \end{bmatrix}, \mathbf{T} = \begin{bmatrix} 1 & 0 & 0 & 0 \\ 0 & 1 & 0 & 0 \\ 0 & 0 & 1 & 0 \\ \Delta x & \Delta y & \Delta z & 1 \end{bmatrix}$$

We could then rotate and translate a point $\mathbf{v}$ to compute a new point $\mathbf{v}'$ as follows:
$$\mathbf{v}' = \mathbf{vRT}$$

Remember that the order of transformations is important, and since we have chosen to use row vectors, the order of transformations coincides with the order in which the matrices are multiplied (from left to right). We are rotating *first* and then translating.

Just like 3×3 matrices, we can concatenate the two matrices into a single transformation matrix, which we'll assign to the matrix $\mathbf{M}$:

$$\begin{aligned} \mathbf{M} &= \mathbf{RT} \\ \mathbf{v}' &= \mathbf{vRT} \\ &= \mathbf{v}(\mathbf{RT}) \\ &= \mathbf{vM} \end{aligned}$$

Let's examine the contents of $\mathbf{M}$:

$$\mathbf{M} = \mathbf{RT} = \begin{bmatrix} r_{11} & r_{12} & r_{13} & 0 \\ r_{21} & r_{22} & r_{23} & 0 \\ r_{31} & r_{32} & r_{33} & 0 \\ 0 & 0 & 0 & 1 \end{bmatrix} \begin{bmatrix} 1 & 0 & 0 & 0 \\ 0 & 1 & 0 & 0 \\ 0 & 0 & 1 & 0 \\ \Delta x & \Delta y & \Delta z & 1 \end{bmatrix} = \begin{bmatrix} r_{11} & r_{12} & r_{13} & 0 \\ r_{21} & r_{22} & r_{23} & 0 \\ r_{31} & r_{32} & r_{33} & 0 \\ \Delta x & \Delta y & \Delta z & 1 \end{bmatrix}$$

Notice that the upper 3×3 portion of $\mathbf{M}$ contains the rotation portion, and the bottom row contains the translation portion. The rightmost column (for now) will be $[0, 0, 0, 1]^T$. Applying this information in reverse, we can take *any* 4×4 matrix and separate it into a linear transformation portion and a translation portion. We can express this succinctly by assigning the translation vector $[\Delta x, \Delta y, \Delta z]$ to the vector $\mathbf{t}$:

$$\mathbf{M} = \begin{bmatrix} \mathbf{R} & \mathbf{0} \\ \mathbf{t} & 1 \end{bmatrix}$$

Note: For the moment, we are assuming that the rightmost column is always $[0, 0, 0, 1]^T$. We will begin to encounter situations where this is not the case in Section 9.4.4.

Let's see what happens with the so-called "points at infinity" when $w = 0$. Multiplying by a "standard" 3×3 linear transformation matrix extended into 4D (a transformation that does *not* contain translation), we get:

$$\begin{bmatrix} x & y & z & 0 \end{bmatrix} \begin{bmatrix} r_{11} & r_{12} & r_{13} & 0 \\ r_{21} & r_{22} & r_{23} & 0 \\ r_{31} & r_{32} & r_{33} & 0 \\ 0 & 0 & 0 & 1 \end{bmatrix}$$

$$= \begin{bmatrix} xr_{11} + yr_{21} + zr_{31} & xr_{12} + yr_{22} + zr_{32} & xr_{13} + yr_{23} + zr_{33} & 0 \end{bmatrix}$$

In other words, when we transform a point at infinity vector of the form $[x, y, z, 0]$ by a transformation matrix containing rotation, scale, etc., the expected transformation occurs. The result is another point at infinity vector of the form $[x', y', z', 0]$.

When we transform a point at infinity vector by a transformation that *does* contain translation, we get the following result:

$$\begin{bmatrix} x & y & z & 0 \end{bmatrix} \begin{bmatrix} r_{11} & r_{12} & r_{13} & 0 \\ r_{21} & r_{22} & r_{23} & 0 \\ r_{31} & r_{32} & r_{33} & 0 \\ \Delta x & \Delta y & \Delta z & 1 \end{bmatrix}$$

$$= \begin{bmatrix} xr_{11} + yr_{21} + zr_{31} & xr_{12} + yr_{22} + zr_{32} & xr_{13} + yr_{23} + zr_{33} & 0 \end{bmatrix}$$

Notice that the result is the same (i.e., no translation occurs). In other words, the w component of a 4D vector can be used to selectively "switch off" the translation portion of a 4×4 matrix. This is useful because some vectors represent "locations" and should be translated, and other vectors represent "directions," such as surface normals, and should not be translated. In a geometric sense, we can think of the first type of data as "points" and the second type of data as "vectors."

One reason why 4×4 matrices are useful is that a 4×4 transformation matrix can contain translation. When we use 4×4 matrices solely for this purpose, the rightmost column of the matrix will always be $[0, 0, 0, 1]^T$. Since this is the case, why don't we just drop the column and use a 4×3 matrix? According to linear algebra rules, 4×3 matrices are undesirable for several reasons:

■ We cannot multiply a 4×3 matrix by another 4×3 matrix.

■ We cannot invert a 4×3 matrix, since the matrix is not square.

■ When we multiply a 4D vector by a 4×3 matrix, the result is a 3D vector.

Strict adherence to linear algebra rules forces us to add the fourth column. Of course, in our code, we are not bound by linear algebra rules. In Section 11.5, we will write a 4×3 matrix class that is useful for representing transformations that contain translation. This matrix class doesn't explicitly store the fourth column.

9.4.3 General Affine Transformations

In Chapter 8, we presented 3×3 matrices for many primitive transformations. Because a 3×3 matrix can only represent *linear* transformations in 3D, translation was not considered. Armed with 4×4 transform matrices, we can now create more general *affine* transformations that contain translation. For example:

- Rotation about an axis that does not pass through the origin
- Scale about a plane that does not pass through the origin
- Reflection about a plane that does not pass through the origin
- Orthographic projection onto a plane that does not pass through the origin

The basic idea is to translate the "center" of the transformation to the origin, perform the linear transformation using the techniques developed in Chapter 8, and then transform the point back to its original location. We will start with a translation matrix $\mathbf{T}$ that translates the point $\mathbf{p}$ to the origin and a linear transform matrix $\mathbf{R}$ from Chapter 8 that performs the linear transformation. The final affine transformation matrix $\mathbf{M}$ will be equal to the matrix product $\mathbf{TRT}^{-1}$. $\mathbf{T}^{-1}$ is a translation matrix with the opposite translation amount as $\mathbf{T}$.

It is interesting to notice the general form of such a matrix. Let's first write $\mathbf{T}, \mathbf{R}, \mathbf{T}^{-1}$ using the "partitioned" form we used earlier:

$$\mathbf{T} = \begin{bmatrix} 1 & 0 & 0 & 0 \\ 0 & 1 & 0 & 0 \\ 0 & 0 & 1 & 0 \\ -\mathbf{p}_x & -\mathbf{p}_y & -\mathbf{p}_z & 1 \end{bmatrix}$$

$$= \begin{bmatrix} \mathbf{I} & 0 \\ -\mathbf{p} & 1 \end{bmatrix}$$

$$\mathbf{R}_{4\times4} = \begin{bmatrix} r_{11} & r_{12} & r_{13} & 0 \\ r_{21} & r_{22} & r_{23} & 0 \\ r_{31} & r_{32} & r_{33} & 0 \\ 0 & 0 & 0 & 1 \end{bmatrix}$$

$$= \begin{bmatrix} \mathbf{R}_{3\times3} & 0 \\ \mathbf{0} & 1 \end{bmatrix}$$

$$\mathbf{T}^{-1} = \begin{bmatrix} 1 & 0 & 0 & 0 \\ 0 & 1 & 0 & 0 \\ 0 & 0 & 1 & 0 \\ \mathbf{p}_x & \mathbf{p}_y & \mathbf{p}_z & 1 \end{bmatrix}$$

$$= \begin{bmatrix} \mathbf{I} & 0 \\ \mathbf{p} & 1 \end{bmatrix}$$

Now we evaluate the matrix multiplications:

$$\mathbf{TR}_{4\times4}\mathbf{T}^{-1} = \begin{bmatrix} \mathbf{I} & 0 \\ -\mathbf{p} & 1 \end{bmatrix} \begin{bmatrix} \mathbf{R}_{3\times3} & 0 \\ \mathbf{0} & 1 \end{bmatrix} \begin{bmatrix} \mathbf{I} & 0 \\ \mathbf{p} & 1 \end{bmatrix}$$

$$= \begin{bmatrix} \mathbf{R}_{3\times3} & 0 \\ -\mathbf{p}\mathbf{R}_{3\times3} + \mathbf{p} & 1 \end{bmatrix}$$

Thus, the extra translation in an affine transformation only changes the last row of the 4×4 matrix. The upper 3×3 portion, which contains the linear transformation, is not affected.

9.4.4 Perspective Projection

Our use of "homogenous" coordinates in the previous section was really nothing more than a mathematical kludge to allow us to include translation in our transformations. We use quotations around "homogenous" because the w value was always one (or zero, in the case of points at infinity). In this section we will remove the quotations and discuss meaningful ways to use 4D coordinates with other w values.

Recall from Section 9.4.1 that when we interpret a 4D homogenous vector in 3D, we divide by w. This gives us a mathematical tool that we did not take advantage of in the previous section, since w was always one (or zero). This division allows us to encapsulate very succinctly some important geometric operations. Most notably, we can perform *perspective projection*.

We can learn a great deal about perspective projection by comparing it to another type of projection we have already discussed, *orthographic* projection. In Section 8.4, we learned how to project 3D space onto a 2D plane, known as the *projection plane*, using orthographic projection. Orthographic projection is also known as *parallel* projection because the *projectors* are parallel. (A *projector* is a line from the original point in space to the resulting projected point on the plane.) The parallel projectors used in orthographic projection are shown below in Figure 9.3:

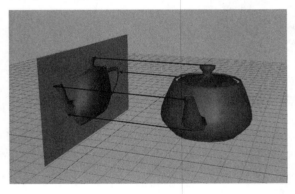

Figure 9.3: Orthographic projection uses parallel projectors

Perspective projection in 3D also projects onto a 2D plane. However, the projectors are not parallel. In fact, they intersect at a point, known as the *center of projection*. This is shown in Figure 9.4:

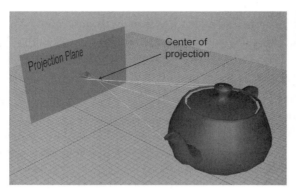

Figure 9.4: Perspective projection. The projectors intersect at the center of projection

Because the center of projection is in front of the projection plane, the projectors cross before striking the plane, and the image is inverted. As we move an object farther away from the center of projection, its orthographic projection remains constant, but the perspective projection gets smaller, as illustrated in Figure 9.5.

Figure 9.5: Perspective foreshortening

The teapot on the right is farther from the projection plane, and the projection is slightly smaller than the closer teapot. This is a very important visual cue known as *perspective foreshortening*.

9.4.5 A Pinhole Camera

Perspective projection is important in graphics because it models the way the human visual system works. Actually, the human visual system is slightly more complicated because we have two eyes, and for each eye, the projection surface (our retina) is not flat. So let's look at the simpler example of a pinhole camera. A pinhole camera is a box with a tiny hole on one end. Rays of light enter the pinhole (converging at a point) and then strike the opposite end of the box, which is the projection plane. This is shown in Figure 9.6.

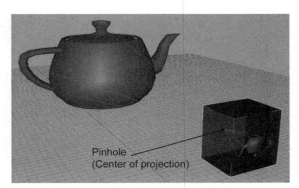

Figure 9.6: A pinhole camera

Pinhole
(Center of projection)

In this view, the left and back sides of the box have been removed so you can see the inside. Notice that the image projected onto the back of the box is inverted. This is because the rays of light (the projectors) cross as they meet at the pinhole (the center of projection).

Let's examine the geometry behind the perspective projection of a pinhole camera. Imagine a 3D coordinate space with the origin at the pinhole and the z-axis perpendicular to the projection plane. The x- and y-axes are parallel to the plane of projection. This is shown below in Figure 9.7:

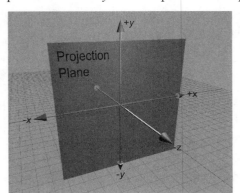

Figure 9.7: A projection plane parallel to the xy plane

Let's see if we can't compute, for an arbitrary point **p**, the 3D coordinates of **p'**, which is **p** projected through the pinhole onto the projection plane. First, we need to know the distance from the pinhole to the projection plane. We'll assign this to the variable d. Thus, the plane is defined by the equation $z = -d$. Now let's view the problem from the side, and solve the problem for y. Examine Figure 9.8.

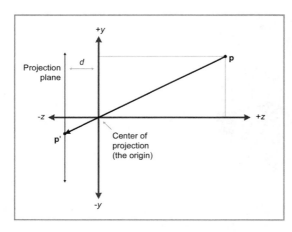

By similar triangles, we can see that:

$$\frac{-\mathbf{P}'_y}{d} = \frac{\mathbf{P}_y}{z} \implies \mathbf{P}'_y = \frac{-d\mathbf{p}_y}{z}$$

Notice that since a pinhole camera flips the image upside down, the signs of $\mathbf{p}_y$ and $\mathbf{p}'_y$ are opposite. The value of $\mathbf{p}'_x$ is computed in a similar manner:

$$\mathbf{P}'_x = \frac{-d\mathbf{p}_x}{z}$$

The z values of all the projected points are the same: $-d$. Thus, the result of projecting a point $\mathbf{p}$ through the origin onto a plane at $z = -d$ is:

Equation 9.11:
Projecting onto
the plane
$z = -d$

$$\mathbf{p} = \begin{bmatrix} x \\ y \\ z \end{bmatrix} \implies \mathbf{p}' = \begin{bmatrix} x' \\ y' \\ z' \end{bmatrix} = \begin{bmatrix} -dx/z \\ -dy/z \\ -d \end{bmatrix}$$

In practice, having negative values creates unnecessary complexities, and so we move the plane of projection *in front* of the center of projection (i.e., the plane $z = d$). This is shown in Figure 9.9.

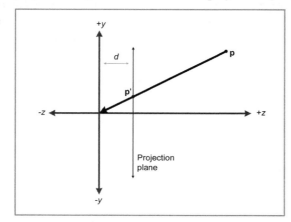

Of course, this would never work for a real pinhole camera, since the purpose of the pinhole in the first place is to only allow in light that passes through a single point. However, in the mathematical universe inside a computer, we can do this. As expected, moving the plane of projection in front of the center of projection removes the annoying minus signs:

Equation 9.12:
Projecting a
point onto the
plane $z = d$

$$\mathbf{p}' = \begin{bmatrix} x' \\ y' \\ z' \end{bmatrix} = \begin{bmatrix} dx/z \\ dy/z \\ d \end{bmatrix}$$

9.4.6 Perspective Projection Using 4×4 Matrices

Because the conversion from 4D to 3D space implies a division, we can encode a perspective projection in a 4×4 matrix. The basic idea is to come up with an equation for **p**' with a common denominator for x, y, and z and then set up a 4×4 matrix which will set w equal to this denominator. We will assume that the original points have $w = 1$.

First we manipulate the equation for **p**' to have a common denominator:

$$\begin{aligned} \mathbf{p}' &= \begin{bmatrix} dx/z & dy/z & d \end{bmatrix} \\ &= \begin{bmatrix} dx/z & dy/z & dz/z \end{bmatrix} \\ &= \frac{\begin{bmatrix} x & y & z \end{bmatrix}}{z/d} \end{aligned}$$

To divide by this denominator, we put the denominator into w, so the 4D point will be of the form:

$$\begin{bmatrix} x & y & z & z/d \end{bmatrix}$$

So we need a 4×4 matrix that takes an "ordinary" homogenous vector of the form $[x, y, z, 1]$ and transforms it into the form given above. The matrix that does this is shown below:

Equation 9.13:
Projecting onto
the plane
$z = d$ using a
4×4 matrix

$$\begin{bmatrix} x & y & z & 1 \end{bmatrix} \begin{bmatrix} 1 & 0 & 0 & 0 \\ 0 & 1 & 0 & 0 \\ 0 & 0 & 1 & 1/d \\ 0 & 0 & 0 & 0 \end{bmatrix} = \begin{bmatrix} x & y & z & z/d \end{bmatrix}$$

Thus, we have derived a 4×4 projection matrix. There are several important points to be made here:

■ Multiplication by this matrix doesn't *actually* perform the perspective transform; it just computes the proper denominator into w. Remember that the perspective division actually occurs when we convert from 4D to 3D by dividing by w.

■ There are many variations. For example, we can place the plane of projection at $z = 0$ and the center of projection at $[0, 0, -d]$. This results in a slightly different equation.

■ This seems overly complicated. It seems like it would be simpler to divide by z, rather than bothering with matrices. So why is homogenous space interesting? First, 4×4 matrices provide a way to express projection as a transformation that can be concatenated with other transformations. Second, projection onto non-axially aligned planes is possible. Basically, we don't *need* homogenous coordinates to perform any operations, but 4×4 matrices provide a compact way to represent and manipulate projection transformations.

■ The projection matrix in a real graphics geometry pipeline is not going to be exactly like the one we derived here. There are many important details that must be considered. For example, our matrix basically discards z, which many graphics systems use for z-buffering. See Chapter 15 for a description of how the graphics geometry pipeline would be implemented.

9.5 Exercises

1. Compute the determinant of the following matrix:
$$\begin{bmatrix} 3 & -2 \\ 1 & 4 \end{bmatrix}$$

2. Compute the determinant, adjoint, and inverse of the following matrix:
$$\begin{bmatrix} 3 & -2 & 0 \\ 1 & 4 & 0 \\ 0 & 0 & 2 \end{bmatrix}$$

3. Is the following matrix orthogonal?
$$\begin{bmatrix} -0.1495 & -0.1986 & 0.9685 \\ -0.8256 & 0.5640 & 0.0117 \\ -0.5439 & -0.8015 & 0.2484 \end{bmatrix}$$

4. Invert the matrix from the previous exercise.

5. Invert the 4×4 matrix:
$$\begin{bmatrix} -0.1495 & -0.1986 & 0.9685 & 0 \\ -0.8256 & 0.5640 & 0.0117 & 0 \\ -0.5439 & -0.8015 & 0.2484 & 0 \\ 1.7928 & -5.3116 & 8.0151 & 1 \end{bmatrix}$$

6. Construct a 4×4 matrix to translate by [4,2,3].

7. Construct a 4×4 matrix to rotate 20° about the x-axis and then translate by [4,2,3].

8. Construct a 4×4 matrix to translate by [4,2,3] and then rotate 20° about the x-axis.

9. Construct a 4×4 matrix to perform a perspective projection onto the plane $x=5$. (Assume the origin is the center of projection.)

10. Use the matrix from the previous exercise to compute the 3D coordinates of the projection of the point (107, –243, 89) onto the plane $x=5$.

Chapter 10

Orientation and Angular Displacement in 3D

This chapter discusses orientation in 3D. It is divided into six sections.

- Section 10.1 discusses the subtle differences between terms like "orientation," "direction," and "angular displacement."
- Section 10.2 describes how to express orientation using a matrix.
- Section 10.3 describes how to express angular displacement using *Euler angles*.
- Section 10.4 describes how to express angular displacement using a *quaternion*.
- Section 10.5 compares and contrasts the three methods.
- Section 10.6 explains how to convert an orientation from one form to another.

In this chapter, we will tackle the difficult problem of describing the orientation of an object in 3D. We will also discuss the closely related concept of *angular displacement*. There are several different ways we can express orientation and angular displacement in 3D. We will discuss the three most important methods — matrices, Euler angles, and quaternions. For each method, we will define precisely how the representation method works and discuss the peculiarities, advantages, and disadvantages of the method.

Different techniques are needed in different circumstances, and each technique has its advantages and disadvantages. It is important to know not only how each method works, but also which technique is most appropriate for a particular situation and how to convert between representations.

In this chapter, we will make extensive use of the terms *object space* and *inertial space*, which were discussed in Section 3.2.

10.1 What is Orientation?

Before we can begin to discuss how to describe orientation in 3D, let us first define exactly what it is that we are attempting to describe. In this section, we will discuss how *orientation* is related to other similar terms:

■ Direction

■ Angular displacement

■ Rotation

Intuitively, we know that the "orientation" of an object basically tells us what direction the object is facing. However, "direction" is not exactly the same as orientation. A vector has "direction," but not "orientation." The difference is that when a vector points in a certain direction, you can "twist" the vector along its length (see Figure 10.1), and there is no real change to the vector (or its direction) since a vector has no thickness or dimension other than its length.

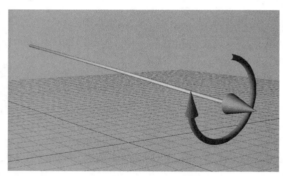

Figure 10.1: "Twisting" a vector along its length results in no appreciable change to the vector

However, if you have an object facing a certain direction and you twist that object in the same way that we twisted the vector (see Figure 10.2), you *will* change the orientation of the object.

Figure 10.2: "Twisting" an object changes its orientation

Technically, this is demonstrated by the fact that we can parameterize a direction in 3D using just two numbers (i.e., polar coordinates), whereas an orientation requires a minimum of three numbers.

When we specify the position of an object, we cannot do so in absolute terms; we must always do so within the context of a specific reference frame. (See Section 4.3.1.) We have seen how specifying a position is actually the same as specifying an amount of *translation* from a given reference point (usually the origin of some coordinate system).

In the same way, when we describe the orientation of an object, orientation cannot be described in absolute terms. Just as a position is given by a translation from some known point, an orientation is given by a *rotation* from some known reference orientation (often called the "identity" or "home" orientation). The amount of rotation is known as an *angular displacement*. In other words, describing an orientation is mathematically equivalent to describing an angular displacement.

We say "mathematically equivalent" because we will make a subtle distinction between "orientation" and terms like "angular displacement" and "rotation" in this book. It is helpful to think of "angular displacement" as having a direction of transformation attached with it. (For example, the angular displacement *from* the old orientation *to* the new orientation, or *from* inertial space *to* object space.) So there is a "source/destination" relationship. "Orientation" will be used in situations where we are not describing a "source/destination" relationship but a "parent/child" relationship. This distinction between "orientation" and "angular displacement" is similar to the distinction between "points" and "vectors" — two other terms that are equivalent mathematically but not identical conceptually. In both cases, the first term is primarily used to describe a single "state," and the second term is used primarily to describe a "difference between two states."

Of course, these conventions are purely a matter of preference, but they can be helpful. In particular, we will think about matrices and quaternions representing "angular displacements" and Euler angles representing "orientations."

10.2 Matrix Form

One way to represent the orientation of a coordinate space in 3D is to list the basis vectors of one coordinate space, expressed using the other coordinate space. When these basis vectors are used to form the rows of a 3×3 matrix, we have expressed the orientation in *matrix form*. Another way to say this is that we can express the relative orientation of two coordinate spaces by giving the rotation matrix that can be used to transform vectors from one coordinate space to the other.

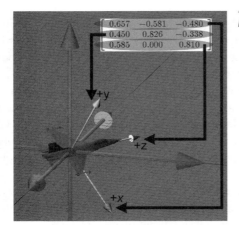

10.2.1 Which Matrix?

We've seen how a matrix can be used to transform points from one coordinate space to another. When we are talking about using a matrix to represent an angular displacement, which transformation are we referring to exactly? Does the matrix transform vectors from inertial space into object space, or is it in the other direction?

For our purposes in this chapter, it doesn't matter. It will be sufficient that a matrix describes an orientation by listing basis vectors after transformation. By describing the rotation from one coordinate space to the other (whichever transformation we chose to represent), we have established the orientation. The actual direction of transformation of the matrix is an implementation detail. Since rotation matrices are orthogonal (see Section 9.3), using one matrix or the other is simply a matter of transposing it to get the inverse transformation, if necessary.

10.2.2 Advantages of Matrix Form

Matrix form is a very explicit form of representing orientation. This explicit nature provides some benefits.

- **Rotation of vectors is immediately available**. The most important property of matrix form is that you can use a matrix to rotate vectors between object and inertial space. No other representation of orientation allows this. In order to rotate vectors, you must convert the orientation to matrix form. (It is an often touted advantage of quaternions that they can be used to perform rotations through quaternion multiplication — see Section 10.4.8. However, if you examine the math, you'll see that this "shortcut" amounts to multiplication by the corresponding rotation matrix.)

- **Format used by graphics APIs**. Partly due to reasons in the previous paragraph, graphics APIs use matrices to express orientation. (API stands for application programming interface — basically, this is the code that you use to communicate with the video hardware.) When you are communicating with the graphics API, you must express your transformations as matrices eventually. How you store transformations internally in your program is up to you, but if you choose another representation, you must convert them into matrices at some point in the graphics pipeline.

- **Concatenation of multiple angular displacements**. A second advantage of matrices is that it is possible to "collapse" nested coordinate space relationships. For example, if we know the orientation of object A relative to object B, and we know the orientation of object B relative to object C, then by using matrices we can determine the orientation of object A relative to object C. We encountered these concepts before when we learned about nested coordinate spaces in Chapter 3, and then we discussed how matrices could be concatenated in Section 8.6.

- **Matrix inversion**. When an angular displacement is represented in matrix form, it is possible to compute the "opposite" angular displacement using matrix inversion. Since rotation matrices are orthogonal, this computation is a trivial matter of transposing the matrix.

10.2.3 Disadvantages of Matrix Form

The explicit nature of a matrix provides some advantages, as we have discussed in the previous section. However, a matrix uses nine numbers to store an orientation, and it is possible to parameterize orientation using only three numbers. These "extra" numbers can cause some problems.

- **Matrices take more memory**. If we need to store many orientations, such as keyframes in an animation sequence, that extra space for nine numbers instead of three can really add up. Let's take a modest example. Let's say we are animating a model of a human that is broken up into 15 pieces for different body parts. Animation is accomplished strictly by controlling the orientation of each part relative to its parent part. Assume we are storing one orientation for each part, per frame, and our animation data is stored at a reasonable rate of 15 Hz. This means we will have 225 orientations per second. Using matrices and 32-bit floating-point numbers, each frame will take 8,100 bytes. Using Euler angles (which we will meet in Section 10.3), the same data would only take 2,700 bytes. For a mere 30 seconds of animation data, matrices would take 162 K more than the same data stored using Euler angles!

- **Difficult for humans to use**. Matrices are not intuitive for humans to work with directly. There are just too many numbers, and they are all between −1 and 1. Also, humans naturally think about orientation in terms of angles, but a matrix is expressed using vectors. With practice, we can learn how to decipher the orientation from a given matrix. (The techniques from Section 7.2.2 for visualizing a matrix help with this.) This is still much more difficult than Euler angles, and going the other way is *much* more difficult. It would take forever to construct the matrix for a nontrivial orientation by hand. In general, matrices just aren't the way people naturally think about orientation.

- **Matrices can be malformed**. A matrix uses nine numbers when only three are necessary. In other words, a matrix contains six degrees of redundancy. There are six constraints that must be satisfied in order for a matrix to be "valid" for representing an orientation. The rows must be unit vectors, and they must be mutually perpendicular. (See Section 9.3.2.)

Let's consider this last point in more detail. If we take any nine numbers at random and create a 3×3 matrix, it is very unlikely that these six constraints will be satisfied. Thus, the nine numbers will not form a valid rotation matrix. In other words, matrices can be ill-formed, at least for purposes of representing an orientation. Ill-formed matrices can be a problem because they can cause numerical exceptions and other unexpected behavior.

How could we end up with a bad matrix? There are several ways:

- First, we may have a matrix that contains scale, skew, or reflection. What is the "orientation" of an object that has been affected by such operations? There really isn't a clear definition for this. Any non-orthogonal matrix is not a well-defined rotation matrix. (See Section 9.3 for a complete discussion on orthogonal matrices.) Reflection matrices, which are orthogonal, are not valid rotation matrices either.

- Second, we may just get bad data from an external source. For example, if we are using a physical data acquisition system, such as motion capture, there could be errors due to the capturing process. Many modeling packages are notorious for producing malformed matrices.

- Finally, we can actually create bad data due to floating-point round-off error. For example, suppose we apply a large number of incremental changes to an orientation, which could routinely happen in a game or simulation that allows a human to interactively control the orientation of an object. The large number of matrix multiplications, which are subject to limited floating-point precision, can result in an ill-formed matrix. This phenomenon is known as *matrix creep*. We can combat matrix creep by *orthogonalizing* the matrix, as we already discussed in Section 9.3.3.

10.2.4 Summary

Let's summarize what we have learned in Section 10.2 about using matrices to represent angular displacement:

- Matrices are a "brute force" method of expressing orientation; we explicitly list the basis vectors of one coordinate system using a different coordinate system.

- The matrix form of representing orientation is useful, primarily because it allows us to rotate vectors between coordinate spaces.

- Modern graphics APIs express orientation using matrices.

- We can use matrix multiplication to collapse matrices for nested coordinate spaces into a single matrix.

- Matrix inversion provides a mechanism for determining the "opposite" angular displacement.

- Matrices take two to three times as much memory as the other techniques we will learn. This can become significant when storing large numbers of orientations, such as animation data.

- Not all matrices are valid for describing an orientation. Some matrices contain mirroring or skew. We can end up with a malformed matrix either by getting bad data from an external source or through matrix creep.

- The numbers in a matrix aren't intuitive for humans to work with.

10.3 Euler Angles

Another common method of representing orientation is known as *Euler angles*. (Euler is pronounced "oiler," not "yoolur.") The technique is named after the famous mathematician Leonhard Euler (1707-1783) who proved that a sequence of angular displacements was equivalent to a single angular displacement.

10.3.1 What are Euler Angles?

The basic idea behind Euler angles is to define an angular displacement as a sequence of three rotations about three mutually perpendicular axes. This sounds complicated, but actually, it is very intuitive. (In fact, its ease of use is one if its primary advantages.) We say "angular displacement" because Euler angles can indeed be used to describe any arbitrary rotation. However, in this book, we will use them primarily to describe the orientation of an object within a parent coordinate space (such as world space).

Euler angles describe orientation as three rotations about three mutually perpendicular axes. But which axes? And in what order? As it turns out, any three axes in any order will work, but it makes the most sense to use the cardinal axes in a particular order. The most common convention, and the one we will use in this book, is the so-called "heading-pitch-bank" convention for Euler angles. In this system, an orientation is defined by a *heading* angle, a *pitch* angle, and a *bank* angle. The basic idea is to start with the object in the "identity" orientation — that is, with the axes aligned with the inertial axes. From there, we apply the rotations for heading, then pitch, and finally bank, so that the object arrives in the orientation we are attempting to describe.

Before we define the terms "heading," "pitch," and "bank" precisely, let us briefly review the coordinate space conventions we use in this book. We use a left-handed system, where +*x* is to the right, +*y* is up, and +*z* is forward. (Check out Figure 2.16 for an illustration.) Also, if you have forgotten how positive rotation is defined according to the left-hand rule, you might want to flip back to Figure 8.5 to refresh your memory.

As shown in Figure 10.4, *heading* measures the amount of rotation about the *y*-axis. Positive rotation rotates to the right (clockwise when viewed from above).

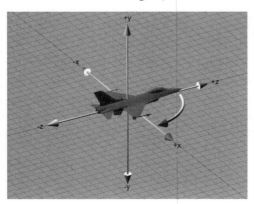

Figure 10.4: Heading is the first rotation and rotates about the y-axis

After heading has been applied, *pitch* measures the amount of rotation about the *x*-axis. This is the object space *x*-axis, *not* the original inertial space *x*-axis. Staying consistent with the left-hand rule, positive rotation rotates downward. In other words, pitch actually measures the angle of declination. This is illustrated in Figure 10.5.

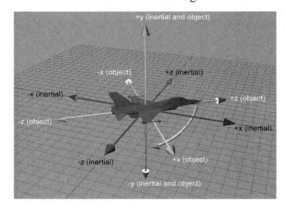

Figure 10.5: Pitch is the second rotation and rotates about the object space x-axis

Finally, after heading and pitch have been applied, *bank* measures the amount of rotation about the *z*-axis. Again, this is the object space *z*-axis, not the original inertial space *z*-axis. The left-hand rule dictates that positive bank rotates counterclockwise when viewed from the origin looking toward +*z*. This is illustrated in Figure 10.6.

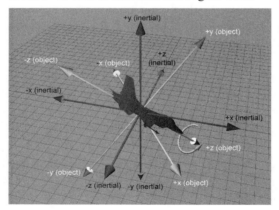

Figure 10.6: Bank is the third and final rotation; it rotates about the object space z-axis

It may seem contradictory that positive bank is counterclockwise, since positive heading is clockwise. Notice that positive heading is clockwise when viewed from the positive end of the axis toward the origin, the opposite perspective from the one used when judging clockwise/counterclockwise for bank. If we look from the origin to the positive end of the *y*-axis, then positive heading does rotate counterclockwise. Or, if we look from the positive end of the *z*-axis toward the origin (looking backward from in front of the object), then positive bank appears to rotate the object clockwise. In either case, the left-hand rule prevails.

Remember, when we say the rotations happen in the order of heading, pitch, and then bank, we are talking about the order in which we rotate the object from inertial space into object space. If we are thinking about rotating from object space into inertial space, the order is reversed.

Another name given to the heading-pitch-bank system is "roll-pitch-yaw," where roll is synonymous with bank, and yaw is synonymous with heading. (Actually, yaw is not precisely the same as heading. More on this in Section 10.3.2.) Notice that in the roll-pitch-yaw system, the angles are named in the order that we rotate from object space to inertial space.

10.3.2 Other Euler Angle Conventions

As we've mentioned, the *heading-pitch-bank* system isn't the only system of Euler angles. Any sequence of rotations about any three mutually perpendicular axes can define an orientation. There are several options that cause the variation in Euler angle conventions:

■ First, the heading-pitch-bank system goes by other names. Of course, calling something by a different name isn't a different convention, but it is worth noting. One common set of terminology is *roll-pitch-yaw*, where *roll* is the same as *bank*, and *yaw* is the basically the same as *heading*. Notice that this order appears to be opposite from *heading-pitch-bank*. This is purely semantics; they are naming the order of rotations when a vector is rotated from object to inertial space. (Actually, there is a technical difference between "yaw" and "heading." Yaw is a rotation about the *object y*-axis, and heading is a rotation about the *inertial y*-axis. Since this rotation is performed at a time when the object y-axis is coincident with the inertial y-axis, this distinction is not important.)

■ Second, any three axes can be used as the axes of rotation. The axes don't have to be the cardinal axes, although it makes the most sense to use these axes.

■ Third, it is not necessary to adhere to the left- or right-hand rule when defining which direction is considered positive for each of the rotations. It is certainly possible and common to define positive pitch to rotate upward, for example.

■ Fourth, and most importantly, the rotations can occur in different order, and the order *does* matter. Any system would work for defining an orientation, but the heading-pitch-bank order is the most common order used because it is the most practical. *Heading* measures rotation about the vertical axes, which is meaningful primarily because the environments we work in frequently have some sort of flat "ground." Knowing the amount of rotation about the inertial x- or z-axis is usually not useful. The orderings for the other two angles were also chosen to be useful: *pitch* is meaningful as an angle of declination from horizontal, and *bank* measures how much we are "twisted" on our z-axis.

If you have to deal with Euler angles that use a different convention from the one you prefer, we offer two pieces of advice:

■ First, make sure you understand *exactly* how the other Euler angle system works. The little details, such as definition of positive rotation and order of rotations, make a big difference.

■ Second, the easiest way to convert the Euler angles to your format is to convert them to matrix form and then convert the matrix back to your style of Euler angles. We will learn how to perform these conversions in Section 10.6. Fiddling with the angles directly is much more difficult than it would seem. See [21] for more information.

10.3.3 Advantages of Euler Angles

Euler angles parameterize orientation using only three numbers, and these numbers are angles. These two characteristics of Euler angles provide certain advantages over other forms of representing orientation.

- **Euler angles are easy for us to use**, considerably easier than matrices or quaternions. Perhaps this is because the numbers in an Euler angle triple are *angles*, which is naturally how people think about orientation. If the conventions most appropriate for the situation are chosen, then the *most important* angles can be expressed directly. For example, the angle of declination is expressed directly using the heading-pitch-bank system. The ease of use is a serious advantage. When an orientation needs to be displayed numerically or entered at the keyboard, Euler angles are really the only choice.

- **Smallest representation possible**. Euler angles use three numbers to describe an orientation. No system can parameterize 3D orientation using fewer than three numbers. If memory is at a premium, then Euler angles are the most economical way to represent an orientation.

- **Any set of three numbers is valid**. If we take any three numbers at random, they form a valid set of Euler angles that we can interpret as an expression of an orientation. In other words, there is no such thing as an "invalid" set of Euler angles. Of course, the numbers may not be correct, but at least they are valid. This is not the case with matrices and quaternions.

10.3.4 Disadvantages of Euler Angles

In this section we discuss some disadvantages of the Euler angle method of representing orientation. These are primarily:

- The representation for a given orientation is not unique.
- Interpolating between two angles is difficult.

Let's address these points in detail. First, we have the problem that for a given orientation, there are many different Euler angle triples that can be used to describe that orientation. This is known as *aliasing* and can be somewhat of an inconvenience. Basic questions such as "do two Euler angle triples represent the same angular displacement?" are difficult to answer due to aliasing.

The first and simplest form of aliasing occurs when we add a multiple of 360° to one of the angles. Obviously, adding a whole number of revolutions does not change the orientation expressed, even though the numbers are different.

A second and more troublesome form of aliasing occurs because the three angles are not completely independent of each other. For example, pitching down 135° is the same as heading 180°, pitching down 45°, and then banking 180°.

In order to guarantee a unique representation for any given orientation, we must restrict the ranges of the angles. One common technique is to limit heading and bank to ±180° and limit pitch to ±90°. This establishes a "canonical" set of Euler angles. For any orientation, there is only one canonical Euler angle set to represent the orientation. (Actually, there is one more irritating singularity that must be handled, which we will describe in just a moment.)

Almost all of the functions in our code that accept Euler angle parameters will work given Euler angles in any range. However, when we write code that computes, or *returns*, Euler angles, we will always try to return the canonical Euler angle triple. Using canonical Euler angles simplifies many basic tests such as "am I facing approximately east?"

The most famous (and irritating) type of aliasing problem suffered by Euler angles is illustrated by this example: if we head right 45° and then pitch down 90°, this is the same as pitching down 90° and then banking 45°. In fact, once we choose ±90° as the pitch angle, we are restricted to rotating about the vertical axis. This phenomenon, where an angle of ±90° for the second rotation can cause the first and third angles to rotate about the same axis, is known as *Gimbal lock*. In order to remove this aliasing from the canonical set of Euler angle triples, we will assign all rotation about the vertical axis to *heading* in the Gimbal lock case. In other words, in the canonical set, if pitch is ±90°, then bank is zero.

For the purposes of representing an orientation, aliasing doesn't pose a huge problem, especially when *canonical* Euler angles are used. But let's say we wish to interpolate between two orientations, A and B. In other words, for a given parameter t, $0 \le t \le 1$, we wish to compute an intermediate orientation C, so that C interpolates smoothly from A to B as t varies from zero to one. This is an extremely useful operation for character animation and automatic camera control, for example.

The naïve approach to this problem is to apply the standard linear interpolation formula to each of the three angles independently. This equation is shown below:

$$\Delta\theta = \theta_1 - \theta_0$$
$$\theta_t = \theta_0 + t\Delta\theta$$

This is fraught with problems.

First, if canonical Euler angles are not used, we may have large angle values. For example, imagine the heading of orientation A is 720°, and the heading of orientation B is 45°. 720° = 2 × 360°, which is the same as 0°. So basically, the heading values are only 45° apart. However, naïve interpolation will spin around nearly twice in the wrong direction, as shown below in Figure 10.7.

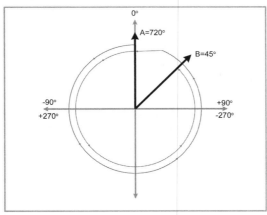

Figure 10.7: Naïve interpolation can cause excessive rotation

Of course, the solution to this problem is to use canonical Euler angles. We could assume that we will always be interpolating between two sets of canonical Euler angles. Or, we could attempt to enforce this by converting to canonical values inside our interpolation routine. (Simply wrapping angles within the $-180°\ldots180°$ range is easy, but dealing with pitch values outside the $-90°\ldots90°$ range is more challenging.)

However, even using canonical angles doesn't completely solve the problem. A second type of interpolation problem can occur because of the cyclic nature of rotation angles. Suppose the heading in A was $-170°$, and the heading in B was $170°$. Notice that these are canonical values for heading, both in range $-180°\ldots180°$. The two heading values are only $20°$ apart, but again, naïve interpolation will not behave correctly, rotating the "long way around" across $340°$ instead of taking the shorter path of $20°$, as shown in Figure 10.8.

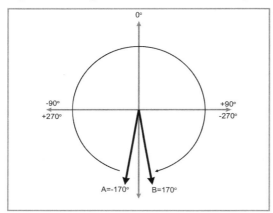

Figure 10.8: Naïve interpolation can rotate "the long way around"

The solution to this second type of problem is to wrap the "delta" angles used in the interpolation equation in range $-180°\ldots180°$ in order to find the shortest arc:

$$\mathrm{wrap}(x) \;=\; x - 360°\lfloor(x+180°)/360°\rfloor$$
$$\Delta\theta \;=\; \mathrm{wrap}(\theta_1 - \theta_0)$$
$$\theta_t \;=\; \theta_0 + t\Delta\theta$$

Even with these two "Band-Aids," Euler angle interpolation still suffers from Gimbal lock, which in many situations causes a jerky, unnatural course. The object whips around suddenly and appears to be "hung" somewhere. The basic problem is that the angular velocity is not constant during the interpolation. If you have never experienced what Gimbal lock looks like, you may wonder what all the fuss is about. Unfortunately, it is very difficult to fully appreciate the problem from illustrations in a book; you need to experience it interactively. Luckily, the companion web page for this book (gamemath.com) has an excellent interactive demonstration of Gimbal lock.

The first two problems with Euler angle interpolation were irritating, but certainly not insurmountable. Using canonical Euler angles and wrapping the delta values in range provided relatively easy workarounds. Gimbal lock, unfortunately, is more than a minor nuisance; it's a fundamental problem. Perhaps we could reformulate our rotations and devise a system that does not suffer from these problems? Unfortunately, this is not possible. There is simply an inherent problem with using three numbers to describe 3D orientation. We could change our problems, but not eliminate them. Any system that parameterizes 3-space orientation using three numbers is guaranteed to have singularities in the parameterization space and, therefore, be subject to problems such as Gimbal lock. In Section 10.4, we will learn how to overcome these problems using quaternions.

10.3.5 Summary

Let's summarize our findings in Section 10.3 concerning Euler angles:

- Euler angles store orientation using three angles. These angles are ordered rotations about three mutually perpendicular axes.
- The most common system of Euler angles is the heading-pitch-bank system.
- In most situations, Euler angles are more intuitive for us to work with compared to other methods of representing orientation.
- When memory is at a premium, Euler angles use the minimum amount of data possible for storing an orientation in 3D.
- There is no such thing as an "invalid" set of Euler angles. Any three numbers have a meaningful interpretation.
- Euler angles suffer from aliasing problems, due to the cyclic nature of rotation angles, and because the rotations are not completely independent of one another.
- Using canonical Euler angles can simplify many basic queries on Euler angles. An Euler angle triple is in the canonical set if heading and bank are in range $-180°\ldots180°$ and pitch is in range $-90°\ldots90°$. Also, if pitch is $\pm90°$, then bank is zero.
- Gimbal lock occurs when pitch is $\pm90°$. In this case, one degree of freedom is lost because heading and bank both rotate about the vertical axis.
- Interpolating between two orientations expressed using Euler angles is problematic. Simple forms of aliasing are irritating, but there are workarounds. Gimbal lock is a more fundamental problem and no easy solution exists.

10.4 Quaternions

The term *quaternion* is somewhat of a buzzword in 3D math. That's probably because most people don't understand quaternions. The mystery surrounding quaternions is largely due to the way quaternions have been presented in most texts. Hopefully, this book will help you resolve any confusion concerning quaternions.

There is a mathematical reason for why using only three numbers to represent a 3-space orientation is guaranteed to cause the problems we discussed with Euler angles, such as Gimbal lock. It has something to do with some fairly advanced math terms like "manifolds." A quaternion avoids these problems by using four numbers to express an orientation (hence the name *quat*ernion).

10.4.1 Quaternion Notation

A quaternion contains a scalar component and a 3D vector component. We usually refer to the scalar component as w. We may refer to the vector component as a single entity $\mathbf{v}$ or as individual components x, y, and z. Both notations are illustrated below:

$$\begin{bmatrix} w & \mathbf{v} \end{bmatrix}$$
$$\begin{bmatrix} w & (x & y & z) \end{bmatrix}$$

In some cases, it will be convenient to use the shorter notation using $\mathbf{v}$, and in some cases, the "expanded" version is clearer. In this chapter, we will present all equations using both forms, when possible. In just a moment, we will describe exactly what these four numbers represent.

We also may write quaternions vertically. This is strictly to make the equations format nicely; there is no significant distinction between "row" and "column" quaternions.

10.4.2 Quaternions as Complex Numbers

We will now make a brief digression into complex math. This material is not completely necessary in order to understand how to use quaternions, since we will be able to interpret quaternions completely from a geometric perspective. However, it is interesting to know the mathematical heritage of quaternions and the circumstances that surrounded their invention.

Recall that the complex pair (a, b) defines the number $a+bi$, where i is the so-called imaginary number such that $i^2 = -1$. a is known as the *real* part, and b is the *imaginary* part. Any real number k (an "ordinary" number) can be expressed as the complex number $(k, 0) = k + 0i$.

Complex numbers can be added, subtracted, and multiplied as follows:

Equation 10.1:
Adding, subtracting, and multiplying complex numbers

$$\begin{aligned}
(a + bi) + (c + di) &= (a + c) + (b + d)i \\
(a + bi) - (c + di) &= (a - c) + (b - d)i \\
(a + bi)(c + di) &= ac + adi + bci + bdi^2 \\
&= ac + (ad + bc)i + bd(-1) \\
&= (ac - bd) + (ad + bc)i
\end{aligned}$$

We also may compute the *conjugate* of a complex number by negating the imaginary portion. The notation is shown below:

Equation 10.2:
Complex conjugate

$$\begin{aligned}
p &= (a + bi) \\
p^* &= (a - bi)
\end{aligned}$$

We may also compute the *magnitude* of a complex number. The notation and interpretation of this operation is similar to the absolute value of a real number, and in fact, when we express a real number as a complex number, they produce the same result. Equation 10.3 shows the magnitude of a complex number.

Equation 10.3:
Magnitude of
a complex
number

$$\|p\| = \sqrt{pp^*}$$

$$\|(a + bi)\| = \sqrt{(a + bi)(a + bi)^*}$$

$$\|(a + bi)\| = \sqrt{(a + bi)(a - bi)}$$

$$= \sqrt{a^2 + b^2}$$

The set of complex numbers "live" in a 2D plane. We can think about this plane as having two axes: the real axis and the imaginary axis. Thus, we interpret the complex number (x, y) as a 2D vector. When complex numbers are interpreted in this fashion, they can be used to perform rotation in the plane (albeit in a roundabout way). A complex number p is rotated about the origin by an angle θ, as shown in Figure 10.9.

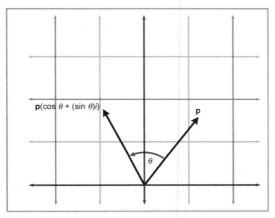

Figure 10.9: Rotating a complex number in the plane

To perform this rotation, we define a second complex number $q = (\cos \theta, \sin \theta)$. Now, the rotated vector p' can be computed by the complex multiplication:

$$p = (x + yi)$$

$$q = (\cos \theta + (\sin \theta)i)$$

$$p' = pq$$

$$= (x + yi)(\cos \theta + (\sin \theta)i)$$

$$= (x \cos \theta - y \sin \theta) + (x \sin \theta + y \cos \theta)i$$

Of course, this is nothing more than the 2×2 rotation matrix from Section 8.2.1. However, complex numbers provide an interesting notation for this. We shall see that quaternions can be used in a similar way in 3D.

The Irish mathematician William Hamilton looked for a way to extend complex numbers from 2D to 3D for years. This new type of complex number, he thought, would have one real part and two imaginary parts. However, Hamilton was unable to create a useful type of complex number with two imaginary parts. Then, as the story goes, in 1843, on his way to a speech at the Royal Irish Academy, he suddenly realized that *three* imaginary parts were needed rather than two. He carved the equations that define the properties of this new type of complex number on the Broome Bridge. (These equations are given on the following page.) Thus, quaternions were invented.

Quaternions extend the complex number system by having three imaginary numbers, i, j, and k, which are related as follows:

$$i^2 = j^2 = k^2 = -1$$
$$ij = k, ji = -k$$
$$jk = i, kj = -i$$
$$ki = j, ik = -j$$

A quaternion $[w, (x, y, z)]$ defines the complex number $w + xi + yj + zk$. As we will soon see, many of the properties of standard complex numbers also apply to quaternions. Most importantly, in a manner analogous to the way complex numbers can be used to rotate vectors in the plane, quaternions can be used to rotate vectors in 3D.

10.4.3 Quaternions as an Axis-Angle Pair

Euler proved that a sequence of rotations was equivalent to a single rotation. Thus, any angular displacement in 3D can be described as a single rotation about a single axis. (The word *axis* here is used in the general sense as a line about which something rotates and is not to be confused with the cardinal axes. Quite often, an axis of rotation for a given orientation is arbitrarily oriented.) When an orientation is represented in this form, it is known as an *axis-angle* representation. (Actually, we could have defined *axis-angle* form as a fourth form for representing orientation. However, axis-angle form is rarely used in practice; usually either quaternions or Euler angles are used instead.)

In Section 8.2.3, we derived a matrix to rotate vectors about an arbitrary axis. As we did then, let us define the vector **n** to be the axis of rotation. The length of **n** is not important for purposes of defining an axis, although it will be convenient at this time for us to restrict **n** to have unit length. The direction of **n** defines which way is considered "positive" rotation, according to the standard "hand" rule for left-hand or right-hand coordinate spaces. (See Figure 8.5 if you have forgotten this rule.) We will also define the scalar θ to be the amount of rotation about this axis. Thus, the pair $(\theta, \mathbf{n})$ defines an angular displacement as a rotation of θ radians about the axis specified by **n**.

A quaternion can be interpreted as an axis-angle representation of angular displacement. Of course, **n** and θ aren't simply stored in the four numbers of the quaternion directly — that would be too easy! They're in there, but it's not quite that straightforward. Equation 10.4 shows how the numbers inside a quaternion **q** are related to θ and **n**. Both forms of quaternion notation are used:

Equation 10.4:
The four values
of a quaternion

$$\mathbf{q} = \begin{bmatrix} \cos(\theta/2) & \sin(\theta/2)\mathbf{n} \end{bmatrix}$$
$$= \begin{bmatrix} \cos(\theta/2) & (\sin(\theta/2)\mathbf{n}_x & \sin(\theta/2)\mathbf{n}_y & \sin(\theta/2)\mathbf{n}_z) \end{bmatrix}$$

Keep in mind that the w component of **q** is related to θ, but they are not the same thing. Likewise, **v** and **n** are related, but not identical.

10.4.4 Quaternion Negation

Quaternions can be negated. This is done in the obvious way of negating each component:

Equation 10.5:
Quaternion
negation

$$-\mathbf{q} = -\big[\ w\ \ (\ x\ \ y\ \ z\ )\ \big] = \big[\ -w\ \ (\ -x\ \ -y\ \ -z\ )\ \big]$$
$$= -\big[\ w\ \ \mathbf{v}\ \big] = \big[\ -w\ \ -\mathbf{v}\ \big]$$

It is surprising to realize that the quaternions $\mathbf{q}$ and $-\mathbf{q}$ actually represent the *same* angular displacement! If we add any multiple of 360° to θ, it doesn't change the angular displacement represented by $\mathbf{q}$, but it negates all four components of $\mathbf{q}$. Thus, any angular displacement in 3D has exactly *two* distinct representations in quaternion format, and they are negatives of each other.

10.4.5 Identity Quaternion(s)

Geometrically, there are two "identity" quaternions, which represent no angular displacement: [1, **0**] and [–1, **0**]. (Note the boldface zero, which indicates the zero-vector.) When θ is an even multiple of 360°, then $\cos(\theta/2) = 1$, and we have the first form. If θ is an odd multiple of 360°, then $\cos(\theta/2) = -1$, and we have the second form. In both cases, $\sin(\theta/2) = 0$, so the value of $\mathbf{n}$ is irrelevant. This makes sense; if the rotation angle θ is a whole number of complete revolutions, then no real change is made to the orientation, and the axis of rotation is irrelevant.

Mathematically, there is really only one identity quaternion: [1, **0**]. When we multiply any quaternion $\mathbf{q}$ by the identity quaternion, the result is $\mathbf{q}$. (We will learn about quaternion multiplication in Section 10.4.8.) When we multiply a quaternion $\mathbf{q}$ by the other "geometric identity" quaternion [–1, **0**], we get $-\mathbf{q}$. Geometrically, this results in the same quaternion, since $\mathbf{q}$ and $-\mathbf{q}$ represent the same angular displacement. Mathematically, $\mathbf{q}$ and $-\mathbf{q}$ are not equal, so [–1, **0**] is not a "true" identity quaternion.

10.4.6 Quaternion Magnitude

We can compute the *magnitude* of a quaternion, just as we can for vectors and complex numbers. The notation and formula, shown below, are similar to that used for vectors:

Equation 10.6:
Quaternion
magnitude

$$\|\mathbf{q}\| = \left\|\big[\ w\ \ (\ x\ \ y\ \ z\ )\ \big]\right\| = \sqrt{w^2 + x^2 + y^2 + z^2}$$
$$= \left\|\big[\ w\ \ \mathbf{v}\ \big]\right\| = \sqrt{w^2 + \|\mathbf{v}\|^2}$$

Let's see what this means geometrically. Substituting using θ and $\mathbf{n}$:

$$\|\mathbf{q}\| = \left\|\big[\ w\ \ \mathbf{v}\ \big]\right\|$$
$$= \sqrt{w^2 + \|\mathbf{v}\|^2}$$
$$= \sqrt{\cos^2(\theta/2) + (\sin(\theta/2)\|\mathbf{n}\|)^2}$$
$$= \sqrt{\cos^2(\theta/2) + \sin^2(\theta/2)\|\mathbf{n}\|^2}$$

Recalling the restriction that **n** has unit length, we have:

$$\|\mathbf{q}\| = \sqrt{\cos^2(\theta/2) + \sin^2(\theta/2)\|\mathbf{n}\|^2}$$
$$= \sqrt{\cos^2(\theta/2) + \sin^2(\theta/2)(1)}$$
$$= \sqrt{\cos^2(\theta/2) + \sin^2(\theta/2)}$$

Applying the trig identity $\sin^2 x + \cos^2 x = 1$ (see Appendix A):

$$\|\mathbf{q}\| = \sqrt{\cos^2(\theta/2) + \sin^2(\theta/2)}$$
$$= \sqrt{1}$$
$$= 1$$

For our purposes of using quaternions to represent orientation, we will only deal with so-called *unit quaternions* that obey this rule. For information concerning non-normalized quaternions, we refer the reader to [3].

10.4.7 Quaternion Conjugate and Inverse

The *conjugate* of a quaternion, denoted $\mathbf{q}^*$, is obtained by negating the vector portion of the quaternion:

Equation 10.7:
Quaternion
conjugate
$$\mathbf{q}^* = \begin{bmatrix} w & \mathbf{v} \end{bmatrix}^* = \begin{bmatrix} w & -\mathbf{v} \end{bmatrix}$$
$$= \begin{bmatrix} w & (x \ y \ z) \end{bmatrix}^* = \begin{bmatrix} w & (-x \ -y \ -z) \end{bmatrix}$$

The *inverse* of a quaternion, denoted $\mathbf{q}^{-1}$, is defined as the conjugate of a quaternion divided by its magnitude:

Equation 10.8:
Quaternion
inverse
$$\mathbf{q}^{-1} = \frac{\mathbf{q}^*}{\|\mathbf{q}\|}$$

The quaternion inverse has an interesting correspondence with the multiplicative inverse for real numbers (scalars). For real numbers, the multiplicative inverse a^{-1} is $1/a$. In other words, $a(a^{-1}) = a^{-1}a = 1$. The same applies to quaternions. When we multiply a quaternion **q** by its inverse $\mathbf{q}^{-1}$, we get the identity quaternion [1, **0**]. (We will discuss quaternion multiplication in the next section.)

Equation 10.8 is the *official* definition of quaternion inverse. However, since we will only be using unit quaternions for our purposes, the quaternion conjugate and inverse will be equivalent.

The conjugate (inverse) is interesting because **q** and $\mathbf{q}^*$ represent opposite angular displacements. It is easy to see why this is the case. By negating **v**, we are negating the axis of rotation **n**, which reverses what we consider to be positive rotation. Thus, **q** rotates about an axis by an amount θ, and $\mathbf{q}^*$ rotates in the opposite direction by the same amount.

For our purposes, an alternative definition of quaternion conjugate could have been to negate w, leaving **v** (and **n**) unchanged. This would negate the amount of rotation θ, rather than reversing what is considered positive rotation by flipping the axis of rotation. This would have been equivalent to the definition given in Equation 10.8 (for our purposes, at least) and provided for a slightly faster implementation and a slightly more intuitive geometric interpretation also. However, the term *conjugate* has a special significance in the context of complex numbers, and so we have chosen to preserve the original definition.

10.4.8 Quaternion Multiplication (Cross Product)

Quaternions can be multiplied according to their complex number interpretation from Section 10.4.2:

$$(w_1 + x_1 i + y_1 j + z_1 k)(w_2 + x_2 i + y_2 j + z_2 k)$$

$$= \quad w_1 w_2 + w_1 x_2 i + w_1 y_2 j + w_1 z_2 k$$
$$+ x_1 w_2 i + x_1 x_2 i^2 + x_1 y_2 ij + x_1 z_2 ik$$
$$+ y_1 w_2 j + y_1 x_2 ji + y_1 y_2 j^2 + y_1 z_2 jk$$
$$+ z_1 w_2 k + z_1 x_2 ki + z_1 y_2 kj + y_1 z_2 k^2$$

$$= \quad w_1 w_2 + w_1 x_2 i + w_1 y_2 j + w_1 z_2 k$$
$$+ x_1 w_2 i + x_1 x_2 (-1) + x_1 y_2 k + x_1 z_2 (-j)$$
$$+ y_1 w_2 j + y_1 x_2 (-k) + y_1 y_2 (-1) + y_1 z_2 i$$
$$+ z_1 w_2 k + z_1 x_2 j + z_1 y_2 (-i) + y_1 z_2 (-1)$$

$$= \quad w_1 w_2 - x_1 x_2 - y_1 y_2 - y_1 z_2$$
$$+ (w_1 x_2 + x_1 w_2 + y_1 z_2 - z_1 y_2) i$$
$$+ (w_1 y_2 + y_1 w_2 + z_1 x_2 - x_1 z_2) j$$
$$+ (w_1 z_2 + z_1 w_2 + x_1 y_2 - y_1 x_2) j$$

This leads us to the standard definition for quaternion multiplication, given below using both quaternion notations.

Equation 10.9:
Standard
definition of
quaternion
product

$$\begin{bmatrix} w_1 & \begin{pmatrix} x_1 & y_1 & z_1 \end{pmatrix} \end{bmatrix} \begin{bmatrix} w_2 & \begin{pmatrix} x_2 & y_2 & z_2 \end{pmatrix} \end{bmatrix}$$

$$= \begin{bmatrix} w_1 w_2 - x_1 x_2 - y_1 y_2 - z_1 z_2 \\ \begin{pmatrix} w_1 x_2 + x_1 w_2 + z_1 y_2 - y_1 z_2 \\ w_1 y_2 + y_1 w_2 + x_1 z_2 - z_1 x_2 \\ w_1 z_2 + z_1 w_2 + y_1 x_2 - x_1 y_2 \end{pmatrix} \end{bmatrix}$$

$$\begin{bmatrix} w_1 & \mathbf{v}_1 \end{bmatrix} \begin{bmatrix} w_2 & \mathbf{v}_2 \end{bmatrix}$$

$$= \begin{bmatrix} w_1 w_2 - \mathbf{v}_1 \cdot \mathbf{v}_2 & w_1 \mathbf{v}_2 + w_2 \mathbf{v}_1 + \mathbf{v}_2 \times \mathbf{v}_1 \end{bmatrix}$$

Note: This is *not* the definition of quaternion multiplication we actually use in this book. We will use a slightly different form. This alternative definition, and the rationale behind it, will be given in a few pages.

We do not use a multiplication symbol for quaternion cross product, and there is no distinction made between "row" and "column" quaternions.

Quaternion multiplication is associative, but it is not commutative:

Equation 10.10:
Quaternion
multiplication is
associative, but
not commutative

$$(\mathbf{ab})\mathbf{c} = \mathbf{a}(\mathbf{bc})$$
$$\mathbf{ab} \neq \mathbf{ba}$$

Let's examine the magnitude of the product of two quaternions.

$$\|\mathbf{q}_1\mathbf{q}_2\| = \left\| \left[\; w_1 \quad (\; x_1 \quad y_1 \quad z_1\;)\; \right]\left[\; w_2 \quad (\; x_2 \quad y_2 \quad z_2\;)\; \right]\right\|$$

$$= \left\| \left[\begin{array}{c} w_1w_2 - x_1x_2 - y_1y_2 - z_1z_2 \\ \left(\begin{array}{c} w_1x_2 + x_1w_2 + y_1z_2 - z_1y_2 \\ w_1y_2 + y_1w_2 + z_1x_2 - x_1z_2 \\ w_1z_2 + z_1w_2 + x_1y_2 - y_1x_2 \end{array} \right) \end{array} \right] \right\|$$

$$= \sqrt{\begin{array}{l} (w_1w_2 - x_1x_2 - y_1y_2 - z_1z_2)^2 \\ +(w_1x_2 + x_1w_2 + y_1z_2 - z_1y_2)^2 \\ +(w_1y_2 + y_1w_2 + z_1x_2 - x_1z_2)^2 \\ +(w_1z_2 + z_1w_2 + x_1y_2 - y_1x_2)^2 \end{array}}$$

After expanding this product and then canceling terms (a step which we have omitted because it is very messy), we then factor:

$$\|\mathbf{q}_1\mathbf{q}_2\| = \sqrt{\begin{array}{l} w_1{}^2w_2{}^2 + x_1{}^2x_2{}^2 + y_1{}^2y_2{}^2 + z_1{}^2z_2{}^2 \\ +w_1{}^2x_2{}^2 + x_1{}^2w_2{}^2 + y_1{}^2z_2{}^2 + z_1{}^2y_2{}^2 \\ +w_1{}^2y_2{}^2 + y_1{}^2w_2{}^2 + z_1{}^2x_2{}^2 + x_1{}^2z_2{}^2 \\ +w_1{}^2z_2{}^2 + z_1{}^2w_2{}^2 + x_1{}^2y_2{}^2 + y_1{}^2x_2{}^2 \end{array}}$$

$$= \sqrt{\begin{array}{l} w_1{}^2(w_2{}^2 + x_2{}^2 + y_2{}^2 + z_2{}^2) \\ +x_1{}^2(w_2{}^2 + x_2{}^2 + y_2{}^2 + z_2{}^2) \\ +y_1{}^2(w_2{}^2 + x_2{}^2 + y_2{}^2 + z_2{}^2) \\ +z_1{}^2(w_2{}^2 + x_2{}^2 + y_2{}^2 + z_2{}^2) \end{array}}$$

$$= \sqrt{(w_1{}^2 + x_1{}^2 + y_1{}^2 + z_1{}^2)(w_2{}^2 + x_2{}^2 + y_2{}^2 + z_2{}^2)}$$

Finally, applying the definition of quaternion magnitude:

Equation 10.11:
Magnitude of
quaternion
product is equal
to the product of
the magnitudes

$$\|\mathbf{q}_1\mathbf{q}_2\| = \sqrt{(w_1{}^2 + x_1{}^2 + y_1{}^2 + z_1{}^2)(w_2{}^2 + x_2{}^2 + y_2{}^2 + z_2{}^2)}$$
$$= \sqrt{\|\mathbf{q}_1\|^2\|\mathbf{q}_2\|^2}$$
$$= \|\mathbf{q}_1\|\|\mathbf{q}_2\|$$

Thus, the magnitude of a quaternion product is equal to the product of the magnitudes. This is very significant, since it guarantees that when we multiply two unit quaternions, the result is a unit quaternion.

The inverse of a quaternion product is equal to the product of the inverses taken in reverse order:

Equation 10.12:
Inverse of
quaternion
product equals
the product of
inverses, taken
in reverse order

$$(\mathbf{ab})^{-1} = \mathbf{b}^{-1}\mathbf{a}^{-1}$$
$$(\mathbf{q}_1\mathbf{q}_2\cdots\mathbf{q}_{n-1}\mathbf{q}_n)^{-1} = \mathbf{q}_n^{-1}\mathbf{q}_{n-1}^{-1}\cdots\mathbf{q}_2^{-1}\mathbf{q}_1^{-1}$$

Now we come to a very interesting property of quaternions. Let us "extend" a standard 3D (x, y, z) point into quaternion space by defining the quaternion $\mathbf{p} = [0, (x, y, z)]$. (Of course, $\mathbf{p}$ will not, in general, be a unit quaternion.) Let $\mathbf{q}$ be a rotation quaternion in the form we have discussed, $[\cos\theta/2, \mathbf{n}\sin\theta/2]$, where $\mathbf{n}$ is a unit vector axis of rotation, and θ is the rotation angle. It is surprising to realize that we can rotate the 3D point $\mathbf{p}$ about $\mathbf{n}$ by performing the following quaternion multiplication:

$$\mathbf{p}' = \mathbf{q}\mathbf{p}\mathbf{q}^{-1}$$

We can prove this by expanding the multiplication, substituting in $\mathbf{n}$ and θ, and comparing the result to Equation 8.5. In fact, this is how most texts on quaternions derive the conversion from quaternion to matrix form. We have chosen to derive the conversion from quaternion to matrix form solely from the geometry of the rotations, which we will do in Section 10.6.3. As it turns out, the correspondence between quaternion multiplication and 3D vector rotations is more of a theoretical interest than a practical one. In practice, it's likely to be just as fast to convert the quaternion to matrix form (using Equation 10.23, which we will derive in Section 10.6.3) and then multiply the vector by the matrix.

Other than this bit of mathematical trivia, what's the point of quaternion multiplication? Examine what happens when we apply multiple rotations. We'll rotate a point $\mathbf{p}$ by the quaternion $\mathbf{a}$ and then rotate that result by another quaternion $\mathbf{b}$:

$$\begin{aligned}
\mathbf{p}' &= \mathbf{b}(\mathbf{a}\mathbf{p}\mathbf{a}^{-1})\mathbf{b}^{-1} \\
&= (\mathbf{b}\mathbf{a})\mathbf{p}(\mathbf{a}^{-1}\mathbf{b}^{-1}) \\
&= (\mathbf{b}\mathbf{a})\mathbf{p}(\mathbf{b}\mathbf{a})^{-1}
\end{aligned}$$

Notice that rotating by $\mathbf{a}$ and then by $\mathbf{b}$ is equivalent to performing a single rotation by the quaternion product $\mathbf{b}\mathbf{a}$. Thus, quaternion multiplication can be used to concatenate multiple rotations, just like matrix multiplication.

According to the standard definition of quaternion multiplication, these rotations occur in order from right to left. This is very unfortunate, since it forces us to write concatenation of multiple rotations "inside out," and it does not mirror the same operations in matrix form. (At least not when row vectors are used.)

Because of this "backwardness" resulting from Equation 10.9, in this book and in our code, we will deviate from the standard definition and define quaternion multiplication with the operands in the opposite order. Notice that only the vector cross product portion is affected:

Equation 10.13:
Definition of
quaternion
multiplication
used in this
book

$$\begin{bmatrix} w_1 & (x_1 & y_1 & z_1) \end{bmatrix} \begin{bmatrix} w_2 & (x_2 & y_2 & z_2) \end{bmatrix}$$

$$= \begin{bmatrix} w_1 w_2 - x_1 x_2 - y_1 y_2 - z_1 z_2 \\ \begin{pmatrix} w_1 x_2 + x_1 w_2 + y_1 z_2 - z_1 y_2 \\ w_1 y_2 + y_1 w_2 + z_1 x_2 - x_1 z_2 \\ w_1 z_2 + z_1 w_2 + x_1 y_2 - y_1 x_2 \end{pmatrix} \end{bmatrix}$$

$$\begin{bmatrix} w_1 & \mathbf{v}_1 \end{bmatrix} \begin{bmatrix} w_2 & \mathbf{v}_2 \end{bmatrix}$$

$$= \begin{bmatrix} w_1 w_2 - \mathbf{v}_1 \cdot \mathbf{v}_2 & w_1 \mathbf{v}_2 + w_2 \mathbf{v}_1 + \mathbf{v}_1 \times \mathbf{v}_2 \end{bmatrix}$$

This does not change the fundamental properties of quaternions or their geometric interpretation using θ and $\mathbf{n}$. We can still use quaternion multiplication to rotate vectors directly, only with our definition, we multiply by the quaternion on the right and its inverse on the left:

$$\mathbf{p}' = \mathbf{q}^{-1} \mathbf{p} \mathbf{q}$$

We see that the product representing the concatenation of multiple rotations does, indeed, read from left to right in the order that rotations occur:

$$\begin{aligned} \mathbf{p}' &= \mathbf{b}^{-1}(\mathbf{a}^{-1} \mathbf{p} \mathbf{a})\mathbf{b} \\ &= (\mathbf{b}^{-1} \mathbf{a}^{-1})\mathbf{p}(\mathbf{a}\mathbf{b}) \\ &= (\mathbf{a}\mathbf{b})^{-1} \mathbf{p}(\mathbf{a}\mathbf{b}) \end{aligned}$$

For the remainder of this book, and in all the code, we will use the definition of quaternion multiplication given above in Equation 10.13. To minimize confusion, we will always point out any area where this deviation from the standard will cause our equations or code to differ from other texts.

We do not take this deviation from the standard lightly, and we have done it for very good reason. We will develop quaternion classes in Section 11.3, which will make direct manipulation of the members of the quaternion class completely unnecessary. For us, quaternions' ease of use in a "high level" capacity as an angular displacement will be much more important than adherence to the official standard. The goal is to understand the nature of quaternions and what operations are available to us, design a class that exports these operations directly, and then use the class through these operations, never having to fiddle around with the numbers inside the class again.

10.4.9 Quaternion "Difference"

Using quaternion multiplication and inverse, we can compute the "difference" between two quaternions, with "difference" being defined as the angular displacement from one orientation to another. In other words, for given orientations $\mathbf{a}$ and $\mathbf{b}$, we can compute the angular displacement $\mathbf{d}$ which rotates from $\mathbf{a}$ to $\mathbf{b}$. This can be expressed compactly using the following quaternion equation:

$$\mathbf{a}\mathbf{d} = \mathbf{b}$$

(Here we are using our more intuitive definition of quaternion multiplication, where the order of rotations corresponds to the order of multiplications from left to right.) Let's solve for **d**. If the variables in the equation represented scalars, we could simply divide by **d**. However, we can't divide quaternions; we can only multiply them. Perhaps multiplication by the inverse will achieve the desired effect? Multiplying both sides by $\mathbf{a}^{-1}$ on the left (we have to be careful since quaternion multiplication is not commutative):

$$\mathbf{a}^{-1}(\mathbf{ad}) = \mathbf{a}^{-1}\mathbf{b}$$

Applying the associative property of quaternion multiplication and simplifying:

$$\begin{aligned}
(\mathbf{a}^{-1}\mathbf{a})\mathbf{d} &= \mathbf{a}^{-1}\mathbf{b} \\
\begin{bmatrix} 1 & \mathbf{0} \end{bmatrix}\mathbf{d} &= \mathbf{a}^{-1}\mathbf{b} \\
\mathbf{d} &= \mathbf{a}^{-1}\mathbf{b}
\end{aligned}$$

Now we have a way to generate a quaternion to represent the angular displacement from one orientation to another. We will use this in Section 10.4.13.

Mathematically, the angular "difference" between two quaternions is actually more similar to a *division* than a true *difference* (subtraction).

10.4.10 Quaternion Dot Product

The dot product operation is defined for quaternions. The notation and definition for this operation is very similar to the vector dot product:

Equation 10.14:
Quaternion dot product

$$\begin{aligned}
\mathbf{q}_1 \cdot \mathbf{q}_2 &= \begin{bmatrix} w_1 & \mathbf{v}_1 \end{bmatrix} \cdot \begin{bmatrix} w_2 & \mathbf{v}_2 \end{bmatrix} = w_1 w_2 + \mathbf{v}_1 \cdot \mathbf{v}_2 \\
&= \begin{bmatrix} w_1 & (x_1 & y_1 & z_1) \end{bmatrix} \cdot \begin{bmatrix} w_2 & (x_2 & y_2 & z_2) \end{bmatrix} = w_1 w_2 + x_1 x_2 + y_1 y_2 + z_1 z_2
\end{aligned}$$

Notice that like the vector dot product, the result is a scalar. For unit quaternions **a** and **b**, $-1 \leq \mathbf{a} \cdot \mathbf{b} \leq 1$. Usually we are only interested in the absolute value of $\mathbf{a} \cdot \mathbf{b}$, since $\mathbf{a} \cdot \mathbf{b} = -(\mathbf{a} \cdot -\mathbf{b})$, even though **b** and $-\mathbf{b}$ represent the same angular displacement.

The geometric interpretation of the quaternion dot product is similar to the interpretation of the vector dot product; the larger the absolute value of the quaternion dot product $\mathbf{a} \cdot \mathbf{b}$, the more "similar" the angular displacements represented by **a** and **b**.

10.4.11 Quaternion Log, Exp, and Multiplication by a Scalar

In this section, we discuss three operations on quaternions that, although they are seldom used directly, are the basis for several important quaternion operations. These operations are quaternion logarithm, exponential, and multiplication by a scalar.

First, let us reformulate our definition of a quaternion by introducing a variable α to equal the half angle, $\theta/2$:

$$\alpha = \theta/2$$
$$\|\mathbf{n}\| = 1$$
$$\mathbf{q} = [\ \cos\alpha \quad \mathbf{n}\sin\alpha\ ]$$
$$= [\ \cos\alpha \quad (\ x\sin\alpha \quad y\sin\alpha \quad z\sin\alpha\ )\ ]$$

Now the logarithm of $\mathbf{q}$ is defined as:

Equation 10.15:
The logarithm of
a quaternion

$$\log\mathbf{q} = \log([\ \cos\alpha \quad \mathbf{n}\sin\alpha\ ])$$
$$\equiv [\ 0 \quad \alpha\mathbf{n}\ ]$$

We use the notation $\equiv$ to mean "equal by definition." Note that the result of $\log\mathbf{q}$ is, in general, not a unit quaternion.

The exponential function is defined in the exact opposite manner. First, we define the quaternion $\mathbf{p}$ to be of the form $[0, \alpha\mathbf{n}]$, with $\mathbf{n}$ a unit vector:

$$\mathbf{p} = [\ 0 \quad \alpha\mathbf{n}\ ]$$
$$= [\ 0 \quad (\ \alpha x \quad \alpha y \quad \alpha z\ )\ ]$$
$$\|\mathbf{n}\| = 1$$

Then the exponential function is defined as:

Equation 10.16:
The exponential
function of a
quaternion

$$\exp\mathbf{p} = \exp([\ 0 \quad \alpha\mathbf{n}\ ])$$
$$\equiv [\ \cos\alpha \quad \mathbf{n}\sin\alpha\ ]$$

By definition, $\exp\mathbf{p}$ always returns a unit quaternion.

The quaternion logarithm and exponential are related to their scalar analogs. Recall that, for any scalar a, the following relation holds:

$$e^{\ln a} = a$$

In the same way, the quaternion exp function is defined to be the inverse of the quaternion log function:

$$\exp(\log\mathbf{q}) = \mathbf{q}$$

Finally, quaternions can be multiplied by a scalar, and the result is computed in the obvious way of multiplying each component by the scalar. Given a scalar k and a quaternion $\mathbf{q}$:

Equation 10.17:
Multiplying a
quaternion by
a scalar

$$k\mathbf{q} = k[\ w \quad \mathbf{v}\ ] = [\ kw \quad k\mathbf{v}\ ]$$
$$= k[\ w \quad (\ x \quad y \quad z\ )\ ] = [\ kw \quad (\ kx \quad ky \quad kz\ )\ ]$$

Usually, this will not result in a unit quaternion, which is why multiplication by a scalar is not a very useful operation in the context of representing angular displacement.

10.4.12 Quaternion Exponentiation

Quaternions can be exponentiated (raised to a power). This is denoted $\mathbf{q}^t$. (Don't confuse this with the exponential function. The exponential function only accepts one quaternion argument. Quaternion exponentiation has two parameters — the quaternion and the exponent.)

Quaternion exponentiation has a similar meaning to the result when a real number is raised to a power. Recall that $a^0 = 1$, and $a^1 = a$, where a is a nonzero scalar. As t varies from $0 \ldots 1$, a^t varies from $1 \ldots a$. A similar statement holds for quaternion exponentiation: as t varies from $0 \ldots 1$, $\mathbf{q}^t$ varies from $[1, \mathbf{0}] \ldots \mathbf{q}$.

Quaternion exponentiation is useful because it allows us to extract a "fraction" of an angular displacement. For example, to compute a quaternion that represents one-third of the angular displacement represented by the quaternion $\mathbf{q}$, we would compute $\mathbf{q}^{1/3}$.

Exponents outside the $0 \ldots 1$ range behave mostly as expected (with one major caveat). For example, $\mathbf{q}^2$ represents twice the angular displacement as $\mathbf{q}$. If $\mathbf{q}$ represents a clockwise rotation of $30°$ about the x-axis, then $\mathbf{q}^2$ represents a clockwise rotation of $60°$ about the x-axis, and $\mathbf{q}^{-1/3}$ represents a counterclockwise rotation of $10°$ about the x-axis.

The caveat we mentioned is this: a quaternion represents angular displacements using the shortest arc. "Multiple spins" cannot be represented. Continuing our example from above, $\mathbf{q}^4$ is not a $240°$ clockwise rotation about the x-axis as expected; it is an $80°$ counterclockwise rotation. Of course, rotating $240°$ in one direction is the same as rotating $80°$ in the opposite direction, so the correct "end result" is properly captured. However, if further operations on this quaternion were performed, it might not behave as expected. For example, $(\mathbf{q}^4)^{1/2}$ is not $\mathbf{q}^2$, as we would intuitively expect. In general, many of the algebraic identities concerning exponentiation of scalars, such as $(a^s)^t = a^{st}$, do not apply to quaternions.

Now that we understand what quaternion exponentiation is used for, let's see how it is mathematically defined. Quaternion exponentiation is defined in terms of the "utility" operations we learned in the previous section. The definition is given below:

Equation 10.18:
Raising a
quaternion to
a power

$$\mathbf{q}^t = \exp\left(t \log \mathbf{q}\right)$$

Notice that a similar statement is true regarding exponentiation of a scalar:

$$a^t = e^{(t \ln a)}$$

It is not too difficult to understand why $\mathbf{q}^t$ interpolates from identity to $\mathbf{q}$ as t varies from $0 \ldots 1$. Notice that the log operation basically extracts the axis $\mathbf{n}$ and angle θ. Then, when we perform the scalar multiplication by the exponent t, the effect is just to multiply θ by t. Finally, the exp "undoes" what the log operation did, recalculating the new w and $\mathbf{v}$ from $t\theta$ and $\mathbf{n}$. Thus, the definitions given above are the official mathematical ones and work elegantly in theory, but direct translation into code is more complicated than necessary. The code below shows how we could compute the value of $\mathbf{q}^t$.

Listing 10.1: Code to raise a quaternion to a power

```
// Quaternion (input and output)

float w,x,y,z;

// Input exponent

float exponent;

// Check for the case of an identity quaternion.
// This will protect against divide by zero

if (fabs(w) < .9999f) {

    // Extract the half angle alpha (alpha = theta/2)

    float alpha = acos(w);

    // Compute new alpha value

    float newAlpha = alpha * exponent;

    // Compute new w value

    w = cos(newAlpha);

    // Compute new xyz values

    float mult = sin(newAlpha) / sin(alpha);
    x *= mult;
    y *= mult;
    z *= mult;
}
```

There are a few points to notice about this code.

■ First, the check for the identity quaternion is necessary, since a value of $w = \pm 1$ would cause the compututation of `mult` to divide by zero. Raising an identity quaternion to any power results in the identity quaternion, so if we detect an identity quaternion on input, we simply ignore the exponent and return the original quaternion.

■ Second, when we compute alpha, we use the `acos` function, which always returns a positive angle. This does not create a loss of generality. Any quaternion can be interpreted as having a positive angle of rotation, since negative rotation about an axis is the same as positive rotation about the axis pointing in the opposite direction.

10.4.13 Quaternion Interpolation — aka "Slerp"

The *raison d'etre* of quaternions in 3D math today is an operation known as *slerp*, which stands for **S**pherical **L**inear int**erp**olation. The slerp operation is useful because it allows us to smoothly interpolate between two interpolations. Slerp avoids all the problems that plagued interpolation of Euler angles (see Section 10.3.4).

Slerp is a ternary operator, meaning it accepts three operands. The first two operands to slerp are the two quaternions between which we wish to interpolate. We'll assign these "starting" and "ending" orientations to the variables $\mathbf{q}_0$ and $\mathbf{q}_1$, respectively. The interpolation parameter will be assigned to the variable t, and as t varies from 0 to 1, the slerp function

$$\text{slerp}(\mathbf{q}_0, \mathbf{q}_1, t)$$

will return an orientation that interpolates from $\mathbf{q}_0$ and $\mathbf{q}_1$.

Let's see if we can't derive the slerp formula using the tools we have so far. If we were interpolating between two scalar values a_0 and a_1, we could use the standard linear interpolation formula below:

$$\Delta a = a_1 - a_0$$
$$\text{lerp}(a_0, a_1, t) = a_0 + t\Delta a$$

The standard linear interpolation formula works by starting at a_0 and adding a tth of the difference between a_1 and a_0. This requires three basic steps:

- Compute the difference between the two values.
- Take a fraction of this difference.
- Take the original value and adjust it by this fraction of the difference.

We can use the same basic idea to interpolate between orientations.

- **Compute the difference between the two values**. We learned how to do this in Section 10.4.9. The angular displacement from $\mathbf{q}_0$ to $\mathbf{q}_1$ is given by:

  $$\Delta \mathbf{q} = \mathbf{q}_0^{-1}\mathbf{q}_1$$

- **Take a fraction of this difference**. To do this, we will use quaternion exponentiation, which we discussed in Section 10.4.12. The fraction of the difference is given by:

  $$\Delta \mathbf{q}^t$$

- **Take the original value and adjust it by this fraction of the difference**. We "adjust" the initial value by composing the angular displacements via quaternion multiplication:

  $$\mathbf{q}_0\Delta \mathbf{q}^t$$

(Again, we use our more intuitive definition of quaternion multiplication that reads from left to right.)

Thus, the equation for slerp is given by:

$$\text{slerp}(\mathbf{q}_0, \mathbf{q}_1, t) = \mathbf{q}_0(\mathbf{q}_0^{-1}\mathbf{q}_1)^t$$

This is how slerp is computed in theory. In practice, a more efficient technique is used.

We start by interpreting the quaternions as existing in a 4D space. Since all of the quaternions we will be interested in are unit quaternions, they "live" on the surface of a 4D "sphere." The basic idea is to interpolate around the arc that connects the two quaternions along the surface of the 4D sphere. (Hence the name *spherical* linear interpolation.)

We can visualize this in the plane. Imagine two 2D vectors $\mathbf{v}_0$ and $\mathbf{v}_1$, both of unit length. We wish to compute the value of $\mathbf{v}_t$, which is the result of smoothly interpolating around the arc by a fraction t of the distance from $\mathbf{v}_0$ to $\mathbf{v}_1$. If we let ω (pronounced "omega") be the angle intercepted by the arc from $\mathbf{v}_0$ to $\mathbf{v}_1$, then $\mathbf{v}_t$ is the result of rotating $\mathbf{v}_1$ around this arc by an angle of $t\omega$. This is illustrated in Figure 10.10.

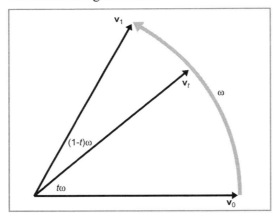

Figure 10.10: Interpolating a rotation

We can express $\mathbf{v}_t$ as a linear combination of $\mathbf{v}_0$ and $\mathbf{v}_1$. In other words, there exists nonnegative constants k_0 and k_1 such that:

$$\mathbf{v}_t = k_0\mathbf{v}_0 + k_1\mathbf{v}_1$$

We can use basic geometry to determine the values of k_0 and k_1. Figure 10.11 shows how this can be done.

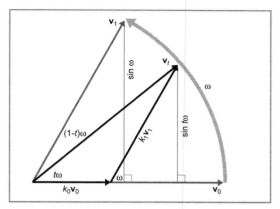

Figure 10.11: Interpolating a vector about an arc

Applying some trig to the right triangle with $k_1 \mathbf{v}_1$ as the hypotenuse (and recalling that $\mathbf{v}_1$ is a unit vector), we see that:

$$\sin \omega = \frac{\sin t\omega}{k_1}$$

$$k_1 = \frac{\sin t\omega}{\sin \omega}$$

Using a similar technique to solve for k_0 yields the following result:

$$k_0 = \frac{\sin(1 - t)\omega}{\sin \omega}$$

Thus, $\mathbf{v}_t$ can be expressed as:

$$\mathbf{v}_t = k_0 \mathbf{v}_0 + k_1 \mathbf{v}_1$$

$$\mathbf{v}_t = \frac{\sin(1 - t)\omega}{\sin \omega} \mathbf{v}_0 + \frac{\sin t\omega}{\sin \omega} \mathbf{v}_1$$

The same basic idea can be extended into quaternion space, and we can reformulate the slerp as:

$$\text{slerp}(\mathbf{q}_0, \mathbf{q}_1, t) = \frac{\sin(1 - t)\omega}{\sin \omega} \mathbf{q}_0 + \frac{\sin t\omega}{\sin \omega} \mathbf{q}_1$$

We can use the quaternion dot product to compute the "angle" between the two quaternions.

There are two slight complications. First, the two quaternions $\mathbf{q}$ and $-\mathbf{q}$ represent the same orientation, but they may produce different results when used as an argument to slerp. This problem doesn't happen in 2D or 3D because the surface of a 4D sphere is not exactly a straightforward extension of Euclidian space. The solution is to choose the signs of $\mathbf{q}_0$ and $\mathbf{q}_1$ such that the dot product $\mathbf{q}_0 \cdot \mathbf{q}_1$ is nonnegative. This has the effect of always selecting the shortest rotational arc from $\mathbf{q}_0$ to $\mathbf{q}_1$. The second consideration is that if $\mathbf{q}_0$ and $\mathbf{q}_1$ are very close, then $\sin \theta$ will be very small, which will cause problems with the division. To avoid this, we will use simple linear interpolation if $\sin \theta$ is very small. Listing 10.2 applies all of this advice to compute the quaternion slerp:

Listing 10.2: How slerp is computed in practice

```
// The two input quaternions

float w0,x0,y0,z0;
float w1,x1,y1,z1;

// The interpolation parameter

float t;

// The output quaternion will be computed here

float w,x,y,z;

// Compute the "cosine of the angle" between the
// quaternions, using the dot product

float cosOmega = w0*w1 + x0*x1 + y0*y1 + z0*z1;

// If negative dot, negate one of the input
// quaternions to take the shorter 4D "arc"

if (cosOmega < 0.0f) {
    w1 = -w1;
    x1 = -x1;
    y1 = -y1;
    z1 = -z1;
    cosOmega = -cosOmega;
}

// Check if they are very close together to protect
// against divide-by-zero

float k0, k1;
if (cosOmega > 0.9999f) {

    // Very close - just use linear interpolation

    k0 = 1.0f-t;
    k1 = t;

} else {

    // Compute the sin of the angle using the
    // trig identity sin^2(omega) + cos^2(omega) = 1

    float sinOmega = sqrt(1.0f - cosOmega*cosOmega);

    // Compute the angle from its sin and cosine

    float omega = atan2(sinOmega, cosOmega);

    // Compute inverse of denominator, so we only have
    // to divide once

    float oneOverSinOmega = 1.0f / sinOmega;

    // Compute interpolation parameters
```

```
        k0 = sin((1.0f - t) * omega) * oneOverSinOmega;
        k1 = sin(t * omega) * oneOverSinOmega;
    }

    // Interpolate

    w = w0*k0 + w1*k1;
    x = x0*k0 + x1*k1;
    y = y0*k0 + y1*k1;
    z = z0*k0 + z1*k1;
```

10.4.14 Quaternion Splines — aka "Squad"

Slerp provides interpolation between two orientations, but what if we have a sequence of more than two orientations which define a "path" we wish to interpolate through? We could use slerp in between the "control points." This is analogous to using simple geometric linear interpolation, which uses straight lines between the control points. Obviously, there is a discontinuity at the control points — something we would like to avoid.

Although a complete discussion is outside the scope of this book, we will present the equation for *squad* (which stands for **s**pherical and **quad**rangle) which can be used to trace out a path between control points. For a detailed analysis of this technique, including a description of some of its shortcomings (the angular velocity is not constant), we refer the interested and mathematically inclined reader to [3]. Fortunately, it is not completely necessary to understand the math involved in order to use squad!

Let our "control points" be defined by a sequence of quaternions:

$$\mathbf{q}_1, \mathbf{q}_2, \mathbf{q}_3, \cdots, \mathbf{q}_{n-2}, \mathbf{q}_{n-1}, \mathbf{q}_n$$

We will also define the "helper" quaternion $\mathbf{s}_i$, which can be thought of as intermediate control points:

$$\mathbf{s}_i = \exp\left(-\frac{\log(\mathbf{q}_{i+1}\mathbf{q}_i^{-1}) + \log(\mathbf{q}_{i-1}\mathbf{q}_i^{-1})}{4}\right)\mathbf{q}_i$$

Notice that $\mathbf{s}_i$ is computed using $\mathbf{q}_{i-1}$ and $\mathbf{q}_{i+1}$, and, therefore, $\mathbf{s}_1$ and $\mathbf{s}_n$ are undefined. In other words, the curve extends from $\mathbf{q}_2...\mathbf{q}_{n-1}$. The first and last control points are only used to control the interior of the curve. If it is necessary that the curve pass through these control points, then we must insert extra dummy control points at the beginning and end, with the obvious choice being to simply duplicate the control points.

Given four adjacent control points, squad is used to compute the correct interpolation between the middle two, much like a cardinal spline.

Let's denote the four control points:

$$\mathbf{q}_{i-1}, \mathbf{q}_i, \mathbf{q}_{i+1}, \mathbf{q}_{i+2}$$

We will also define an interpolation parameter h. As h varies from $0...1$, squad traces out the segment of the curve between $\mathbf{q}_i$ and $\mathbf{q}_{i+1}$:

$$\text{squad}(\mathbf{q}_i, \mathbf{q}_{i+1}, \mathbf{s}_i, \mathbf{s}_{i+1}, h) = \text{slerp}\left(\text{slerp}(\mathbf{q}_i, \mathbf{q}_{i+1}, h), \text{slerp}(\mathbf{s}_i, \mathbf{s}_{i+1}, h), 2h(1-h)\right)$$

(As always, we are using our left-to-right definition of quaternion multiplication.) The entire curve can be generated by applying squad piecewise.

10.4.15 Advantages/Disadvantages of Quaternions

Using quaternions offers a number of advantages over other methods of representing angular displacement:

- **Smooth interpolation.** The interpolation provided by the *slerp* and *squad* operations provides smooth interpolation between orientations. No other representation method provides smooth interpolation.

- **Fast concatenation and inversion of angular displacements.** We can concatenate a sequence of angular displacements into a single angular displacement using the quaternion cross product. The same operation using matrices is considerably slower. Quaternion conjugate provides a way to compute the opposite angular displacement very efficiently. This can be done by transposing a rotation matrix, but it is not easy with Euler angles.

- **Fast conversion to/from matrix form.** As we will see in Section 10.6, quaternions can be converted to and from matrix form slightly faster than Euler angles.

- **Only four numbers.** Since a quaternion contains four scalar values, it is considerably more economical than a matrix, which uses nine numbers. (However, it still is 33% larger than Euler angles.)

These advantages do come at some cost. Quaternions suffer from a few of the problems that plague matrices, only to a lesser degree:

- **Slightly bigger than Euler angles.** This one additional number may not seem like much, but an extra 33% can make a difference when large amounts of angular displacements are needed, such as when storing animation data.

- **Quaternions can become invalid.** This can happen either through bad input data or from accumulated floating-point round-off error. (We can address this problem by normalizing the quaternion to ensure that it has unit magnitude.)

- **Difficult for us to work with.** Of the three representation methods, quaternions are the most difficult for us to work with directly.

10.5 Comparison of Methods

Let's summarize our discoveries in the previous sections. Figure 10.12 summarizes the differences between the three representation methods.

Task/Property	Matrix	Euler Angles	Quaternion
Rotating points between coordinate spaces (object and inertial)	Possible	Impossible (must convert to matrix)	Impossible (must convert to matrix)
Concatenation or incremental rotation	Possible but usually slower than quaternion form; watch out for matrix creep	Impossible	Possible, and usually faster than matrix form
Interpolation	Basically impossible	Possible, but aliasing causes Gimbal lock and other problems	Slerp provides smooth interpolation
Human interpretation	Difficult	Easy	Difficult
Storing in memory or in a file	Nine numbers	Three numbers	Four numbers
Representation is unique for a given orientation	Yes	No — an infinite number of Euler angle triples alias to the same orientation	Exactly two distinct representations for any orientation, and they are negates of each other
Possible to become invalid	Matrix creep can occur	Any three numbers form a valid orientation	Error creep can occur

Figure 10.12: Comparison of matrices, Euler angles, and quaternions

Some situations are better suited for one orientation format or another. Here are a few words of advice to aid you in selecting the right format:

▇   Euler angles are easiest for us to work with. Using Euler angles greatly simplifies human interaction when specifying the orientation of objects in the world. This includes direct keyboard entry of an orientation, specifying orientations directly in the code (i.e., positioning the camera for rendering), and examination in the debugger. This advantage should not be underestimated. Certainly don't sacrifice ease of use in the name of "optimization" until you are certain that it will make a difference.

▇   Matrix form must eventually be used if vector coordinate space transformations are needed. However, this doesn't mean you can't store the orientation using another format and then generate a rotation matrix when you need it. An alternative solution is to store the "main copy" of the orientation using Euler angles, but also maintain a matrix for rotations, recomputing this matrix anytime the Euler angles change.

- For storage of large numbers of orientations (i.e., animation data), use Euler angles or quaternions. Euler angles will take 25 % less memory, but they will be slightly slower to convert to matrix form. If the animation data requires concatenation of nested coordinate spaces, quaternions will probably be the better choice.

- Decent interpolation can only be accomplished using quaternions. However, even if you are using a different form, you can always convert to quaternions, perform the interpolation, and then convert back to the original form.

10.6 Converting between Representations

We have established that different methods of representing orientation are appropriate in different situations, and we have also provided some guidelines for choosing the most appropriate method. In this section, we discuss how to convert angular displacement from one form to another.

10.6.1 Converting Euler Angles to a Matrix

Euler angles define a sequence of rotations. We can compute the matrix for each individual rotation and then concatenate these matrices into one matrix that defines the total angular displacement. Of course, it matters whether we want the object-to-inertial matrix or the inertial-to-object matrix. In this section, we show how to compute both.

We have chosen to formulate our Euler angles as a sequence of rotations that transform an object (and its coordinate space) from inertial space into object space. Thus, the generation of the inertial-to-object rotation matrix is a straightforward translation of the definition of our Euler angles:

$$\mathbf{M}_{inertial \to object} = \mathbf{HPB}$$

$\mathbf{H}$, $\mathbf{P}$, and $\mathbf{B}$ are the rotation matrices for heading, pitch, and bank, which rotate about the y, x, and z-axis, respectively. We learned how to compute these elementary rotation matrices in Section 8.2.2. However, there is a slight complication. As we discussed in Section 8.1, rotating a coordinate space is the exact opposite of rotating a point. Imagine a point that is fixed in space while these rotations are occurring. When we pitch the coordinate space down, for example, the point actually rotates *up*, with respect to the coordinate space. Our formulation of Euler angles specifies that the object and its coordinate space are rotated. Since we are seeking to compute a matrix to transform points, when we compute our primitive matrices $\mathbf{H}$, $\mathbf{P}$, and $\mathbf{B}$, we will rotate by the *opposite* rotation amounts. Let us assign the rotation angles heading, pitch, and bank to the variables h, p, and b, respectively.

$$\mathbf{H} = \mathbf{R}_y(-h) = \begin{bmatrix} \cos(-h) & 0 & -\sin(-h) \\ 0 & 1 & 0 \\ \sin(-h) & 0 & \cos(-h) \end{bmatrix} = \begin{bmatrix} \cos h & 0 & \sin h \\ 0 & 1 & 0 \\ -\sin h & 0 & \cos h \end{bmatrix}$$

$$\mathbf{P} = \mathbf{R}_x(-p) = \begin{bmatrix} 1 & 0 & 0 \\ 0 & \cos(-p) & \sin(-p) \\ 0 & -\sin(-p) & \cos(-p) \end{bmatrix} = \begin{bmatrix} 1 & 0 & 0 \\ 0 & \cos p & -\sin p \\ 0 & \sin p & \cos p \end{bmatrix}$$

$$\mathbf{B} = \mathbf{R}_z(-b) = \begin{bmatrix} \cos(-b) & \sin(-b) & 0 \\ -\sin(-b) & \cos(-b) & 0 \\ 0 & 0 & 1 \end{bmatrix} = \begin{bmatrix} \cos b & -\sin b & 0 \\ \sin b & \cos b & 0 \\ 0 & 0 & 1 \end{bmatrix}$$

Concatenating these matrices in the proper order yields Equation 10.21:

Equation 10.21:
Computing the
inertial-to-object
rotation matrix
from a set of
Euler angles

$$\mathbf{M}_{inertial \to object} = \mathbf{HPB}$$

$$= \begin{bmatrix} \cos h & 0 & \sin h \\ 0 & 1 & 0 \\ -\sin h & 0 & \cos h \end{bmatrix} \begin{bmatrix} 1 & 0 & 0 \\ 0 & \cos p & -\sin p \\ 0 & \sin p & \cos p \end{bmatrix} \begin{bmatrix} \cos b & -\sin b & 0 \\ \sin b & \cos b & 0 \\ 0 & 0 & 1 \end{bmatrix}$$

$$= \begin{bmatrix} \cos h \cos b + \sin h \sin p \sin b & -\cos h \sin b + \sin h \sin p \cos b & \sin h \cos p \\ \sin b \cos p & \cos b \cos p & -\sin p \\ -\sin h \cos b + \cos h \sin p \sin b & \sin b \sin h + \cos h \sin p \cos b & \cos h \cos p \end{bmatrix}$$

If we wish to rotate vectors from object to inertial space, then we will use the inverse of the inertial-to-object matrix. We know that since a rotation matrix is orthogonal, the inverse is simply the transpose. However, let's verify this.

To transform from object to inertial space, we will effectively "un-bank," "un-pitch," and then "un-heading," in that order. In other words:

$$\mathbf{M}_{object \to inertial} = (\mathbf{M}_{inertial \to object})^{-1}$$
$$= (\mathbf{HPB})^{-1}$$
$$= \mathbf{B}^{-1}\mathbf{P}^{-1}\mathbf{H}^{-1}$$

Notice that we can either think of the rotation matrices $\mathbf{B}^{-1}$, $\mathbf{P}^{-1}$, and $\mathbf{H}^{-1}$ as the inverse matrices of their counterparts or as normal rotation matrices, using the opposite rotation angles b, p, and h. (Remember that for the inertial-to-object matrix, we used the negatives of the rotation matrices. So in this case, the angles will not be negated.)

$$\mathbf{B}^{-1} = \mathbf{R}_z(b) = \begin{bmatrix} \cos b & \sin b & 0 \\ -\sin b & \cos b & 0 \\ 0 & 0 & 1 \end{bmatrix}$$

$$\mathbf{P}^{-1} = \mathbf{R}_x(p) = \begin{bmatrix} 1 & 0 & 0 \\ 0 & \cos p & \sin p \\ 0 & -\sin p & \cos p \end{bmatrix}$$

$$\mathbf{H}^{-1} = \mathbf{R}_y(h) = \begin{bmatrix} \cos h & 0 & -\sin h \\ 0 & 1 & 0 \\ \sin h & 0 & \cos h \end{bmatrix}$$

Just as we did before, let's concatenate these in the correct order:

Equation 10.22:
Computing the
object-to-inertia
l rotation matrix
from a set of
Euler angles

$$\mathbf{M}_{inertial \to object} = \mathbf{B}^{-1}\mathbf{P}^{-1}\mathbf{H}^{-1}$$

$$= \begin{bmatrix} \cos b & \sin b & 0 \\ -\sin b & \cos b & 0 \\ 0 & 0 & 1 \end{bmatrix} \begin{bmatrix} 1 & 0 & 0 \\ 0 & \cos p & \sin p \\ 0 & -\sin p & \cos p \end{bmatrix} \begin{bmatrix} \cos h & 0 & -\sin h \\ 0 & 1 & 0 \\ \sin h & 0 & \cos h \end{bmatrix}$$

$$= \begin{bmatrix} \cos h \cos b + \sin h \sin p \sin b & \sin b \cos p & -\sin h \cos b + \cos h \sin p \sin b \\ -\cos h \sin b + \sin h \sin p \cos b & \cos b \cos p & \sin b \sin h + \cos h \sin p \cos b \\ \sin h \cos p & -\sin p & \cos h \cos p \end{bmatrix}$$

When we compare Equation 10.21 with Equation 10.22, we see that the object-to-inertial matrix is indeed the transpose of the inertial-to-object matrix as expected.

10.6.2 Converting a Matrix to Euler Angles

Converting an angular displacement from matrix form to Euler angle representation entails several considerations:

◼ We must know which rotation the matrix performs: either object-to-inertial or inertial-to-object. In this section, we will develop a technique using the inertial-to-object matrix. The process of converting an object-to-inertial matrix to Euler angles is very similar.

◼ For any given angular displacement, there are an infinite number of Euler angle representations due to Euler angle aliasing. (See Section 10.3.4.) The technique we present here will always return "canonical" Euler angles, with heading and bank in range $\pm 180°$ and pitch in range $\pm 90°$.

◼ Some matrices may be malformed, and so we must be tolerant of floating-point precision errors. Some matrices contain transformations other than rotation, such as scale, mirroring, or skew. For now, we will discuss a technique that works only on proper rotation matrices.

With those considerations in mind, we set out to solve for the Euler angles from Equation 10.21 directly:

$$\mathbf{M}_{inertial \to object} = \begin{bmatrix} \cos h \cos b + \sin h \sin p \sin b & -\cos h \sin b + \sin h \sin p \cos b & \sin h \cos p \\ \sin b \cos p & \cos b \cos p & -\sin p \\ -\sin h \cos b + \cos h \sin p \sin b & \sin b \sin h + \cos h \sin p \cos b & \cos h \cos p \end{bmatrix}$$

We can solve for p immediately from m_{23}:

$$m_{23} = -\sin p$$
$$-m_{23} = \sin p$$
$$\operatorname{asin}(-m_{23}) = p$$

The C standard library function `asin` returns a value in the range $-\pi/2$ to $\pi/2$ radians, which is $-90°$ to $+90°$, exactly the range of values we wish to return for pitch.

Now that we know p, we also know $\cos p$. Let us first assume that $\cos p \neq 0$. We can determine $\sin h$ and $\cos h$ by dividing m_{13} and m_{33} by $\cos p$, as follows:

$$
\begin{aligned}
m_{13} &= \sin h \cos p \\
m_{13}/\cos p &= \sin h \\
m_{33} &= \cos h \cos p \\
m_{33}/\cos p &= \cos h
\end{aligned}
$$

Once we know the sine and cosine of an angle, we can compute the value of the angle using the C standard library function `atan2`. This function returns an angle from $-\pi$ to π radians, which is in our desired output range. A straightforward translation from the equations above yields:

$$
\begin{aligned}
h &= \text{atan2}(\sin h, \cos h) \\
&= \text{atan2}(m_{13}/\cos p, m_{33}/\cos p)
\end{aligned}
$$

However, we can actually simplify this because `atan2(y,x)` works by taking the arctangent of the quotient y/x, using the signs of the two arguments to determine the quadrant of the returned angle. Since $\cos p > 0$, the divisions do not affect the quotient and are, therefore, unnecessary. Thus, heading can be computed more simply by:

$$
\begin{aligned}
h &= \text{atan2}(m_{13}/\cos p, m_{33}/\cos p) \\
&= \text{atan2}(m_{13}, m_{33})
\end{aligned}
$$

We can compute bank in a similar manner from m_{21} and m_{22}:

$$
\begin{aligned}
m_{21} &= \sin b \cos p \\
m_{21}/\cos p &= \sin b \\
m_{22} &= \cos b \cos p \\
m_{22}/\cos p &= \cos b \\
b &= \text{atan2}(\sin b, \cos b) \\
&= \text{atan2}(m_{21}/\cos p, m_{22}/\cos p) \\
&= \text{atan2}(m_{21}, m_{22})
\end{aligned}
$$

If $\cos p = 0$, then we cannot use the above trick since all the matrix elements involved are zero. However, notice that when $\cos p = 0$, then $p = \pm 90°$, which means we are either looking straight up or straight down. This is the Gimbal lock situation, where heading and bank effectively rotate about the same physical axis (the vertical axis). In this case, we will arbitrarily assign all rotation about the vertical axis to heading and set bank equal to zero. Now we know the value of pitch and bank, and all we have left is to solve for heading. Armed with the following simplifying assumptions:

$$
\begin{aligned}
\cos p &= 0 \\
b &= 0 \\
\sin b &= 0 \\
\cos b &= 1
\end{aligned}
$$

we can substitute these assumptions into Equation 10.21:

$$\mathbf{M}_{inertial \to object} = \begin{bmatrix} \cos h \cos b + \sin h \sin p \sin b & -\cos h \sin b + \sin h \sin p \cos b & \sin h \cos p \\ \sin b \cos p & \cos b \cos p & -\sin p \\ -\sin h \cos b + \cos h \sin p \sin b & \sin b \sin h + \cos h \sin p \cos b & \cos h \cos p \end{bmatrix}$$

$$= \begin{bmatrix} \cos h(1) + \sin h \sin p(0) & -\cos h(0) + \sin h \sin p(1) & \sin h(0) \\ (0)(0) & (1)(0) & -\sin p \\ -\sin h(1) + \cos h \sin p(0) & (0)\sin h + \cos h \sin p(1) & \cos h(0) \end{bmatrix}$$

$$= \begin{bmatrix} \cos h & \sin h \sin p & 0 \\ 0 & 0 & -\sin p \\ -\sin h & \cos h \sin p & 0 \end{bmatrix}$$

Now we can compute h from $-m_{31}$ and m_{11}, which contain the sine and cosine of the heading, respectively.

Let's look at some code to extract the Euler angles from an inertial-to-object rotation matrix using the technique developed above. To make the example simple, we will assume global variables for input and output:

Listing 10.3: Extracting Euler angles from an inertial-to-object rotation matrix

```
// Assume the matrix is stored in these variables:

float m11,m12,m13;
float m21,m22,m23;
float m31,m32,m33;

// We will compute the Euler angle values in radians and store them here:

float h,p,b;

// Extract pitch from m23, being careful for domain errors with asin(). We could have
// values slightly out of range due to floating point arithmetic.

float sp = -m23;
if (sp <= -1.0f) {
    p = -1.570796f; // -pi/2
} else if (sp >= 1.0) {
    p = 1.570796; // pi/2
} else {
    p = asin(sp);
}

// Check for the Gimbal lock case, giving a slight tolerance
// for numerical imprecision

if (sp > 0.9999f) {

    // We are looking straight up or down.
    // Slam bank to zero and just set heading

    b = 0.0f;
    h = atan2(-m31, m11);

} else {

    // Compute heading from m13 and m33

    h = atan2(m13, m33);
```

```
// Compute bank from m21 and m22

b = atan2(m21, m22);

}
```

10.6.3 Converting a Quaternion to a Matrix

To convert an angular displacement from quaternion form to matrix form, we will use the matrix from Section 8.2.3, which rotates about an arbitrary axis:

$$\mathbf{R}(\mathbf{n}, \theta) = \begin{bmatrix} \mathbf{n}_x{}^2(1 - \cos\theta) + \cos\theta & \mathbf{n}_x\mathbf{n}_y(1 - \cos\theta) + \mathbf{n}_z\sin\theta & \mathbf{n}_x\mathbf{n}_z(1 - \cos\theta) - \mathbf{n}_y\sin\theta \\ \mathbf{n}_x\mathbf{n}_y(1 - \cos\theta) - \mathbf{n}_z\sin\theta & \mathbf{n}_y{}^2(1 - \cos\theta) + \cos\theta & \mathbf{n}_y\mathbf{n}_z(1 - \cos\theta) + \mathbf{n}_x\sin\theta \\ \mathbf{n}_x\mathbf{n}_z(1 - \cos\theta) + \mathbf{n}_y\sin\theta & \mathbf{n}_y\mathbf{n}_z(1 - \cos\theta) - \mathbf{n}_x\sin\theta & \mathbf{n}_z{}^2(1 - \cos\theta) + \cos\theta \end{bmatrix}$$

This matrix is in terms of $\mathbf{n}$ and θ, but remember that the components of a quaternion are:

$$\begin{aligned} w &= \cos(\theta/2) \\ x &= \mathbf{n}_x \sin(\theta/2) \\ y &= \mathbf{n}_y \sin(\theta/2) \\ z &= \mathbf{n}_z \sin(\theta/2) \end{aligned}$$

Let's see if we can manipulate the matrix into a form so that we can substitute in w, x, y, and z. We need to do this for all nine elements of the matrix. Luckily, the matrix has a great deal of structure; once we have a technique for computing one element on the diagonal, the other elements can be solved in the same way. Likewise, the non-diagonal elements are very similar to each other.

Note: This is a tricky derivation, and it is not necessary to understand how the matrix is derived in order to *use* the matrix. If you're not interested in the math, skip to Equation 10.23.

Let's examine the elements along the diagonal of the matrix. We'll work through m_{11} completely; m_{22} and m_{33} can be solved similarly.

$$m_{11} = \mathbf{n}_x{}^2(1 - \cos\theta) + \cos\theta$$

We'll start by manipulating the above expression in a manner that may seem to be a detour. The purpose of these steps will become apparent in just a moment.

$$\begin{aligned} m_{11} &= \mathbf{n}_x{}^2(1 - \cos\theta) + \cos\theta \\ &= \mathbf{n}_x{}^2 - \mathbf{n}_x{}^2\cos\theta + \cos\theta \\ &= 1 - 1 + \mathbf{n}_x{}^2 - \mathbf{n}_x{}^2\cos\theta + \cos\theta \\ &= 1 - (1 - \mathbf{n}_x{}^2 + \mathbf{n}_x{}^2\cos\theta - \cos\theta) \\ &= 1 - (1 - \cos\theta - \mathbf{n}_x{}^2 + \mathbf{n}_x{}^2\cos\theta) \\ &= 1 - (1 - \mathbf{n}_x{}^2)(1 - \cos\theta) \end{aligned}$$

Now we need to get rid of the $\cos\theta$ term, and we'd like to replace it with something that contains $\cos\theta/2$ or $\sin\theta/2$, since that's what the elements of a quaternion are in terms of. As we have done before, let $\alpha = \theta/2$. We'll write one of the double-angle formulas for cosine from Appendix A in terms of α, and then substitute in θ:

$$\cos 2\alpha \;=\; 1 - 2\sin^2\alpha$$
$$\cos\theta \;=\; 1 - 2\sin^2(\theta/2)$$

Substituting for $\cos\theta$:

$$
\begin{aligned}
m_{11} &= 1 - (1 - \mathbf{n}_x{}^2)(1 - \cos\theta) \\
&= 1 - (1 - \mathbf{n}_x{}^2)\left(1 - \left(1 - 2\sin^2(\theta/2)\right)\right) \\
&= 1 - (1 - \mathbf{n}_x{}^2)\left(2\sin^2(\theta/2)\right)
\end{aligned}
$$

Expanding the product and simplifying (Notice that we use the trig identity $\sin^2 x = 1 - \cos^2 x$.):

$$
\begin{aligned}
m_{11} &= 1 - (1 - \mathbf{n}_x{}^2)\left(2\sin^2(\theta/2)\right) \\
&= 1 - \left(2\sin^2(\theta/2) - 2\mathbf{n}_x{}^2\sin^2(\theta/2)\right) \\
&= 1 - 2\sin^2(\theta/2) + 2\mathbf{n}_x{}^2\sin^2(\theta/2) \\
&= 1 - 2\left(1 - \cos^2(\theta/2)\right) + 2\mathbf{n}_x{}^2\sin^2(\theta/2) \\
&= 1 - 2 + 2\cos^2(\theta/2) + 2\mathbf{n}_x{}^2\sin^2(\theta/2) \\
&= -1 + 2\left(\cos(\theta/2)\right)^2 + 2\left(\mathbf{n}_x\sin(\theta/2)\right)^2
\end{aligned}
$$

Finally, we can substitute using w and x:

$$
\begin{aligned}
m_{11} &= -1 + 2\left(\cos(\theta/2)\right)^2 + 2\left(\mathbf{n}_x\sin(\theta/2)\right)^2 \\
&= -1 + 2w^2 + 2x^2
\end{aligned}
$$

The above equation is correct; however, it is not the standard equation given in other texts:

$$m_{11} = 1 - 2y^2 - 2z^2$$

In fact, other forms exist, most notably the one found in a very authoritative text on quaternions [22], which gives m_{11} as $w^2 + x^2 - y^2 - z^2$. Since $w^2 + x^2 + y^2 + z^2 = 1$, the three forms are equivalent. However, let's back up and see if we can't derive the "standard" form directly. In the first step, we'll use the fact that since $\mathbf{n}$ is a unit vector, $\mathbf{n}_x{}^2 + \mathbf{n}_y{}^2 + \mathbf{n}_z{}^2 = 1$, and then $1 - \mathbf{n}_x{}^2 = \mathbf{n}_y{}^2 + \mathbf{n}_z{}^2$.

$$
\begin{aligned}
m_{11} &= 1 - (1 - \mathbf{n}_x{}^2)\left(2\sin^2(\theta/2)\right) \\
&= 1 - (\mathbf{n}_y{}^2 + \mathbf{n}_z{}^2)\left(2\sin^2(\theta/2)\right) \\
&= 1 - 2\mathbf{n}_y{}^2\sin^2(\theta/2) - \mathbf{n}_z{}^2\sin^2(\theta/2) \\
&= 1 - 2y^2 - 2z^2
\end{aligned}
$$

Elements m_{22} and m_{33} are derived in a similar fashion. The results are presented in Equation 10.23 when we give the complete matrix.

Let's look at the non-diagonal elements of the matrix; they are easier than the diagonal elements. We'll use m_{12} as an example.

$$m_{12} = \mathbf{n}_x\mathbf{n}_y(1 - \cos\theta) + \mathbf{n}_z\sin\theta$$

We'll need the reverse of the double-angle formula for sine (see Appendix A):

$$\sin 2\alpha = 2 \sin \alpha \cos \alpha$$
$$\sin \theta = 2 \sin(\theta/2) \cos(\theta/2)$$

Substituting and simplifying:

$$
\begin{aligned}
m_{12} &= \mathbf{n}_x \mathbf{n}_y \left(1 - \cos \theta\right) + \mathbf{n}_z \sin \theta \\
&= \mathbf{n}_x \mathbf{n}_y \left(1 - \left(1 - 2 \sin^2(\theta/2)\right)\right) + \mathbf{n}_z \left(2 \sin(\theta/2) \cos(\theta/2)\right) \\
&= \mathbf{n}_x \mathbf{n}_y \left(2 \sin^2(\theta/2)\right) + 2 \mathbf{n}_z \sin(\theta/2) \cos(\theta/2) \\
&= 2 \left(\mathbf{n}_x \sin(\theta/2)\right) \left(\mathbf{n}_y \sin(\theta/2)\right) + 2 \cos(\theta/2) \left(\mathbf{n}_z \sin(\theta/2)\right) \\
&= 2xy + 2wz
\end{aligned}
$$

The other non-diagonal elements are derived in a similar fashion.

Finally, we present the complete rotation matrix constructed from a quaternion:

Equation 10.23:
Converting a
quaternion to
matrix form

$$
\begin{bmatrix}
1 - 2y^2 - 2z^2 & 2xy + 2wz & 2xz - 2wy \\
2xy - 2wz & 1 - 2x^2 - 2z^2 & 2yz + 2wx \\
2xz + 2wy & 2yz - 2wx & 1 - 2x^2 - 2y^2
\end{bmatrix}
$$

10.6.4 Converting a Matrix to a Quaternion

To extract a quaternion from the corresponding rotation matrix, we will reverse engineer Equation 10.23 directly. Examining the sum of the diagonal elements (known as the *trace* of the matrix) we get:

$$
\begin{aligned}
\text{tr}(\mathbf{M}) &= m_{11} + m_{22} + m_{33} \\
&= (1 - 2y^2 - 2z^2) + (1 - 2x^2 - 2z^2) + (1 - 2x^2 - 2y^2) \\
&= 3 - 4(x^2 + y^2 + z^2) \\
&= 3 - 4(1 - w^2) \\
&= 4w^2 - 1
\end{aligned}
$$

Therefore, we can compute w by:

$$w = \frac{\sqrt{m_{11} + m_{22} + m_{33} + 1}}{2}$$

The other three elements can be computed in a similar way by negating two of the three elements in the trace:

$$m_{11} - m_{22} - m_{33} = (1 - 2y^2 - 2z^2) - (1 - 2x^2 - 2z^2) - (1 - 2x^2 - 2y^2)$$
$$= 4x^2 - 1$$
$$-m_{11} + m_{22} - m_{33} = -(1 - 2y^2 - 2z^2) + (1 - 2x^2 - 2z^2) - (1 - 2x^2 - 2y^2)$$
$$= 4y^2 - 1$$
$$-m_{11} - m_{22} + m_{33} = -(1 - 2y^2 - 2z^2) - (1 - 2x^2 - 2z^2) + (1 - 2x^2 - 2y^2)$$
$$= 4z^2 - 1$$
$$x = \frac{\sqrt{m_{11} - m_{22} - m_{33} + 1}}{2}$$
$$y = \frac{\sqrt{-m_{11} + m_{22} - m_{33} + 1}}{2}$$
$$z = \frac{\sqrt{-m_{11} - m_{22} + m_{33} + 1}}{2}$$

Unfortunately, this does not always work, since the square root will always yield positive results. (More accurately, we have no basis for choosing the positive or negative root.) However, since **q** and −**q** represent the same orientation, we can arbitrarily choose to use the nonnegative root for *one* of the four components and still always return a correct quaternion. We just can't use the above technique for *all four* values of the quaternion.

Another trick that works is to examine the sum and difference of diagonally opposite matrix elements:

$$m_{12} + m_{21} = (2xy + 2wz) + (2xy - 2wz) = 4xy$$
$$m_{12} - m_{21} = (2xy + 2wz) - (2xy - 2wz) = 4wz$$
$$m_{31} + m_{13} = (2xz + 2wy) + (2xz - 2wy) = 4xz$$
$$m_{31} - m_{13} = (2xz + 2wy) - (2xz - 2wy) = 4wy$$
$$m_{23} + m_{32} = (2yz + 2wx) + (2yz - 2wx) = 4yz$$
$$m_{23} - m_{32} = (2yz + 2wx) - (2yz - 2wx) = 4wx$$

Thus, once we know one of the four values using the square root of the sum/difference of diagonal elements, we can compute the other three, as shown below:

$$w = \frac{\sqrt{m_{11} + m_{22} + m_{33} + 1}}{2} \implies x = \frac{m_{23} - m_{32}}{4w} \quad y = \frac{m_{31} - m_{13}}{4w} \quad z = \frac{m_{12} - m_{21}}{4w}$$

$$x = \frac{\sqrt{m_{11} - m_{22} - m_{33} + 1}}{2} \implies w = \frac{m_{23} - m_{32}}{4x} \quad y = \frac{m_{12} + m_{21}}{4x} \quad z = \frac{m_{31} + m_{13}}{4x}$$

$$y = \frac{\sqrt{-m_{11} + m_{22} - m_{33} + 1}}{2} \implies w = \frac{m_{31} - m_{13}}{4y} \quad x = \frac{m_{12} + m_{21}}{4y} \quad z = \frac{m_{23} + m_{32}}{4y}$$

$$z = \frac{\sqrt{-m_{11} - m_{22} + m_{33} + 1}}{2} \implies w = \frac{m_{12} - m_{21}}{4z} \quad x = \frac{m_{31} + m_{13}}{4z} \quad y = \frac{m_{23} + m_{32}}{4z}$$

Which of the four should we use? It seems that the simplest strategy would be to always use the same component, say *w*, and then compute *x*, *y*, and *z* by diving the sums of diagonally opposite matrix elements by 4*w*. This is fraught with problems. If *w* = 0, then the division is undefined. If *w* is very small, then numeric instability can result. Shoemake [22] suggests first determining which of w, x, y, and z is the largest (which can be done without performing any square roots), computing that component using the diagonal of the matrix, and then using it to compute the other three, according to the table above.

The code snippet below implements this strategy in a straightforward manner.

Listing 10.4: Converting a rotation matrix to a quaternion

```
// Input matrix:

float  m11,m12,m13;
float  m21,m22,m23;
float  m31,m32,m33;

// Output quaternion

float  w,x,y,z;

// Determine which of w, x, y, or z has the largest absolute value

float  fourWSquaredMinus1 = m11 + m22 + m33;
float  fourXSquaredMinus1 = m11 - m22 - m33;
float  fourYSquaredMinus1 = m22 - m11 - m33;
float  fourZSquaredMinus1 = m33 - m11 - m22;

int    biggestIndex = 0;
float  fourBiggestSquaredMinus1 = fourWSquaredMinus1;
if (fourXSquaredMinus1 > fourBiggestSquaredMinus1) {
        fourBiggestSquaredMinus1 = fourXSquaredMinus1;
        biggestIndex = 1;
}
if (fourYSquaredMinus1 > fourBiggestSquaredMinus1) {
        fourBiggestSquaredMinus1 = fourYSquaredMinus1;
        biggestIndex = 2;
}
if (fourZSquaredMinus1 > fourBiggestSquaredMinus1) {
        fourBiggestSquaredMinus1 = fourZSquaredMinus1;
        biggestIndex = 3;
}

// Perform square root and division

float biggestVal = sqrt(fourBiggestSquaredMinus1 + 1.0f) * 0.5f;
float mult = 0.25f / biggestVal;

// Apply table to compute quaternion values

switch (biggestIndex) {
        case 0:
                w = biggestVal;
                x = (m23 - m32) * mult;
                y = (m31 - m13) * mult;
                z = (m12 - m21) * mult;
                break;

        case 1:
                x = biggestVal;
                w = (m23 - m32) * mult;
```

```
            y = (m12 + m21) * mult;
            z = (m31 + m13) * mult;
            break;

    case 2:
            y = biggestVal;
            w = (m31 - m13) * mult;
            x = (m12 + m21) * mult;
            z = (m23 + m32) * mult;
            break;

    case 3:
            z = biggestVal;
            w = (m12 - m21) * mult;
            x = (m31 + m13) * mult;
            y = (m23 + m32) * mult;
            break;
}
```

10.6.5 Converting Euler Angles to a Quaternion

To convert an angular displacement from Euler angle form to quaternion, we will use a technique similar to the one used in Section 10.6.1 to generate a rotation matrix from Euler angles. We first convert the three rotations to quaternion format individually, which is a trivial operation. Then we concatenate these three quaternions in the proper format. As with matrices, there are two cases to consider: one when we wish to generate an inertial-to-object quaternion, and a second when we want the object-to-inertial quaternion. Since the two are conjugates of each other, we will only walk through the derivation for the inertial-to-object quaternion.

As we did in Section 10.6.1, we'll assign the Euler angles to the variables h, p, and b. Let $\mathbf{h}$, $\mathbf{p}$, and $\mathbf{b}$ be quaternions which perform the rotations about the y, x, and z-axes, respectively. Remember, we'll use the negative rotation amounts, since they specify rotation angles for the coordinate space. (See Section 10.6.1 for an explanation of why we negate the rotation angles.)

$$\mathbf{h} = \left[\begin{pmatrix} \cos(-h/2) \\ 0 \\ \sin(-h/2) \\ 0 \end{pmatrix} \right] = \left[\begin{pmatrix} \cos(h/2) \\ 0 \\ -\sin(h/2) \\ 0 \end{pmatrix} \right]$$

$$\mathbf{p} = \left[\begin{pmatrix} \cos(-p/2) \\ \sin(-p/2) \\ 0 \\ 0 \end{pmatrix} \right] = \left[\begin{pmatrix} \cos(p/2) \\ -\sin(p/2) \\ 0 \\ 0 \end{pmatrix} \right]$$

$$\mathbf{b} = \left[\begin{pmatrix} \cos(-b/2) \\ 0 \\ 0 \\ \sin(-b/2) \end{pmatrix} \right] = \left[\begin{pmatrix} \cos(b/2) \\ 0 \\ 0 \\ -\sin(b/2) \end{pmatrix} \right]$$

Concatenating these in the correct order, we get:

Equation 10.24:
Computing the
inertial-to-object
quaternion from
a set of Euler
angles

$$\mathbf{q}_{inertial \to object}(h, p, b)$$

$$= \mathbf{hpb}$$

$$= \begin{bmatrix} \cos(h/2) \\ \begin{pmatrix} 0 \\ -\sin(h/2) \\ 0 \end{pmatrix} \end{bmatrix} \begin{bmatrix} \cos(p/2) \\ \begin{pmatrix} -\sin(p/2) \\ 0 \\ 0 \end{pmatrix} \end{bmatrix} \begin{bmatrix} \cos(b/2) \\ \begin{pmatrix} 0 \\ 0 \\ -\sin(b/2) \end{pmatrix} \end{bmatrix}$$

$$= \begin{bmatrix} \cos(h/2)\cos(p/2) \\ \begin{pmatrix} -\cos(h/2)\sin(p/2) \\ \sin(h/2)\cos(p/2) \\ \sin(h/2)\sin(p/2) \end{pmatrix} \end{bmatrix} \begin{bmatrix} \cos(b/2) \\ \begin{pmatrix} 0 \\ 0 \\ \sin(b/2) \end{pmatrix} \end{bmatrix}$$

$$= \begin{bmatrix} \cos(h/2)\cos(p/2)\cos(b/2) + \sin(h/2)\sin(p/2)\sin(b/2) \\ \begin{pmatrix} -\cos(h/2)\sin(p/2)\cos(b/2) - \sin(h/2)\cos(p/2)\sin(b/2) \\ \cos(h/2)\sin(p/2)\sin(b/2) - \sin(h/2)\cos(p/2)\cos(b/2) \\ \sin(h/2)\sin(p/2)\cos(b/2) - \cos(h/2)\cos(p/2)\sin(b/2) \end{pmatrix} \end{bmatrix}$$

(Remember that our definition of quaternion multiplication allows us to perform the multiplications from left to right in the order that the rotations occur. See Section 10.4.8 for more on this.)

The object-to-inertial quaternion is the conjugate of the inertial-to-object quaternion:

Equation 10.25:
Computing the
object-to-inertial
quaternion from
a set of Euler
angles

$$\mathbf{q}_{object \to inertial}(h, p, b)$$

$$= \mathbf{q}_{inertial \to object}(h, p, b)^*$$

$$= \begin{bmatrix} \cos(h/2)\cos(p/2)\cos(b/2) + \sin(h/2)\sin(p/2)\sin(b/2) \\ \begin{pmatrix} \cos(h/2)\sin(p/2)\cos(b/2) + \sin(h/2)\cos(p/2)\sin(b/2) \\ \sin(h/2)\cos(p/2)\cos(b/2) - \cos(h/2)\sin(p/2)\sin(b/2) \\ \cos(h/2)\cos(p/2)\sin(b/2) - \sin(h/2)\sin(p/2)\cos(b/2) \end{pmatrix} \end{bmatrix}$$

10.6.6 Converting a Quaternion to Euler Angles

To extract Euler angles from a quaternion, we could solve for the Euler angles from Equation 10.24 directly. However, let's see if we can't take advantage of our work in previous sections and arrive at the answer without going through so much effort. We've already come up with a technique to extract Euler angles from a matrix in Section 10.6.2, and we learned how to convert a quaternion to a matrix. Let's take our technique for converting a matrix to Euler angles and see if we can plug in our results from Equation 10.23.

Summarizing our findings from Section 10.6.2:

$$p = \mathrm{asin}\,(-m_{23})$$

$$h = \begin{cases} \mathrm{atan2}(m_{13}, m_{33}) & \text{if } \cos p \neq 0 \\ \mathrm{atan2}(-m_{31}, m_{11}) & \text{otherwise} \end{cases}$$

$$b = \begin{cases} \mathrm{atan2}(m_{21}, m_{22}) & \text{if } \cos p \neq 0 \\ 0 & \text{otherwise} \end{cases}$$

Here are the values of the matrix elements involved from Equation 10.23:

$$m_{23} = 2yz + 2wx$$
$$m_{13} = 2xz - 2wy$$
$$m_{33} = 1 - 2x^2 - 2y^2$$
$$m_{31} = 2xz + 2wy$$
$$m_{11} = 1 - 2y^2 - 2z^2$$
$$m_{21} = 2xy - 2wz$$
$$m_{22} = 1 - 2x^2 - 2z^2$$

Substituting and simplifying, we have:

$$p = \text{asin}\,(-m_{23})$$
$$= \text{asin}\,(-2(yz + wx))$$

$$h = \begin{cases} \begin{aligned} &\text{atan2}(m_{13}, m_{33}) \\ &= \text{atan2}(2xz - 2wy, 1 - 2x^2 - 2y^2) \\ &= \text{atan2}(xz - wy, 1/2 - x^2 - y^2) \end{aligned} & \text{if } \cos p \neq 0 \\[1em] \begin{aligned} &\text{atan2}(-m_{31}, m_{11}) \\ &= \text{atan2}(-2xz - 2wy, 1 - 2y^2 - 2z^2) \\ &= \text{atan2}(-xz - wy, 1/2 - y^2 - z^2) \end{aligned} & \text{otherwise} \end{cases}$$

$$b = \begin{cases} \begin{aligned} &\text{atan2}(m_{21}, m_{22}) \\ &= \text{atan2}(2xy - 2wz, 1 - 2x^2 - 2z^2) \\ &= \text{atan2}(xy - wz, 1/2 - x^2 - z^2) \end{aligned} & \text{if } \cos p \neq 0 \\[1em] 0 & \text{otherwise} \end{cases}$$

Now we can translate this directly into code, as shown in the listing below, which converts an inertial-to-object quaternion into Euler angles:

Listing 10.5: Converting an inertial-to-object quaternion to Euler angles

```
// Use global variables for input and output

float w,x,y,z;
float h,p,b;

// Extract sin(pitch)

float sp = -2.0f * (y*z + w*x);

// Check for Gimbal lock, giving slight tolerance for numerical imprecision

if (fabs(sp) > 0.9999f) {

        // Looking straight up or down

        p = 1.570796f * sp; // pi/2

        // Compute heading, slam bank to zero

        h = atan2(-x*z - w*y, 0.5f - y*y - z*z);
        b = 0.0f;
```

```
} else {

        // Compute angles

        p = asin(sp);
        h = atan2(x*z - w*y, 0.5f - x*x - y*y);
        b = atan2(x*y - w*z, 0.5f - x*x - z*z);
}
```

To convert an object-to-inertial quaternion to Euler angle format, we use code very similar to the above code. We just negate the x, y, and z values, since we assume the object-to-inertial quaternion is the conjugate of the inertial-to-object quaternion.

Listing 10.6: Converting an object-to-inertial quaternion to Euler angles

```
// Extract sin(pitch)

float sp = -2.0f * (y*z - w*x);

// Check for Gimbal lock, giving slight tolerance for numerical imprecision

if (fabs(sp) > 0.9999f) {

        // Looking straight up or down

        p = 1.570796f * sp; // pi/2

        // Compute heading, slam bank to zero

        h = atan2(-x*z + w*y, 0.5f - y*y - z*z);
        b = 0.0f;

} else {

        // Compute angles

        p = asin(sp);
        h = atan2(x*z + w*y, 0.5f - x*x - y*y);
        b = atan2(x*y + w*z, 0.5f - x*x - z*z);
}
```

10.7 Exercises

1. Construct a quaternion to rotate 30° about the x-axis. What is the magnitude of this quaternion? What is its conjugate? What type of rotation is expressed by the conjugate?

2. What type of rotation is represented by the quaternion:

    $$\left[\; 0.965 \quad (\; 0.149 \quad -0.149 \quad 0.149 \;) \;\right]$$

    Compute a quaternion which performs one-fifth of this rotation.

3. Consider the quaternions.

$$\mathbf{a} = \begin{bmatrix} 0.233 & (0.060 & -0.257 & -0.935) \end{bmatrix}$$
$$\mathbf{b} = \begin{bmatrix} -0.752 & (0.286 & 0.374 & 0.459) \end{bmatrix}$$

Compute the dot product $\mathbf{a} \cdot \mathbf{b}$. Compute the difference from $\mathbf{a}$ to $\mathbf{b}$. Compute the quaternion product $\mathbf{ab}$.

4. Convert the quaternion in Exercise 2 to matrix form.

5. Write the C++ code to convert an object-to-inertial matrix to Euler angle form.

Chapter 11
Transformations in C++

This chapter gives code for representing orientation and performing transformations. It is divided into five sections.

- Section 11.1 discusses a few ground rules that are common to all the helper classes.
- Section 11.2 presents class `EulerAngles`, which is used to store an orientation in Euler angle format.
- Section 11.3 presents class `Quaternion`, which is used to store an angular displacement in quaternion format.
- Section 11.4 presents class `RotationMatrix`, which is a special matrix class tailored specifically for the purpose of rotating vectors between object and inertial space.
- Section 11.5 presents class `Matrix4×3`, which is a more general matrix class to perform arbitrary transformations from a "source" coordinate space to a "destination" coordinate space.

In this chapter, we will put to use the knowledge we have gained in Chapters 7 through 10. We will present some C++ classes we can use to represent orientation in 3D and perform rotations and coordinate space transformations.

For each of the classes in turn, we will begin by showing the header file and discussing the interface that is exported. Then we will show the complete implementation in the .cpp file and discuss any significant implementation details.

We will not go into the theory behind the operations again; that has been covered in previous chapters. At this point, we will focus primarily on interface and implementation issues.

11.1 Overview

Before we can dive into the specific classes, let's first cover a few points that apply to the code in all of the remaining sections. Many of the comments from Chapter 6 also apply to the code in this chapter.

Dealing with transformations can be confusing. Matrices are just tricky. If you've ever written matrix code without the use of well-designed classes, you know that you frequently end up twiddling minus signs, transposing matrices, or concatenating things in the opposite order until it looks right.

The classes in these sections have been designed to eliminate the guesswork usually associated with this type of programming. For example, direct access to the matrix and quaternion elements are seldom needed. We have specifically limited the number of available operations in order to prevent possible confusion. For example, there are no functions to invert or concatenate a `RotationMatrix` because if you use a `RotationMatrix` for its intended purpose, these operations are not useful or even meaningful.

We use a set of simple, common math constants and utility functions. These are provided in MathUtil.h and MathUtil.cpp.

MathUtil.h is shown below:

Listing 11.1: MathUtil.h

```
/////////////////////////////////////////////////////////////////////////////
//
// 3D Math Primer for Graphics and Game Development
//
// MathUtil.h - Declarations for miscellaneous math utilities
//
// Visit gamemath.com for the latest version of this file.
//
/////////////////////////////////////////////////////////////////////////////

#ifndef __MATHUTIL_H_INCLUDED__
#define __MATHUTIL_H_INCLUDED__

#include <math.h>

// Declare a global constant for pi and a few multiples.

const float kPi = 3.14159265f;
const float k2Pi = kPi * 2.0f;
const float kPiOver2 = kPi / 2.0f;
const float k1OverPi = 1.0f / kPi;
const float k1Over2Pi = 1.0f / k2Pi;

// "Wrap" an angle in range -pi...pi by adding the correct multiple
// of 2 pi

extern float wrapPi(float theta);

// "Safe" inverse trig functions
```

```
extern float safeAcos(float x);

// Compute the sin and cosine of an angle. On some platforms, if we know
// that we need both values, it can be computed faster than computing
// the two values seperately.

inline void sinCos(float *returnSin, float *returnCos, float theta) {

    // For simplicity, we'll just use the normal trig functions.
    // Note that on some platforms we may be able to do better

    *returnSin = sin(theta);
    *returnCos = cos(theta);
}

/////////////////////////////////////////////////////////////////////////
#endif // #ifndef __MATHUTIL_H_INCLUDED__
```

The definitions for a few out-of-line functions are in MathUtil.cpp, shown below:

```
/////////////////////////////////////////////////////////////////////////
//
// 3D Math Primer for Graphics and Game Development
//
// MathUtil.cpp - Miscellaneous math utilities
//
// Visit gamemath.com for the latest version of this file.
//
/////////////////////////////////////////////////////////////////////////

#include <math.h>

#include "MathUtil.h"

//-------------------------------------------------------------------------
// "Wrap" an angle in range -pi...pi by adding the correct multiple
// of 2 pi

float wrapPi(float theta) {
    theta += kPi;
    theta -= floor(theta * k1Over2Pi) * k2Pi;
    theta -= kPi;
    return theta;
}

//-------------------------------------------------------------------------
// safeAcos
//
// Same as acos(x), but if x is out of range, it is "clamped" to the nearest
// valid value. The value returned is in range 0...pi, the same as the
// standard C acos() function

extern float safeAcos(float x) {

    // Check limit conditions

    if (x <= -1.0f) {
        return kPi;
    }
    if (x >= 1.0f) {
```

```
        return 0.0f;
    }

    // Value is in the domain - use standard C function

    return acos(x);
}
```

11.2 Class EulerAngles

The EulerAngles class is used to store an orientation in Euler angle form using the heading-pitch-bank convention. For more information on Euler angles, and the heading-pitch-bank convention in particular, see Section 10.3.

The class is fairly straightforward. For simplicity,we have chosen not to implement many operations. Notably, we have not implemented addition and subtraction, multiplication by a scalar, etc. These functions can be handy if the class is used to store not an orientation, but an angular velocity or rate of change.

The interface file for class EulerAngles is EulerAngles.h. The few out-of-line functions are implemented in EulerAngles.cpp. Below is the complete listing of EulerAngles.h:

Listing 11.2: EulerAngles.h

```
/////////////////////////////////////////////////////////////////////////
//
// 3D Math Primer for Graphics and Game Development
//
// EulerAngles.h - Declarations for class EulerAngles
//
// Visit gamemath.com for the latest version of this file.
//
// For more details, see EulerAngles.cpp
//
/////////////////////////////////////////////////////////////////////////

#ifndef __EULERANGLES_H_INCLUDED__
#define __EULERANGLES_H_INCLUDED__

// Forward declarations

class Quaternion;
class Matrix4x3;
class RotationMatrix;

//-------------------------------------------------------------------------
// class EulerAngles
//
// This class represents a heading-pitch-bank Euler angle triple.

class EulerAngles {
public:

// Public data

    // Straightforward representation. Store the three angles, in
```

```
                    // radians

                    float heading;
                    float pitch;
                    float bank;

            // Public operations

                    // Default constructor does nothing

                    EulerAngles() {}

                    // Construct from three values

                    EulerAngles(float h, float p, float b) :
                            heading(h), pitch(p), bank(b) {}

                    // Set to identity triple (all zeros)

                    void   identity() { pitch = bank = heading = 0.0f; }

                    // Determine "canonical" Euler angle triple

                    void   canonize();

                    // Convert the quaternion to Euler angle format. The input quaternion
                    // is assumed to perform the rotation from object-to-inertial
                    // or inertial-to-object, as indicated.

                    void   fromObjectToInertialQuaternion(const Quaternion &q);
                    void   fromInertialToObjectQuaternion(const Quaternion &q);

                    // Convert the transform matrix to Euler angle format. The input
                    // matrix is assumed to perform the transformation from
                    // object-to-world, or world-to-object, as indicated. The
                    // translation portion of the matrix is ignored. The
                    // matrix is assumed to be orthogonal.

                    void   fromObjectToWorldMatrix(const Matrix4×3 &m);
                    void   fromWorldToObjectMatrix(const Matrix4×3 &m);

                    // Convert a rotation matrix to Euler Angle form.

                    void   fromRotationMatrix(const RotationMatrix &m);
            };

            // A global "identity" Euler angle constant

            extern const EulerAngles kEulerAnglesIdentity;

//////////////////////////////////////////////////////////////////////////////
#endif // #ifndef __EULERANGLES_H_INCLUDED__
```

Use of class `EulerAngles` is fairly straightforward. Only a few items warrant elaboration:

■ The `canonize()` member function ensures that the angles are in the "canonical set" of Euler angles as described in Section 10.3.4.

■ The `fromObjectToInertialQuaternion()` and `fromInertialToObject-Quaternion()` functions compute Euler angles from a quaternion. The first function accepts a quaternion that is assumed to rotate from object to inertial space, and the second assumes the input quaternion rotates from object to inertial space. See Section 10.6.6 for more on this conversion and why there are two different versions.

- Likewise, the `fromObjectToWorldMatrix()` and `fromWorldToObjectMatrix()` functions convert orientation contained in the rotation portion of the matrix, which is assumed to be orthogonal, into Euler angle form.

A few out-of-line functions are implemented in EulerAngles.cpp, which is shown below:

Listing 11.3: EulerAngles.cpp

```
/////////////////////////////////////////////////////////////////////////////
//
// 3D Math Primer for Graphics and Game Development
//
// EulerAngles.cpp - Implementation of class EulerAngles
//
// Visit gamemath.com for the latest version of this file.
//
/////////////////////////////////////////////////////////////////////////////

#include <math.h>

#include "EulerAngles.h"
#include "Quaternion.h"
#include "MathUtil.h"
#include "Matrix4×3.h"
#include "RotationMatrix.h"

/////////////////////////////////////////////////////////////////////////////
//
// Notes:
//
// See Chapter 11 for more information on class design decisions.
//
// See section 10.3 for more information on the Euler angle conventions
// assumed.
//
/////////////////////////////////////////////////////////////////////////////

/////////////////////////////////////////////////////////////////////////////
//
// global data
//
/////////////////////////////////////////////////////////////////////////////

// The global "identity" Euler angle constant. Now we may not know exactly
// when this object may get constructed, in relation to other objects, so
// it is possible for the object to be referenced before it is initialized.
// However, on most implementations, it will be zero-initialized at program
// startup anyway, before any other objects are constructed.

const EulerAngles kEulerAnglesIdentity(0.0f, 0.0f, 0.0f);

/////////////////////////////////////////////////////////////////////////////
//
// class EulerAngles Implementation
//
```

```
/////////////////////////////////////////////////////////////////////////
//---------------------------------------------------------------------------
// EulerAngles::canonize
//
// Set the Euler angle triple to its "canonical" value. This does not change
// the meaning of the Euler angles as a representation of orientation in 3D,
// but if the angles are for other purposes such as angular velocities, etc.,
// then the operation might not be valid.
//
// See section 10.3 for more information.

void   EulerAngles::canonize() {

      // First, wrap pitch in range -pi ... pi

      pitch = wrapPi(pitch);

      // Now, check for "the back side" of the matrix pitch outside
      // the canonical range of -pi/2 ... pi/2

      if (pitch < -kPiOver2) {
            pitch = -kPi - pitch;
            heading += kPi;
            bank += kPi;
      } else if (pitch > kPiOver2) {
            pitch = kPi - pitch;
            heading += kPi;
            bank += kPi;
      }

      // Now check for the gimbel lock case (within a slight tolerance)

      if (fabs(pitch) > kPiOver2 - 1e-4) {

            // We are in gimbel lock. Assign all rotation
            // about the vertical axis to heading

            heading += bank;
            bank = 0.0f;

      } else {

            // Not in gimbel lock. Wrap the bank angle in
            // canonical range

            bank = wrapPi(bank);
      }

      // Wrap heading in canonical range

      heading = wrapPi(heading);
}


//---------------------------------------------------------------------------
// EulerAngles::fromObjectToInertialQuaternion
//
// Setup the Euler angles, given an object->inertial rotation quaternion
//
```

```
// See 10.6.6 for more information.

void  EulerAngles::fromObjectToInertialQuaternion(const Quaternion &q) {

      // Extract sin(pitch)

      float sp = -2.0f * (q.y*q.z - q.w*q.x);

      // Check for Gimbel lock, giving slight tolerance for numerical imprecision

      if (fabs(sp) > 0.9999f) {

            // Looking straight up or down

            pitch = kPiOver2 * sp;

            // Compute heading, slam bank to zero

            heading = atan2(-q.x*q.z + q.w*q.y, 0.5f - q.y*q.y - q.z*q.z);
            bank = 0.0f;

      } else {

            // Compute angles. We don't have to use the "safe" asin
            // function because we already checked for range errors when
            // checking for Gimbel lock

            pitch = asin(sp);
            heading = atan2(q.x*q.z + q.w*q.y, 0.5f - q.x*q.x - q.y*q.y);
            bank = atan2(q.x*q.y + q.w*q.z, 0.5f - q.x*q.x - q.z*q.z);
      }
}

//-------------------------------------------------------------------------
// EulerAngles::fromInertialToObjectQuaternion
//
// Setup the Euler angles, given an inertial->object rotation quaternion
//
// See 10.6.6 for more information.

void  EulerAngles::fromInertialToObjectQuaternion(const Quaternion &q) {

      // Extract sin(pitch)

      float sp = -2.0f * (q.y*q.z + q.w*q.x);

      // Check for Gimbel lock, giving slight tolerance for numerical imprecision

      if (fabs(sp) > 0.9999f) {

            // Looking straight up or down

            pitch = kPiOver2 * sp;

            // Compute heading, slam bank to zero

            heading = atan2(-q.x*q.z - q.w*q.y, 0.5f - q.y*q.y - q.z*q.z);
            bank = 0.0f;
```

```
        } else {

                // Compute angles. We don't have to use the "safe" asin
                // function because we already checked for range errors when
                // checking for Gimbel lock

                pitch = asin(sp);
                heading = atan2(q.x*q.z - q.w*q.y, 0.5f - q.x*q.x - q.y*q.y);
                bank = atan2(q.x*q.y - q.w*q.z, 0.5f - q.x*q.x - q.z*q.z);
        }
}

//---------------------------------------------------------------------------
// EulerAngles::fromObjectToWorldMatrix
//
// Setup the Euler angles, given an object->world transformation matrix.
//
// The matrix is assumed to be orthogonal. The translation portion is
// ignored.
//
// See 10.6.2 for more information.

void    EulerAngles::fromObjectToWorldMatrix(const Matrix4x3 &m) {

        // Extract sin(pitch) from m32.

        float  sp = -m.m32;

        // Check for Gimbel lock

        if (fabs(sp) > 9.99999f) {

                // Looking straight up or down

                pitch = kPiOver2 * sp;

                // Compute heading, slam bank to zero

                heading = atan2(-m.m23, m.m11);
                bank = 0.0f;

        } else {

                // Compute angles. We don't have to use the "safe" asin
                // function because we already checked for range errors when
                // checking for Gimbel lock

                heading = atan2(m.m31, m.m33);
                pitch = asin(sp);
                bank = atan2(m.m12, m.m22);
        }
}

//---------------------------------------------------------------------------
// EulerAngles::fromWorldToObjectMatrix
//
// Setup the Euler angles, given a world->object transformation matrix.
//
// The matrix is assumed to be orthogonal. The translation portion is
// ignored.
```

```
//
// See 10.6.2 for more information.

void   EulerAngles::fromWorldToObjectMatrix(const Matrix4×3 &m) {

        // Extract sin(pitch) from m23.

        float  sp = —m.m23;

        // Check for Gimbel lock

        if (fabs(sp) > 9.99999f) {

                // Looking straight up or down

                pitch = kPiOver2 * sp;

                // Compute heading, slam bank to zero

                heading = atan2(—m.m31, m.m11);
                bank = 0.0f;

        } else {

                // Compute angles. We don't have to use the "safe" asin
                // function because we already checked for range errors when
                // checking for Gimbel lock

                heading = atan2(m.m13, m.m33);
                pitch = asin(sp);
                bank = atan2(m.m21, m.m22);
        }
}

//---------------------------------------------------------------------------
// EulerAngles::fromRotationMatrix
//
// Setup the Euler angles, given a rotation matrix.
//
// See 10.6.2 for more information.

void   EulerAngles::fromRotationMatrix(const RotationMatrix &m) {

        // Extract sin(pitch) from m23.

        float  sp = —m.m23;

        // Check for Gimbel lock

        if (fabs(sp) > 9.99999f) {

                // Looking straight up or down

                pitch = kPiOver2 * sp;

                // Compute heading, slam bank to zero

                heading = atan2(—m.m31, m.m11);
                bank = 0.0f;
```

```
        } else {

            // Compute angles. We don't have to use the "safe" asin
            // function because we already checked for range errors when
            // checking for Gimbel lock

            heading = atan2(m.m13, m.m33);
            pitch = asin(sp);
            bank = atan2(m.m21, m.m22);
        }
    }
```

11.3 Class Quaternion

Class `Quaternion` is used to store an orientation or angular displacement in quaternion form. For more information on quaternions, see Section 10.4. From the complete set of mathematical operations that can be performed on quaternions, only those operations that are meaningful for unit quaternions are used for storing angular displacement. For example, quaternion negation, addition, subtraction, multiplication by a scalar, log, and exp are not provided.

The quaternion class is defined in Quaternion.h, which is shown below:

Listing 11.4: Quaternion.h

```
/////////////////////////////////////////////////////////////////////
//
// 3D Math Primer for Graphics and Game Development
//
// Quaternion.h - Declarations for class Quaternion
//
// Visit gamemath.com for the latest version of this file.
//
// For more details, see Quaternion.cpp
//
/////////////////////////////////////////////////////////////////////

#ifndef __QUATERNION_H_INCLUDED__
#define __QUATERNION_H_INCLUDED__

class Vector3;
class EulerAngles;

//---------------------------------------------------------------------
// class Quaternion
//
// Implement a quaternion for the purpose of representing an angular
// displacement (orientation) in 3D.

class Quaternion {
public:

// Public data

        // The four values of the quaternion. Normally, it will not
        // be necessary to manipulate these directly. However,
        // we leave them public, since prohibiting direct access
```

```
            // makes some operations, such as file I/O, unnecessarily
            // complicated.

            float  w, x, y, z;

    // Public operations

            // Set to identity

            void   identity() { w = 1.0f; x = y = z = 0.0f; }

            // Setup the quaternion to a specific rotation

            void   setToRotateAboutX(float theta);
            void   setToRotateAboutY(float theta);
            void   setToRotateAboutZ(float theta);
            void   setToRotateAboutAxis(const Vector3 &axis, float theta);

            // Setup to perform object<->inertial rotations,
            // given orientation in Euler angle format

            void   setToRotateObjectToInertial(const EulerAngles &orientation);
            void   setToRotateInertialToObject(const EulerAngles &orientation);

            // Cross product

            Quaternion operator *(const Quaternion &a) const;

            // Multiplication with assignment, as per C++ convention

            Quaternion &operator *=(const Quaternion &a);

            // Normalize the quaternion.

            void   normalize();

            // Extract and return the rotation angle and axis.

            float         getRotationAngle() const;
            Vector3       getRotationAxis() const;
    };

    // A global "identity" quaternion constant

    extern const Quaternion kQuaternionIdentity;

    // Quaternion dot product.

    extern float dotProduct(const Quaternion &a, const Quaternion &b);

    // Spherical linear interpolation

    extern Quaternion slerp(const Quaternion &p, const Quaternion &q, float t);

    // Quaternion conjugation

    extern Quaternion conjugate(const Quaternion &q);

    // Quaternion exponentiation
```

```
extern Quaternion pow(const Quaternion &q, float exponent);

/////////////////////////////////////////////////////////////////////
#endif // #ifndef __QUATERNION_H_INCLUDED__
```

Assuming a basic understanding of quaternions, most of the functionality of this class should be obvious from the function names and/or comments. To create a quaternion that represents a specific angular displacement, we would use one of the setTo*XXX* functions. setToRotateObjectToInertial() and setToRotateInertialToObject() are used to convert Euler angles to quaternion form. The first function creates a quaternion that specifies the rotation from object to inertial space, and the latter returns a rotation from inertial to object space. See Section 10.6.5 for more information on these conversions and why there are two different functions.

Angular displacements are manipulated using functions that perform the mathematical operations exactly as they have been described in the preceding sections. Angular displacements are concatenated using operator*(). (As always, the order of concatenations reads left to right.) The conjugate() function returns a quaternion representing the opposite angular displacement of the input quaternion.

The axis and angle of rotation can be extracted from a quaternion using getRotationAngle() and getRotationAxis().

normalize() can be called to combat floating-point error creep. If you perform more than a few hundred successive operations on the same quaternion, you might want to call this function. Converting from Euler angles always generates a normalized quaternion and, therefore, removes the possibility of error creep. However, conversion between matrix and quaternion forms does not have the same effect.

The quaternion operations are implemented in Quaternion.cpp, which is listed below:

Listing 11.5: Quaternion.cpp

```
/////////////////////////////////////////////////////////////////////
//
// 3D Math Primer for Graphics and Game Development
//
// Quaternion.cpp - Quaternion implementation
//
// Visit gamemath.com for the latest version of this file.
//
// For more details see section 11.3.
//
/////////////////////////////////////////////////////////////////////

#include <assert.h>
#include <math.h>

#include "Quaternion.h"
#include "MathUtil.h"
#include "vector3.h"
#include "EulerAngles.h"

/////////////////////////////////////////////////////////////////////
//
// global data
//
```

```
////////////////////////////////////////////////////////////////////////

// The global identity quaternion. Notice that there are no constructors
// to the Quaternion class, since we really don't need any.

const Quaternion kQuaternionIdentity = {
    1.0f, 0.0f, 0.0f, 0.0f
};

////////////////////////////////////////////////////////////////////////
//
// class Quaternion members
//
////////////////////////////////////////////////////////////////////////

//---------------------------------------------------------------------------
// Quaternion::setToRotateAboutX
// Quaternion::setToRotateAboutY
// Quaternion::setToRotateAboutZ
// Quaternion::setToRotateAboutAxis
//
// Setup the quaternion to rotate about the specified axis

void    Quaternion::setToRotateAboutX(float theta) {

    // Compute the half angle

    float thetaOver2 = theta * .5f;

    // Set the values

    w = cos(thetaOver2);
    x = sin(thetaOver2);
    y = 0.0f;
    z = 0.0f;
}

void    Quaternion::setToRotateAboutY(float theta) {

    // Compute the half angle

    float thetaOver2 = theta * .5f;

    // Set the values

    w = cos(thetaOver2);
    x = 0.0f;
    y = sin(thetaOver2);
    z = 0.0f;
}

void    Quaternion::setToRotateAboutZ(float theta) {

    // Compute the half angle

    float thetaOver2 = theta * .5f;

    // Set the values

    w = cos(thetaOver2);
```

```
        x = 0.0f;
        y = 0.0f;
        z = sin(thetaOver2);
}

void   Quaternion::setToRotateAboutAxis(const Vector3 &axis, float theta) {

        // The axis of rotation must be normalized

        assert(fabs(vectorMag(axis) - 1.0f) < .01f);

        // Compute the half angle and its sin

        float  thetaOver2 = theta * .5f;
        float  sinThetaOver2 = sin(thetaOver2);

        // Set the values

        w = cos(thetaOver2);
        x = axis.x * sinThetaOver2;
        y = axis.y * sinThetaOver2;
        z = axis.z * sinThetaOver2;
}

//---------------------------------------------------------------------------
// EulerAngles::setToRotateObjectToInertial
//
// Setup the quaternion to perform an object->inertial rotation, given the
// orientation in Euler angle format
//
// See 10.6.5 for more information.

void   Quaternion::setToRotateObjectToInertial(const EulerAngles &orientation) {

        // Compute sine and cosine of the half angles

        float  sp, sb, sh;
        float  cp, cb, ch;
        sinCos(&sp, &cp, orientation.pitch * 0.5f);
        sinCos(&sb, &cb, orientation.bank * 0.5f);
        sinCos(&sh, &ch, orientation.heading * 0.5f);

        // Compute values

        w = ch*cp*cb + sh*sp*sb;
        x = ch*sp*cb + sh*cp*sb;
        y = -ch*sp*sb + sh*cp*cb;
        z = -sh*sp*cb + ch*cp*sb;
}

//---------------------------------------------------------------------------
// EulerAngles::setToRotateInertialToObject
//
// Setup the quaternion to perform an object->inertial rotation, given the
// orientation in Euler angle format
//
// See 10.6.5 for more information.

void   Quaternion::setToRotateInertialToObject(const EulerAngles &orientation) {
```

```
        // Compute sine and cosine of the half angles

        float sp, sb, sh;
        float cp, cb, ch;
        sinCos(&sp, &cp, orientation.pitch * 0.5f);
        sinCos(&sb, &cb, orientation.bank * 0.5f);
        sinCos(&sh, &ch, orientation.heading * 0.5f);

        // Compute values

        w = ch*cp*cb + sh*sp*sb;
        x = -ch*sp*cb - sh*cp*sb;
        y = ch*sp*sb - sh*cb*cp;
        z = sh*sp*cb - ch*cp*sb;
}


//-------------------------------------------------------------------------
// Quaternion::operator *
//
// Quaternion cross product, which concatenates multiple angular
// displacements. The order of multiplication, from left to right,
// corresponds to the order that the angular displacements are
// applied. This is backward from the *standard* definition of
// quaternion multiplication. See section 10.4.8 for the rationale
// behind this deviation from the standard.

Quaternion Quaternion::operator *(const Quaternion &a) const {
        Quaternion result;

        result.w = w*a.w - x*a.x - y*a.y - z*a.z;
        result.x = w*a.x + x*a.w + z*a.y - y*a.z;
        result.y = w*a.y + y*a.w + x*a.z - z*a.x;
        result.z = w*a.z + z*a.w + y*a.x - x*a.y;

        return result;
}


//-------------------------------------------------------------------------
// Quaternion::operator *=
//
// Combined cross product and assignment, as per C++ convention

Quaternion &Quaternion::operator *=(const Quaternion &a) {

        // Multuiply and assign

        *this = *this * a;

        // Return reference to l-value

        return *this;
}


//-------------------------------------------------------------------------
// Quaternion::normalize
//
// "Normalize" a quaternion. Note that normally, quaternions
// are always normalized (within limits of numerical precision).
// See section 10.4.6 for more information.
//
```

```
// This function is provided primarily to combat floating point "error
// creep," which can occur when many successive quaternion operations
// are applied.

void  Quaternion::normalize() {

      // Compute magnitude of the quaternion

      float  mag = (float)sqrt(w*w + x*x + y*y + z*z);

      // Check for bogus length to protect against divide by zero

      if (mag > 0.0f) {

             // Normalize it

             float  oneOverMag = 1.0f / mag;
             w *= oneOverMag;
             x *= oneOverMag;
             y *= oneOverMag;
             z *= oneOverMag;

      } else {

             // Houston, we have a problem

             assert(false);

             // In a release build, just slam it to something

             identity();
      }
}

//-------------------------------------------------------------------------
// Quaternion::getRotationAngle
//
// Return the rotation angle theta

float Quaternion::getRotationAngle() const {

      // Compute the half angle. Remember that w = cos(theta / 2)

      float thetaOver2 = safeAcos(w);

      // Return the rotation angle

      return thetaOver2 * 2.0f;
}

//-------------------------------------------------------------------------
// Quaternion::getRotationAxis
//
// Return the rotation axis

Vector3     Quaternion::getRotationAxis() const {

      // Compute sin^2(theta/2). Remember that w = cos(theta/2),
      // and sin^2(x) + cos^2(x) = 1
```

```
            float sinThetaOver2Sq = 1.0f - w*w;

            // Protect against numerical imprecision

            if (sinThetaOver2Sq <= 0.0f) {

                    // Identity quaternion, or numerical imprecision. Just
                    // return any valid vector, since it doesn't matter

                    return Vector3(1.0f, 0.0f, 0.0f);
            }

            // Compute 1 / sin(theta/2)

            float oneOverSinThetaOver2 = 1.0f / sqrt(sinThetaOver2Sq);

            // Return axis of rotation

            return Vector3(
                    x * oneOverSinThetaOver2,
                    y * oneOverSinThetaOver2,
                    z * oneOverSinThetaOver2
            );
    }

    /////////////////////////////////////////////////////////////////////////
    //
    // Nonmember functions
    //
    /////////////////////////////////////////////////////////////////////////

    //-------------------------------------------------------------------------
    // dotProduct
    //
    // Quaternion dot product. We use a nonmember function so we can
    // pass quaternion expressions as operands without having "funky syntax"
    //
    // See 10.4.10

    float dotProduct(const Quaternion &a, const Quaternion &b) {
            return a.w*b.w + a.x*b.x + a.y*b.y + a.z*b.z;
    }

    //-------------------------------------------------------------------------
    // slerp
    //
    // Spherical linear interpolation.
    //
    // See 10.4.13

    Quaternion slerp(const Quaternion &q0, const Quaternion &q1, float t) {

            // Check for out-of range parameter and return edge points if so

            if (t <= 0.0f) return q0;
            if (t >= 1.0f) return q1;

            // Compute "cosine of angle between quaternions" using dot product
```

```
float cosOmega = dotProduct(q0, q1);

// If negative dot, use -q1. Two quaternions q and -q
// represent the same rotation, but may produce
// different slerp. We chose q or -q to rotate using
// the acute angle.

float q1w = q1.w;
float q1x = q1.x;
float q1y = q1.y;
float q1z = q1.z;
if (cosOmega < 0.0f) {
      q1w = -q1w;
      q1x = -q1x;
      q1y = -q1y;
      q1z = -q1z;
      cosOmega = -cosOmega;
}

// We should have two unit quaternions, so dot should be <= 1.0

assert(cosOmega < 1.1f);

// Compute interpolation fraction, checking for quaternions
// almost exactly the same

float k0, k1;
if (cosOmega > 0.9999f) {

      // Very close - just use linear interpolation,
      // which will protect againt a divide by zero

      k0 = 1.0f-t;
      k1 = t;

} else {

      // Compute the sin of the angle using the
      // trig identity sin^2(omega) + cos^2(omega) = 1

      float sinOmega = sqrt(1.0f - cosOmega*cosOmega);

      // Compute the angle from its sin and cosine

      float omega = atan2(sinOmega, cosOmega);

      // Compute inverse of denominator, so we only have
      // to divide once

      float oneOverSinOmega = 1.0f / sinOmega;

      // Compute interpolation parameters

      k0 = sin((1.0f - t) * omega) * oneOverSinOmega;
      k1 = sin(t * omega) * oneOverSinOmega;
}

// Interpolate

Quaternion result;
```

```
        result.x = k0*q0.x + k1*q1x;
        result.y = k0*q0.y + k1*q1y;
        result.z = k0*q0.z + k1*q1z;
        result.w = k0*q0.w + k1*q1w;

        // Return it

        return result;
}

//---------------------------------------------------------------------------
// conjugate
//
// Compute the quaternion conjugate. This is the quaternion
// with the opposite rotation as the original quaternion. See 10.4.7

Quaternion conjugate(const Quaternion &q) {
        Quaternion result;

        // Same rotation amount

        result.w = q.w;

        // Opposite axis of rotation

        result.x = -q.x;
        result.y = -q.y;
        result.z = -q.z;

        // Return it

        return result;
}

//---------------------------------------------------------------------------
// pow
//
// Quaternion exponentiation.
//
// See 10.4.12

Quaternion pow(const Quaternion &q, float exponent) {

        // Check for the case of an identity quaternion.
        // This will protect against divide by zero

        if (fabs(q.w) > .9999f) {
                return q;
        }

        // Extract the half angle alpha (alpha = theta/2)

        float alpha = acos(q.w);

        // Compute new alpha value

        float newAlpha = alpha * exponent;

        // Compute new w value
```

```
            Quaternion result;
            result.w = cos(newAlpha);

            // Compute new xyz values

            float mult = sin(newAlpha) / sin(alpha);
            result.x = q.x * mult;
            result.y = q.y * mult;
            result.z = q.z * mult;

            // Return it

            return result;
        }
```

11.4 Class RotationMatrix

Class `RotationMatrix` is the first of two matrix classes we present in this chapter. The purpose of the class is to handle the very specific (but extremely common) task of rotating between object and inertial space. See Section 3.2 if you have forgotten what these terms mean.

This matrix class is not a general transformation class. We assume that the matrix contains rotation only and, therefore, is orthogonal. Using our specific terminology from Section 10.1, the matrix contains an *orientation*, not an *angular displacement*. When you create the matrix, you do not specify a direction of transformation (either from object to inertial, or inertial to object). The direction of transformation is specified at the time you wish to actually perform the transformation, and there are two specific functions that are used, one for each direction. All of this is in comparison to class `Matrix4×3`, which is presented in Section 11.5.

Class `RotationMatrix` is defined in RotationMatrix.h. The full listing is below:

Listing 11.6: RotationMatrix.h

```
/////////////////////////////////////////////////////////////////////////////
//
// 3D Math Primer for Graphics and Game Development
//
// RotationMatrix.h - Declarations for class RotationMatrix
//
// Visit gamemath.com for the latest version of this file.
//
// For more details, see RotationMatrix.cpp
//
/////////////////////////////////////////////////////////////////////////////

#ifndef __ROTATIONMATRIX_H_INCLUDED__
#define __ROTATIONMATRIX_H_INCLUDED__

class Vector3;
class EulerAngles;
class Quaternion;

//---------------------------------------------------------------------------
// class RotationMatrix
//
```

```
// Implement a simple 3x3 matrix that is used for ROTATION ONLY. The
// matrix is assumed to be orthogonal. The direction of transformation
// is specified at the time of transformation.

class RotationMatrix {
public:

// Public data

        // The 9 values of the matrix. See RotationMatrix.cpp file for
        // the details of the layout

        float m11, m12, m13;
        float m21, m22, m23;
        float m31, m32, m33;

// Public operations

        // Set to identity

        void   identity();

        // Setup the matrix with a specified orientation

        void   setup(const EulerAngles &orientation);

        // Setup the matrix from a quaternion, assuming the
        // quaternion performs the rotation in the
        // specified direction of transformation

        void   fromInertialToObjectQuaternion(const Quaternion &q);
        void   fromObjectToInertialQuaternion(const Quaternion &q);

        // Perform rotations

        Vector3     inertialToObject(const Vector3 &v) const;
        Vector3     objectToInertial(const Vector3 &v) const;
};

///////////////////////////////////////////////////////////////////////
#endif // #ifndef __ROTATIONMATRIX_H_INCLUDED__
```

Because of its tight focus, class RotationMatrix is extremely easy to use. First, we set up the matrix using Euler angles or a quaternion. If we are using a quaternion, then we must specify which sort of angular displacement the quaternion represents. Once we have created the matrix, we perform rotations using the `inertialToObject()` and `objectToInertial()` functions.

The implementation for class `RotationMatrix` is in RotationMatrix.cpp. The full listing is below:

Listing 11.7: RotationMatrix.cpp

```
///////////////////////////////////////////////////////////////////////
//
// 3D Math Primer for Graphics and Game Development
//
// RotationMatrix.cpp - Implementation of class RotationMatrix
//
// Visit gamemath.com for the latest version of this file.
```

```
//
// For more details see section 11.4.
//
/////////////////////////////////////////////////////////////////////

#include "vector3.h"
#include "RotationMatrix.h"
#include "MathUtil.h"
#include "Quaternion.h"
#include "EulerAngles.h"


/////////////////////////////////////////////////////////////////////
//
// class RotationMatrix
//
//-------------------------------------------------------------------
//
// MATRIX ORGANIZATION
//
// A user of this class should rarely care how the matrix is organized.
// However, it is, of course, important that internally we keep everything
// straight.
//
// The matrix is assumed to be a rotation matrix only and, therefore,
// orthogonal. The "forward" direction of transformation (if that really
// even applies in this case) will be from inertial to object space.
// To perform an object->inertial rotation, we will multiply by the
// transpose.
//
// In other words:
//
// Inertial to object:
//
//                  | m11 m12 m13 |
//      [ ix iy iz ]| m21 m22 m23 | = [ ox oy oz ]
//                  | m31 m32 m33 |
//
// Object to inertial:
//
//                  | m11 m21 m31 |
//      [ ox oy oz ]| m12 m22 m32 | = [ ix iy iz ]
//                  | m13 m23 m33 |
//
// Or, using column vector notation:
//
// Inertial to object:
//
//      | m11 m21 m31 | | ix |   | ox |
//      | m12 m22 m32 | | iy | = | oy |
//      | m13 m23 m33 | | iz |   | oz |
//
// Object to inertial:
//
//      | m11 m12 m13 | | ox |   | ix |
//      | m21 m22 m23 | | oy | = | iy |
//      | m31 m32 m33 | | oz |   | iz |
//
/////////////////////////////////////////////////////////////////////

//-------------------------------------------------------------------
```

```
// RotationMatrix::identity
//
// Set the matrix to the identity matrix

void  RotationMatrix::identity() {
     m11 = 1.0f; m12 = 0.0f; m13 = 0.0f;
     m21 = 0.0f; m22 = 1.0f; m23 = 0.0f;
     m31 = 0.0f; m32 = 0.0f; m33 = 1.0f;
}

//---------------------------------------------------------------------------
// RotationMatrix::setup
//
// Setup the matrix with the specified orientation
//
// See 10.6.1

void  RotationMatrix::setup(const EulerAngles &orientation) {

     // Fetch sine and cosine of angles

     float  sh,ch, sp,cp, sb,cb;
     sinCos(&sh, &ch, orientation.heading);
     sinCos(&sp, &cp, orientation.pitch);
     sinCos(&sb, &cb, orientation.bank);

     // Fill in the matrix elements

     m11 = ch * cb + sh * sp * sb;
     m12 = -ch * sb + sh * sp * cb;
     m13 = sh * cp;

     m21 = sb * cp;
     m22 = cb * cp;
     m23 = -sp;

     m31 = -sh * cb + ch * sp * sb;
     m32 = sb * sh + ch * sp * cb;
     m33 = ch * cp;
}

//---------------------------------------------------------------------------
// RotationMatrix::fromInertialToObjectQuaternion
//
// Setup the matrix, given a quaternion that performs an inertial->object
// rotation
//
// See 10.6.3

void  RotationMatrix::fromInertialToObjectQuaternion(const Quaternion &q) {

     // Fill in the matrix elements.  This could possibly be
     // optimized, since there are many common subexpressions.
     // We'll leave that up to the compiler...

     m11 = 1.0f - 2.0f * (q.y*q.y + q.z*q.z);
     m12 = 2.0f * (q.x*q.y + q.w*q.z);
     m13 = 2.0f * (q.x*q.z - q.w*q.y);

     m21 = 2.0f * (q.x*q.y - q.w*q.z);
```

```
        m22 = 1.0f - 2.0f * (q.x*q.x + q.z*q.z);
        m23 = 2.0f * (q.y*q.z + q.w*q.x);

        m31 = 2.0f * (q.x*q.z + q.w*q.y);
        m32 = 2.0f * (q.y*q.z - q.w*q.x);
        m33 = 1.0f - 2.0f * (q.x*q.x + q.y*q.y);

}


//---------------------------------------------------------------------------
// RotationMatrix::fromObjectToInertialQuaternion
//
// Setup the matrix, given a quaternion that performs an object->inertial
// rotation
//
// See 10.6.3

void  RotationMatrix::fromObjectToInertialQuaternion(const Quaternion &q) {

        // Fill in the matrix elements.  This could possibly be
        // optimized since there are many common subexpressions.
        // We'll leave that up to the compiler...

        m11 = 1.0f - 2.0f * (q.y*q.y + q.z*q.z);
        m12 = 2.0f * (q.x*q.y - q.w*q.z);
        m13 = 2.0f * (q.x*q.z + q.w*q.y);

        m21 = 2.0f * (q.x*q.y + q.w*q.z);
        m22 = 1.0f - 2.0f * (q.x*q.x + q.z*q.z);
        m23 = 2.0f * (q.y*q.z - q.w*q.x);

        m31 = 2.0f * (q.x*q.z - q.w*q.y);
        m32 = 2.0f * (q.y*q.z + q.w*q.x);
        m33 = 1.0f - 2.0f * (q.x*q.x + q.y*q.y);
}

//---------------------------------------------------------------------------
// RotationMatrix::inertialToObject
//
// Rotate a vector from inertial to object space

Vector3    RotationMatrix::inertialToObject(const Vector3 &v) const {

        // Perform the matrix multiplication in the "standard" way.

        return Vector3(
                m11*v.x + m21*v.y + m31*v.z,
                m12*v.x + m22*v.y + m32*v.z,
                m13*v.x + m23*v.y + m33*v.z
        );
}

//---------------------------------------------------------------------------
// RotationMatrix::objectToInertial
//
// Rotate a vector from object to inertial space

Vector3    RotationMatrix::objectToInertial(const Vector3 &v) const {
```

```
        // Multiply by the transpose

        return Vector3(
                m11*v.x + m12*v.y + m13*v.z,
                m21*v.x + m22*v.y + m23*v.z,
                m31*v.x + m32*v.y + m33*v.z
        );
}
```

11.5 Class Matrix4×3

Class `RotationMatrix` is extremely useful for the very specific purpose for which it was designed. However, it is very limited. Class `Matrix4×3` is a more general-purpose matrix class designed to handle more complicated transformations. This matrix class stores a general affine transformation matrix. Rotation, scale, skew, reflection, projection, and translation are all supported. Matrices can be inverted and concatenated.

Because of this, the semantics of class `Matrix4×3` are different from class `RotationMatrix`. Whereas class `RotationMatrix` applies specifically to object space and inertial space, class `Matrix4×3` will have more general application, so we will use the more generic terms "source" and "destination" coordinate space instead. Unlike class `Rotation-Matrix`, the direction of transformation is specified when the matrix is created, and then points may only be transformed in that direction (from source to destination). If you need to transform in the other direction, you must compute the inverse of the matrix.

We use linear algebra notation for the multiplications. `operator*()` is used both to transform points and to concatenate matrices. Since our convention is to use row vectors rather than column vectors, the order of transformations reads like a sentence from left to right.

Class `Matrix4×3` is defined in Matrix4×3.h. The full listing is below:

Listing 11.8: Matrix4×3.h

```
/////////////////////////////////////////////////////////////////////////////
//
// 3D Math Primer for Graphics and Game Development
//
// Matrix4×3.h - Declarations for class Matrix4×3
//
// Visit gamemath.com for the latest version of this file.
//
// For more details, see Matrix4×3.cpp
//
/////////////////////////////////////////////////////////////////////////////

#ifndef __MATRIX4×3_H_INCLUDED__
#define __MATRIX4×3_H_INCLUDED__

class Vector3;
class EulerAngles;
class Quaternion;
class RotationMatrix;

//-------------------------------------------------------------------------
```

```
// class Matrix4×3
//
// Implement a 4×3 transformation matrix. This class can represent
// any 3D affine transformation.

class Matrix4×3 {
public:

// Public data

        // The values of the matrix. Basically, the upper 3×3 portion
        // contains a linear transformation, and the last row is the
        // translation portion. See the Matrix4×3.cpp for more
        // details.

        float  m11, m12, m13;
        float  m21, m22, m23;
        float  m31, m32, m33;
        float  tx,  ty,  tz;

// Public operations

        // Set to identity

        void   identity();

        // Access the translation portion of the matrix directly

        void   zeroTranslation();
        void   setTranslation(const Vector3 &d);
        void   setupTranslation(const Vector3 &d);

        // Setup the matrix to perform a specific transforms from parent <->
        // local space, assuming the local space is in the specified position
        // and orientation within the parent space. The orientation may be
        // specified using either Euler angles or a rotation matrix

        void   setupLocalToParent(const Vector3 &pos, const EulerAngles &orient);
        void   setupLocalToParent(const Vector3 &pos, const RotationMatrix &orient);
        void   setupParentToLocal(const Vector3 &pos, const EulerAngles &orient);
        void   setupParentToLocal(const Vector3 &pos, const RotationMatrix &orient);

        // Setup the matrix to perform a rotation about a cardinal axis

        void   setupRotate(int axis, float theta);

        // Setup the matrix to perform a rotation about an arbitrary axis

        void   setupRotate(const Vector3 &axis, float theta);

        // Setup the matrix to perform a rotation, given
        // the angular displacement in quaternion form

        void   fromQuaternion(const Quaternion &q);

        // Setup the matrix to perform scale on each axis

        void   setupScale(const Vector3 &s);
```

```
        // Setup the matrix to perform scale along an arbitrary axis

        void  setupScaleAlongAxis(const Vector3 &axis, float k);

        // Setup the matrix to perform a shear

        void  setupShear(int axis, float s, float t);

        // Setup the matrix to perform a projection onto a plane passing
        // through the origin

        void  setupProject(const Vector3 &n);

        // Setup the matrix to perform a reflection about a plane parallel
        // to a cardinal plane

        void  setupReflect(int axis, float k = 0.0f);

        // Setup the matrix to perform a reflection about an arbitrary plane
        // through the origin

        void  setupReflect(const Vector3 &n);
};

// Operator * is used to transform a point, and it also concatenates matrices.
// The order of multiplications from left to right is the same as
// the order of transformations

Vector3     operator *(const Vector3 &p, const Matrix4×3 &m);
Matrix4×3   operator *(const Matrix4×3 &a, const Matrix4×3 &b);

// Operator *= for conformance to C++ standards

Vector3     &operator *=(Vector3 &p, const Matrix4×3 &m);
Matrix4×3   &operator *=(const Matrix4×3 &a, const Matrix4×3 &m);

// Compute the determinant of the 3×3 portion of the matrix

float determinant(const Matrix4×3 &m);

// Compute the inverse of a matrix

Matrix4×3 inverse(const Matrix4×3 &m);

// Extract the translation portion of the matrix

Vector3     getTranslation(const Matrix4×3 &m);

// Extract the position/orientation from a local->parent matrix,
// or a parent->local matrix

Vector3     getPositionFromParentToLocalMatrix(const Matrix4×3 &m);
Vector3     getPositionFromLocalToParentMatrix(const Matrix4×3 &m);

/////////////////////////////////////////////////////////////////////////////
#endif // #ifndef __ROTATIONMATRIX_H_INCLUDED__
```

Let's look at the functionality provided by this class. Hopefully, the function names and comments make elaboration unnecessary, but let's review just for the sake of clarity.

All of the member functions in class `Matrix4×3` are designed to set up the matrix with a primitive transformation:

- `identity()` sets the matrix to the identity matrix.

- `zeroTranslation()` removes the translation portion of the matrix by setting the last row to [0,0,0], leaving the linear translation portion (the 3×3 portion) unaffected. `setTranslation()` sets the translation portion of the matrix to the specified value, without changing the 3×3 portion. `setupTranslation()` sets up the matrix to perform a translation; the upper 3×3 portion is set to identity, and the translation row is set to the vector specified.

- `setupLocalToParent()` creates a matrix that can be used to transform points from a "local" coordinate space to its "parent" coordinate space, given the position and orientation of the local space within the parent space. The most common use of this function will probably be to transform points from object space to world space, but these terms were not used since other types of nested relationships work as well. The orientation of the local space can be specified using either Euler angles or a rotation matrix. The rotation matrix version is faster, since no real math is necessary, only the copying of matrix elements. `setupParent-ToLocal()` sets up the matrix to perform the exact opposite transformation.

- Both overloads of `setupRotate()` create a matrix to rotate about an axis. If the axis is a cardinal axis, then an integer axis number may be used. As documented in the .cpp file, 1 specifies the x-axis, 2 specifies the y-axis, and 3 specifies the z-axis. To rotate about an arbitrarily oriented axis, use the second version of `setupRotate()`, which specifies the axis of rotation using a unit vector.

- `fromQuaternion()` converts a quaternion to matrix form. The translation portion of the matrix is zeroed.

- `setupScale()` creates a matrix that performs uniform or non-uniform scale along the cardinal axes. The input vector contains the scale factors on the x-, y-, and z-axes. For uniform scale, simply use a vector with the same value for each axis.

- `setupScaleAlongAxis()` creates a matrix which scales in an arbitrary direction. The scale occurs about a plane through the origin — the plane is perpendicular to the vector parameter, which must be normalized.

- `setupShear()` creates a shear matrix. See the comments near the implementation of this function for the details of the parameters.

- `setupProject()` creates a matrix to project orthographically onto the plane through the origin that is perpendicular to the given normal vector.

- `setupReflect()` creates a matrix to reflect about a plane. In the first version, a cardinal axis is specified by integer index, and the plane does not necessarily have to pass through the origin. For the second version, an arbitrary normal may be specified, but the plane must pass through the origin. (For a reflection about an arbitrary plane that *doesn't* pass through the origin, you must concatenate this matrix with the appropriate translation matrices.)

As we have mentioned, the actual transformation operation is performed using `operator*()`, according to linear algebra notation. Matrix concatenation also uses this syntax.

The `determinant()` function computes the determinant of the matrix. Only the 3×3 portion is actually used. If we assume a rightmost column of $[0,0,0,1]^T$, then the last row (the translation portion) is canceled out by the first three 0's of this assumed rightmost column.

`inverse()` computes and returns the inverse of a matrix. As we noted in the source comments, it is not technically possible to invert a 4×3 matrix, since only square matrices can be inverted. Once again, assuming a rightmost column of $[0,0,0,1]^T$ will circumvent these legalities.

`getTranslation()` is a handy shorthand function for extracting the translation portion of a matrix in vector form.

`getPositionFromLocalToParentMatrix()` and `getPositionFromParent-ToLocalMatrix()` are functions (with extremely long names) that extract the position of a local coordinate space within a parent coordinate space, given a matrix that performs the specified transformation. In a way, these functions reverse-engineer the position part of `setupLocalTo-Parent()` and `setupparentToLocal()`. Of course, you can call `getPosition-FromLocalToParentMatrix()` and `getPositionFromParentToLocalMatrix()` on *any* matrix (provided that it is a rigid body transform), not just a matrix that was created using `setupLocalToParent()` or `setupParentToLocal()`. To extract the orientation from a transform matrix in Euler angle form, use one of the member functions in class `EulerAngles`.

Class `Matrix4×3` is implemented in Matrix4×3.cpp. The full listing is below:

Listing 11.9: Matrix4×3.cpp

```
/////////////////////////////////////////////////////////////////////////////
//
// 3D Math Primer for Graphics and Game Development
//
// Matrix4×3.cpp - Implementation of class Matrix4×3
//
// Visit gamemath.com for the latest version of this file.
//
// For more details see section 11.5.
//
/////////////////////////////////////////////////////////////////////////////

#include <assert.h>
#include <math.h>

#include "Vector3.h"
#include "EulerAngles.h"
#include "Quaternion.h"
#include "RotationMatrix.h"
#include "Matrix4×3.h"
#include "MathUtil.h"

/////////////////////////////////////////////////////////////////////////////
//
// Notes:
//
// See Chapter 11 for more information on class design decisions.
//
//-------------------------------------------------------------------------
//// MATRIX ORGANIZATION
//
// The purpose of this class is so that a user might perform transformations
```

```
// without fiddling with plus or minus signs or transposing the matrix
// until the output "looks right." Of course, the specifics of the
// internal representation is important, not only for the implementation
// in this file to be correct, but occasionally direct access to the
// matrix variables is necessary, or beneficial for optimization. Thus,
// we document our matrix conventions here.
//
// We use row vectors, so multiplying by our matrix looks like this:
//
//                  | m11 m12 m13 |
//      [ x y z ]   | m21 m22 m23 | = [ x' y' z' ]
//                  | m31 m32 m33 |
//                  | tx   ty   tz  |
//
// Strict adherance to linear algebra rules dictates that this
// multiplication is actually undefined. To circumvent this, we can
// consider the input and output vectors as having an assumed fourth
// coordinate of 1. Also, since we cannot technically invert a 4×3 matrix
// according to linear algebra rules, we will also assume a rightmost
// column of [ 0 0 0 1 ]. This is shown below:
//
//                  | m11 m12 m13 0 |
//      [ x y z 1 ] | m21 m22 m23 0 | = [ x' y' z' 1 ]
//                  | m31 m32 m33 0 |
//                  |  tx   ty   tz 1 |
//
// In case you have forgotten your linear algebra rules for multiplying
// matrices (which are described in section 7.1.6 and 7.1.7), see the
// definition of operator * for the expanded computations.
//
/////////////////////////////////////////////////////////////////////////

/////////////////////////////////////////////////////////////////////////
//
// Matrix4×3 class members
//
/////////////////////////////////////////////////////////////////////////

//-----------------------------------------------------------------------
// Matrix4×3::identity
//
// Set the matrix to identity

void  Matrix4×3::identity() {
      m11 = 1.0f; m12 = 0.0f; m13 = 0.0f;
      m21 = 0.0f; m22 = 1.0f; m23 = 0.0f;
      m31 = 0.0f; m32 = 0.0f; m33 = 1.0f;
      tx  = 0.0f; ty  = 0.0f; tz  = 1.0f;
}

//-----------------------------------------------------------------------
// Matrix4×3::zeroTranslation
//
// Zero the fourth row of the matrix, which contains the translation portion.

void  Matrix4×3::zeroTranslation() {
      tx = ty = tz = 0.0f;
}

//-----------------------------------------------------------------------
```

```
// Matrix4×3::setTranslation
//
// Sets the translation portion of the matrix in vector form

void  Matrix4×3::setTranslation(const Vector3 &d) {
    tx = d.x; ty = d.y; tz = d.z;
}

//---------------------------------------------------------------------------
// Matrix4×3::setTranslation
//
// Sets the translation portion of the matrix in vector form

void  Matrix4×3::setupTranslation(const Vector3 &d) {

    // Set the linear transformation portion to identity

    m11 = 1.0f; m12 = 0.0f; m13 = 0.0f;
    m21 = 0.0f; m22 = 1.0f; m23 = 0.0f;
    m31 = 0.0f; m32 = 0.0f; m33 = 1.0f;

    // Set the translation portion

    tx = d.x; ty = d.y; tz = d.z;
}

//---------------------------------------------------------------------------
// Matrix4×3::setupLocalToParent
//
// Setup the matrix to perform a local -> parent transformation, given
// the position and orientation of the local reference frame within the
// parent reference frame.
//
// A very common use of this will be to construct an object -> world matrix.
// As an example, the transformation in this case is straightforward. We
// first rotate from object space into inertial space, and then we translate
// into world space.
//
// We allow the orientation to be specified using either Euler angles,
// or a RotationMatrix

void  Matrix4×3::setupLocalToParent(const Vector3 &pos, const EulerAngles &orient) {

    // Create a rotation matrix.

    RotationMatrix orientMatrix;
    orientMatrix.setup(orient);

    // Setup the 4×3 matrix. Note: if we were really concerned with
    // speed, we could create the matrix directly into these variables,
    // without using the temporary RotationMatrix object. This would
    // save us a function call and a few copy operations.

    setupLocalToParent(pos, orientMatrix);
}

void  Matrix4×3::setupLocalToParent(const Vector3 &pos, const RotationMatrix &orient) {

    // Copy the rotation portion of the matrix. According to
    // the comments in RotationMatrix.cpp, the rotation matrix
```

```
        // is "normally" an inertial->object matrix, which is
        // parent->local. We want a local->parent rotation, so we
        // must transpose while copying

        m11 = orient.m11; m12 = orient.m21; m13 = orient.m31;
        m21 = orient.m12; m22 = orient.m22; m23 = orient.m32;
        m31 = orient.m13; m32 = orient.m23; m33 = orient.m33;

        // Now set the translation portion. Translation happens "after"
        // the 3×3 portion, so we can simply copy the position
        // field directly

        tx = pos.x; ty = pos.y; tz = pos.z;
}


//---------------------------------------------------------------------------
// Matrix4×3::setupParentToLocal
//
// Setup the matrix to perform a parent -> local transformation, given
// the position and orientation of the local reference frame within the
// parent reference frame.
//
// A very common use of this will be to construct a world -> object matrix.
// To perform this transformation, we would normally first transform
// from world to inertial space and then rotate from inertial space into
// object space. However, our 4×3 matrix always translates last. So
// we think about creating two matrices T and R, and then concatenating
// M = TR.
//
// We allow the orientation to be specified using either Euler angles,
// or a RotationMatrix

void    Matrix4×3::setupParentToLocal(const Vector3 &pos, const EulerAngles &orient) {

        // Create a rotation matrix.

        RotationMatrix orientMatrix;
        orientMatrix.setup(orient);

        // Setup the 4×3 matrix.

        setupParentToLocal(pos, orientMatrix);
}

void    Matrix4×3::setupParentToLocal(const Vector3 &pos, const RotationMatrix &orient) {

        // Copy the rotation portion of the matrix. We can copy the
        // elements directly (without transposing), according
        // to the layout as commented in RotationMatrix.cpp

        m11 = orient.m11; m12 = orient.m12; m13 = orient.m13;
        m21 = orient.m21; m22 = orient.m22; m23 = orient.m23;
        m31 = orient.m31; m32 = orient.m32; m33 = orient.m33;

        // Now set the translation portion. Normally, we would
        // translate by the negative of the position to translate
        // from world to inertial space. However, we must correct
        // for the fact that the rotation occurs "first." So we
        // must rotate the translation portion. This is the same
        // as creating a translation matrix T to translate by -pos
```

```
            // and a rotation matrix R and then creating the matrix
            // as the concatenation of TR

            tx = -(pos.x*m11 + pos.y*m21 + pos.z*m31);
            ty = -(pos.x*m12 + pos.y*m22 + pos.z*m32);
            tz = -(pos.x*m13 + pos.y*m23 + pos.z*m33);
    }

    //---------------------------------------------------------------------------
    // Matrix4×3::setupRotate
    //
    // Setup the matrix to perform a rotation about a cardinal axis
    //
    // The axis of rotation is specified using a 1-based index:
    //
    //      1 => rotate about the x-axis
    //      2 => rotate about the y-axis
    //      3 => rotate about the z-axis
    //
    // Theta is the amount of rotation, in radians. The left-hand rule is
    // used to define "positive" rotation.
    //
    // The translation portion is reset.
    //
    // See 8.2.2 for more info.

    void    Matrix4×3::setupRotate(int axis, float theta) {

            // Get sin and cosine of rotation angle

            float s, c;
            sinCos(&s, &c, theta);

            // Check which axis they are rotating about

            switch (axis) {

                    case 1: // Rotate about the x-axis

                            m11 = 1.0f; m12 = 0.0f; m13 = 0.0f;
                            m21 = 0.0f; m22 = c;    m23 = s;
                            m31 = 0.0f; m32 = -s;   m33 = c;
                            break;

                    case 2: // Rotate about the y-axis

                            m11 = c;    m12 = 0.0f; m13 = -s;
                            m21 = 0.0f; m22 = 1.0f; m23 = 0.0f;
                            m31 = s;    m32 = 0.0f; m33 = c;
                            break;

                    case 3: // Rotate about the z-axis

                            m11 = c;    m12 = s;    m13 = 0.0f;
                            m21 = -s;   m22 = c;    m23 = 0.0f;
                            m31 = 0.0f; m32 = 0.0f; m33 = 1.0f;
                            break;

                    default:
```

```
                        // bogus axis index

                    assert(false);

        }

        // Reset the translation portion

        tx = ty = tz = 0.0f;
}

//---------------------------------------------------------------------------
// Matrix4×3::setupRotate
//
// Setup the matrix to perform a rotation about an arbitrary axis.
// The axis of rotation must pass through the origin.
//
// Axis defines the axis of rotation, and must be a unit vector.
//
// Theta is the amount of rotation, in radians. The left-hand rule is
// used to define "positive" rotation.
//
// The translation portion is reset.
//
// See 8.2.3 for more info.

void  Matrix4×3::setupRotate(const Vector3 &axis, float theta) {

        // Quick sanity check to make sure they passed in a unit vector
        // to specify the axis

        assert(fabs(axis*axis - 1.0f) < .01f);

        // Get sin and cosine of rotation angle

        float  s, c;
        sinCos(&s, &c, theta);

        // Compute 1 - cos(theta) and some common subexpressions

        float  a = 1.0f - c;
        float  ax = a * axis.x;
        float  ay = a * axis.y;
        float  az = a * axis.z;

        // Set the matrix elements. There is still a little more
        // opportunity for optimization due to the many common
        // subexpressions. We'll let the compiler handle that...

        m11 = ax*axis.x + c;
        m12 = ax*axis.y + axis.z*s;
        m13 = ax*axis.z - axis.y*s;

        m21 = ay*axis.x - axis.z*s;
        m22 = ay*axis.y + c;
        m23 = ay*axis.z + axis.x*s;

        m31 = az*axis.x + axis.y*s;
        m32 = az*axis.y - axis.x*s;
        m33 = az*axis.z + c;
```

```
        // Reset the translation portion

        tx = ty = tz = 0.0f;
}


//---------------------------------------------------------------------------
// Matrix4×3::fromQuaternion
//
// Setup the matrix to perform a rotation, given the angular displacement
// in quaternion form.
//
// The translation portion is reset.
//
// See 10.6.3 for more info.

void   Matrix4×3::fromQuaternion(const Quaternion &q) {

        // Compute a few values to optimize common subexpressions

        float  ww = 2.0f * q.w;
        float  xx = 2.0f * q.x;
        float  yy = 2.0f * q.y;
        float  zz = 2.0f * q.z;

        // Set the matrix elements. There is still a little more
        // opportunity for optimization due to the many common
        // subexpressions. We'll let the compiler handle that...

        m11 = 1.0f - yy*q.y - zz*q.z;
        m12 = xx*q.y + ww*q.z;
        m13 = xx*q.z - ww*q.x;

        m21 = xx*q.y - ww*q.z;
        m22 = 1.0f - xx*q.x - zz*q.z;
        m23 = yy*q.z + ww*q.x;

        m31 = xx*q.z + ww*q.y;
        m32 = yy*q.z - ww*q.x;
        m33 = 1.0f - xx*q.x - yy*q.y;

        // Reset the translation portion

        tx = ty = tz = 0.0f;
}


//---------------------------------------------------------------------------
// Matrix4×3::setupScale
//
// Setup the matrix to perform scale on each axis. For uniform scale by k,
// use a vector of the form Vector3(k,k,k)
//
// The translation portion is reset.
//
// See 8.3.1 for more info.

void   Matrix4×3::setupScale(const Vector3 &s) {

        // Set the matrix elements. Pretty straightforward:

        m11 = s.x;  m12 = 0.0f; m13 = 0.0f;
```

```
        m21 = 0.0f; m22 = s.y;  m23 = 0.0f;
        m31 = 0.0f; m32 = 0.0f; m33 = s.z;

        // Reset the translation portion

        tx = ty = tz = 0.0f;
}


//---------------------------------------------------------------------------
// Matrix4×3::setupScaleAlongAxis
//
// Setup the matrix to perform scale along an arbitrary axis.
//
// The axis is specified using a unit vector.
//
// The translation portion is reset.
//
// See 8.3.2 for more info.

void  Matrix4×3::setupScaleAlongAxis(const Vector3 &axis, float k) {

        // Quick sanity check to make sure they passed in a unit vector
        // to specify the axis

        assert(fabs(axis*axis - 1.0f) < .01f);

        // Compute k-1 and some common subexpressions

        float  a = k - 1.0f;
        float  ax = a * axis.x;
        float  ay = a * axis.y;
        float  az = a * axis.z;

        // Fill in the matrix elements. We'll do the common
        // subexpression optimization ourselves here, since diagonally
        // opposite matrix elements are equal

        m11 = ax*axis.x + 1.0f;
        m22 = ay*axis.y + 1.0f;
        m32 = az*axis.z + 1.0f;

        m12 = m21 = ax*axis.y;
        m13 = m31 = ax*axis.z;
        m23 = m32 = ay*axis.z;

        // Reset the translation portion

        tx = ty = tz = 0.0f;
}


//---------------------------------------------------------------------------
// Matrix4×3::setupShear
//
// Setup the matrix to perform a shear
//
// The type of shear is specified by the 1-based "axis" index. The effect
// of transforming a point by the matrix is described by the pseudocode
// below:
//
//     axis == 1  =>  y += s*x, z += t*x
```

```
//     axis == 2   =>   x += s*y, z += t*y
//     axis == 3   =>   x += s*z, y += t*z
//
// The translation portion is reset.
//
// See 8.6 for more info.

void   Matrix4x3::setupShear(int axis, float s, float t) {

      // Check which type of shear they want

      switch (axis) {

            case 1: // Shear y and z using x

                  m11 = 1.0f; m12 = s;    m13 = t;
                  m21 = 0.0f; m22 = 1.0f; m23 = 0.0f;
                  m31 = 0.0f; m32 = 0.0f; m33 = 1.0f;
                  break;

            case 2: // Shear x and z using y

                  m11 = 1.0f; m12 = 0.0f; m13 = 0.0f;
                  m21 = s;    m22 = 1.0f; m23 = t;
                  m31 = 0.0f; m32 = 0.0f; m33 = 1.0f;
                  break;

            case 3: // Shear x and y using z

                  m11 = 1.0f; m12 = 0.0f; m13 = 0.0f;
                  m21 = 0.0f; m22 = 1.0f; m23 = 0.0f;
                  m31 = s;    m32 = t;    m33 = 1.0f;
                  break;

            default:

                  // bogus axis index

                  assert(false);
      }

      // Reset the translation portion

      tx = ty = tz = 0.0f;
}

//---------------------------------------------------------------------------
// Matrix4x3::setupProject
//
// Setup the matrix to perform a projection onto a plane passing
// through the origin. The plane is perpendicular to the
// unit vector n.
//
// See 8.4.2 for more info.

void   Matrix4x3::setupProject(const Vector3 &n) {

      // Quick sanity check to make sure they passed in a unit vector
      // to specify the axis
```

```
        assert(fabs(n*n - 1.0f) < .01f);

        // Fill in the matrix elements. We'll do the common
        // subexpression optimization ourselves here, since diagonally
        // opposite matrix elements are equal

        m11 = 1.0f - n.x*n.x;
        m22 = 1.0f - n.y*n.y;
        m33 = 1.0f - n.z*n.z;

        m12 = m21 = -n.x*n.y;
        m13 = m31 = -n.x*n.z;
        m23 = m32 = -n.y*n.z;

        // Reset the translation portion

        tx = ty = tz = 0.0f;
}

//---------------------------------------------------------------------------
// Matrix4×3::setupReflect
//
// Setup the matrix to perform a reflection about a plane parallel
// to a cardinal plane.
//
// Axis is a 1-based index, which specifies the plane to project about:
//
//      1 => reflect about the plane x=k
//      2 => reflect about the plane y=k
//      3 => reflect about the plane z=k
//
// The translation is set appropriately, since translation must occur if
// k != 0
//
// See 8.5 for more info.

void   Matrix4×3::setupReflect(int axis, float k) {

        // Check which plane they want to reflect about

        switch (axis) {

                case 1: // Reflect about the plane x=k

                        m11 = -1.0f; m12 =  0.0f; m13 =  0.0f;
                        m21 =  0.0f; m22 =  1.0f; m23 =  0.0f;
                        m31 =  0.0f; m32 =  0.0f; m33 =  1.0f;

                        tx = 2.0f * k;
                        ty = 0.0f;
                        tz = 0.0f;

                        break;

                case 2: // Reflect about the plane y=k

                        m11 =  1.0f; m12 =  0.0f; m13 =  0.0f;
                        m21 =  0.0f; m22 = -1.0f; m23 =  0.0f;
                        m31 =  0.0f; m32 =  0.0f; m33 =  1.0f;
```

```
                            tx = 0.0f;
                            ty = 2.0f * k;
                            tz = 0.0f;

                            break;

                    case 3: // Reflect about the plane z=k

                            m11 =   1.0f; m12 =   0.0f; m13 =   0.0f;
                            m21 =   0.0f; m22 =   1.0f; m23 =   0.0f;
                            m31 =   0.0f; m32 =   0.0f; m33 =  -1.0f;

                            tx = 0.0f;
                            ty = 0.0f;
                            tz = 2.0f * k;

                            break;

                    default:

                            // bogus axis index

                            assert(false);

            }

    }

//---------------------------------------------------------------------------
// Matrix4×3::setupReflect
//
// Setup the matrix to perform a reflection about an arbitrary plane
// through the origin.  The unit vector n is perpendicular to the plane.
//
// The translation portion is reset.
//
// See 8.5 for more info.

void   Matrix4×3::setupReflect(const Vector3 &n) {

        // Quick sanity check to make sure they passed in a unit vector
        // to specify the axis

        assert(fabs(n*n - 1.0f) < .01f);

        // Compute common subexpressions

        float  ax = -2.0f * n.x;
        float  ay = -2.0f * n.y;
        float  az = -2.0f * n.z;

        // Fill in the matrix elements. We'll do the common
        // subexpression optimization ourselves here, since diagonally
        // opposite matrix elements are equal

        m11 = 1.0f + ax*n.x;
        m22 = 1.0f + ay*n.y;
        m32 = 1.0f + az*n.z;

        m12 = m21 = ax*n.y;
        m13 = m31 = ax*n.z;
```

```
        m23 = m32 = ay*n.z;

        // Reset the translation portion

        tx = ty = tz = 0.0f;
}

//----------------------------------------------------------------------
// Vector * Matrix4×3
//
// Transform the point. This makes using the vector class look like it
// does with linear algebra notation on paper.
//
// We also provide a *= operator, as per C convention.
//
// See 7.1.7


Vector3        operator*(const Vector3 &p, const Matrix4×3 &m) {

        // Grind through the linear algebra.

        return Vector3(
                p.x*m.m11 + p.y*m.m21 + p.z*m.m31 + m.tx,
                p.x*m.m12 + p.y*m.m22 + p.z*m.m32 + m.ty,
                p.x*m.m13 + p.y*m.m23 + p.z*m.m33 + m.tz
        );
}

Vector3 &operator*=(Vector3 &p, const Matrix4×3 &m) {
        p = p * m;
        return p;
}

//----------------------------------------------------------------------
// Matrix4×3 * Matrix4×3
//
// Matrix concatenation. This makes using the vector class look like it
// does with linear algebra notation on paper.
//
// We also provide a *= operator, as per C convention.
//
// See 7.1.6

Matrix4×3 operator*(const Matrix4×3 &a, const Matrix4×3 &b) {

        Matrix4×3 r;

        // Compute the upper 3×3 (linear transformation) portion

        r.m11 = a.m11*b.m11 + a.m12*b.m21 + a.m13*b.m31;
        r.m12 = a.m11*b.m12 + a.m12*b.m22 + a.m13*b.m32;
        r.m13 = a.m11*b.m13 + a.m12*b.m23 + a.m13*b.m33;

        r.m21 = a.m21*b.m11 + a.m22*b.m21 + a.m23*b.m31;
        r.m22 = a.m21*b.m12 + a.m22*b.m22 + a.m23*b.m32;
        r.m23 = a.m21*b.m13 + a.m22*b.m23 + a.m23*b.m33;

        r.m31 = a.m31*b.m11 + a.m32*b.m21 + a.m33*b.m31;
        r.m32 = a.m31*b.m12 + a.m32*b.m22 + a.m33*b.m32;
```

```
        r.m33 = a.m31*b.m13 + a.m32*b.m23 + a.m33*b.m33;

        // Compute the translation portion

        r.tx = a.tx*b.m11 + a.ty*b.m21 + a.tz*b.m31 + b.tx;
        r.ty = a.tx*b.m12 + a.ty*b.m22 + a.tz*b.m32 + b.ty;
        r.tz = a.tx*b.m13 + a.ty*b.m23 + a.tz*b.m33 + b.tz;

        // Return it. Ouch - involves a copy constructor call. If speed
        // is critical, we may need a separate function which places the
        // result where we want it...

        return r;
}

Matrix4x3 &operator*=(Matrix4x3 &a, const Matrix4x3 &b) {
        a = a * b;
        return a;
}

//-------------------------------------------------------------------------
// determinant
//
c// Compute the determinant of the 3x3 portion of the matrix.
//
// See 9.1.1 for more info.

float determinant(const Matrix4x3 &m) {
        return
                  m.m11 * (m.m22*m.m33 - m.m23*m.m32)
                + m.m12 * (m.m23*m.m31 - m.m21*m.m33)
                + m.m13 * (m.m21*m.m32 - m.m22*m.m31);
}

//-------------------------------------------------------------------------
// inverse
//
// Compute the inverse of a matrix. We use the classical adjoint divided
// by the determinant method.
//
// See 9.2.1 for more info.

Matrix4x3 inverse(const Matrix4x3 &m) {

        // Compute the determinant

        float det = determinant(m);

        // If we're singular, then the determinant is zero and there's
        // no inverse

        assert(fabs(det) > 0.000001f);

        // Compute one over the determinant, so we divide once and
        // can *multiply* per element

        float oneOverDet = 1.0f / det;

        // Compute the 3x3 portion of the inverse, by
```

```
        // dividing the adjoint by the determinant

        Matrix4×3   r;

        r.m11 = (m.m22*m.m33 - m.m23*m.m32) * oneOverDet;
        r.m12 = (m.m13*m.m32 - m.m12*m.m33) * oneOverDet;
        r.m13 = (m.m12*m.m23 - m.m13*m.m22) * oneOverDet;

        r.m21 = (m.m23*m.m31 - m.m21*m.m33) * oneOverDet;
        r.m22 = (m.m11*m.m33 - m.m13*m.m31) * oneOverDet;
        r.m23 = (m.m13*m.m21 - m.m11*m.m23) * oneOverDet;

        r.m31 = (m.m21*m.m32 - m.m22*m.m31) * oneOverDet;
        r.m32 = (m.m12*m.m31 - m.m11*m.m32) * oneOverDet;
        r.m33 = (m.m11*m.m22 - m.m12*m.m21) * oneOverDet;

        // Compute the translation portion of the inverse

        r.tx = -(m.tx*r.m11 + m.ty*r.m21 + m.tz*r.m31);
        r.ty = -(m.tx*r.m12 + m.ty*r.m22 + m.tz*r.m32);
        r.tz = -(m.tx*r.m13 + m.ty*r.m23 + m.tz*r.m33);

        // Return it. Ouch - involves a copy constructor call. If speed
        // is critical, we may need a seperate function which places the
        // result where we want it...

        return r;
}

//---------------------------------------------------------------------------
// getTranslation
//
// Return the translation row of the matrix in vector form

Vector3     getTranslation(const Matrix4×3 &m) {
        return Vector3(m.tx, m.ty, m.tz);
}

//---------------------------------------------------------------------------
// getPositionFromParentToLocalMatrix
//
// Extract the position of an object given a parent -> local transformation
// matrix (such as a world -> object matrix)
//
// We assume that the matrix represents a rigid transformation. (No scale,
// skew, or mirroring)

Vector3     getPositionFromParentToLocalMatrix(const Matrix4×3 &m) {

        // Multiply negative translation value by the
        // transpose of the 3×3 portion. By using the transpose,
        // we assume that the matrix is orthogonal. (This function
        // doesn't really make sense for non-rigid transformations...)

        return Vector3(
                -(m.tx*m.m11 + m.ty*m.m12 + m.tz*m.m13),
                -(m.tx*m.m21 + m.ty*m.m22 + m.tz*m.m23),
                -(m.tx*m.m31 + m.ty*m.m32 + m.tz*m.m33)
```

```
        );
}

//---------------------------------------------------------------------------
// getPositionFromLocalToParentMatrix
//
// Extract the position of an object given a local -> parent transformation
// matrix (such as an object -> world matrix)

Vector3     getPositionFromLocalToParentMatrix(const Matrix4×3 &m) {

        // Position is simply the translation portion

        return Vector3(m.tx, m.ty, m.tz);
}
```

Chapter 12
Geometric Primitives

This chapter discusses the fundamental properties of many different geometric primitives. It is divided into seven sections:

- Section 12.1 discusses methods for representing primitives in general.
- Section 12.2 discusses lines and rays.
- Section 12.3 discusses spheres and circles.
- Section 12.4 discusses bounding boxes.
- Section 12.5 discusses planes.
- Section 12.6 discusses triangles.
- Section 12.7 discusses polygons.

This chapter is about geometric primitives in general and specifically. First, we will discuss some general principles related to representing geometric primitives. We will also cover a number of specific important geometric primitives. We will talk about how to represent those primitives and some important properties and operations. However, this chapter is not all theory. Along the way, we'll present some C++ code for representing primitives and performing the computations as they are discussed.

12.1 Representation Techniques

In this section, we will discuss representation techniques in general. For any given primitive, one or more of these techniques may be applicable. Different techniques are useful in different situations.

12.1.1 Implicit Form

We can represent an object *implicitly* by defining a Boolean function $f(x,y,z)$ that is true for all points of the primitive and false for all other points. For example, the equation

$$x^2 + y^2 + z^2 = 1$$

is true for all points on the surface of a unit sphere centered at the origin. Implicit form is sometimes useful for point inclusion tests and the like.

12.1.2 Parametric Form

An object may be represented *parametrically*. We'll begin with a simple 2D example. Let us define the following two functions of t:

$$x(t) = \cos 2\pi t$$
$$y(t) = \sin 2\pi t$$

The argument t is known as the *parameter* and is independent of the coordinate system used. As t varies from $0\ldots1$, the point $(x(t), y(t))$ traces out the outline of the shape we are describing. In this case, it is a unit circle centered at the origin. (See Figure 12.1.)

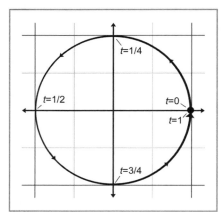

Figure 12.1: Parametric circle

It is often convenient to restrict the parameter in range $0\ldots1$, although we may allow t to assume any range of values we wish. Another common choice is $0\ldots l$, where l is the "length" of the primitive.

When our functions are in terms of one parameter, we say that the functions are *univariate*. Univariate functions trace out a curve. We may use more than one parameter. A *bivariate* function accepts two parameters, usually assigned to the variables s and t. Bivariate functions trace out a curved surface rather than a line.

12.1.3 "Straightforward" Forms

For lack of a better term, we have named this group of representation techniques "straightforward" forms. They vary depending on the type of primitive, and they usually capture the most important and obvious information directly. For example, to store a line segment, we could give two endpoints. For a sphere, we could give its center and radius. The straightforward forms are the easiest for humans to work with directly.

12.1.4 Degrees of Freedom

Each geometric primitive has an inherent number of *degrees of freedom*. This is the minimum number of "pieces of information" which are required to describe the entity unambiguously. It is interesting to notice that for the same geometric primitive, some representation forms use more numbers than others. However, we will always find that any "extra" numbers are always due to a redundancy in the parameterization of the primitive that could be eliminated by assuming the appropriate constraint, such as a vector having unit length.

12.2 Lines and Rays

In this section, we consider lines and rays in 2D and 3D. Terminology is very important here. In classical geometry, the following definitions are used:

- A *line* extends infinitely in two directions.
- A *line segment* is a finite portion of a line that has two endpoints.
- A *ray* is "half" of a line that has an origin and extends infinitely in one direction.

In computer science and computational geometry, there are variations on these definitions. In this book, we will use the classical definitions for "line" and "line segment." However, we will alter our definition of "ray" slightly:

- A *ray* is a directed line segment.

To us, a ray will have an origin and an endpoint. Thus, a ray defines a position, a finite length, and (unless the ray has zero length) a direction. Any ray also defines a line and a line segment (that contain the ray). Rays are of fundamental importance in computational geometry and graphics, and they will be the focus of this section. (See Figure 12.2.)

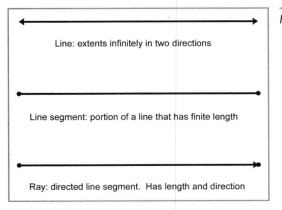

Figure 12.2: Line vs. line segment vs. ray

Line: extents infinitely in two directions

Line segment: portion of a line that has finite length

Ray: directed line segment. Has length and direction

12.2.1 Two Points Representation

The most obvious way to describe a ray is to give the two points that are the ray origin and the ray endpoint: $\mathbf{p}_{org}$ and $\mathbf{p}_{end}$.

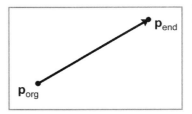

Figure 12.3: Defining a ray using the starting and ending points

12.2.2 Parametric Representation of Rays

A ray may be specified parametrically in 2D or 3D. A 2D ray is defined parametrically using the two functions:

Equation 12.1:
Parametric
definition of
a 2D ray

$$x(t) = x_0 + t\Delta x$$
$$y(t) = y_0 + t\Delta y$$

A 3D ray is a straightforward extension, adding a third function $z(t)$. We restrict the parameter t in range $0\ldots1$.

We may write the parametric equations for a ray more compactly using vector notation. This form applies in any dimension:

Equation 12.2:
Parametric
definition of a
ray using vector
notation

$$\mathbf{p}(t) = \mathbf{p}_0 + t\mathbf{d}$$

The ray starts at the point $\mathbf{p}(0) = \mathbf{p}_0$. Thus, $\mathbf{p}_0$ contains information about the *position* of the ray, while the "delta vector" $\mathbf{d}$ contains its length and direction. The ray ends at the point $\mathbf{p}(1) = \mathbf{p}_0 + \mathbf{d}$, as shown below.

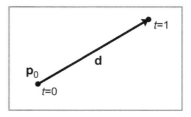

Figure 12.4: Defining a ray parametrically

A slight variation on Equation 12.2 that we will use in some of the intersection tests is to use a unit vector $\mathbf{d}$ and vary the parameter t from $0\ldots l$, where l is the length of the ray.

12.2.3 Special 2D Representations of Lines

In this section, we will describe some ways to describe (infinite) lines. These methods are only applicable in 2D. Similar techniques are used in 3D to define a plane. (See Section 12.5.)

In 2D, we may represent a line implicitly using the following equation:

Equation 12.3:
Implicit
definition of
infinite line
in 2D

$$ax + by = d$$

Note: Many sources use $ax + by + d = 0$. This flips the sign of d. We will use the form in Equation 12.3 because it has fewer terms.

Alternatively, we may assign the vector $\mathbf{n} = [a, b]$ and write Equation 12.3 using vector notation:

Equation 12.4:
Implicit
definition of
infinite 2D line
using vector
notation

$$\mathbf{p} \cdot \mathbf{n} = d$$

Multiplying both sides of the equation by any constant k scales $\mathbf{n}$ and d without changing the line defined. It is often convenient for $\mathbf{n}$ to be a unit vector. This gives $\mathbf{n}$ and d interesting geometric interpretations, which we will discuss later on in this section.

Alternatively, this equation can be manipulated to express the line in *slope-intercept* form:

Equation 12.5:
Slope-intercept
form

$$y = mx + b$$

m is the "slope" of the line, expressed as a ratio of *rise* over *run*: for every *rise* unit that we move up, we will move *run* units to the right. b is the *y-intercept*. (This is not the same b used in the first implicit form.) b is called the *y*-intercept because that's where the line crosses the *y*-axis. Substituting $x = 0$ clearly shows that the line crosses the *y-axis* at $y = b$, as shown in Figure 12.5.

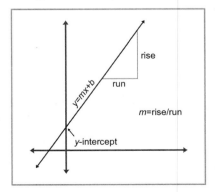

Figure 12.5: The slope and y-intercept of a line

The slope of a horizontal line is zero. A vertical line has infinite slope and cannot be represented in slope-intercept form since the implicit form of a vertical line is $x = k$.

Another way to specify a line is to give a normal vector **n** perpendicular to the line and the perpendicular distance d from the line to the origin. The normal describes the *direction* of the line, and the distance describes its *location*.

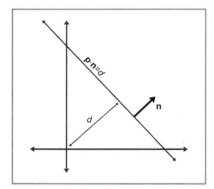

Figure 12.6: Defining a line using a perpendicular vector and distance to the origin

Note that this is just a special case of the implicit form from Equation 12.4. **n** is the unit vector normal to the line, and d gives the signed distance from the origin to the line. This distance is measured perpendicular to the line (parallel to **n**). By *signed distance*, we mean that d is positive if the line is on the same side of the origin as the normal points. As d increases, the line moves in the direction of **n**.

A variation on this theme is to describe the location of the line by giving a point **q** that is on the line, rather than the distance to the origin. Of course, any point will do. The direction of the line is described using a normal to the line **n,** as before.

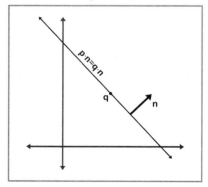

Figure 12.7: Defining a line using a perpendicular vector and a point on the line

One final way to define a line is as the perpendicular bisector of two points **q** and **r**, as shown in Figure 12.8. In fact, this is one of the earliest definitions of a line: the set of all points equidistant from two given points.

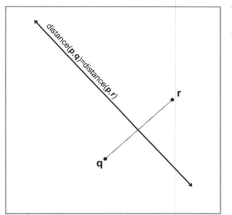

12.2.4 Converting between Representations

In this section, we give a few examples of how to convert a ray or line between the various representation techniques. We will not cover all of the combinations. Remember that the techniques we learned for infinite lines are only applicable in 2D.

To convert a ray defined using two points to parametric form:

$$\mathbf{p}_0 = \mathbf{p}_{org}$$
$$\mathbf{d} = \mathbf{p}_{end} - \mathbf{p}_{org}$$

The opposite conversion, from parametric form to two-points form:

$$\mathbf{p}_{org} = \mathbf{p}_0$$
$$\mathbf{p}_{end} = \mathbf{p}_0 + \mathbf{d}$$

Given a parametric ray, we can compute the implicit line that contains this ray:

$$a = \mathbf{d}_y$$
$$b = -\mathbf{d}_x$$
$$d = \mathbf{p}_{org_x}\mathbf{d}_y - \mathbf{p}_{org_y}\mathbf{d}_x$$

To convert a line expressed implicitly to slope-intercept form:

$$m = -a/b$$
$$b = d/b$$

Note that the b on the left side of the equal sign refers to the slope in the slope-intercept equation $y = mx + b$. The bs on the right side of the equal sign refer to the y coefficient in the implicit equation $ax + by = d$.

Converting a line expressed implicitly to "normal and distance" form:

$$\mathbf{n} = \begin{bmatrix} a & b \end{bmatrix} / \sqrt{a^2 + b^2}$$

$$distance = d / \sqrt{a^2 + b^2}$$

Converting a normal and a point on line to normal and distance form:

$$\mathbf{n} = \mathbf{n}$$

$$distance = \mathbf{n} \cdot \mathbf{q}$$

(This assumes that $\mathbf{n}$ is a unit vector.)

Finally, perpendicular bisector form to implicit form:

$$a = \mathbf{q}_y - \mathbf{r}_y$$
$$b = \mathbf{r}_x - \mathbf{q}_x$$
$$\begin{aligned} d &= \frac{\mathbf{q}+\mathbf{r}}{2} \cdot \begin{bmatrix} a & b \end{bmatrix} \\ &= \frac{\mathbf{q}+\mathbf{r}}{2} \cdot \begin{bmatrix} \mathbf{q}_y - \mathbf{r}_y & \mathbf{r}_x - \mathbf{q}_x \end{bmatrix} \\ &= \frac{(\mathbf{q}_x + \mathbf{r}_x)(\mathbf{q}_y - \mathbf{r}_y) + (\mathbf{q}_y + \mathbf{r}_y)(\mathbf{r}_x - \mathbf{q}_x)}{2} \\ &= \frac{(\mathbf{q}_x\mathbf{q}_y - \mathbf{q}_x\mathbf{r}_y + \mathbf{r}_x\mathbf{q}_y - \mathbf{r}_x\mathbf{r}_y) + (\mathbf{q}_y\mathbf{r}_x - \mathbf{q}_y\mathbf{q}_x + \mathbf{r}_y\mathbf{r}_x - \mathbf{r}_y\mathbf{q}_x)}{2} \\ &= \mathbf{r}_x\mathbf{q}_y - \mathbf{q}_x\mathbf{r}_y \end{aligned}$$

12.3 Spheres and Circles

A sphere is a 3D object defined as the set of all points that are a given distance from a given point. The distance from the center of the sphere to a point is known as the *radius* of the sphere. The straightforward representation of a sphere is to describe its center $\mathbf{c}$ and radius r:

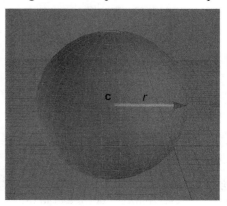

Figure 12.9: A sphere is defined by its center and radius

Spheres are ubiquitous in computational geometry and graphics because of their simplicity. A "bounding sphere" is often used for trivial rejection because the equations for intersection with a sphere are simple. Rotating a sphere does not change its shape, and so a bounding sphere can be used for an object regardless of the orientation of the object.

The implicit form of a sphere comes directly from its definition: the set of all points that are a given distance from the center. The implicit form of a sphere with center c and radius r is:

Equation 12.6:
Implicit definition of a sphere using vector notation

$$\|\mathbf{p} - \mathbf{c}\| = r$$

Notice that $\mathbf{p}$ is any point on the surface of the sphere. For a point $\mathbf{p}$ inside the sphere to satisfy the equation, we must change the " = " to a " ≤ ". Equation 12.6 is also the implicit definition of a circle in 2D. Expanding Equation 12.6 in 3D and squaring both sides yields:

Equation 12.7:
Implicit definition of a sphere

$$(x - \mathbf{c}_x)^2 + (y - \mathbf{c}_y)^2 + (z - \mathbf{c}_z)^2 = r^2$$

For both circles and spheres, we compute the diameter (distance from one point to a point on the exact opposite side), and circumference (distance all the way around the circle):

Equation 12.8:
Diameter and circumference of circles and spheres

$$
\begin{aligned}
D &= 2r \\
C &= 2\pi r \\
&= \pi D
\end{aligned}
$$

The area of a circle is given by:

Equation 12.9:
Area of a circle

$$A = \pi r^2$$

The surface area and volume of a sphere are given by:

Equation 12.10:
Surface area and volume of a sphere

$$
\begin{aligned}
S &= 4\pi r^2 \\
V &= \frac{4}{3}\pi r^3
\end{aligned}
$$

For the calculus buffs, it is interesting to notice that the derivative of the area of a circle is its circumference, and the derivative for the volume of a sphere is its surface area.

12.4 Bounding Boxes

Another simple geometric primitive commonly used as a bounding volume is the bounding box. Bounding boxes may be either axially aligned or arbitrarily oriented. Axially aligned bounding boxes have the restriction that their sides must be perpendicular to principal axes. The acronym AABB is often used for axially aligned bounding box, and OBB is used for oriented bounding box. Axially aligned bounding boxes are simpler to create and use, and they will be the focus of this section.

A 3D AABB is a simple six-sided box with each side parallel to one of the cardinal planes. The box is not necessarily a cube — the length, width, and height of the box may each be different. Figure 12.10 shows a few simple 3D objects and their axially aligned bounding boxes.

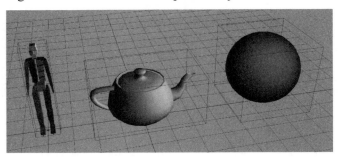

Figure 12.10: 3D objects and their AABBs

12.4.1 Representing AABBs

Let us introduce several important properties of an AABB and the notation we will use when referring to these values. The points inside an AABB satisfy the inequalities:

$$x_{min} \leq x \leq x_{max}$$
$$y_{min} \leq y \leq y_{max}$$
$$z_{min} \leq z \leq z_{max}$$

Two corner points of special significance are:

$$\mathbf{p}_{min} = \begin{bmatrix} x_{min} & y_{min} & z_{min} \end{bmatrix}$$
$$\mathbf{p}_{max} = \begin{bmatrix} x_{max} & y_{max} & z_{max} \end{bmatrix}$$

The center point $\mathbf{c}$ is given by:

$$\mathbf{c} = (\mathbf{p}_{min} + \mathbf{p}_{max})/2$$

The "size vector" $\mathbf{s}$ is the vector from $\mathbf{p}_{min}$ to $\mathbf{p}_{max}$ and contains the width, height, and length of the box:

$$\mathbf{s} = \mathbf{p}_{max} - \mathbf{p}_{min}$$

We can also refer to the "radius vector" $\mathbf{r}$ of the box, which is the vector from the center to $\mathbf{p}_{max}$:

$$\mathbf{r} = \mathbf{p}_{max} - \mathbf{c}$$
$$= \mathbf{s}/2$$

To unambiguously define an AABB requires only *two* of the five vectors $\mathbf{p}_{min}$, $\mathbf{p}_{max}$, $\mathbf{c}$, $\mathbf{s}$, and $\mathbf{r}$. Other than the pair $\mathbf{s}$ and $\mathbf{r}$, any pair may be used. Some representation forms are more useful in particular situations than others. We advise representing a bounding box using $\mathbf{p}_{min}$ and $\mathbf{p}_{max}$, since in practice these are needed far more frequently that $\mathbf{s}$, $\mathbf{c}$, and $\mathbf{r}$. Of course, computing any of these three from $\mathbf{p}_{min}$ and $\mathbf{p}_{max}$ is very fast.

In our C++ code, we will use the following simple representation for an AABB. This is an abbreviated listing with only the data members. (See Section 13.20 for the complete listing.)

```
class AABB3 {
public:
        Vector3     min;
        Vector3     max;
};
```

12.4.2 Computing AABBs

Computing an AABB for a set of points is a simple process. We first reset the minimum and maximum values to "infinity," or what is effectively bigger than any number we will encounter in practice. Then, we pass through the list of points, expanding our box as necessary to contain each point.

In our AABB class, we will define two functions to help with this. The first function "empties" the AABB:

```
void   AABB3::empty() {
        const float kBigNumber = 1e37f;
        min.x = min.y = min.z = kBigNumber;
        max.x = max.y = max.z = -kBigNumber;
}
```

The other function "adds" a single point into the AABB by expanding the AABB if necessary to contain the point:

```
void   AABB3::add(const Vector3 &p) {
        if (p.x < min.x) min.x = p.x;
        if (p.x > max.x) max.x = p.x;
        if (p.y < min.x) min.y = p.y;
        if (p.y > max.x) max.y = p.y;
        if (p.z < min.x) min.z = p.z;
        if (p.z > max.x) max.z = p.z;
}
```

Now, to create a bounding box from a set of points, we could use the following code:

Listing 12.1: Computing the AABB for a set of points

```
// Our list of points

const int n;
Vector3     list[n];

// First, empty the box

AABB3       box;
box.empty();

// Add each point into the box
```

```
for (int i = 0 ; i < n ; ++i) {
    box.add(list[i]);
}
```

12.4.3 AABBs vs. Bounding Spheres

In many cases, AABBs are preferable to spheres as a bounding volume:

- Computing the optimal AABB for a set of points is easy to program and can be run in linear time. Computing the optimal bounding sphere is a much more difficult problem. (See [4] and [16] for algorithms on bounding spheres.)

- For many objects that arise in practice, AABBs usually provide a "tighter" bounding volume, and thus, better trivial rejection. Of course, for some objects, the bounding sphere is better. (Imagine an object that is itself a sphere!) Even in the worst case, an AABB will have a volume of just under twice the volume of the sphere. However, when a sphere is bad, it can be *really* bad. Compare the bounding sphere and AABB of a telephone pole.

Figure 12.11: The AABB and bounding sphere for various objects

The basic problem with spheres is that there is only one degree of freedom to their shape — the radius of the sphere. An AABB has three degrees of freedom — the length, width, and height. Thus, it can usually adapt to differently shaped objects better. For most of the objects in Figure 12.11, the AABB is smaller than the bounding sphere, except the star in the upper-right corner. For the star, the bounding sphere is slightly smaller than the AABB. Notice that the AABB is highly sensitive to the orientation of the object; compare the AABBs for the two rifles on the bottom. In each case, the size of the rifle is the same: only the orientation is different between the two. Also, notice that the bounding spheres are the same size, since bounding spheres are not sensitive to the orientation of the object.

12.4.4 Transforming AABBs

As an object moves around in our virtual world, its AABB needs to move around with it. We have two choices — either we compute a new AABB from the transformed object, or we can try applying the same transform to the AABB as we did to the object. What we get as a result is not necessarily axially aligned (if the object rotated), and it is not necessarily a box (if the object skewed). However, computing an AABB for the "transformed AABB" (we should perhaps call it a NNAABNNB — a "not-necessarily axially aligned bounding not-necessarily box") should be faster than computing a new AABB for the transformed object because AABBs have only eight points.

So, to compute an AABB for a transformed AABB, it is not enough to simply transform the eight corner points. Nor can we simply compute new $\mathbf{p}_{min}$ and $\mathbf{p}_{max}$ by transforming the original $\mathbf{p}_{min}$ and $\mathbf{p}_{max}$ — this could result in $x_{min} > x_{max}$, for example. To compute a new AABB, we must transform the eight corner points and then form an AABB from these eight points.

Depending on the transformation, this may result in a bounding box that is larger than the original bounding box. For example, in 2D, a rotation of 45° will increase the size of the bounding box significantly, as shown in Figure 12.12.

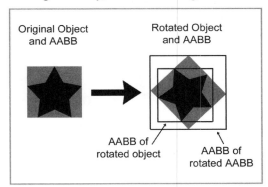

Figure 12.12: The AABB of a transformed box

Compare the size of the original AABB in Figure 12.12 (the gray box) with the new AABB (the largest box on the right), which was computed solely from the rotated AABB. The new AABB is almost twice as big. Notice that if we were able to compute an AABB from the rotated object rather than the rotated AABB, it would be about the same size as the original AABB.

As it turns out, the structure of an AABB can be exploited to speed up the generation of the new AABB so that it is not necessary to actually transform all eight corner points and build a new AABB from these points.

Let's quickly review what happens when we transform a 3D point by a 3×3 matrix. (See Section 7.1.7 if you have forgotten how to multiply a vector by a matrix.)

$$\begin{bmatrix} x' & y' & z' \end{bmatrix} = \begin{bmatrix} x & y & z \end{bmatrix} \begin{bmatrix} m_{11} & m_{12} & m_{13} \\ m_{21} & m_{22} & m_{23} \\ m_{31} & m_{32} & m_{33} \end{bmatrix}$$

$$x' = m_{11}x + m_{21}y + m_{31}z$$
$$y' = m_{12}x + m_{22}y + m_{32}z$$
$$z' = m_{13}x + m_{23}y + m_{33}z$$

Assume the original bounding box is in x_{min}, x_{max}, y_{min}, etc., and the new bounding box will be computed into x'_{min}, x'_{max}, y'_{min}, etc. Let's examine how we might more quickly compute x'_{min} as an example. In other words, we wish to find the minimum value of

$$m_{11}x + m_{21}y + m_{31}z$$

where $[x, y, z]$ is any of the original eight corner points. Our job is to figure out which of these corner points would have the smallest x value after transformation. The trick to minimizing the entire sum is to minimize each of the products individually. Let's look at the first product, $m_{11}x$. We must decide which of x_{min} or x_{max} to substitute for x in order to minimize the product. Obviously, if $m_{11} > 0$, then the smaller of the two, x_{min}, will result in the smaller product. Conversely, if $m_{11} < 0$, then x_{max} gives a smaller product. Conveniently, whichever of x_{min} or x_{max} we use for computing x'_{min}, we use the *other* value for computing x'_{max}. We then apply this process for each of the nine elements in the matrix, as illustrated in `AABB3::setToTransformedBox()`, which is in Listing 13.4 (see page 304).

12.5 Planes

A *plane* in 3D is the set of points equidistant from two points. A plane is perfectly flat, has no thickness, and extends infinitely.

12.5.1 Implicit Definition — The Plane Equation

We can represent planes using techniques similar to the ones we used to describe infinite 2D lines in Section 12.2.3. The implicit form of a plane is given by all points $\mathbf{p} = (x, y, z)$ that satisfy the *plane equation*, which is shown below using both notation forms:

Equation 12.11: The plane equation

$$ax + by + cz = d$$
$$\mathbf{p} \cdot \mathbf{n} = d$$

Note that in the second form, $\mathbf{n} = [a, b, c]$. Once we know $\mathbf{n}$, we can compute d from any point known to be in the plane.

Reminder: Many sources give the plane equation as $ax + by + cz + d = 0$. This has the effect of flipping the sign of d.

The vector **n** is called the plane *normal* because it is perpendicular ("normal") to the plane. Let's verify this. Assume **p** and **q** are both in the plane, and, therefore, satisfy the plane equation. Substituting **p** and **q** into Equation 12.11:

$$\mathbf{n} \cdot \mathbf{p} = d$$
$$\mathbf{n} \cdot \mathbf{q} = d$$
$$\mathbf{n} \cdot \mathbf{p} = \mathbf{n} \cdot \mathbf{q}$$
$$\mathbf{n} \cdot \mathbf{p} - \mathbf{n} \cdot \mathbf{q} = 0$$
$$\mathbf{n} \cdot (\mathbf{p} - \mathbf{q}) = 0$$

The geometric implication of the last line is that **n** is perpendicular to the vector from **q** to **p**. This is true for any points **p** and **q** in the plane, and, therefore, **n** is perpendicular to every vector in the plane.

We may consider a plane to have a "front" side and a "back" side. Normally, the front side of the plane is the direction that **n** points; for example, when looking from the head of **n** toward the tail, we are looking at the front side.

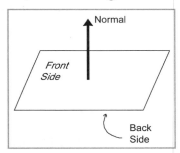

Figure 12.13: The front and back sides of a plane

We can restrict **n** to have unit length without loss of generality, and it will often be convenient to do so.

12.5.2 Definition Using Three Points

Another way we can define a plane is to give three noncollinear points that are in the plane, that is, three points that are not on the same straight line. (If the three points are in a line, there would be an infinite number of planes that contain that line, and there would be no way of telling which one we mean.)

Let's compute **n** and d from three points $\mathbf{p}_1$, $\mathbf{p}_2$, and $\mathbf{p}_3$ known to be in the plane. First, we must compute **n**. Which way will **n** point? The standard way to do this in a left-handed coordinate system is to assume that $\mathbf{p}_1$, $\mathbf{p}_2$, and $\mathbf{p}_3$ are listed in clockwise order when viewed from the front side of the plane. (In a right-handed coordinate system, we usually assume the points are listed in counter-clockwise order. This way, the equations are the same no matter what coordinate system is used.)

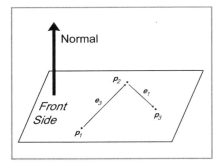

Figure 12.14: Computing a plane normal from three points in the plane

We will construct two vectors according to the clockwise ordering. (See Figure 12.14.) The "e" stands for "edge" vector, since these equations commonly arise when computing the plane equation for a triangle. (The seemingly strange indexing agrees with the indices used in Section 12.6 where triangles are discussed in more detail.) The cross product of these two vectors yields the perpendicular vector $\mathbf{n}$, but this vector is not necessarily of unit length. As mentioned earlier, we will usually normalize $\mathbf{n}$. All of this is summarized succinctly by the following equations:

Equation 12.12: The normal of a plane containing three points

$$\mathbf{e}_3 = \mathbf{p}_2 - \mathbf{p}_1$$
$$\mathbf{e}_1 = \mathbf{p}_3 - \mathbf{p}_2$$
$$\mathbf{n} = \frac{\mathbf{e}_3 \times \mathbf{e}_1}{\|\mathbf{e}_3 \times \mathbf{e}_1\|}$$

Notice that if the points are collinear, then $\mathbf{e}_3$ and $\mathbf{e}_1$ will be parallel, and thus, the cross product will be $\mathbf{0}$, which cannot be normalized. This mathematical singularity coincides with the physical singularity that collinear points do not unambiguously define a plane.

Now that we know $\mathbf{n}$, all that is left to do is compute d. This is done by taking the dot product of one of the points and $\mathbf{n}$.

12.5.3 "Best-fit" Plane for More Than Three Points

Occasionally, we may wish to compute the plane equation for a set of more than three points. The most common example of such a set of points is the vertices of a polygon. In this case, the vertices are assumed to be enumerated in a clockwise fashion around the polygon. (The ordering matters because it is how we decide which side is the "front" and which is the "back," which in turn determines in what direction our normal will point.)

One naïve solution is to arbitrarily select three consecutive points and compute the plane equation from those three points. However, the three points we chose may be collinear, or nearly collinear, which is almost as bad because it is numerically inaccurate. Or, perhaps the polygon is concave and the three points we have chosen are a point of concavity and form a counterclockwise turn (which would result in a normal that points the wrong direction). Or, the vertices of the polygon may not be coplanar, which can happen due to numeric imprecision or the method used to generate the polygons. What we really want is a way to compute the "best fit" plane for a set of points, which takes into account *all* of the points. Given n points:

$$\mathbf{p}_1 = \begin{bmatrix} x_1 & y_1 & z_1 \end{bmatrix}$$
$$\mathbf{p}_2 = \begin{bmatrix} x_2 & y_2 & z_2 \end{bmatrix}$$
$$\vdots$$
$$\mathbf{p}_{n-1} = \begin{bmatrix} x_{n-1} & y_{n-1} & z_{n-1} \end{bmatrix}$$
$$\mathbf{p}_n = \begin{bmatrix} x_n & y_n & z_n \end{bmatrix}$$

The "best-fit" perpendicular vector $\mathbf{n}$ is given by:

Equation 12.13:
Computing the
best-fit plane
normal from n
points

$$\mathbf{n}_x = (z_1 + z_2)(y_1 - y_2) + (z_2 + z_3)(x_2 - y_3) + \cdots + (z_{n-1} + z_n)(y_{n-1} - y_n) + (z_n + z_1)(y_n - y_1)$$
$$\mathbf{n}_y = (x_1 + x_2)(z_1 - z_2) + (x_2 + x_3)(x_2 - z_3) + \cdots + (x_{n-1} + x_n)(z_{n-1} - z_n) + (x_n + x_1)(z_n - z_1)$$
$$\mathbf{n}_z = (y_1 + y_2)(x_1 - x_2) + (y_2 + y_3)(x_2 - x_3) + \cdots + (y_{n-1} + y_n)(x_{n-1} - x_n) + (y_n + y_1)(x_n - x_1)$$

This vector must then be normalized if we wish to enforce the restriction that $\mathbf{n}$ be of unit length.

We can express Equation 12.13 succinctly using summation notation. If we let $\mathbf{p}_{n+1} = \mathbf{p}_1$, then:

$$\mathbf{n}_x = \sum_{i=1}^{n}(z_i + z_{i+1})(y_i - y_{i+1})$$
$$\mathbf{n}_y = \sum_{i=1}^{n}(x_i + x_{i+1})(z_i - z_{i+1})$$
$$\mathbf{n}_z = \sum_{i=1}^{n}(y_i + y_{i+1})(x_i - x_{i+1})$$

The following code illustrates how we might compute a best-fit normal for a set of points:

Listing 12.2: Computing the best-fit plane normal for a set of points

```
Vector3 computeBestFitNormal(const Vector3 v[], int n) {

    // Zero out sum

    Vector3 result = kZeroVector;

    // Start with the "previous" vertex as the last one.
    // This avoids an if-statement in the loop

    const Vector3 *p = &v[n-1];

    // Iterate through the vertices

    for (int i = 0 ; i < n ; ++i) {

        // Get shortcut to the "current" vertex

        const Vector3 *c = &v[i];

        // Add in edge vector products appropriately

        result.x += (p->z + c->z) * (p->y - c->y);
        result.y += (p->x + c->x) * (p->z - c->z);
```

```
            result.z += (p->y + c->y) * (p->x - c->x);

            // Next vertex, please

            p = c;
        }

        // Normalize the result and return it

        result.normalize();
        return result;
    }
```

The best-fit d value can be computed as the average of the d values for each point:

$$d = \frac{1}{n} \sum_{i=1}^{n} (\mathbf{p}_i \cdot \mathbf{n})$$

$$= \frac{1}{n} \left(\sum_{i=1}^{n} \mathbf{p}_i \right) \cdot \mathbf{n}$$

12.5.4 Distance from Point to Plane

Imagine a plane and a point $\mathbf{q}$ that is not in the plane. There exists a point $\mathbf{p}$ that lies in the plane and is the closest point in the plane to $\mathbf{q}$. Clearly, the vector from $\mathbf{p}$ to $\mathbf{q}$ is perpendicular to the plane and is of the form $a\mathbf{n}$. This is shown in Figure 12.15.

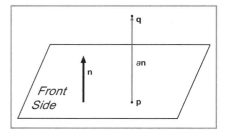

Figure 12.15: Computing the distance between a point and a plane

If we assume $\mathbf{n}$ is a unit vector, then the distance from $\mathbf{p}$ to $\mathbf{q}$ (and thus, the distance from $\mathbf{q}$ to the plane) is simply a. (This "distance" will be negative when $\mathbf{q}$ is on the back side of the plane.) What's surprising is that we can compute a without knowing the location of $\mathbf{p}$. We go back to our original definition of $\mathbf{q}$ and then perform some vector algebra to eliminate $\mathbf{p}$:

Equation 12.14:
Computing the
signed distance
from a plane to
an arbitrary 3D
point

$$\begin{aligned}
\mathbf{p} + a\mathbf{n} &= \mathbf{q} \\
(\mathbf{p} + a\mathbf{n}) \cdot \mathbf{n} &= \mathbf{q} \cdot \mathbf{n} \\
\mathbf{p} \cdot \mathbf{n} + (a\mathbf{n}) \cdot \mathbf{n} &= \mathbf{q} \cdot \mathbf{n} \\
d + a &= \mathbf{q} \cdot \mathbf{n} \\
a &= \mathbf{q} \cdot \mathbf{n} - d
\end{aligned}$$

12.6 Triangles

Triangles are of fundamental importance in modeling and graphics. The surface of a complex 3D object, such as a car or a human body, is approximated with many triangles. Such a group of connected triangles forms a *triangle mesh*, which is the topic of Chapter 14. Before we can learn how to manipulate many triangles though, we must first learn how to manipulate one triangle.

12.6.1 Basic Properties of a Triangle

A triangle is defined by listing its three vertices. The order that these points are listed is significant. In a left-handed coordinate system, we typically enumerate the points in clockwise order when viewed from the "front" side of the triangle. We will refer to the three vertices as v_1, v_2, and v_3.

A triangle lies in a plane. The equation of this plane (the normal $\mathbf{n}$ and distance to origin d) is important in a number of applications. For more information on planes, including how to compute the plane equation given three points, see Section 12.5.2.

Let us label the interior angles, clockwise edge vectors, and side lengths as shown in Figure 12.16.

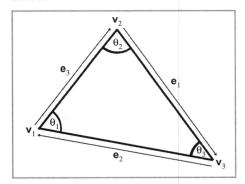

Figure 12.16: Labeling triangles

Let l_i denote the length of $\mathbf{e}_i$. Notice that $\mathbf{e}_i$ and l_i are opposite v_i, the vertex with the corresponding index, and they are given by:

$$\mathbf{e}_1 = \mathbf{v}_3 - \mathbf{v}_2 \qquad l_1 = \|\mathbf{e}_1\|$$

$$\mathbf{e}_2 = \mathbf{v}_1 - \mathbf{v}_3 \qquad l_2 = \|\mathbf{e}_2\|$$

$$\mathbf{e}_3 = \mathbf{v}_2 - \mathbf{v}_1 \qquad l_3 = \|\mathbf{e}_3\|$$

Writing the law of sines and law of cosines using this notation:

Equation 12.15:
Law of sines
$$\frac{\sin \theta_1}{l_1} = \frac{\sin \theta_2}{l_2} = \frac{\sin \theta_3}{l_3}$$

Equation 12.16:
Law of cosines

$$l_1{}^2 = l_2{}^2 + l_3{}^2 - 2l_2 l_3 \cos\theta_1$$
$$l_2{}^2 = l_1{}^2 + l_3{}^2 - 2l_1 l_3 \cos\theta_2$$
$$l_3{}^2 = l_1{}^2 + l_2{}^2 - 2l_1 l_2 \cos\theta_3$$

The perimeter of the triangle is often an important value, and it is computed trivially by summing the three sides:

Equation 12.17:
Perimeter of a triangle

$$p = l_1 + l_2 + l_3$$

12.6.2 Area of a Triangle

In this section, we investigate several techniques for computing the area of a triangle. The most well-known method is to compute the area from the *base* and *height* (also known at the *altitude*). Examine the parallelogram and enclosed triangle below.

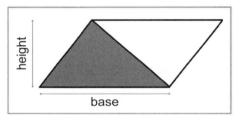

Figure 12.17: A triangle enclosed in a parallelogram

From classical geometry, we know that the area of a parallelogram is equal to the product of the base and height. (See Section 5.11.2 for an explanation on why this is true.) Since the triangle occupies exactly one-half of this area, the area of a triangle, given the base and height is:

Equation 12.18:
The area of a triangle is half the area of the parallelogram that shares two sides with the triangle

$$A = bh/2$$

If the altitude is not known, then *Heron's formula* can be used, which requires only the lengths of the three sides. Let s equal one-half the perimeter (also known as the *semiperimeter*). Then the area is given by:

Equation 12.19:
Heron's formula for the area of a triangle

$$s = \frac{l_1 + l_2 + l_3}{2} = \frac{p}{2}$$
$$A = \sqrt{s(s - l_1)(s - l_2)(s - l_3)}$$

Heron's formula is particularly interesting because of the ease with which it can be applied in 3D.

Sometimes the altitude or lengths of the sides are not readily available and all we have are the Cartesian coordinates of the vertices. (Of course, we could always compute the side lengths from the coordinates, but there are situations where we wish to avoid this relatively costly computation.) Let's see if we can compute the area of a triangle using only the coordinates of the vertices.

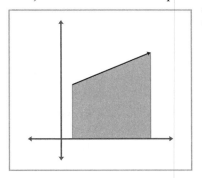

Figure 12.18: The area "beneath" an edge vector

Let's tackle this problem in 2D. The basic idea is to compute, for each of the three edges of the triangle, the signed area of the trapezoid bounded above by the edge and below by the *x*-axis, as shown in Figure 12.18. By "signed area" we mean that the area is positive if the edge points from left to right, and it is negative if the edge points from right to left. Notice that no matter how the triangle is oriented, there will always be at least one positive edge and at least one negative edge. A vertical edge will have zero area. The formula for the areas under each edge are given below:

$$A(\mathbf{e}_1) = \frac{(y_3 + y_2)(x_3 - x_2)}{2}$$

$$A(\mathbf{e}_2) = \frac{(y_1 + y_3)(x_1 - x_3)}{2}$$

$$A(\mathbf{e}_3) = \frac{(y_2 + y_1)(x_2 - x_1)}{2}$$

As it turns out, the formula above works even when some (or all) of the triangle extends below the *x*-axis.

By summing the signed areas of the three trapezoids, we arrive at the area of the triangle itself. In fact, the same idea can be used to compute the area of a polygon with any number of sides, although we will not need to do so in this book.

We assume a clockwise ordering of the vertices around the triangle. Enumerating the vertices in the opposite order flips the sign of the area. With these considerations in mind, we sum the areas of the trapezoids to compute the signed area of the triangle:

$$
\begin{aligned}
A &= A(\mathbf{e}_1) + A(\mathbf{e}_2) + A(\mathbf{e}_3) \\
&= \frac{(y_3 + y_2)(x_3 - x_2) + (y_1 + y_3)(x_1 - x_3) + (y_2 + y_1)(x_2 - x_1)}{2} \\
&= \frac{(y_3 x_3 - y_3 x_2 + y_2 x_3 - y_2 x_2) + (y_1 x_1 - y_1 x_3 + y_3 x_1 - y_3 x_3) + (y_2 x_2 - y_2 x_1 + y_1 x_2 - y_1 x_1)}{2} \\
&= \frac{-y_3 x_2 + y_2 x_3 - y_1 x_3 + y_3 x_1 - y_2 x_1 + y_1 x_2}{2} \\
&= \frac{y_1(x_2 - x_3) + y_2(x_3 - x_1) + y_3(x_1 - x_2)}{2}
\end{aligned}
$$

We can actually simplify this further. The basic idea is to realize that we can translate the triangle without affecting the area. In this case, we will shift the triangle vertically by subtracting y_3 from each of the y coordinates. (You can achieve the same simplifications using only algebraic manipulations.)

Equation 12.20: Computing the area of a 2D triangle from the coordinates of the vertices

$$A = \frac{y_1(x_2 - x_3) + y_2(x_3 - x_1) + y_3(x_1 - x_2)}{2}$$

$$= \frac{(y_1 - y_3)(x_2 - x_3) + (y_2 - y_3)(x_3 - x_1) + (y_3 - y_3)(x_1 - x_2)}{2}$$

$$= \frac{(y_1 - y_3)(x_2 - x_3) + (y_2 - y_3)(x_3 - x_1)}{2}$$

In 3D we can use the cross product to compute the area of a triangle. Recall from Section 5.11.2 that the magnitude of the cross product of two vectors $\mathbf{a}$ and $\mathbf{b}$ is equal to the area of the parallelogram formed on two sides by $\mathbf{a}$ and $\mathbf{b}$. Since the area of a triangle is half the area of the enclosing parallelogram, we have a simple way to calculate the area of the triangle. Given two edge vectors from the triangle, $\mathbf{e}_1$ and $\mathbf{e}_2$, the area of the triangle is given by:

$$A = \frac{\|\mathbf{e}_1 \times \mathbf{e}_2\|}{2}$$

12.6.3 Barycentric Space

Although we certainly use triangles in 3D, the surface of a triangle lies in a plane and is inherently a 2D object. Moving around on the surface of a triangle that is arbitrarily oriented in 3D is somewhat awkward. It would be nice to have a coordinate space that is related to the surface of the triangle and is independent of the 3D space in which the triangle "lives." *Barycentric space* is just such a coordinate space.

Any point in the plane of a triangle can be expressed as the weighted average of the vertices. The weights are known as *barycentric coordinates*. The conversion from barycentric coordinates (b_1, b_2, b_3) to standard 3D space is defined by:

Equation 12.21: Computing a 3D point from barycentric coordinates

$$(b_1, b_2, b_3) \iff b_1 \mathbf{v}_1 + b_2 \mathbf{v}_2 + b_3 \mathbf{v}_3$$

The sum of the coordinates is always one:
$$b_1 + b_2 + b_3 = 1$$

The values b_1, b_2, and b_3 are the "contributions" or "weights" that each vertex contributes to the point. Figure 12.19 shows some examples of points and their barycentric coordinates.

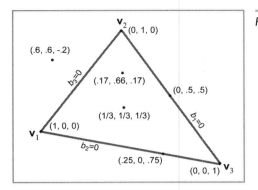

Figure 12.19: Examples of barycentric coordinates

A few important observations can be made:

■ First, notice that the three vertices of the triangle have a trivial form in barycentric space:

$$(1, 0, 0) \iff \mathbf{v}_1$$
$$(0, 1, 0) \iff \mathbf{v}_2$$
$$(0, 0, 1) \iff \mathbf{v}_3$$

■ Second, all points on the side opposite a vertex will have a zero for the barycentric coordinate corresponding to that vertex. For example, $b_1 = 0$ for all points on the line containing the side opposite $\mathbf{v}_1$.

■ Third, *any* point in the plane can be described using barycentric coordinates, not just the points inside the triangle. The barycentric coordinates of a point *inside* the triangle will all be in range 0...1. A point *outside* the triangle will have at least one negative coordinate. Barycentric space tessellates the plane into triangles of the same size as the original triangle, as shown in Figure 12.20.

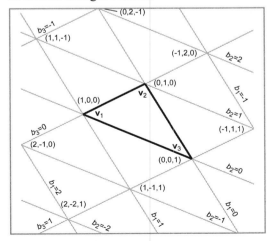

Figure 12.20: Barycentric coordinates tessellate the plane

The nature of barycentric space is not exactly the same as Cartesian space. This is because barycentric space is 2D, but there are three coordinates. Since the sum of the coordinates is one, barycentric space only has two degrees of freedom; there is one degree of redundancy. In other words, we could completely describe a point in barycentric space using only two of the coordinates and compute the third from the other two.

To convert a point from barycentric coordinates to normal 3D coordinates, we simply compute the weighted average of the vertices by applying Equation 12.21. Computing the barycentric coordinates for an arbitrary point in 2D or 3D is slightly more difficult. Let's see how we might do this in 2D. Examine Figure 12.21, which shows the three vertices $\mathbf{v}_1$, $\mathbf{v}_2$, and $\mathbf{v}_3$ and the point $\mathbf{p}$. We have also labeled the three "subtriangles" T_1, T_2, and T_3, which are opposite the vertex of the same index. These will become useful in a moment.

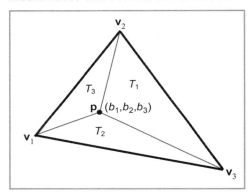

Figure 12.21: Computing the barycentric coordinates for an arbitrary point p

Now, we know the Cartesian coordinates of the three vertices and the point $\mathbf{p}$. Our task is to compute the barycentric coordinates b_1, b_2, and b_3. This gives us three equations and three unknowns:

$$\mathbf{p}_x = b_1 x_1 + b_2 x_2 + b_3 x_3$$
$$\mathbf{p}_y = b_1 y_1 + b_2 y_2 + b_3 y_3$$
$$b_1 + b_2 + b_3 = 1$$

Solving the system of equations yields:

Equation 12.22: Computing barycentric coordinates for a 2D point

$$b_1 = \frac{(\mathbf{p}_y - y_3)(x_2 - x_3) + (y_2 - y_3)(x_3 - \mathbf{p}_x)}{(y_1 - y_3)(x_2 - x_3) + (y_2 - y_3)(x_3 - x_1)}$$

$$b_2 = \frac{(\mathbf{p}_y - y_1)(x_3 - x_1) + (y_3 - y_1)(x_1 - \mathbf{p}_x)}{(y_1 - y_3)(x_2 - x_3) + (y_2 - y_3)(x_3 - x_1)}$$

$$b_3 = \frac{(\mathbf{p}_y - y_2)(x_1 - x_2) + (y_1 - y_2)(x_2 - \mathbf{p}_x)}{(y_1 - y_3)(x_2 - x_3) + (y_2 - y_3)(x_3 - x_1)}$$

Examining Equation 12.22 closely, we see that the denominator is the same in each expression, and it is equal to twice the area of the triangle, according to Equation 12.20. Also, for each barycentric coordinate b_i, the numerator is equal to twice the area of the "subtriangle" T_i. In other words:

Equation 12.23:
Interpreting
barycentric
coordinates as
ratios of areas

$$b_1 = A(T_1)/A(T)$$
$$b_2 = A(T_2)/A(T)$$
$$b_3 = A(T_3)/A(T)$$

Note that this interpretation applies even if **p** is outside the triangle, since our equation for computing area yields a negative result if the vertices are enumerated in a counterclockwise order. If the three vertices of the triangle are collinear, then the area in the denominator will be zero, and thus, the barycentric coordinates cannot be computed.

Computing barycentric coordinates for an arbitrary point **p** in 3D is more complicated than in 2D. We cannot solve a system of equations as we did before, since we have three unknowns and four equations. Another complication is that **p** may not lie in the plane that contains the triangle, in which case the barycentric coordinates are undefined. For now, let's assume that **p** lies in the plane containing the triangle.

One trick that works is to turn the 3D problem into a 2D one, simply by discarding one of x, y, or z. This has the effect of projecting the triangle onto one of the three cardinal planes. Intuitively, this works because the projected areas are proportional to the original areas.

Which coordinate should we discard? We can't always discard the same one, since the projected points will be collinear if the triangle is perpendicular to the projection plane. If our triangle is *nearly* perpendicular to the plane of projection, we will have problems with floating-point accuracy. A solution to this dilemma is to choose the plane of projection so as to maximize the area of the projected triangle. This can be done by examining the plane normal; the coordinate that has the largest absolute value is the coordinate that we will discard. For example, if the normal is $[-1, 0, 0]$, then we would discard the x values of the vertices and **p**, projecting onto the yz plane. The code below shows how to compute the barycentric coordinates for an arbitrary 3D point.

Listing 12.3: Computing barycentric coordinates in 3D

```
bool    computeBarycentricCoords3d(
        const Vector3 v[3],      // vertices of the triangle
        const Vector3 &p,        // point that we wish to compute coords for
        float b[3]               // barycentric coords returned here
) {

        // First, compute two clockwise edge vectors

        Vector3      d1 = v[1] - v[0];
        Vector3      d2 = v[2] - v[1];

        // Compute surface normal using cross product. In many cases
        // this step could be skipped, since we would have the surface
        // normal precomputed. We do not need to normalize it, although
        // if a precomputed normal was normalized, it would be OK.

        Vector3      n = crossProduct(d1, d2);
```

```
// Locate dominant axis of normal, and select plane of projection

float u1, u2, u3, u4;
float v1, v2, v3, v4;
if ((fabs(n.x) >= fabs(n.y)) && (fabs(n.x) >= fabs(n.z))) {

        // Discard x, project onto yz plane

        u1 = v[0].y - v[2].y;
        u2 = v[1].y - v[2].y;
        u3 = p.y - v[0].y;
        u4 = p.y - v[2].y;

        v1 = v[0].z - v[2].z;
        v2 = v[1].z - v[2].z;
        v3 = p.z - v[0].z;
        v4 = p.z - v[2].z;

} else if (fabs(n.y) >= fabs(n.z)) {

        // Discard y, project onto xz plane

        u1 = v[0].z - v[2].z;
        u2 = v[1].z - v[2].z;
        u3 = p.z - v[0].z;
        u4 = p.z - v[2].z;

        v1 = v[0].x - v[2].x;
        v2 = v[1].x - v[2].x;
        v3 = p.x - v[0].x;
        v4 = p.x - v[2].x;

} else {

        u1 = v[0].x - v[2].x;
        u2 = v[1].x - v[2].x;
        u3 = p.x - v[0].x;
        u4 = p.x - v[2].x;

        v1 = v[0].y - v[2].y;
        v2 = v[1].y - v[2].y;
        v3 = p.y - v[0].y;
        v4 = p.y - v[2].y;
}

// Compute denominator, check for invalid

float denom = v1 * u2 - v2 * u1;
if (denom == 0.0f) {

        // Bogus triangle - probably triangle has zero area

        return false;
}

// Compute barycentric coordinates

float oneOverDenom = 1.0f / denom;
b[0] = (v4*u2 - v2*u4) * oneOverDenom;
b[1] = (v1*u3 - v3*u1) * oneOverDenom;
```

```
        b[2] = 1.0f - b[0] - b[1];

        // OK

        return true;
    }
```

Another technique for computing barycentric coordinates in 3D is based on the method for computing the area of a 3D triangle using the cross product, which we discussed in Section 12.6.2. Recall that given two edge vectors e_1 and e_2 of a triangle, we can compute the area of the triangle as $\|e_1 \times e_2\|/2$. Once we have the area of the entire triangle, and the areas of the three "subtriangles," we can compute the barycentric coordinates.

There is one slight problem with this: the magnitude of the cross product is not sensitive to the ordering of the vertices. Magnitude is, by definition, always positive. This will not work for points outside the triangle, since these points must always have at least one negative barycentric coordinate.

Let's see if we can find a way to work around this problem. It seems like we need a way to calculate the length of the cross product vector that would yield a negative value if the vertices were enumerated in the "incorrect" order. As it turns out, there is a very simple way to do this using the dot product.

Let's assign c as the cross product of two edge vectors of a triangle. Remember that the magnitude of c will equal twice the area of the triangle. Assume we have a normal n of unit length. Now, n and c are parallel, since they are both perpendicular to the plane containing the triangle. However, they may point in opposite directions. Recall from Section 5.10.2 that the dot product of two vectors is equal to the product of their magnitudes times the cosine of the angle between them. Since we know that n is a unit vector, and the vectors are either pointing in the same or exact opposite direction, we have:

$$\begin{aligned} c \cdot n &= \|c\|\|n\| \cos\theta \\ &= \|c\|(1)(\pm 1) \\ &= \pm\|c\| \end{aligned}$$

Dividing this result by two, we have a way to compute the "signed area" of a triangle in 3D. Armed with this trick, we can now apply the observation from the previous section that each barycentric coordinate b_i is proportional to the area of the "subtriangle" T_i. We will first label all of the vectors involved, as shown in Figure 12.22.

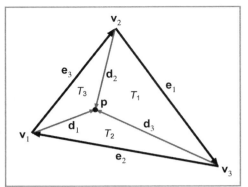

As you can see in Figure 12.22, each vertex has a vector from $\mathbf{v}_i$ to $\mathbf{p}$ named $\mathbf{d}_i$. Summarizing the equations for the vectors:

$$\mathbf{e}_1 = \mathbf{v}_3 - \mathbf{v}_2$$
$$\mathbf{e}_2 = \mathbf{v}_1 - \mathbf{v}_3$$
$$\mathbf{e}_3 = \mathbf{v}_2 - \mathbf{v}_1$$
$$\mathbf{d}_1 = \mathbf{p} - \mathbf{v}_1$$
$$\mathbf{d}_2 = \mathbf{p} - \mathbf{v}_2$$
$$\mathbf{d}_3 = \mathbf{p} - \mathbf{v}_3$$

We'll also need a surface normal, which can be computed by:

$$\mathbf{n} = \frac{\mathbf{e}_1 \times \mathbf{e}_2}{\|\mathbf{e}_1 \times \mathbf{e}_2\|}$$

Now the areas for the entire triangle (which we'll call T) and the three subtriangles are given by:

$$A(T) = ((\mathbf{e}_1 \times \mathbf{e}_2) \cdot \mathbf{n})/2$$
$$A(T_1) = ((\mathbf{e}_1 \times \mathbf{d}_3) \cdot \mathbf{n})/2$$
$$A(T_2) = ((\mathbf{e}_2 \times \mathbf{d}_1) \cdot \mathbf{n})/2$$
$$A(T_3) = ((\mathbf{e}_3 \times \mathbf{d}_2) \cdot \mathbf{n})/2$$

Each barycentric coordinate b_i is given by $A(T_i) / A(T)$, as shown below:

Equation 12.24: Computing barycentric coordinates in 3D

$$b_1 = A(T_1)/A(T) = \frac{(\mathbf{e}_1 \times \mathbf{d}_3) \cdot \mathbf{n}}{(\mathbf{e}_1 \times \mathbf{e}_2) \cdot \mathbf{n}}$$

$$b_2 = A(T_2)/A(T) = \frac{(\mathbf{e}_2 \times \mathbf{d}_1) \cdot \mathbf{n}}{(\mathbf{e}_1 \times \mathbf{e}_2) \cdot \mathbf{n}}$$

$$b_3 = A(T_3)/A(T) = \frac{(\mathbf{e}_3 \times \mathbf{d}_2) \cdot \mathbf{n}}{(\mathbf{e}_1 \times \mathbf{e}_2) \cdot \mathbf{n}}$$

Notice that $\mathbf{n}$ is used in all of the numerators *and* all of the denominators. Thus, it is not actually necessary that $\mathbf{n}$ be normalized. In this case, the denominator is simply $\mathbf{n}{\cdot}\mathbf{n}$.

This technique for computing barycentric coordinates involves more scalar math operations than the method of projection into 2D. However, it is branchless and offers considerable opportunity for optimization by a vector coprocessor. Thus, it may be faster on a superscalar processor with a vector coprocessor.

12.6.4 Special Points

In this section, we discuss three points on a triangle that have special geometric significance:

- Center of gravity
- Incenter
- Circumcenter

Much of this section is inspired by [12]. For each point, we will discuss its geometric significance and construction and give its barycentric coordinates.

The *center of gravity* is the point where the triangle would balance perfectly. It is the intersection of the medians. (A *median* is a line from one vertex to the midpoint of the opposite side.) Figure 12.23 shows the center of gravity of a triangle.

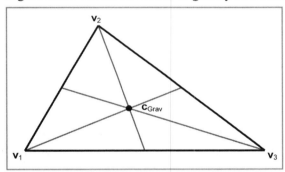

Figure 12.23: The center of gravity of a triangle

The center of gravity is the geometric average of the three vertices:

$$\mathbf{c}_{\text{Grav}} = \frac{\mathbf{v}_1 + \mathbf{v}_2 + \mathbf{v}_3}{3}$$

The barycentric coordinates are:

$$\left(\frac{1}{3}, \frac{1}{3}, \frac{1}{3} \right)$$

The center of gravity is also known as the *centroid*.

The *incenter* is the point in the triangle that is equidistant from the sides. It is called the incenter because it is the center of the circle inscribed in the triangle. The incenter is constructed as the intersection of the angle bisectors.

Figure 12.24 shows the incenter of a triangle.

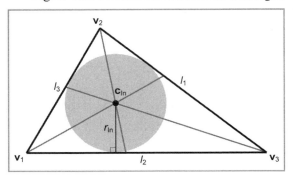

The incenter is computed by:

$$\mathbf{c}_{\text{In}} = \frac{l_1\mathbf{v}_1 + l_2\mathbf{v}_2 + l_3\mathbf{v}_3}{p}$$

where $p = l_1 + l_2 + l_3$ is the perimeter of the triangle. Thus, the barycentric coordinates of the incenter are:

$$\left(\frac{l_1}{p}, \frac{l_2}{p}, \frac{l_3}{p}\right)$$

The radius of the inscribed circle can be computed by dividing the area of the triangle by its perimeter:

$$r_{\text{In}} = \frac{A}{p}$$

The inscribed circle solves the problem of finding a circle tangent to three lines.

The *circumcenter* is the point in the triangle that is equidistant from the vertices. It is the center of the circle that circumscribes the triangle. The circumcenter is constructed as the intersection of the perpendicular bisectors of the sides. Figure 12.25 shows the circumcenter of a triangle.

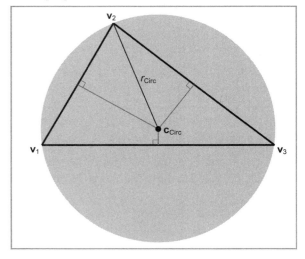

Figure 12.25: The circumcenter of a triangle

To compute the circumcenter, we will first define the following intermediate values:

$$
\begin{aligned}
d_1 &= -\mathbf{e}_2 \cdot \mathbf{e}_3 \\
d_2 &= -\mathbf{e}_3 \cdot \mathbf{e}_1 \\
d_3 &= -\mathbf{e}_1 \cdot \mathbf{e}_2 \\
c_1 &= d_2 d_3 \\
c_2 &= d_3 d_1 \\
c_3 &= d_1 d_2 \\
c &= c_1 + c_2 + c_3
\end{aligned}
$$

With those intermediate values, the barycentric coordinates for the circumcenter are given by:

$$
\left(\frac{c_2 + c_3}{2c}, \frac{c_3 + c_1}{2c}, \frac{c_1 + c_2}{2c} \right)
$$

Thus, the circumcenter is given by:

$$
\mathbf{c}_{\text{Circ}} = \frac{(c_2 + c_3)\mathbf{v}_1 + (c_3 + c_1)\mathbf{v}_2 + (c_1 + c_2)\mathbf{v}_3}{2c}
$$

The circumradius is given by:

$$
r_{\text{Circ}} = \frac{\sqrt{(d_1 + d_2)(d_2 + d_3)(d_3 + d_1)/c}}{2}
$$

The circumradius and circumcenter solve the problem of finding a circle that passes through three points.

12.7 Polygons

It is difficult to come up with a simple definition for *polygon*, since the precise definition usually varies depending on the context. In general, a polygon is a flat object made up of *vertices* and *edges*. In the next few sections, we discuss several ways in which polygons may be classified.

12.7.1 Simple vs. Complex Polygons

A *simple* polygon does not have any "holes," whereas a *complex* polygon may have holes (see Figure 12.26). A simple polygon can be described by enumerating the vertices in order around the polygon. (Recall that in a left-handed world, we usually enumerate them in clockwise order when viewed from the "front" side of the polygon.) Simple polygons are used much more frequently than complex polygons.

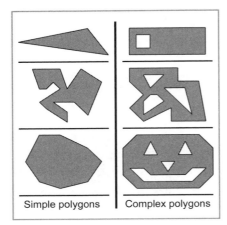

Figure 12.26: Simple vs. complex polygons

We can turn any complex polygon into a simple one by adding pairs of "seam" edges, as shown in Figure 12.27. As the close-up on the right shows, we add two edges per "seam." The edges are actually coincidental, although in the close-up they have been separated so you can see them. When we think about the edges being ordered around the polygon, the two seam edges point in opposite directions.

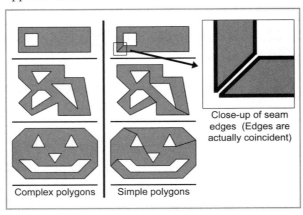

Figure 12.27: Turning complex polygons into simple ones by adding pairs of seam edges

12.7.2 Self-intersecting Polygons

The edges of most simple polygons do not intersect each another. If the edges do intersect, the polygon is considered a *self-intersecting* polygon. A simple example of a self-intersecting polygon is shown in Figure 12.28.

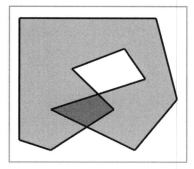

Figure 12.28: A self-intersecting polygon

Most people usually work with non-self-intersecting polygons.

12.7.3 Convex vs. Concave Polygons

Non-self-intersecting simple polygons may be further classified as either *convex* or *concave*. Giving a precise definition for "convex" is actually somewhat tricky, since there are many sticky degenerate cases. For most polygons, the following commonly used definitions are equivalent, although some degenerate polygons may be classified as convex according to one definition and concave according to another.

- Intuitively, a convex polygon doesn't have any "dents." A concave polygon has at least one vertex that is a "dent" — a point of concavity.

- In a convex polygon, the line between any two points in the polygon is completely contained within the polygon. In a concave polygon, we can find a pair of points in the polygon where the line between the points is partially outside the polygon.

- As we move around the perimeter of a convex polygon, we will turn in the same direction at each vertex. In a concave polygon, we will make some left-hand turns and some right-hand turns. We will turn the opposite direction at the point(s) of concavity. (Note that this applies to non-self-intersecting polygons only.)

As we mentioned, degenerate cases can make even these relatively clear-cut definitions blurry. For example, what about a polygon with two consecutive coincident vertices, or an edge that doubles back on itself? Are those polygons considered "convex"? In practice, the following definitions for convexity are often used:

- If my code that is only supposed to work for convex polygons can deal with it, then it's convex. (This is the "If it ain't broke, don't fix it" definition.)

- If my algorithm that tests for convexity decides it's convex, then it's convex. (This is an "Algorithm as definition" explanation.)

For now, let's ignore the pathological cases and give some examples of polygons that we can all agree are definitely convex or definitely concave. Some examples are shown in Figure 12.29. The concave polygon in the upper-right corner has one point of concavity. The bottom concave polygon has five points of concavity.

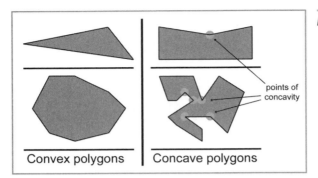

Figure 12.29: Convex vs. concave polygons

Any concave polygon may be divided into convex pieces. For techniques on how this can be done, see [19]. The basic idea is to locate the points of concavity (called "reflex vertices" in that text) and systematically remove them by adding diagonals. In [4], an algorithm is given that works for complex polygons as well simple polygons.

How can we know if a polygon is convex or concave? One method is to examine the sum of the angles at the vertices. Consider a convex polygon with n vertices. The sum of interior angles in a convex polygon is $(n-2)180°$. We have two ways to show this to be true.

- First, let θ_i measure the interior angle at vertex i. Clearly, $\theta_i \leq 180°$ (assuming the polygon is convex). The amount of "turn" that occurs at each vertex will be $180° - \theta_i$. A closed polygon will, of course, "turn" one complete revolution, or $360°$. Therefore:

$$\sum_{i=1}^{n}(180° - \theta_i) = 360°$$

$$n180° - \sum_{i=1}^{n}\theta_i = 360°$$

$$-\sum_{i=1}^{n}\theta_i = 360° - n180°$$

$$\sum_{i=1}^{n}\theta_i = n180° - 360°$$

$$\sum_{i=1}^{n}\theta_i = (n-2)180°$$

- Second, as we will show in Section 12.7.4, any convex polygon with n vertices can be triangulated into $n-2$ triangles. From classical geometry, the sum of the interior angles of a triangle is $180°$. The sum of the interior angles of all of the triangles is $(n-2)180°$, and we can see that this sum must also be equal to the sum of the interior angles of the polygon itself.

Unfortunately, the sum of the interior angles is $(n-2)180°$ for concave as well as convex polygons. So how does this get us any closer to determining whether or not a polygon is convex? For a convex polygon, the interior angle is not larger than the exterior angle. (The exterior angle is not the same as the "turn amount." The interior and exterior angles sum to $360°$.)

So, if we take the sum of the smaller angle (interior or exterior) at each vertex, then the sum will be $(n-2)180°$ for convex polygons and less than that if the polygon is concave. How do we measure the smaller angle? Luckily, we have a tool that does just that — the dot product. In Section 5.10.2, we learned how to compute the angle between two vectors using the dot product. The angle returned using this method always measured the shortest arc.

The code below shows how to determine if a polygon is convex by summing the angles:

Listing 12.4: 3D polygon convexity test using angle sum

```
// Function to determine if a polygon is convex. The polygon is
// assumed to be planar.
//
// Input:
//    n      Number of vertices
//    vl     pointer to array of of vertices

bool   isConvex(int n, const Vector3 vl[]) {

    // Initialize sum to 0 radians

    float angleSum = 0.0f;

    // Go around the polygon and sum the angle at each vertex

    for (int i = 0 ; i < n ; ++i) {

        // Get edge vectors. We have to be careful on
        // the first and last vertices. Also, note that
        // this could be optimized considerably…

        Vector3 e1;
        if (i == 0) {
            e1 = vl[n−1] − vl[i];
        } else {
            e1 = vl[i−1] − vl[i];
        }

        Vector3 e2;
        if (i == n−1) {
            e2 = vl[0] − vl[i];
        } else {
            e2 = vl[i+1] − vl[i];
        }

        // Normalize and compute dot product

        e1.normalize();
        e2.normalize();
        float dot = e1 * e2;

        // Compute smaller angle using "safe" function that protects
        // against range errors which could be caused by
        // numerical imprecision

        float theta = safeAcos(dot);

        // Sum it up
```

```
        angleSum += theta;
    }

    // Figure out what the sum of the angles should be, assuming
    // we are convex. Remember that pi/2 rad = 180 degrees

    float convexAngleSum = (float)(n - 2) * kPiOverTwo;

    // Now, check if the sum of the angles is less than it should be;
    // then we're concave. We give a slight tolerance for
    // numerical imprecision

    if (angleSum < convexAngleSum - (float)n * 0.0001f) {

        // We're concave

        return false;
    }

    // We're convex, within tolerance

    return true;
}
```

Another method for determining convexity is to search for vertices that are points of concavity. If none are found, then the polygon is convex. The basic idea is that each vertex should turn in the same direction. Any vertex that turns in the opposite direction is a point of concavity.

How do we know which way a vertex turns? One trick is to use the cross product on the edge vectors. Recall from Section 5.11.2 that in a left-handed coordinate system, the cross product will point toward you if the vectors form a clockwise turn.

What does "toward you" mean in this case? We'll view the polygon from the front, as determined by the polygon normal. If this normal is not available to us initially, we have to exercise some care in computing it. The techniques in Section 12.5.3 for computing the best-fit normal from a set of points can be used in this case.

In 2D, we can simply act as if the polygon were in 3D at the plane $z = 0$, and we'll assume the normal is $[0, 0, -1]$.

Once we have a normal, we check each vertex of the polygon, computing a normal at that vertex using the adjacent clockwise edge vectors. We take the dot product of the polygon normal with the normal computed at that vertex to determine if they point in opposite directions. If so (the dot product is negative), then we have located a point of concavity.

For more on determining the convexity of a polygon, see [20].

12.7.4 Triangulation and Fanning

Any polygon can be divided into triangles. Thus, all of the operations and calculations for triangles can be applied to polygons. Triangulating complex, self-intersecting, or even simple concave polygons is no trivial task and is slightly out of the scope of this book. For more information, we refer the reader to [4] and [19], both of which cover the intricacies of this task in excellent detail.

Luckily, triangulating simple convex polygons is a trivial matter. One obvious triangulation technique is to pick one vertex (say, the first one) and "fan" the polygon around this vertex. Given a polygon with n vertices, enumerated $\mathbf{v}_1 \ldots \mathbf{v}_n$ around the polygon, we can easily form $n-2$ triangles each of the form $\{ \mathbf{v}_1, \mathbf{v}_{i-1}, \mathbf{v}_i \}$, with the index i going from $3 \ldots n$, as shown in Figure 12.30.

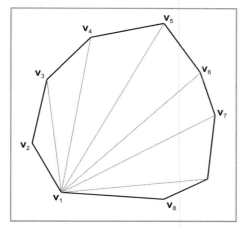

Figure 12.30: Triangulating a convex polygon by fanning

Fanning tends to create many long, thin "sliver" triangles, which can be troublesome in some situations. Numerical inaccuracies inherent in measuring extremely small angles can be problematic, like when computing a surface normal.

A "smarter" technique is to triangulate as follows: consider that we can divide a polygon into two pieces with a diagonal between two vertices. When this occurs, the two interior angles at the vertices of the diagonal are each divided into two new interior angles. Thus, a total of four new interior angles are created. To subdivide a polygon, select the diagonal that maximizes the smallest of these four new interior angles. Divide the polygon in two using this diagonal. Recursively, apply the procedure to each half until only triangles remain.

This algorithm results in a triangulation with fewer slivers, but, in practice, it is often overkill. Depending on the geometry and the application, fanning may be perfectly adequate (and much simpler).

12.8 Exercises

1. Give the slope and y-intercept of the 2D line defined implicitly by $4x + 7y = 42$.
2. Consider a triangle defined by the clockwise enumeration of the vertices $(6, 10, -2)$, $(3, -1, 17)$, $(-9, 8, 0)$.
    a. What is the plane equation of the plane containing this triangle?
    b. Is the point $(3, 4, 5)$ on the front or back side of this plane?
    c. How far is this point from the plane?
    d. Compute the barycentric coordinates of the point $(-3.3, 12.4, 33.2)$.
    e. What is the center of gravity? Incenter? Circumcenter?

Chapter 13

Geometric Tests

This chapter is about geometric tests that can be performed on primitives. It is divided into twenty sections.

- Sections 13.1 through 13.5 present a number of *closest point* tests, which determine the closest point on a given primitive to an arbitrary point.
- Section 13.6 discusses a few general issues related to *intersection tests*, which are used to detect the 3D overlap of a pair of geometric primitives.
- Sections 13.7 through 13.18 present a variety of intersection tests.
- Section 13.19 discusses other intersection tests not covered in this book.
- Section 13.20 presents the complete listing for class AABB3.

In the previous chapter, we discussed a number of calculations that can be performed on a single primitive. In this chapter, we will discuss calculations that relate more than one primitive.

13.1 Closest Point on 2D Implicit Line

Consider an infinite line L in 2D defined implicitly by all points $\mathbf{p}$ such that:
$$\mathbf{p} \cdot \mathbf{n} = d$$

where $\mathbf{n}$ is a unit vector. Our goal is to find, for any point $\mathbf{q}$, the point $\mathbf{q}'$ that is the closest point on L to $\mathbf{q}$. This is the result of projecting $\mathbf{q}$ onto L. Let us draw a second line M through $\mathbf{q}$, parallel to L, as shown in Figure 13.1. Let $\mathbf{n}_M$ and d_M be the normal and d value of the line equation for M. Since L and M are parallel, they have the same normal: $\mathbf{n}_M = \mathbf{n}$. Since $\mathbf{q}$ is on M, d_M can be computed as $\mathbf{q} \cdot \mathbf{n}$.

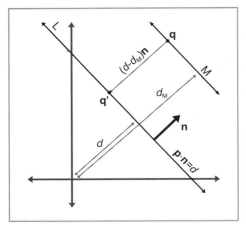

Figure 13.1: Finding the closest point on a 2D implicit line

Now the signed distance from M to L measured parallel to $\mathbf{n}$ is simply $d - d_M = d - \mathbf{q} \cdot \mathbf{n}$. This distance is obviously the same as the distance from $\mathbf{q}$ to $\mathbf{q}'$. (If we only need the distance and not the value of $\mathbf{q}'$, then we can stop here.) To compute the value of $\mathbf{q}'$, we can simply take $\mathbf{q}$ and displace by a multiple of $\mathbf{n}$:

Equation 13.1: Computing the closest point on a 2D implicit line

$$\mathbf{q}' = \mathbf{q} + (d - \mathbf{q} \cdot \mathbf{n})\mathbf{n}$$

13.2 Closest Point on Parametric Ray

Consider the parametric ray R in 2D or 3D defined by:

$$\mathbf{p}(t) = \mathbf{p}_{\text{org}} + t\mathbf{d}$$

where $\mathbf{d}$ is a unit vector, and the parameter t varies from $0 \ldots l$, where l is the length of R. For a given point $\mathbf{q}$, we wish to find the point $\mathbf{q}'$ on R that is closest to $\mathbf{q}$.

This is a simple matter of projecting one vector onto another, which we learned how to do in Section 5.10.3. Let $\mathbf{v}$ be the vector from $\mathbf{p}_{\text{org}}$ to $\mathbf{q}$. We wish to compute the result of projecting $\mathbf{v}$ onto $\mathbf{d}$, or the portion of $\mathbf{v}$ parallel to $\mathbf{d}$. This is illustrated in Figure 13.2.

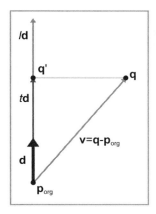

Figure 13.2: Finding the closest point on a ray

The value of the dot product $\mathbf{v} \cdot \mathbf{d}$ is the value t such that $\mathbf{p}(t) = \mathbf{q}'$.

Equation 13.2:
Computing the
closest point on
a parametric ray

$$
\begin{aligned}
t &= \mathbf{d} \cdot \mathbf{v} \\
&= \mathbf{d} \cdot (\mathbf{q} - \mathbf{p}_{\text{org}}) \\
\mathbf{q}' &= \mathbf{p}(t) \\
&= \mathbf{p}_{\text{org}} + t\mathbf{d} \\
&= \mathbf{p}_{\text{org}} + (\mathbf{d} \cdot (\mathbf{q} - \mathbf{p}_{\text{org}}))\mathbf{d}
\end{aligned}
$$

Actually, the equation for $\mathbf{p}(t)$ above computes the point closest to $\mathbf{q}$ on the *infinite line* containing R. If $t < 0$ or $t > l$, then $\mathbf{p}(t)$ is not in the portion contained by R. In this case, the closest point on R to $\mathbf{q}$ will be the origin (if $t < 0$) or endpoint (if $t > l$).

If the ray is defined where t varies from $0 \ldots 1$ and $\mathbf{d}$ is not necessarily a unit vector, then we must divide by the magnitude of $\mathbf{d}$ to compute the t value:

$$
t = \frac{\mathbf{d} \cdot (\mathbf{q} - \mathbf{p}_{\text{org}})}{\|\mathbf{d}\|}
$$

13.3 Closest Point on Plane

Consider a plane P defined in the standard implicit manner as all points $\mathbf{p}$ that satisfy
$\mathbf{p} \cdot \mathbf{n} = d$

where $\mathbf{n}$ is a unit vector. Given a point $\mathbf{q}$, we wish to find the point $\mathbf{q}'$, which is the result of projecting $\mathbf{q}$ onto P. $\mathbf{q}'$ is the closest point on P to $\mathbf{q}$.

We learned how to compute the distance from a point to a plane in Section 12.5.4. To compute $\mathbf{q}'$, we simply displace by this distance, parallel to $\mathbf{n}$:

Equation 13.3:
Computing the
closest point on
a plane

$$
\mathbf{q}' = \mathbf{q} + (d - \mathbf{q} \cdot \mathbf{n})\mathbf{n}
$$

Notice that this is the same as Equation 13.1, which computes the closest point to an implicit line in 2D.

13.4 Closest Point on Circle/Sphere

Imagine a 2D point q and a circle with center c and radius r. (The following discussion will also apply to a sphere in 3D.) We wish to find q', which is the closest point on the circle to q.

Let d be the vector from q to c. This vector intersects the circle at q'. Let b be the vector from q to q', as shown in Figure 13.3.

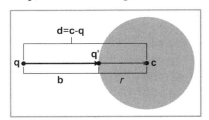

Figure 13.3: Finding the closest point on a circle

Now clearly, $\|b\| = \|d\| - r$. Therefore:

$$b = \frac{\|d\| - r}{\|d\|} d$$

Adding this displacement to q to project onto the circle:

Equation 13.4:
Computing the
closest point on
a circle or sphere

$$
\begin{aligned}
q' &= q + b \\
&= q + \frac{\|d\| - r}{\|d\|} d
\end{aligned}
$$

If $\|d\| < r$, then q is inside the circle. There is some question as to what we should do with this situation. Should $q' = q$, or should we project q onto the surface of the circle? Certain circumstances might call for either behavior. If we decide we wish to project the points onto the surface of the circle, then we will have a problem deciding what to do when $q = c$.

13.5 Closest Point in AABB

Let B be an AABB defined by the extreme points p_{min} and p_{max}. For any point q we can easily compute q', the closest point in B to q. This is done by "pushing" q into B along each axis in turn, as illustrated in Listing 13.1.

Listing 13.1: Computing the closest point in an AABB to a point

```
if (x < minX) {
        x = minX;
} else if (x > maxX) {
        x = maxX;
}

if (y < minY) {
        y = minY;
```

```
    } else if (y > maxY) {
        y = maxY;
    }

    if (z < minZ) {
        z = minZ;
    } else if (z > maxZ) {
        z = maxZ;
    }
```

Notice that if the point is already inside the box, then this code returns the original point.

13.6 Intersection Tests

In the following sections, we will present an assortment of intersection tests. These tests are designed to determine if two geometric primitives intersect and (in some cases) locate the intersection. These primitive tests form the foundation for a collision detection system, which is used to prevent objects from passing through each other and to make things appear to bounce off each other convincingly.

We will consider two different types of intersection tests:

- A **static** test checks two stationary primitives and detects if the two primitives intersect. It is a Boolean test — that is, it usually only returns true (there is an intersection) or false (there is no intersection). More information may be available if there is an intersection, but in general, the test is primarily designed to return a Boolean result.

- A **dynamic** test checks two moving primitives and detects if and when two primitives intersect. Usually the movement is expressed parametrically, and therefore, the result of such a test is not only a Boolean true/false result but also a time value (the value of the parameter t) that indicates when the primitives intersect. For the tests that we will consider here, the movement value is a simple linear displacement — a vector offset that the primitive moves as t varies from $0\ldots1$. Each primitive may have its own movement value. However, it will be easier to view the problem from the point of view of one of the primitives; that primitive is considered to be "still" while the other primitive does all of the "moving." We can easily do this by combining the two displacement vectors to get a single relative displacement vector that describes how the two primitives move in relation to each other. Thus, all of the dynamic tests will usually involve one stationary primitive and one moving primitive.

Notice that many important tests involving rays are actually dynamic tests, since a ray can be viewed as a moving point.

13.7 Intersection of Two Implicit Lines in 2D

Finding the intersection of two lines defined implicitly in 2D is a straightforward matter of solving a system of linear equations. We have two equations (the two implicit equations of the lines) and two unknowns (the x and y coordinates of the point of intersection). Our two equations are:

$$a_1 x + b_1 y = d_1$$
$$a_2 x + b_2 y = d_2$$

Solving this system of equations yields:

Equation 13.5: Computing the intersection of two lines in 2D

$$x = \frac{b_2 d_1 - b_1 d_2}{a_1 b_2 - a_2 b_1}$$
$$y = \frac{a_1 d_2 - a_2 d_1}{a_1 b_2 - a_2 b_1}$$

Just like any system of linear equations, there are three possibilities (as illustrated in Figure 13.4):

■ There is one solution. In this case, the denominators in Equation 13.5 will be nonzero.

■ There are no solutions. This indicates that the lines are parallel and not intersecting. The denominators are zero.

■ There are an infinite number of solutions. This is the case when the two lines are coincident. The denominators are zero.

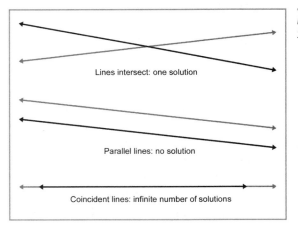

Figure 13.4: Intersection of two lines in 2D — the three cases

Lines intersect: one solution

Parallel lines: no solution

Coincident lines: infinite number of solutions

13.8 Intersection of Two Rays in 3D

Consider two rays in 3D defined parametrically by:

$$\mathbf{r}_1(t_1) = \mathbf{p}_1 + t_1\mathbf{d}_1$$
$$\mathbf{r}_2(t_2) = \mathbf{p}_2 + t_2\mathbf{d}_2$$

We can solve for their point of intersection. For a moment, let us not restrict the range of t_1 and t_2, and therefore, we consider the rays to be infinite in length. Also, the delta vectors $\mathbf{d}_1$ and $\mathbf{d}_2$ do not necessarily have to be unit vectors. If the rays lie in a plane, then we have the same three cases possible from the previous section:

- The rays intersect at exactly one point.
- The rays are parallel, and there is no intersection.
- The rays are coincident, and there are an infinite number of solutions

However, in 3D we have a fourth case where the rays are *skew* and do not share a common plane. An example of skew lines is illustrated in Figure 13.5.

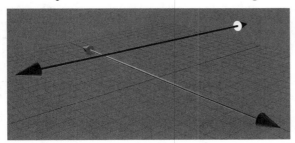

Figure 13.5: Skew lines in 3D do not share a common plane or intersect

We can solve for t_1 and t_2. At the point of intersection:

$$\mathbf{r}_1(t_1) = \mathbf{r}_2(t_2)$$
$$\mathbf{p}_1 + t_1\mathbf{d}_1 = \mathbf{p}_2 + t_2\mathbf{d}_2$$
$$t_1\mathbf{d}_1 = \mathbf{p}_2 + t_2\mathbf{d}_2 - \mathbf{p}_1$$
$$(t_1\mathbf{d}_1) \times \mathbf{d}_2 = (\mathbf{p}_2 + t_2\mathbf{d}_2 - \mathbf{p}_1) \times \mathbf{d}_2$$
$$t_1(\mathbf{d}_1 \times \mathbf{d}_2) = (t_2\mathbf{d}_2) \times \mathbf{d}_2 + (\mathbf{p}_2 - \mathbf{p}_1) \times \mathbf{d}_2$$
$$t_1(\mathbf{d}_1 \times \mathbf{d}_2) = t_2(\mathbf{d}_2 \times \mathbf{d}_2) + (\mathbf{p}_2 - \mathbf{p}_1) \times \mathbf{d}_2$$
$$t_1(\mathbf{d}_1 \times \mathbf{d}_2) = t_2\mathbf{0} + (\mathbf{p}_2 - \mathbf{p}_1) \times \mathbf{d}_2$$
$$t_1(\mathbf{d}_1 \times \mathbf{d}_2) = (\mathbf{p}_2 - \mathbf{p}_1) \times \mathbf{d}_2$$
$$t_1(\mathbf{d}_1 \times \mathbf{d}_2) \cdot (\mathbf{d}_1 \times \mathbf{d}_2) = ((\mathbf{p}_2 - \mathbf{p}_1) \times \mathbf{d}_2) \cdot (\mathbf{d}_1 \times \mathbf{d}_2)$$
$$t_1 = \frac{((\mathbf{p}_2 - \mathbf{p}_1) \times \mathbf{d}_2) \cdot (\mathbf{d}_1 \times \mathbf{d}_2)}{\|\mathbf{d}_1 \times \mathbf{d}_2\|^2}$$

t_2 is obtained in a similar fashion:

$$t_2 = \frac{((\mathbf{p}_2 - \mathbf{p}_1) \times \mathbf{d}_1) \cdot (\mathbf{d}_1 \times \mathbf{d}_2)}{\|\mathbf{d}_1 \times \mathbf{d}_2\|^2}$$

If the lines are parallel (or coincident), then the cross product of $\mathbf{d}_1$ and $\mathbf{d}_2$ is the zero vector, and the denominator of both equations is zero. If the lines are skew, then $\mathbf{p}_1(t_1)$ and $\mathbf{p}_2(t_2)$ are the points of closest approach. To distinguish between skew and intersecting lines, we examine the distance between $\mathbf{p}_1(t_1)$ and $\mathbf{p}_2(t_2)$. Of course, in practice, an exact intersection rarely occurs due to floating-point imprecision, and a tolerance must be used.

The above discussion assumes that the range of the parameters t_1 and t_2 is not restricted. If the rays have finite length (or only extend in one direction), then the appropriate boundary tests would be applied after computing t_1 and t_2.

13.9 Intersection of Ray and Plane

A ray intersects a plane in 3D at a point. Let the ray be defined parametrically by:
$$\mathbf{p}(t) = \mathbf{p}_0 + t\mathbf{d}$$

The plane will be defined in the standard manner, by all points $\mathbf{p}$ such that:
$$\mathbf{p} \cdot \mathbf{n} = d$$

Although we often restrict $\mathbf{n}$ and d to be unit vectors, in this case neither restriction is necessary.

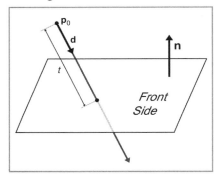

Figure 13.6: Intersection of a ray and plane in 3D

Let us solve for t at the point of intersection, assuming an infinite ray for the moment:

Equation 13.6:
Parametric intersection of a ray and a plane

$$\begin{aligned}
(\mathbf{p}_0 + t\mathbf{d}) \cdot \mathbf{n} &= d \\
\mathbf{p}_0 \cdot \mathbf{n} + t\mathbf{d} \cdot \mathbf{n} &= d \\
t\mathbf{d} \cdot \mathbf{n} &= d - \mathbf{p}_0 \cdot \mathbf{n} \\
t &= \frac{d - \mathbf{p}_0 \cdot \mathbf{n}}{\mathbf{d} \cdot \mathbf{n}}
\end{aligned}$$

If the ray is parallel to the plane, then the denominator $\mathbf{d} \cdot \mathbf{n}$ is zero and there is no intersection. (We may also only wish to intersect with the front of the plane. In this case, we say there is an intersection only if the ray points in an opposite direction as the normal of the plane, i.e., $\mathbf{d} \cdot \mathbf{n} < 0$.) If the value of t is out of range, then the ray does not intersect the plane.

13.10 Intersection of AABB and Plane

Consider a 3D AABB defined by extreme points $\mathbf{p}_{min}$ and $\mathbf{p}_{max}$ and a plane defined in the standard implicit manner by all points $\mathbf{p}$ that satisfy:

$$\mathbf{p} \cdot \mathbf{n} = d$$

where $\mathbf{n}$ is a unit vector. The plane must be expressed in the same coordinate space as the AABB. For techniques on transforming AABBs, see Section 12.4.4. Transforming the plane is probably faster.

The obvious place to start when designing a simple static intersection test is to check whether the box is completely on one side of the plane or the other by taking the dot product of the corner points with $\mathbf{n}$ and comparing these dot products with d. If all of the dot products are greater than d, then the box is completely on the front side of the plane. If all of the dot products are less than d, then the box is completely on the back side of the plane.

Actually, we don't have to check all eight corner points. We'll use a trick similar to the one used in Section 12.4.4 to transform an AABB. For example, if $\mathbf{n}_x > 0$, then the corner with the minimal dot product has $x=x_{min}$ and the corner with the maximal dot product has $x=x_{max}$. If $\mathbf{n}_x < 0$, then the opposite is true. Similar statements apply to $\mathbf{n}_y$ and $\mathbf{n}_z$. We compute the minimum and maximum dot product values. If the minimum dot product value is greater than d or if the maximum dot product is less than d, then there is no intersection. Otherwise, if two corners are found that are on opposite sides of the plane, then an intersection is detected.

A dynamic test goes one step further. We'll consider the plane to be stationary. (Recall from Section 13.6 that it is simpler to view the test from the frame of reference of one of the moving objects.) The displacement of the box will be defined by a unit vector $\mathbf{d}$ and a length l. As before, we first locate the corner points with the minimum and maximum dot product and check for an intersection at $t = 0$. If the box is not initially intersecting the plane, then it must strike the plane at the corner point closest to the plane. This will be one of the two corner points identified in the first step. If we are only interested in colliding with the "front" of the plane, then we can always use the corner with the minimum dot product value. Once we have determined which corner will strike the plane, we use the ray-plane intersection test in Section 13.9.

Class `AABB3` has working implementations of static and dynamic AABB-plane intersection tests. See page 310.

13.11 Intersection of Three Planes

In 3D, three planes intersect at a point, as shown in Figure 13.7.

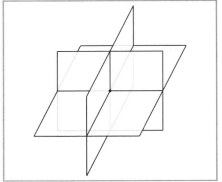

Figure 13.7: Three planes intersect at a point in 3D

Let the three planes be defined implicitly as:

$$\mathbf{p} \cdot \mathbf{n}_1 = d_1$$
$$\mathbf{p} \cdot \mathbf{n}_2 = d_2$$
$$\mathbf{p} \cdot \mathbf{n}_3 = d_3$$

Although we usually use unit vectors for the plane normals, in this case, it is not necessary that $\mathbf{n}_i$ be of unit length. The equations above give us a system of linear equations with three equations and three unknowns (the x, y, and z coordinates of the point of intersection). Solving this system of equations yields the following result, from [11]:

Equation 13.7: Three planes intersect at a point

$$\mathbf{p} = \frac{d_1(\mathbf{n}_2 \times \mathbf{n}_3) + d_2(\mathbf{n}_3 \times \mathbf{n}_1) + d_3(\mathbf{n}_1 \times \mathbf{n}_2)}{(\mathbf{n}_1 \times \mathbf{n}_2) \cdot \mathbf{n}_3}$$

If any pair of planes is parallel, then the point of intersection either does not exist or is not unique. In either case, the denominator is zero.

13.12 Intersection of Ray and Circle/Sphere

In this section, we discuss how to compute the intersection of a ray and a circle in 2D. This also works for computing the intersection of a ray and a sphere in 3D, since we can operate in the plane that contains the ray and the center of the circle and turn the 3D problem into a 2D one. (If the ray lies on a line that passes through the center of the sphere, the plane is not uniquely defined. However, this is not a problem because any of the infinitely many planes that pass through the ray and the center of the sphere can be used.)

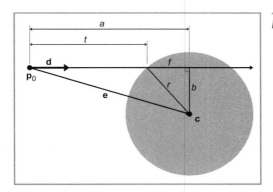

Figure 13.8: Intersection of a ray and sphere

We will use a construction inspired by [15]. See Figure 13.8. The sphere is defined by its center $\mathbf{c}$ and radius r. The ray will be defined by:

$$\mathbf{p}(t) = \mathbf{p}_0 + t\mathbf{d}$$

In this case, we will use a unit vector $\mathbf{d}$ and vary t from 0 to l, the length of the ray. We are solving for the value of t at the point of intersection.

$$t = a - f$$

We can compute a as follows. Let $\mathbf{e}$ be the vector from $\mathbf{p}_0$ to $\mathbf{c}$:

$$\mathbf{e} = \mathbf{c} - \mathbf{p}_0$$

Now project $\mathbf{e}$ onto $\mathbf{d}$. (See Section 5.10.3.) The length of this vector is a, and it can be computed by:

$$a = \mathbf{e} \cdot \mathbf{d}$$

Now, all that remains is to compute f. First, by the Pythagorean theorem, we clearly see that:

$$f^2 + b^2 = r^2$$

We can solve for b^2 using the Pythagorean theorem on the larger triangle:

$$
\begin{aligned}
a^2 + b^2 &= e^2 \\
b^2 &= e^2 - a^2
\end{aligned}
$$

e is the distance from the origin of the ray to the center, i.e., the length of the vector $\mathbf{e}$. Thus, e^2 can be computed by:

$$e^2 = \mathbf{e} \cdot \mathbf{e}$$

Substituting and solving for f:

$$
\begin{aligned}
f^2 + b^2 &= r^2 \\
f^2 + (e^2 - a^2) &= r^2 \\
f^2 &= r^2 - e^2 + a^2 \\
f &= \sqrt{r^2 - e^2 + a^2}
\end{aligned}
$$

And finally, solving for t:

Equation 13.8:
Parametric
intersection of
a ray and
circle/sphere

$$t = a - f$$
$$= a - \sqrt{r^2 - e^2 + a^2}$$

A few notes:

- If the argument $r^2 - e^2 + a^2$ to the square root is negative, then the ray does not intersect the sphere.
- The origin of the ray could be inside the sphere. This is indicated by $e^2 < r^2$. Appropriate behavior in this case would vary depending on the purpose of the test.

13.13 Intersection of Two Circles/Spheres

Detecting the static intersection of two spheres is relatively easy. (The discussion in this section will also apply to circles. In fact, we use circles in the diagrams.) Consider two spheres defined by centers c_1 and c_2 and radii r_1 and r_2, as shown in Figure 13.9. Let d be the distance between their centers. Clearly, the spheres intersect if $d < r_1 + r_2$. In practice, we can avoid the square root involved in the calculation of d by checking if $d^2 < (r_1 + r_2)^2$.

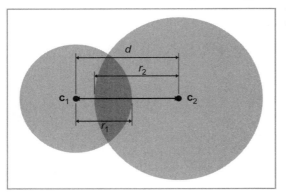

Figure 13.9: Intersection of two spheres

Detecting the intersection of two moving spheres is slightly more difficult. Assume for the moment that we have two separate displacement vectors d_1 and d_2, one for each sphere, that describe how the spheres will move during the period of time under consideration. This is shown in Figure 13.10.

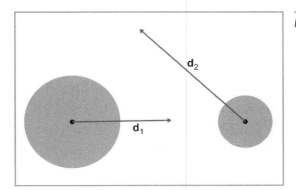

Figure 13.10: Two moving spheres

We can simplify the problem by viewing it from the point of view of the first sphere. Consider that sphere to be "stationary," while the other sphere is the "moving" sphere. This gives us a single displacement vector $\mathbf{d}$, computed as the difference of the two movement vectors $\mathbf{d}_2 - \mathbf{d}_1$. This is illustrated in Figure 13.11.

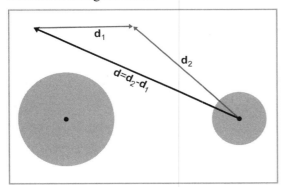

Figure 13.11: Combining displacement vectors so that one sphere is considered stationary

Let the stationary sphere be defined by its center $\mathbf{c}_s$ and radius r_s. The radius of the moving sphere is r_m. The center of the moving sphere is $\mathbf{c}_m$ at $t{=}0$. Rather than varying t from $0\ldots1$, we will normalize $\mathbf{d}$ and vary t from $0\ldots l$, where l is the distance traveled. So the position of the center of the moving sphere at time t is given by $\mathbf{c}_m + t\mathbf{d}$. Our goal is to find t, the time at which the moving sphere touches the stationary sphere. The geometry involved is illustrated in Figure 13.12.

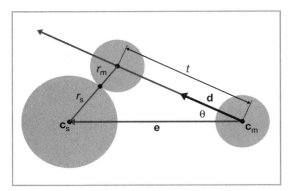

Figure 13.12: Dynamic intersection of circles/ spheres

To solve for t, we begin by calculating an intermediate vector $\mathbf{e}$ as the vector from $\mathbf{c}_m$ to $\mathbf{c}_s$ and set r equal to the sum of the radii:

$$\mathbf{e} = \mathbf{c}_s - \mathbf{c}_m$$

$$r = r_m + r_s$$

According to the law of cosines (see Appendix A), we have:

$$r^2 = t^2 + \|\mathbf{e}\|^2 - 2t\|\mathbf{e}\|\cos\theta$$

Apply the geometric interpretation of the dot product (see Section 5.10.2) and simplify:

$$r^2 = t^2 + \|\mathbf{e}\|^2 - 2t\|\mathbf{e}\|\cos\theta$$
$$r^2 = t^2 + \mathbf{e}\cdot\mathbf{e} - 2t(\mathbf{e}\cdot\mathbf{d})$$
$$0 = t^2 - 2(\mathbf{e}\cdot\mathbf{d})t + \mathbf{e}\cdot\mathbf{e} - r^2$$

Apply the quadratic formula:

$$0 = t^2 - 2(\mathbf{e}\cdot\mathbf{d})t + \mathbf{e}\cdot\mathbf{e} - r^2$$

$$t = \frac{2(\mathbf{e}\cdot\mathbf{d}) \pm \sqrt{(-2(\mathbf{e}\cdot\mathbf{d}))^2 - 4(\mathbf{e}\cdot\mathbf{e} - r^2)}}{2}$$

$$t = \frac{2(\mathbf{e}\cdot\mathbf{d}) \pm \sqrt{4(\mathbf{e}\cdot\mathbf{d})^2 - 4(\mathbf{e}\cdot\mathbf{e} - r^2)}}{2}$$

$$t = \mathbf{e}\cdot\mathbf{d} \pm \sqrt{(\mathbf{e}\cdot\mathbf{d})^2 + r^2 - \mathbf{e}\cdot\mathbf{e}}$$

Which root do we pick? The lower number (the negative root) is the t value when the spheres begin intersecting. The greater number (the positive root) is the point where the spheres cease to intersect. We are interested in the first intersection:

$$t = \mathbf{e}\cdot\mathbf{d} - \sqrt{(\mathbf{e}\cdot\mathbf{d})^2 + r^2 - \mathbf{e}\cdot\mathbf{e}}$$

A few important notes:

- If $\|\mathbf{e}\| < r$, then the spheres are intersecting at $t=0$.
- If $t < 0$ or $t > l$, then the intersection does not occur within the period of time being considered.
- If the value inside the square root is negative, then there is no intersection.

13.14 Intersection of Sphere and AABB

To detect the static intersection of a sphere and an axially aligned bounding box (AABB), we first find the point on the axially aligned bounding box that is closest to the center of the sphere using the techniques from Section 13.5. We compute the distance from this point to the center of the sphere, and we compare this distance with the radius. (Actually, in practice, we compare the distance squared against the radius squared to avoid the square root in the distance computation.) If the distance is smaller than the radius, then the sphere intersects the AABB.

In [1], Arvo discusses this technique, which he uses for intersecting spheres with "solid" boxes. He also discusses some tricks for intersecting spheres with "hollow" boxes.

The static test was relatively simple. Unfortunately, the dynamic test is more complicated. For details, see [16].

13.15 Intersection of Sphere and Plane

Detecting the static intersection of a sphere and a plane is relatively easy. We simply compute the distance from the center of the sphere to the plane using Equation 12.14 (see Section 12.5.4). If this distance is less than the radius of the sphere, then the sphere intersects the plane. We can actually make a more robust test, which classifies the sphere as being completely on the front, completely on the back, or straddling the sphere. Examine Listing 13.2.

Listing 13.2: Determining which side of a plane a sphere is on

```
// Given a sphere and plane, determine which side of the plane
// the sphere is on.
//
// Return values:
//
// < 0 Sphere is completely on the back
// > 0 Sphere is completely on the front
// 0   Sphere straddles plane

int   classifySpherePlane(
      const Vector3    &planeNormal,     // must be normalized
      float       planeD,                // p * planeNormal = planeD
      const Vector3    &sphereCenter,    // center of sphere
      float       sphereRadius           // radius of sphere
) {
```

```
// Compute distance from center of sphere to the plane

float d = planeNormal * sphereCenter - planeD;

// Completely on the front side?

if (d >= sphereRadius) {
    return +1;
}

// Completely on the back side?

if (d <= -sphereRadius) {
    return -1;
}

// Sphere intersects the plane

return 0;
}
```

The dynamic situation is only slightly more complicated. We will consider the plane to be stationary, assigning all relative displacement to the sphere.

We will define the plane in the usual manner using a normalized surface normal $\mathbf{n}$ and distance value d, such that all points $\mathbf{p}$ in the plane satisfy the equation $\mathbf{p} \cdot \mathbf{n} = d$. The sphere is defined by its radius r and the initial position of the center $\mathbf{c}$. The displacement of the sphere will be given by a unit vector $\mathbf{d}$ specifying the direction and a distance l. As t varies from $0 \ldots l$, the motion of the center of the sphere is given by the line equation $\mathbf{c} + t\mathbf{d}$. This situation is shown viewing the plane edge-on in Figure 13.13.

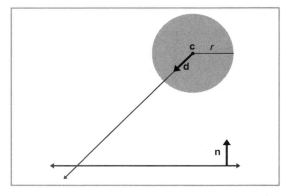

Figure 13.13: A sphere moving toward a plane

The problem is greatly simplified by realizing that no matter where on the surface of the plane the intersection occurs, the point of contact on the surface of the sphere is always the same. That point of contact is given by $\mathbf{c} - r\mathbf{n}$, as shown in Figure 13.14.

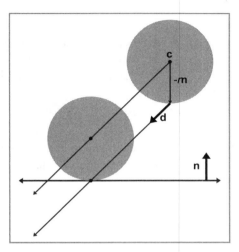

Figure 13.14: Point of contact between a sphere and a plane

Now that we know where the point of contact will occur on the sphere, we can use a simple ray-plane intersection test from Section 13.9. We start with our solution to the ray-plane intersection test from Equation 13.6, and then we substitute in for $\mathbf{p}_0$:

Equation 13.9:
Dynamic
intersection of
a sphere and
plane

$$
\begin{aligned}
t &= \frac{d - \mathbf{p}_0 \cdot \mathbf{n}}{\mathbf{d} \cdot \mathbf{n}} \\
&= \frac{d - (\mathbf{c} - r\mathbf{n}) \cdot \mathbf{n}}{\mathbf{d} \cdot \mathbf{n}} \\
&= \frac{d - \mathbf{c} \cdot \mathbf{n} + r}{\mathbf{d} \cdot \mathbf{n}}
\end{aligned}
$$

13.16 Intersection of Ray and Triangle

The ray-triangle intersection test is very important in graphics and computational geometry. In the absence of a special ray trace test against a given complex object, we can always represent (or at least approximate) the surface of the object using a triangle mesh and then ray trace against this triangle mesh representation.

We will use a simple strategy from [2]. The first step is to compute the point where the ray intersects the plane containing the triangle. We learned how to compute the intersection of a plane and a ray in Section 13.9. Then, we test to see if that point is inside the triangle by computing the barycentric coordinates of the point. We learned how to do this in Section 12.6.3.

To make this test as fast as possible, we use a few tricks:

- Detect and return a negative result (no collision) as soon as possible. This is known as "early out."

- Defer expensive mathematical operations, such as division, as long as possible. This is for two reasons. First, if the result of the expensive calculation is not needed, for example, if we took an early out, then the time we spent performing the operation was wasted. Second, it gives the compiler plenty of room to take advantage of the operator pipeline in modern processors. If an operation such as division has a long latency, then the compiler may be able to look ahead and generate code that begins the division operation early. It then generates code that performs other tests (possibly taking an early out) while the division operation is under way. Then at execution time, when and if the result of the division is actually needed, the result will be available, or at least partially completed.

■ Only detect collisions where the ray approaches the triangle from the front side. This allows us to take a very early out on approximately half of the triangles.

The code below implements these techniques. Although it is commented in the listing, we have chosen to perform some floating-point comparisons "backward" since this behaves better in the presence of invalid floating-point input data (NANs).

```
// Ray-triangle intersection test.
//
// Algorithm from Didier Badouel, Graphics Gems I, pp 390-393

float rayTriangleIntersect(
      const Vector3 &rayOrg,    // origin of the ray
      const Vector3 &rayDelta,  // ray length and direction
      const Vector3 &p0,        // triangle vertices
      const Vector3 &p1,        // .
      const Vector3 &p2,        // .
      float minT                // closest intersection found so far. (Start with 1.0)
) {

      // We'll return this huge number if no intersection is detected

      const float kNoIntersection = 1e30f;

      // Compute clockwise edge vectors.

      Vector3    e1 = p1 - p0;
      Vector3    e2 = p2 - p1;

      // Compute surface normal. (Unnormalized)

      Vector3    n = crossProduct(e1, e2);

      // Compute gradient, which tells us how steep of an angle
      // we are approaching the *front* side of the triangle

      float  dot = n * rayDelta;

      // Check for a ray that is parallel to the triangle or not
      // pointing toward the front face of the triangle.
      //
      // Note that this also will reject degenerate triangles and
      // rays as well. We code this in a very particular
      // way so that NANs will bail here. (This does not
      // behave the same as "dot >= 0.0f" when NANs are involved.)

      if (!(dot < 0.0f)) {
            return kNoIntersection;
      }

      // Compute d value for the plane equation. We will
      // use the plane equation with d on the right side:
```

```
//
// Ax + By + Cz = d

float d = n * p0;

// Compute parametric point of intersection with the plane
// containing the triangle, checking at the earliest
// possible stages for trivial rejection

float t = d - n * rayOrg;

// Is ray origin on the backside of the polygon? Again,
// we phrase the check so that NANs will bail

if (!(t <= 0.0f)) {
    return kNoIntersection;
}

// Closer intersection already found? (Or does
// ray not reach the plane?)
//
// since dot < 0:
//
//     t/dot > minT
//
// is the same as
//
//     t < dot*minT
//
// (And then we invert it for NAN checking...)

if (!(t >= dot*minT)) {
    return kNoIntersection;
}

// OK, ray intersects the plane. Compute actual parametric
// point of intersection

t /= dot;
assert(t >= 0.0f);
assert(t <= minT);

// Compute 3D point of intersection

Vector3 p = rayOrg + rayDelta*t;

// Find dominant axis to select which plane
// to project onto, and compute u's and v's

float u0, u1, u2;
float v0, v1, v2;
if (fabs(n.x) > fabs(n.y)) {
    if (fabs(n.x) > fabs(n.z)) {
        u0 = p.y - p0.y;
        u1 = p1.y - p0.y;
        u2 = p2.y - p0.y;

        v0 = p.z - p0.z;
        v1 = p1.z - p0.z;
        v2 = p2.z - p0.z;
```

```
        } else {
                u0 = p.x - p0.x;
                u1 = p1.x - p0.x;
                u2 = p2.x - p0.x;

                v0 = p.y - p0.y;
                v1 = p1.y - p0.y;
                v2 = p2.y - p0.y;
        }
    } else {
        if (fabs(n.y) > fabs(n.z)) {
                u0 = p.x - p0.x;
                u1 = p1.x - p0.x;
                u2 = p2.x - p0.x;

                v0 = p.z - p0.z;
                v1 = p1.z - p0.z;
                v2 = p2.z - p0.z;
        } else {
                u0 = p.x - p0.x;
                u1 = p1.x - p0.x;
                u2 = p2.x - p0.x;

                v0 = p.y - p0.y;
                v1 = p1.y - p0.y;
                v2 = p2.y - p0.y;
        }
    }

    // Compute denominator, check for invalid

    float temp = u1 * v2 - v1 * u2;
    if (!(temp != 0.0f)) {
        return kNoIntersection;
    }
    temp = 1.0f / temp;

    // Compute barycentric coords, checking for out-of-range
    // at each step

    float alpha = (u0 * v2 - v0 * u2) * temp;
    if (!(alpha >= 0.0f)) {
        return kNoIntersection;
    }

    float beta = (u1 * v0 - v1 * u0) * temp;
    if (!(beta >= 0.0f)) {
        return kNoIntersection;
    }

    float gamma = 1.0f - alpha - beta;
    if (!(gamma >= 0.0f)) {
        return kNoIntersection;
    }

    // Return parametric point of intersection

    return t;
}
```

There is one more significant strategy not illustrated above for optimizing expensive calculations: precompute their results. If values such as the polygon normal can be computed ahead of time, then different strategies may be used.

Because of the fundamental importance of this test, programmers are always looking for ways to make it faster. Tomas Möller has a slightly different strategy that works faster in many cases. For links to his and others' research, visit the web site for this book, gamemath.com.

13.17 Intersection of Ray and AABB

Computing the intersection of a ray with an AABB is an important calculation, since the result of this test is commonly used for trivial rejection on more complicated objects. (For example, if we wish to ray trace against multiple triangle meshes, we can first ray trace against the AABBs of the meshes to trivially reject entire meshes at once, rather than having to check each triangle.)

In [24], Woo describes a method that first determines which side of the box will be intersected, and then performs a ray-plane intersection test against the plane containing that side. If the point of intersection with the plane is within the box, then there is an intersection. Otherwise, there is no intersection.

Woo's technique is applied in the definition of AABB3::rayIntersect(). See page 307.

13.18 Intersection of Two AABBs

Detecting the intersection of two static AABBs is trivial. We simply check for overlapping extents on each dimension independently. If there is no overlap on a particular dimension, then the two AABBs do not intersect. This technique is used in intersectAABBs() in AABB3.cpp (see page 312).

Dynamic intersection of AABBs is only slightly more complicated. Consider a stationary AABB defined by extreme points s_{min} and s_{max} and a moving AABB defined by extreme points m_{min} and m_{max} (in the initial position, at $t = 0$). The moving AABB displaces by an amount given by the vector d, as t varies from $0\ldots1$.

Our task is to compute t, the parametric point in time where the moving box first collides with the stationary box. (We assume that the boxes are not initially intersecting.) To do this, we will attempt to determine the first point in time when the boxes overlap in all dimensions simultaneously. Since this applies in 2D or 3D, we will illustrate the problem in 2D. (Extending the technique into 3D is straightforward.) We will analyze each coordinate separately, solving two (or three, in 3D) separate one-dimensional problems, and then combine these results to give the answer.

The problem is now one-dimensional. We need to know the interval of time when the two boxes overlap on a particular dimension. Imagine projecting the problem onto the x-axis, for example, as shown in Figure 13.15.

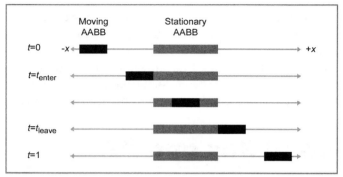

Figure 13.15: Projecting the dynamic AABB intersection problem onto one axis

As we advance in time, the black rectangle representing the moving box will slide along the number line. At $t = 0$ in Figure 13.15, the moving box is completely to the left of the stationary box, and at $t = 1$, the moving box is completely to the right of the stationary box. There is a point t_{enter} where the boxes first begin to overlap and a point t_{leave} where the boxes cease to overlap. For the dimension we are considering, let $m_{min}(t)$ and $m_{max}(t)$ be the minimum and maximum values of the moving box at time t, given by:

$$m_{min}(t) = m_{min}(0) + td$$
$$m_{max}(t) = m_{max}(0) + td$$

$m_{min}(0)$ and $m_{max}(0)$ are the initial extents of the moving box and d is the component of the displacement vector $\mathbf{d}$ for this axis. Let s_{min} and s_{max} have similar definitions for the stationary box. (Of course, these values are independent of t since the box is stationary.) t_{enter} is the t value for which $m_{max}(t)$ is equal to s_{min}. Solving, we get:

$$m_{max}(t_{enter}) = s_{min}$$
$$m_{max}(0) + t_{enter}d = s_{min}$$
$$t_{enter}d = s_{min} - m_{max}(0)$$
$$t_{enter} = \frac{s_{min} - m_{max}(0)}{d}$$

Likewise, we can solve for t_{leave}:

$$m_{min}(t_{leave}) = s_{max}$$
$$m_{min}(0) + t_{leave}d = s_{max}$$
$$t_{leave}d = s_{max} - m_{min}(0)$$
$$t_{leave} = \frac{s_{max} - m_{min}(0)}{d}$$

Three important notes:

- If the denominator d is zero, then boxes either *always* overlap or *never* overlap. We will show how to handle these cases in our code.

- If the moving box begins on the right side of the stationary box and moves left, then t_{enter} will be greater than t_{leave}. We will handle this scenario by swapping their values to ensure that $t_{enter} < t_{leave}$.

- The values for t_{enter} and t_{leave} may be outside the range of $0 \ldots 1$. To accommodate t values outside this range, we can think of the moving box as moving along an infinite trajectory parallel to $\mathbf{d}$. If $t_{enter} > 1$ or $t_{leave} < 0$, then there is no overlap in the period of time under consideration.

We now have a way to find the interval of time, bounded by t_{enter} and t_{leave}, where the two boxes overlap on a single dimension. The intersection of these intervals on all dimensions gives the interval of time where the boxes intersect with each other. This is illustrated in Figure 13.16 for two time intervals in 2D. (Don't confuse this with Figure 13.15. In Figure 13.16, the axis is the *time* axis. In Figure 13.15, the axis shown is the *x*-axis.)

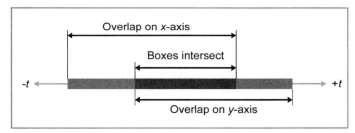

Figure 13.16: Intersecting two intervals of time

If the interval is empty, then the boxes never collide. If the interval lies completely outside the range $t = 0 \ldots 1$, then there is no collision over the period of time we are interested in. Actually, the interval during which the boxes overlap is more information than we want, since we are only interested in the point in time where the boxes begin intersecting, not when they cease to intersect. Still, we will need to maintain this interval, mainly to determine if it is empty.

For a complete implementation, see the definition of `intersectMovingAABBs()` on page 313.

Unfortunately, in practice, bounding boxes for objects are rarely axially aligned in the same coordinate space. However, because this test is relatively fast, it is useful as a preliminary trivial rejection test to be followed by a more specific (and usually more expensive) test.

An alternative test allows one of the boxes to be arbitrarily oriented. For links to more information on this test, visit `gamemath.com`.

13.19 Other Tests

There are a number of other important geometric tests that were not discussed due to time constraints:

- Triangle-triangle intersection tests
- AABB-OBB (oriented bounding box) intersection tests
- Triangle-box intersection tests

■ Tests using more "exotic" primitives, such as cylinders, cones, and tori (that's plural for torus, which is the doughnut-shaped thing).

More information on these tests can be found through some of the links at gamemath.com.

13.20 Class AABB3

Previous sections have used class AABB3, which is used to represent a 3D axially aligned bounding box (AABB). In this section, we give the complete class definition and implementation.

The class is declared in AABB3.h, which is listed below:

Listing 13.3: AABB3.h

```
/////////////////////////////////////////////////////////////////////
//
// 3D Math Primer for Graphics and Game Development
//
// AABB3.h - Declarations for class AABB3
//
// Visit gamemath.com for the latest version of this file.
//
// For more details, see AABB3.cpp
//
/////////////////////////////////////////////////////////////////////

#ifndef __AABB3_H_INCLUDED__
#define __AABB3_H_INCLUDED__

#ifndef __VECTOR3_H_INCLUDED__
    #include "Vector3.h"
#endif

class Matrix4x3;

//---------------------------------------------------------------------
// class AABB3
//
// Implement a 3D axially aligned bounding box

class AABB3 {
public:

// Public data

    // Min and max values. Pretty simple.

    Vector3     min;
    Vector3     max;

// Query for dimentions

    Vector3     size() const { return max - min; }
    float       xSize() { return max.x - min.x; }
    float       ySize() { return max.y - min.y; }
```

```
        float       zSize() { return max.z - min.z; }
        Vector3     center() const { return (min + max) * .5f; }

        // Fetch one of the eight corner points. See the
        // .cpp for numbering conventions

        Vector3     corner(int i) const;

// Box operations

        // "Empty" the box by setting the values to really
        // large/small numbers

        void   empty();

        // Add a point to the box

        void   add(const Vector3 &p);

        // Add an AABB to the box

        void   add(const AABB3 &box);

        // Transform the box and compute the new AABB

        void   setToTransformedBox(const AABB3 &box, const Matrix4×3 &m);

// Containment/intersection tests

        // Return true if the box is empty

        bool   isEmpty() const;

        // Return true if the box contains a point

        bool   contains(const Vector3 &p) const;

        // Return the closest point on this box to another point

        Vector3     closestPointTo(const Vector3 &p) const;

        // Return true if we intersect a sphere

        bool   intersectsSphere(const Vector3 &center, float radius) const;

        // Parametric intersection with a ray. Returns >1 if no intresection

        float rayIntersect(const Vector3 &rayOrg, const Vector3 &rayDelta,
                Vector3 *returnNormal = 0) const;

        // Classify box as being on one side or the other of a plane

        int    classifyPlane(const Vector3 &n, float d) const;

        // Dynamic intersection with plane

        float intersectPlane(const Vector3 n, float planeD,
                const Vector3 &dir) const;
};
```

```
// Check if two AABBs intersect, and return true if so. Optionally, return
// the AABB of their intersection if an intersection is detected.

bool    intersectAABBs(const AABB3 &box1, const AABB3 &box2,
        AABB3 *boxIntersect = 0);

// Return parametric point in time when a moving AABB collides
// with a stationary AABB. Returns > 1 if no intersection

float  intersectMovingAABB(
       const AABB3 &stationaryBox,
       const AABB3 &movingBox,
       const Vector3 &d
);

//////////////////////////////////////////////////////////////////////////
#endif // #ifndef __AABB3_H_INCLUDED__
```

Implementation for class AABB3 is in AABB3.cpp, listed below:

Listing 13.4: AABB3.cpp

```
//////////////////////////////////////////////////////////////////////////
//
// 3D Math Primer for Graphics and Game Development
//
// AABB3.cpp - Implementation for class AABB3
//
// Visit gamemath.com for the latest version of this file.
//
// For more details, see Chapter 12
//
//////////////////////////////////////////////////////////////////////////

#include <assert.h>
#include <stdlib.h>

#include "AABB3.h"
#include "Matrix4x3.h"
#include "CommonStuff.h"

//////////////////////////////////////////////////////////////////////////
//
// class AABB3 member functions
//
//////////////////////////////////////////////////////////////////////////

//-------------------------------------------------------------------------
// AABB3::corner
//
```

```
// Return one of the eight corner points. The points are numbered as follows:
//
//             6                              7
//              ----------------------------
//            /|                          /|
//           / |                         / |
//          /  |                        /  |
//         /   |                       /   |
//        /    |                      /    |
//       /     |                     /     |
//      /      |                    /      |
//     /       |                   /       |
//   2/        |                 3/        |
//   /---------------------------/         |
//   |         |                 |         |
//   |       4 |                 |         |    +Y
//   |         |-----------------|---------|
//   |        /                  |        /  5  |
//   |       /                   |       /      |    +Z
//   |      /                    |      /       |
//   |     /                     |     /        |
//   |    /                      |    /         |   /
//   |   /                       |   /          |  /
//   |  /                        |  /           | /
//   | /                         | /            |/
//   |/                          |/    ---------------- +X
//    ----------------------------
//   0                           1
//
// Bit 0 selects min.x vs. max.x
// Bit 1 selects min.y vs. max.y
// Bit 2 selects min.z vs. max.z

Vector3     AABB3::corner(int i) const {

    // Make sure index is in range...

    assert(i >= 0);
    assert(i <= 7);

    // Return it

    return Vector3(
        (i & 1) ? max.x : min.x,
        (i & 2) ? max.y : min.y,
        (i & 4) ? max.z : min.z
    );
}


//-------------------------------------------------------------------------
// AABB3::empty
//
// "Empty" the box by setting the values to really
// large/small numbers
```

```
void  AABB3::empty() {
    const float kBigNumber = 1e37f;
    min.x = min.y = min.z = kBigNumber;
    max.x = max.y = max.z = -kBigNumber;
}

//---------------------------------------------------------------------------
// AABB3::add
//
// Add a point to the box

void  AABB3::add(const Vector3 &p) {

    // Expand the box as necessary to contain the point.

    if (p.x < min.x) min.x = p.x;
    if (p.x > max.x) max.x = p.x;
    if (p.y < min.x) min.y = p.y;
    if (p.y > max.x) max.y = p.y;
    if (p.z < min.x) min.z = p.z;
    if (p.z > max.x) max.z = p.z;
}

//---------------------------------------------------------------------------
// AABB3::add
//
// Add an AABB to the box

void  AABB3::add(const AABB3 &box) {

    // Expand the box as necessary.

    if (box.min.x < min.x) min.x = box.min.x;
    if (box.min.x > max.x) max.x = box.min.x;
    if (box.min.y < min.x) min.y = box.min.y;
    if (box.min.y > max.x) max.y = box.min.y;
    if (box.min.z < min.x) min.z = box.min.z;
    if (box.min.z > max.x) max.z = box.min.z;
}

//---------------------------------------------------------------------------
// AABB3::setToTransformedBox
//
// Transform the box and compute the new AABB.  Remember, this always
// results in an AABB that is at least as big as the origin, and it may be
// considerably bigger.
//
// See 12.4.4

void  AABB3::setToTransformedBox(const AABB3 &box, const Matrix4×3 &m) {

    // If we're empty, then bail

    if (box.isEmpty()) {
        empty();
        return;
    }

    // Start with the translation portion
```

```
      min = max = getTranslation(m);

      // Examine each of the nine matrix elements
      // and compute the new AABB

      if (m.m11 > 0.0f) {
            min.x += m.m11 * box.min.x; max.x += m.m11 * box.max.x;
      } else {
            min.x += m.m11 * box.max.x; max.x += m.m11 * box.min.x;
      }

      if (m.m12 > 0.0f) {
            min.y += m.m12 * box.min.x; max.y += m.m12 * box.max.x;
      } else {
            min.y += m.m12 * box.max.x; max.y += m.m12 * box.min.x;
      }

      if (m.m13 > 0.0f) {
            min.z += m.m13 * box.min.x; max.z += m.m13 * box.max.x;
      } else {
            min.z += m.m13 * box.max.x; max.z += m.m13 * box.min.x;
      }

      if (m.m21 > 0.0f) {
            min.x += m.m21 * box.min.y; max.x += m.m21 * box.max.y;
      } else {
            min.x += m.m21 * box.max.y; max.x += m.m21 * box.min.y;
      }

      if (m.m22 > 0.0f) {
            min.y += m.m22 * box.min.y; max.y += m.m22 * box.max.y;
      } else {
            min.y += m.m22 * box.max.y; max.y += m.m22 * box.min.y;
      }

      if (m.m23 > 0.0f) {
            min.z += m.m23 * box.min.y; max.z += m.m23 * box.max.y;
      } else {
            min.z += m.m23 * box.max.y; max.z += m.m23 * box.min.y;
      }

      if (m.m31 > 0.0f) {
            min.x += m.m31 * box.min.z; max.x += m.m31 * box.max.z;
      } else {
            min.x += m.m31 * box.max.z; max.x += m.m31 * box.min.z;
      }

      if (m.m32 > 0.0f) {
            min.y += m.m32 * box.min.z; max.y += m.m32 * box.max.z;
      } else {
            min.y += m.m32 * box.max.z; max.y += m.m32 * box.min.z;
      }

      if (m.m33 > 0.0f) {
            min.z += m.m33 * box.min.z; max.z += m.m33 * box.max.z;
      } else {
            min.z += m.m33 * box.max.z; max.z += m.m33 * box.min.z;
      }
}
```

```
//-------------------------------------------------------------------------
// AABB3::isEmpty
//
// Return true if the box is empty

bool   AABB3::isEmpty() const {

    // Check if we're inverted on any axis

    return (min.x > max.x) || (min.y > max.y) || (min.z > max.z);
}

//-------------------------------------------------------------------------
// AABB3::contains
//
// Return true if the box contains a point

bool   AABB3::contains(const Vector3 &p) const {

    // Check for overlap on each axis

    return
        (p.x >= min.x) && (p.x <= max.x) &&
        (p.y >= min.y) && (p.y <= max.y) &&
        (p.z >= min.z) && (p.z <= max.z);
}

//-------------------------------------------------------------------------
// AABB3::closestPointTo
//
// Return the closest point on this box to another point

Vector3    AABB3::closestPointTo(const Vector3 &p) const {

    // "Push" p into the box on each dimension

    Vector3 r;

    if (p.x < min.x) {
        r.x = min.x;
    } else if (p.x > max.x) {
        r.x = max.x;
    } else {
        r.x = p.x;
    }

    if (p.y < min.y) {
        r.y = min.y;
    } else if (p.y > max.y) {
        r.y = max.y;
    } else {
        r.y = p.y;
    }

    if (p.z < min.z) {
        r.z = min.z;
    } else if (p.z > max.z) {
        r.z = max.z;
    } else {
        r.z = p.z;
```

```
        }

        // Return it

        return r;
}

//---------------------------------------------------------------------------
// AABB3::intersectsSphere
//
// Return true if we intersect a sphere.  Uses Arvo's algorithm.

bool    AABB3::intersectsSphere(const Vector3 &center, float radius) const {

        // Find the closest point on box to the point

        Vector3     closestPoint = closestPointTo(center);

        // Check if it's within range

        return distanceSquared(center, closestPoint) < radius*radius;
}

//---------------------------------------------------------------------------
// AABB3::rayIntersect
//
// Parametric intersection with a ray.  Returns parametric point
// of intsersection in range 0...1 or a really big number (>1) if no
// intersection.
//
// From "Fast Ray-Box Intersection," by Woo in Graphics Gems I,
// page 395.
//
// See 12.9.11

float AABB3::rayIntersect(
        const Vector3 &rayOrg,          // orgin of the ray
        const Vector3 &rayDelta,        // length and direction of the ray
        Vector3 *returnNormal           // optionally, the normal is returned
) const {

        // We'll return this huge number if no intersection

        const float kNoIntersection = 1e30f;

        // Check for point inside box, trivial reject, and determine parametric
        // distance to each front face

        bool inside = true;

        float xt, xn;
        if (rayOrg.x < min.x) {
                xt = min.x — rayOrg.x;
                if (xt > rayDelta.x) return kNoIntersection;
                xt /= rayDelta.x;
                inside = false;
                xn = —1.0f;
        } else if (rayOrg.x > max.x) {
                xt = max.x — rayOrg.x;
                if (xt < rayDelta.x) return kNoIntersection;
```

```
            xt /= rayDelta.x;
            inside = false;
            xn = 1.0f;
    } else {
            xt = -1.0f;
    }

    float yt, yn;
    if (rayOrg.y < min.y) {
            yt = min.y - rayOrg.y;
            if (yt > rayDelta.y) return kNoIntersection;
            yt /= rayDelta.y;
            inside = false;
            yn = -1.0f;
    } else if (rayOrg.y > max.y) {
            yt = max.y - rayOrg.y;
            if (yt < rayDelta.y) return kNoIntersection;
            yt /= rayDelta.y;
            inside = false;
            yn = 1.0f;
    } else {
            yt = -1.0f;
    }

    float zt, zn;
    if (rayOrg.z < min.z) {
            zt = min.z - rayOrg.z;
            if (zt > rayDelta.z) return kNoIntersection;
            zt /= rayDelta.z;
            inside = false;
            zn = -1.0f;
    } else if (rayOrg.z > max.z) {
            zt = max.z - rayOrg.z;
            if (zt < rayDelta.z) return kNoIntersection;
            zt /= rayDelta.z;
            inside = false;
            zn = 1.0f;
    } else {
            zt = -1.0f;
    }

    // Inside box?

    if (inside) {
            if (returnNormal != NULL) {
                    *returnNormal = -rayDelta;
                    returnNormal->normalize();
            }
            return 0.0f;
    }

    // Select farthest plane - this is
    // the plane of intersection.

    int which = 0;
    float t = xt;
    if (yt > t) {
            which = 1;
            t = yt;
    }
```

```
        if (zt > t) {
              which = 2;
              t = zt;
        }

        switch (which) {

              case 0: // intersect with yz plane
              {
                    float y = rayOrg.y + rayDelta.y*t;
                    if (y < min.y || y > max.y) return kNoIntersection;
                    float z = rayOrg.z + rayDelta.z*t;
                    if (z < min.z || z > max.z) return kNoIntersection;

                    if (returnNormal != NULL) {
                          returnNormal->x = xn;
                          returnNormal->y = 0.0f;
                          returnNormal->z = 0.0f;
                    }

              } break;

              case 1: // intersect with xz plane
              {
                    float x = rayOrg.x + rayDelta.x*t;
                    if (x < min.x || x > max.x) return kNoIntersection;
                    float z = rayOrg.z + rayDelta.z*t;
                    if (z < min.z || z > max.z) return kNoIntersection;

                    if (returnNormal != NULL) {
                          returnNormal->x = 0.0f;
                          returnNormal->y = yn;
                          returnNormal->z = 0.0f;
                    }

              } break;

              case 2: // intersect with xy plane
              {
                    float x = rayOrg.x + rayDelta.x*t;
                    if (x < min.x || x > max.x) return kNoIntersection;
                    float y = rayOrg.y + rayDelta.y*t;
                    if (y < min.y || y > max.y) return kNoIntersection;

                    if (returnNormal != NULL) {
                          returnNormal->x = 0.0f;
                          returnNormal->y = 0.0f;
                          returnNormal->z = zn;
                    }

              } break;
        }

        // Return parametric point of intersection

        return t;

}

//-------------------------------------------------------------------------
```

```
// AABB3::classifyPlane
//
// Perform static AABB-plane intersection test.  Returns:
//
// <0  Box is completely on the BACK side of the plane
// >0  Box is completely on the FRONT side of the plane
// 0   Box intersects the plane

int    AABB3::classifyPlane(const Vector3 &n, float d) const {

        // Inspect the normal and compute the minimum and maximum
        // D values.

        float minD, maxD;

        if (n.x > 0.0f) {
                minD = n.x*min.x; maxD = n.x*max.x;
        } else {
                minD = n.x*max.x; maxD = n.x*min.x;
        }

        if (n.y > 0.0f) {
                minD += n.y*min.y; maxD += n.y*max.y;
        } else {
                minD += n.y*max.y; maxD += n.y*min.y;
        }

        if (n.z > 0.0f) {
                minD += n.z*min.z; maxD += n.z*max.z;
        } else {
                minD += n.z*max.z; maxD += n.z*min.z;
        }

        // Check if completely on the front side of the plane

        if (minD >= d) {
                return +1;
        }

        // Check if completely on the back side of the plane

        if (maxD <= d) {
                return -1;
        }

        // We straddle the plane

        return 0;
}

//----------------------------------------------------------------------------
// AABB3::intersectPlane
//
// Perform dynamic AABB-plane intersection test.
//
// n is the plane normal (assumed to be normalized)
// planeD is the D value of the plane equation p.n = d
// dir dir is the direction of movement of the AABB.
//
```

```
        // The plane is assumed to be stationary.
        //
        // Returns the parametric point of intersection - the distance traveled
        // before an intersection occurs.  If no intersection, a REALLY big
        // number is returned.  You must check against the length of the
        // displacement.
        //
        // Only intersections with the front side of the plane are detected

        float AABB3::intersectPlane(
            const Vector3      &n,
            float              planeD,
            const Vector3      &dir
        ) const {

            // Make sure they are passing in normalized vectors

            assert(fabs(n*n - 1.0) < .01);
            assert(fabs(dir*dir - 1.0) < .01);

            // We'll return this huge number if no intersection

            const float kNoIntersection = 1e30f;

            // Compute glancing angle. Make sure we are moving toward
            // the front of the plane.

            float dot = n * dir;
            if (dot >= 0.0f) {
                return kNoIntersection;
            }

            // Inspect the normal and compute the minimum and maximum
            // D values.  minD is the D value of the "frontmost" corner point

            float minD, maxD;

            if (n.x > 0.0f) {
                minD = n.x*min.x; maxD = n.x*max.x;
            } else {
                minD = n.x*max.x; maxD = n.x*min.x;
            }

            if (n.y > 0.0f) {
                minD += n.y*min.y; maxD += n.y*max.y;
            } else {
                minD += n.y*max.y; maxD += n.y*min.y;
            }

            if (n.z > 0.0f) {
                minD += n.z*min.z; maxD += n.z*max.z;
            } else {
                minD += n.z*max.z; maxD += n.z*min.z;
            }

            // Check if we're already completely on the other
            // side of the plane

            if (maxD <= planeD) {
                return kNoIntersection;
```

```
        }

        // Perform standard ray trace equation using the
        // frontmost corner point

        float  t = (planeD - minD) / dot;

        // Were we already penetrating?

        if (t < 0.0f) {
            return 0.0f;
        }

        // Return it.  If > 1, then we didn't hit in time.  That's
        // the condition that the caller should be checking for.

        return t;
}

////////////////////////////////////////////////////////////////////////
//
// Global nonmember code
//
////////////////////////////////////////////////////////////////////////

//-------------------------------------------------------------------------
// intersectAABBs
//
// Check if two AABBs intersect, and return true if so.  Optionally, return
// the AABB of their intersection if an intersection is detected

bool   intersectAABBs(
       const AABB3 &box1,
       const AABB3 &box2,
       AABB3 *boxIntersect
) {

       // Check for no overlap

       if (box1.min.x > box2.max.x) return false;
       if (box1.max.x < box2.min.x) return false;
       if (box1.min.y > box2.max.y) return false;
       if (box1.max.y < box2.min.y) return false;
       if (box1.min.z > box2.max.z) return false;
       if (box1.max.z < box2.min.z) return false;

       // We have overlap.  Compute AABB of intersection, if they want it

       if (boxIntersect != NULL) {
            boxIntersect->min.x = max(box1.min.x, box2.min.x);
            boxIntersect->max.x = min(box1.max.x, box2.max.x);
            boxIntersect->min.y = max(box1.min.y, box2.min.y);
            boxIntersect->max.y = min(box1.max.y, box2.max.y);
            boxIntersect->min.z = max(box1.min.z, box2.min.z);
            boxIntersect->max.z = min(box1.max.z, box2.max.z);
       }

       // They intersected

       return true;
```

```
}

//---------------------------------------------------------------------
// intersectMovingAABB
//
// Return parametric point in time when a moving AABB collides
// with a stationary AABB.  Returns > 1 if no intersection

float intersectMovingAABB(
      const AABB3 &stationaryBox,
      const AABB3 &movingBox,
      const Vector3 &d
) {

      // We'll return this huge number if no intersection

      const float kNoIntersection = 1e30f;

      // Initialize interval to contain all the time under consideration

      float tEnter = 0.0f;
      float tLeave = 1.0f;

      //
      // Compute interval of overlap on each dimension, and intersect
      // this interval with the interval accumulated so far.  As soon as
      // an empty interval is detected, return a negative result
      // (no intersection). In each case, we have to be careful for
      // an infinite of empty interval on each dimension.
      //

      // Check x-axis

      if (d.x == 0.0f) {

            // Empty or infinite inverval on x

            if (
                  (stationaryBox.min.x >= movingBox.max.x) ||
                  (stationaryBox.max.x <= movingBox.min.x)
            ) {

                  // Empty time interval so no intersection

                  return kNoIntersection;
            }

            // Inifinite time interval - no update necessary

      } else {

            // Divide once

            float oneOverD = 1.0f / d.x;

            // Compute time value when they begin and end overlapping

            float xEnter = (stationaryBox.min.x - movingBox.max.x) * oneOverD;
            float xLeave = (stationaryBox.max.x - movingBox.min.x) * oneOverD;
```

```
            // Check for interval out of order

            if (xEnter > xLeave) {
                  swap(xEnter, xLeave);
            }

            // Update interval

            if (xEnter > tEnter) tEnter = xEnter;
            if (xLeave < tLeave) tLeave = xLeave;

            // Check if this resulted in empty interval

            if (tEnter > tLeave) {
                  return kNoIntersection;
            }
      }

// Check y-axis

if (d.y == 0.0f) {

      // Empty or infinite inverval on y

      if (
            (stationaryBox.min.y >= movingBox.max.y) ||
            (stationaryBox.max.y <= movingBox.min.y)
      ) {

            // Empty time interval, so no intersection

            return kNoIntersection;
      }

      // Infinite time interval - no update necessary

} else {

      // Divide once

      float oneOverD = 1.0f / d.y;

      // Compute time value when they begin and end overlapping

      float yEnter = (stationaryBox.min.y - movingBox.max.y) * oneOverD;
      float yLeave = (stationaryBox.max.y - movingBox.min.y) * oneOverD;

      // Check for interval out of order

      if (yEnter > yLeave) {
            swap(yEnter, yLeave);
      }

      // Update interval

      if (yEnter > tEnter) tEnter = yEnter;
      if (yLeave < tLeave) tLeave = yLeave;

      // Check if this resulted in empty interval
```

```
            if (tEnter > tLeave) {
                  return kNoIntersection;
            }
      }

      // Check z-axis

      if (d.z == 0.0f) {

            // Empty or infinite inverval on z

            if (
                  (stationaryBox.min.z >= movingBox.max.z) ||
                  (stationaryBox.max.z <= movingBox.min.z)
            ) {

                  // Empty time interval, so no intersection

                  return kNoIntersection;
            }

            // Infinite time interval - no update necessary

      } else {

            // Divide once

            float oneOverD = 1.0f / d.z;

            // Compute time value when they begin and end overlapping

            float zEnter = (stationaryBox.min.z – movingBox.max.z) * oneOverD;
            float zLeave = (stationaryBox.max.z – movingBox.min.z) * oneOverD;

            // Check for interval out of order

            if (zEnter > zLeave) {
                  swap(zEnter, zLeave);
            }

            // Update interval

            if (zEnter > tEnter) tEnter = zEnter;
            if (zLeave < tLeave) tLeave = zLeave;

            // Check if this resulted in empty interval

            if (tEnter > tLeave) {
                  return kNoIntersection;
            }
      }

      // OK, we have an intersection.  Return the parametric point in time
      // where the intersection occurs

      return tEnter;
}
```

13.21 Exercises

 Note: You may assume that all vectors that "look" like they are close to being unit vectors are, in fact, unit vectors. (No trick questions in this section.)

1. Consider the infinite line in 2D consisting of all points **p** such that

   $$\mathbf{p} \cdot \begin{bmatrix} 0.3511 & 0.9363 \end{bmatrix} = 6$$

   Find the point on the line closest to (10,20). Find the point on the line closest to (4,3). Find the distance from the line to both of these points.

2. Consider the parametric ray in 3D defined by

   $$\mathbf{p}(t) = \begin{bmatrix} 3 & 4 & 5 \end{bmatrix} + t \begin{bmatrix} .2673 & 0.8018 & 0.5345 \end{bmatrix}$$

   where t varies from 0 to 50. Find the value of t for the point on the ray closest to (18,7,32). Find the value of t for the point on the ray closest to (13,52,26). Find the Cartesian coordinates of both of these points.

3. Consider the plane formed by all points **p** such that

   $$\mathbf{p} \cdot \begin{bmatrix} 0.4838 & 0.8602 & -0.1613 \end{bmatrix} = 42$$

   Find the point on the plane that is closest to (3,6,9). Find the point on the plane that is closest to (7,9,42).

4. Consider a unit sphere (a sphere of radius 1) centered at (2,6,9). Find the point on the sphere closest to (3,–17,6).

5. Consider the AABB defined by $\mathbf{p}_{min}$=(2,4,6) and $\mathbf{p}_{max}$=(8,14,26). Find the point in the AABB that is closest to (23,–9,12).

6. Find the point of intersection of the two 2D lines defined parametrically by:

   $$\mathbf{p} \cdot \begin{bmatrix} -0.7863 & 0.6178 \end{bmatrix} = 8$$
   $$\mathbf{p} \cdot \begin{bmatrix} 0.2688 & 0.9632 \end{bmatrix} = 2$$

7. Consider the parametric rays in 3D defined by

   $$\mathbf{r}_1(t_1) = \begin{bmatrix} 2 & 8 & 3 \end{bmatrix} + t_1 \begin{bmatrix} 0.3429 & -0.9077 & 0.2420 \end{bmatrix}$$
   $$\mathbf{r}_2(t_2) = \begin{bmatrix} 1 & 6 & 13 \end{bmatrix} + t_2 \begin{bmatrix} -0.7079 & -0.6926 & 0.1385 \end{bmatrix}$$

   Find the values of t_1 and t_2 at the point of closest approach of these lines. What are the Cartesian coordinates of these points?

8. Consider the infinite 3D ray through the origin given by

   $$\mathbf{r}(t) = t \begin{bmatrix} 0.4417 & 0.5822 & 0.6826 \end{bmatrix}$$

   and the plane consisting of all points **p** such that

   $$\mathbf{p} \cdot \begin{bmatrix} 0.6125 & 0.4261 & 0.6658 \end{bmatrix} = 11$$

Find the point of intersection of the infinite ray with the plane. Does it intersect with the front or the back of the plane?

9. Consider the AABB defined by $\mathbf{p}_{min}=(7,-4,16)$ and $\mathbf{p}_{max}=(18,4,26)$ and the plane consisting of all points $\mathbf{p}$ such that

$$\mathbf{p} \cdot \begin{bmatrix} -0.4472 & 0 & -0.8944 \end{bmatrix} = 13$$

Does the plane intersect the AABB, and if not, does it lie in front of or behind the plane?

10. Find the point of intersection of the planes defined by the following equations:

$$\mathbf{p} \cdot \begin{bmatrix} -0.5973 & 0.6652 & -0.4480 \end{bmatrix} = 2$$
$$\mathbf{p} \cdot \begin{bmatrix} 0.7613 & 0.2900 & -0.5800 \end{bmatrix} = 3$$
$$\mathbf{p} \cdot \begin{bmatrix} 0.3128 & 0.8096 & 0.4968 \end{bmatrix} = 5$$

11. Consider a sphere of radius 10 centered at the origin. Find the points of intersection of the sphere with the infinite ray

$$\mathbf{r}(t) = \begin{bmatrix} -10.1275 & -9.6922 & -9.7103 \end{bmatrix} + t\begin{bmatrix} 0.5179 & 0.6330 & 0.5754 \end{bmatrix}$$

12. Consider a sphere S_1 of radius 7 centered at (42,9,90), and a sphere S_2 of radius 5 centered at (41,80,41). The spheres start moving at time $t=0$. The velocity vector of S_1 in units per second is [27,38,−37]. The velocity vector of S_2 in units per second is [24,−38,10]. Determine whether the two spheres intersect, and if so, find the time t at which they first intersect.

13. Consider a sphere of radius 3 centered at (78,43,43) and a plane given by all points $\mathbf{p}$ such that
$$\mathbf{p} \cdot \begin{bmatrix} 0.5358 & -0.7778 & -0.3284 \end{bmatrix} = 900$$

The sphere starts moving at time $t=0$ with velocity vector [9,2,1] given in units per second. Does the sphere eventually intersect with the plane? If so, at what time does it first touch the plane? Repeat the computation using the velocity vector [−9,−2,−1].

14. Consider the triangle given by the clockwise enumeration of the points (78,59,29), (21,172,65), and (7,6,0). Compute the plane equation of the plane containing the triangle. For each of the following infinite rays from the origin, compute the point at which the ray intersects the plane of the triangle, compute the barycentric coordinates of that point, and finally, use this information to determine whether the ray intersects the triangle:

$$\mathbf{r}(t) = t\begin{bmatrix} 0.6956 & 0.6068 & 0.3848 \end{bmatrix}$$
$$\mathbf{r}(t) = t\begin{bmatrix} 0.3839 & 0.3839 & 0.8398 \end{bmatrix}$$
$$\mathbf{r}(t) = t\begin{bmatrix} 0.7208 & 0.1941 & 0.6654 \end{bmatrix}$$

15. Calculate AABBs for the spheres in Problem 13. Determine whether the AABBs will eventually overlap, and if so, compute the times t_{enter} and t_{leave} when they first and last overlap.

Chapter 14

Triangle Meshes

This chapter discusses a number of issues related to storing and manipulating triangle meshes. It is divided into five sections.

- Section 14.1 discusses a number of different ways to represent triangle meshes in a computer.
- Section 14.2 discusses different types of data that we store with triangle meshes, other than the basic geometric information.
- Section 14.3 introduces mesh topology.
- Section 14.4 covers a number of operations that are performed on triangle meshes.
- Section 14.5 presents the declaration for a triangle mesh class.

In the previous chapters, we discussed techniques for manipulating one triangle or one polygon at a time. In this chapter, we discuss polygon and triangle *meshes*. In its simplest form, a polygon mesh is nothing more than a list of polygons. Triangle meshes, which are of special importance, are polygon meshes made entirely of triangles. Polygon and triangle meshes are ubiquitous in graphics and modeling; they are used to approximate the surface of arbitrarily complex objects, such as buildings, vehicles, human beings, and of course, teapots. Figure 14.1 shows some examples of triangle meshes.

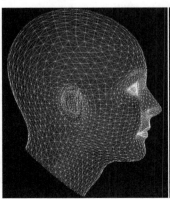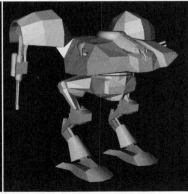

Figure 14.1: Examples of triangle meshes

Mech model by Grant Gosler. Used by permission of Terminal Reality.

In this chapter, we will focus on *triangle* meshes specifically. Of course, any polygon mesh can be tessellated into triangles. (See Section 12.7.4 for more information on polygon triangulation.) Many of the concepts we will discuss are applicable to both triangle and polygon meshes. Triangle meshes are attractive because of their simplicity. Many operations are more easily performed on triangles than general polygons. However, polygons offer advantages in some cases. We will discuss the significant differences between triangles and polygons as they are encountered.

14.1 Representing Meshes

A triangle mesh is a list of triangles, so the most straightforward way to represent a triangle mesh would be to use an array of triangles:

Listing 14.1: A trivial representation of a triangle mesh

```
struct Triangle {
    Vector3     p[3];
};

struct TriangleMesh {
    int         triCount;
    Triangle    *triList;
};
```

For some applications, this trivial representation is adequate. However, the term "mesh" implies a degree of connectivity between adjacent triangles, and this connectivity is not expressed in our trivial representation above. For most triangle meshes that arise in practice, each triangle edge is shared by another triangle from the mesh. Thus, there are three basic types of information in a triangle mesh:

- **Vertices**. Each triangle has exactly three vertices. Each vertex may be shared by multiple triangles.
- **Edges**. An edge connects two vertices. Each triangle has three edges.
- **Faces**. These are the surfaces of the triangles. We can store a face as either a list of three vertices or a list of three edges.

There are a variety of different ways to represent this information efficiently depending on the operations to be performed most often on the mesh. In this chapter, we will focus on a standard storage format known as an *indexed triangle mesh*.

14.1.1 Indexed Triangle Mesh

In an indexed triangle mesh, we maintain two lists: a list of vertices and a list of triangles.

- Each vertex contains a position in 3D. We may also store other information at the vertex level, such as texture mapping coordinates, surface normals, or lighting values.
- A triangle is represented using three indices in the vertex list. Often, the order that these vertices are listed is significant, since we may consider faces to have "front" and "back" sides. We

will list the vertices in a clockwise fashion when viewed from the front side. Other information may also be stored at the triangle level, such as a precomputed normal of the plane containing the triangle, surface properties (such as a texture map), etc.

Listing 14.2 shows a highly simplified example of how an indexed triangle mesh might be stored in C++:

Listing 14.2: Indexed triangle mesh

```
// struct Vertex is the information we store at the vertex level

struct Vertex {

    // 3D position of the vertex

    Vector3     p;

    // Other information could include
    // texture mapping coordinates, a
    // surface normal, lighting values, etc.
}

// struct Triangle is the information we store at the triangle level

struct Triangle {

    // Indices into the vertex list

    int    vertex[3];

    // Other information could include
    // a normal, material information, etc.
}

// struct TriangleMesh stores an indexed triangle mesh

struct TriangleMesh {

    // The vertices

    int         vertexCount;
    Vertex *vertexList;

    // The triangles

    int         triangleCount;
    Triangle    *triangleList;
};
```

In practice, the `TriangleMesh` struct would be a class with a set of operations to access and maintain the vertex and triangle lists. In Section 14.5, we will look at such a class and offer some design advice. Of course, to store a polygon mesh, we would define a `Polygon` struct that could accommodate faces with an arbitrary number of vertices. We could impose a maximum number of vertices per polygon for simplicity and efficiency.

Notice that the adjacency information contained in an indexed triangle list is stored implicitly. For example, the edges are not stored explicitly, but we can locate shared edges between triangles by searching the triangle list. This "extra" adjacency information actually comes with a memory *savings* compared with the trivial "array of triangles" format given at the beginning of this chapter. The reason for this is that the information stored at the vertex level, which is duplicated in the trivial format, is relatively large compared to a single integer index. (At the minimum, we store a 3D vector position most.) There is typically a large degree of connectivity in triangle meshes encountered in practice, like those shown in Figure 14.1.

14.1.2 Advanced Techniques

The simple indexed triangle mesh scheme is appropriate for many basic applications. However, some changes need to be made in order for some operations on triangle meshes to be implemented more efficiently. The basic problem is that the adjacency between triangles is not expressed explicitly and must be extracted by searching the triangle list. Other representation techniques exist which make this information available in constant time.

One idea is to maintain an edge list explicitly. Each edge is defined by listing the two vertices on the ends. We also maintain a list of triangles that share the edge. Then the triangles can be viewed as a list of three edges rather than a list of three vertices, so that they are stored as three indices into the edge list rather than the vertex list. An extension of this idea is known as the *winged edge* model, which also stores, for each vertex, a reference to one edge that uses the vertex. The edges and triangles may be traversed intelligently to quickly locate all edges and triangles that use the vertex. For more information, see [8] and [9].

14.1.3 Specialized Representations for Rendering

Most graphics cards do not natively operate on indexed triangle meshes. In order to render a triangle mesh, we typically submit three vertices of a triangle at a time. The shared vertices must be submitted multiple times, once for each triangle in which they are used. Since the transfer of data between memory and the graphics hardware is often a bottleneck, many graphics hardware and APIs support specialized mesh formats designed to send as few vertices per triangle as possible to the graphics accelerator. The basic idea is to order the faces and vertices in such a way that the vertices for a triangle are already present in memory on the graphics processor (due to a prior triangle that used the vertex) and therefore do not need to be transferred again.

In order of most flexible to least flexible, we will discuss these three common techniques:

- Vertex caching
- Triangle strips
- Triangle fans

14.1.4 Vertex Caching

Vertex caching is not so much a specialized storage format as a strategy of coordination between the API and graphics hardware to exploit the coherency between consecutive triangles. Typically, the higher level code does not need to be aware that vertex caching is being performed in order to function properly, although we'll see later that steps can be taken to maximize the benefit from vertex caching.

Just like any caching scheme, vertex caching works on the simple heuristic that *recently accessed data is likely to be needed again*. The processor on the graphics card has a cache that holds a small number (say, 16) of recently submitted vertices. When the API needs to send a vertex to the graphics hardware, it first checks to see which vertices are in the cache. Naturally, the API must be familiar with the size and replacement strategy of the graphics card's cache. If the vertex is not already on board, then a *cache miss* occurs and the vertex is submitted to the graphics card (and entered in the cache). Otherwise, when the vertex is already on board, we have a *cache hit* and the API dispatches a special code that says to the graphics card "use the vertex in slot x in the cache."

As mentioned earlier, vertex caching is not really a special mesh format but an optimization strategy employed at the lower level. Any triangle mesh can be rendered properly without special action by the higher level code. However, we can take maximum advantage of a vertex cache (if it exists) simply by reordering the faces of the mesh so that triangles that share a vertex are submitted reasonably close together in time. This reordering of triangles only needs to be done once, and in fact, it can be done offline. It can only help performance, since it doesn't slow down a system *without* vertex caching. Algorithms for reordering faces to maximize vertex cache hits can be found in [14].

With proper use of the vertex cache, it is possible to send the graphics card less than one vertex per triangle on average.

14.1.5 Triangle Strips

A *triangle strip* is a list of triangles in which each triangle shares an edge with the previous triangle. Figure 14.2 shows an example of a triangle strip. Notice that the vertices are listed in an order that implicitly defines the triangles so that every set of three consecutive indices forms a triangle. For example:

- Vertices 1, 2, 3 form the first triangle.
- Vertices 2, 3, 4 form the second triangle.
- Vertices 3, 4, 5 form the third triangle, etc.

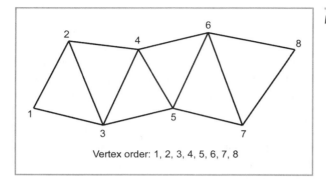

Vertex order: 1, 2, 3, 4, 5, 6, 7, 8

In Figure 14.2, the vertices are numbered according to the order in which they would be used to specify the strip. No "index" information is necessary, since the order of the vertices defines the triangles implicitly. Usually, the vertex list is preceded with the number of vertices or a special code is used to indicate "end of list."

Notice that the ordering of the vertices of the triangle alternates between clockwise and counterclockwise (see Figure 14.3). On some platforms, we may specify the vertex ordering of the first triangle, while on other platforms the ordering is fixed and may not be specified.

Vertex	Triangle	Vertex Ordering
1	(none)	
2	(none)	
3	1,2,3	Clockwise
4	2,3,4	Counterclockwise
5	3,4,5	Clockwise
6	4,5,6	Counterclockwise
7	5,6,7	Clockwise
8	6,7,8	Counterclockwise

Figure 14.3: The triangles in a triangle strip alternate between clockwise and counterclockwise vertex ordering

In the best case, a triangle strip can store a mesh with n faces using $n+2$ vertices. As n gets large, we send just over one vertex on average per triangle. Unfortunately, this is the best case. In practice, there are many meshes for which a single long strip cannot be found. Not only that, but vertices shared by more than three triangles are sent to the graphics card multiple times. In other words, *at least* one vertex must be sent per triangle. With a vertex caching scheme, for example, it is actually possible to average fewer than one vertex per triangle downloaded to the graphics hardware. Of course, with vertex caching, there is extra bookkeeping information (the indices and cache management data). However, since the data for one vertex may be relatively large, or the operations performed on a vertex relatively slow, a system that attempts to minimize the number of vertices may be fastest on that particular system.

Assuming a straightforward generation of triangle strips, the number of vertices used to represent a triangle mesh as a triangle strip is $t + 2s$, where t is the number of triangles and s is the number of strips. It takes three vertices for the first triangle in each strip and one vertex per triangle thereafter. Since we want to minimize the number of vertices downloaded to the graphics hardware, we wish to have as few strips as possible. This means that they need to be as long as possible. An efficient stripping algorithm known as *STRIPE* exists that produces a number of strips that is very close to the theoretical lower bound. For more information on STRIPE, see [6].

Another reason we want to minimize the number of strips is because there is usually additional setup time associated with each strip. In other words, in many cases rendering two strips with n vertices each may be slower than rendering one strip with $2n$ vertices, even if the single strip contains more triangles than the two separate ones put together. As it turns out, we can always turn the entire mesh into one continuous strip by "seaming" together the strips using degenerate triangles. *Degenerate* means that they have zero area. Figure 14.4 shows how two triangle strips were seamed together by repeating two vertices in the strip.

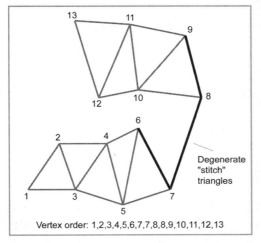

Vertex order: 1,2,3,4,5,6,7,7,8,8,9,10,11,12,13

Figure 14.4: Stitching together two triangle strips using degenerate triangles

It's not immediately apparent in Figure 14.4, but *four* degenerate triangles are needed to stitch together two triangle strips in order to maintain proper alternating clockwise/counterclockwise order. The edge between vertices 7 and 8 actually contains two degenerate triangles. Figure 14.5 shows the triangles that are created using the vertex order from Figure 14.4. The degenerate triangles (whose rows have been shaded in Figure 14.5) do not usually impose much overhead since they have zero area and do not result in anything being rendered. What actually gets sent to the graphics card is still the first column of vertices:

1,2,3,4,5,6,7,7,8,8,9,10,11,12,13

This follows the same convention that every set of three consecutive indices in the list forms a triangle.

Vertex	Triangle	Vertex Ordering
1	(none)	
2	(none)	
3	1,2,3	Clockwise
4	2,3,4	Counterclockwise
5	3,4,5	Clockwise
6	4,5,6	Counterclockwise
7	5,6,7	Clockwise
7	6,7,7	Counterclockwise
8	7,7,8	Clockwise
8	7,8,8	Counterclockwise
9	8,8,9	Clockwise
10	8,9,10	Counterclockwise
11	9,10,11	Clockwise
12	10,11,12	Counterclockwise
13	11,12,13	Clockwise

Figure 14.5: The triangles obtained by stitching together two triangle strips

Some graphics hardware (such as the GS on the Playstation II) supports the ability to skip triangles in the strip by marking certain vertices with a bit that means "don't draw the triangle." This gives us a means to effectively start a new triangle strip at any point without duplicating vertices or using degenerate triangles. For example, the two triangle strips in Figure 14.4 could have been joined as shown in Figure 14.6. The shaded rows indicate where a vertex would be flagged as "don't draw the triangle."

Vertex	Triangle	Vertex Ordering
1	(none)	
2	(none)	
3	1,2,3	Clockwise
4	2,3,4	Counterclockwise
5	3,4,5	Clockwise
6	4,5,6	Counterclockwise
7	5,6,7	Clockwise
8	6,7,8	Counterclockwise
9	7,8,9	Clockwise
10	8,9,10	Counterclockwise
11	9,10,11	Clockwise
12	10,11,12	Counterclockwise
13	11,12,13	Clockwise

Figure 14.6: Joining two triangle strips by skipping vertices

14.1.6 Triangle Fans

Triangle fans are similar to triangle strips, but they are less flexible and thus used less often. The simplest way to describe triangle fans is with an illustration (see Figure 14.7).

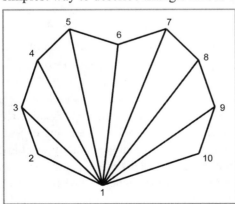

Figure 14.7: A triangle fan

A triangle fan stores n faces using $n+2$ vertices, the same as triangle strips. However, since the first vertex must be used by every triangle, we usually cannot find many places in an arbitrary mesh where large triangle fans can be used. Also, triangle fans can't be stitched together like triangle strips can. Thus, triangle fans can work well in some specialized cases, but in general, strips are more flexible.

14.2 Additional Mesh Information

A triangle mesh may have additional information stored at the triangle or vertex level.

14.2.1 Texture Mapping Coordinates

Texture mapping is the practice of applying a bitmap image (known as a "texture map" or simply "texture") to the surface of a polygon mesh. We will discuss texture mapping in more detail in Section 15.6, but a greatly simplified explanation of the idea is that we wish to "paint" from a 2D texture onto a polygon, taking into account the polygon's orientation in camera space. For each pixel on the polygon to be rendered, a set of 2D *texture mapping coordinates* is computed, and these 2D coordinates are used to index into the texture map and fetch the surface color to be drawn on the pixel.

Usually, texture mapping coordinates are stored at the vertex level and then interpolated across the face of the triangle for rendering.

14.2.2 Surface Normals

In many applications, we need a surface normal for a point on the surface of the mesh. For example, the surface normal can be used:

- To compute proper lighting (Section 15.4).
- To perform backface culling (Section 15.9.1).
- To simulate a particle "bouncing" off the surface of the mesh.
- To speed up collision detection by only intersecting with the "front" side of a surface.

The surface normals may be stored at the triangle level, the vertex level, or both.

The surface normals for triangles can be computed easily using the techniques from Section 12.5.2. Computing normals at the vertex level is more difficult. First, it should be noted that there is not a true surface normal at a vertex (or an edge for that matter) since these locations mark discontinuities in the surface of the mesh. Rather, we must remember that a triangle mesh is typically used as an approximation for some continuous surface. So what we actually want is (an approximation of) the surface normal of the continuous surface. This information may or may not be readily available, depending on how the triangle mesh was generated. If the mesh is generated procedurally, such as from a parametric curved surface, then the vertex normals can be supplied at that time.

If the surface normals are not provided, then we must approximate them by interpreting the information available to us (the vertex positions and the triangles). One trick that works is to average the normals of the adjacent triangles and then renormalize the result. Of course, this requires that we have valid triangle normals. Usually we can compute outward facing normals using the cross product and assume a clockwise enumeration of triangle vertices. If a vertex enumeration order cannot be assumed, then techniques described by Glassner in [10] can be used.

Averaging triangle normals to compute vertex normals is a tried-and-true technique that works well in most cases. However, there are a few situations worth mentioning where the results are not desirable.

The most notable case is when two triangles with exactly opposite surface normals share a vertex. This situation can arise with triangles in "billboard" type objects (these are exactly what they sound like — flat objects on which to display images), which typically have two triangles placed back to back. The two normals point in exactly opposite directions, and averaging the normals results in the zero vector which cannot be normalized. To solve this problem, these so-called "double-sided" triangles must be detached (see Section 14.4.3).

Another problem caused by averaging vertex normals occurs with Gouraud shading. We'll discuss Gouraud shading in detail in Section 15.4.10, but for now it will suffice to say that a lighting value is computed per vertex using the vertex normal. If we compute vertex normals by averaging the triangle normals, some areas that should have sharp edges appear to get "smoothed out." Take the very simple example of a box. There should be a sharp lighting discontinuity at its edges. However, if we use vertex normals computed from the average of the face surface normals, then there is no lighting discontinuity. This is shown in Figure 14.8.

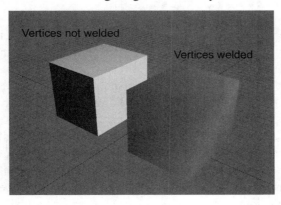

Figure 14.8: On the right, the box edges are not visible because there is only one normal at each corner

The basic problem is that there is supposed to be a surface discontinuity at the box edges, but this discontinuity cannot be properly represented because there is only one normal stored per vertex. Again, the solution to this problem is to detach the faces; in other words, duplicate the vertices where there is a true geometric discontinuity. In doing so, we create a discontinuity to prevent the vertex normals from being averaged. This "seam" in the topology of the mesh may cause a problem for some applications. However, for many important tasks, such as rendering and ray tracing, this is not a problem. Class `EditTriMesh`, which is previewed in Section 14.5, illustrates techniques for handling such discontinuities.

Another slight problem is that the averaging is biased toward large numbers of triangles with the same normal. For example, suppose several triangles share a vertex, and two of them are coplanar. The vertex normal computed by averaging the triangle normals will be biased because the normal shared by the coplanar triangles essentially gets twice as many "votes" as the other triangle normals. Thus, tessellating a triangle can cause vertex normals to change even though the surface really doesn't change. We could devise techniques to correct this situation, but fortunately in practice this isn't a big problem because the vertex normal is just an approximation to begin with.

14.2.3 Lighting Values

Another piece of information often maintained at the vertex level is a lighting value. These light values are then interpolated across the surface of the face, a practice known as *Gouraud shading* (see Section 15.4.10).

In some situations, we may only store a surface normal per vertex and dynamically compute a lighting value during rendering. See Section 15.8.2 for the details of this computation. In other situations, we will specify the lighting value ourselves. See Section 15.7.2 for more information on different vertex formats.

14.3 Topology and Consistency

The *topology* of a triangle mesh refers to the logical connectivity of the triangles in the mesh without regard to the 3D position of the vertices or other geometric properties. Thus, two meshes with the same number of vertices and triangles connected in the same manner have identical topology, even though they may describe completely different objects. Another way to say this is if we "pull" the vertices of a mesh and stretch the triangles without breaking apart adjacent triangles, we change the shape but not the topology of the mesh.

One special type of mesh is the *closed* mesh, also known as a *manifold*. Conceptually, a closed mesh perfectly covers the surface of the object. There are no gaps in the mesh, and you cannot see the back of any triangles from outside the object. This is a very important type of mesh. The vertices and edges of a closed mesh form a *planar graph*. This means that if we draw vertices as points and edges with straight line segments joining them, then a closed mesh can actually be drawn (very distortedly) on a 2D plane without crossing edges. Planar graphs obey Euler's equation $v - e + f = 2$, where v is the number of vertices, e is the number of edges, and f is the number of faces in the mesh.

In practice, we frequently encounter meshes (even — or perhaps we should say *particularly* — those generated by professional 3D modeling software) with abnormalities in the topology which cause them to not be closed:

- ■ **Isolated vertices**. A vertex in the vertex list is not used by any triangles.
- ■ **Duplicate vertices**. Two vertices in the vertex list are identical. In this case, the triangles (and edges) that use these vertices are geometrically adjacent, but they are not logically adjacent.

In most cases, we do not want this seam to exist, and we will *weld* the vertices. (More on this in Section 14.4.2.)

■ **Degenerate triangles**. A triangle uses a vertex more than once. This means the triangle has no area. Typically, these triangles should be deleted. (However, we saw an example in Section 14.1.3 where degenerate faces are intentionally created in order to stitch together triangle strips.)

■ **Open edges**. An edge is used by only one triangle.

■ **Edges used by more than two triangles**. Each edge in a closed mesh must be used by *exactly* two triangles.

■ **Duplicate faces**. The mesh contains two or more identical faces. In most cases, this is undesirable, and all but one of the faces should be deleted.

Depending on the application, these abnormalities may be a fundamental problem, a minor nuisance, or safely ignored.

For an excellent discussion on topology, see [18].

14.4 Triangle Mesh Operations

Now that we know how to store a triangle mesh, it's time to learn what we can do to one. In this section, we discuss a number of important operations that are performed on triangle meshes.

14.4.1 Piecewise Operations

A mesh is a list of triangles and vertices. A number of simple operations can be performed on the mesh as a whole by performing a basic operation on each of the vertices or triangles individually. Most notably, rendering and transformation are performed in this way. To render a triangle mesh, we render each of the triangles. To apply a transformation to the triangle mesh, such as rotation or scale, we transform each of the vertices.

14.4.2 Welding Vertices

When two or more vertices are coincident (within some tolerant distance), it is often beneficial to *weld* them into a single vertex. More accurately, we delete all but one of the vertices. For example, assume we wish to weld vertices A and B in Figure 14.9. Welding two vertices together is a two-step process:

■ **Step 1**. We scan the triangle list, replacing each reference to vertex B with a reference to vertex A.

■ **Step 2**. Now vertex B is isolated and can be removed from the vertex list.

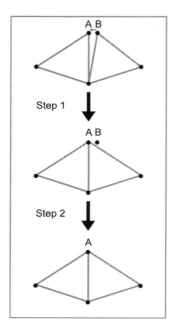

Step 1

Step 2

Figure 14.9: Welding two nearly coincident vertices

Vertex welding is useful for two reasons. First, it allows us to remove redundancy and use less memory. This is an important optimization and can make operations on the mesh, such as rendering and transformation, faster. Second, it logically connects edges and triangles that are geometrically adjacent.

The discussion above focused on welding two vertices. In practice, we frequently wish to locate and weld all pairs (or groups) of coincident vertices. This is fairly straightforward, but there are a few important details.

First, we usually remove isolated vertices before vertex welding. We don't want any unused vertex to influence any vertices that are used, as shown in Figure 14.10.

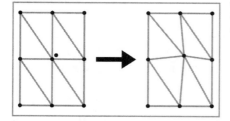

Figure 14.10: A vertex is welded to an isolated vertex, causing unnecessary distortion to the mesh

Second, welding vertices can create degenerate triangles when two vertices from a "sliver" triangle are welded, as shown in Figure 14.11. (This is equivalent to an edge collapse, which is discussed in Section 14.4.4.) These triangles should be deleted. Usually, the number of such triangles is small. Welding vertices can frequently reduce the number of vertices significantly, while removing only a few, if any, sliver faces.

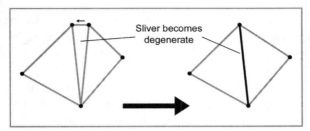

Figure 14.11: Welding two vertices of a sliver triangle causes the triangle to become degenerate

Third, it would seem that when we weld two (or more) vertices, we should compute the new, welded vertex position as the average of the original vertex positions rather than just choosing one vertex to keep and one to discard. This way the welding is not biased toward one vertex or another. This is probably a good idea when small groups of vertices are welded interactively. However, when vertex welding is automated, a "domino effect" can occur, resulting in three or more vertices that were not originally within the tolerance range to become welded together.

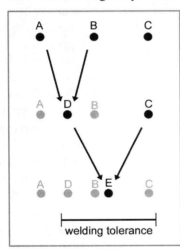

Figure 14.12: A domino effect created by averaging vertex positions during welding

In Figure 14.12, vertices A and B are within the tolerance to be welded. We weld these vertices, and being "smart," we compute a new vertex position from the average of A and B, resulting in vertex D. Now C and D are within tolerance and are welded, resulting in vertex E. The end result is that vertices A and C have become welded, even though they were not originally within tolerance of each other. Also, our attempt to be "smart" has failed because vertices A, B, and C are welded, but the resulting vertex is not in the middle of where the three vertices were originally.

This is not even the worst-case scenario. At least in the example above, no vertex moved more than the welding tolerance distance. Other perverse examples can be constructed using more vertices and a different vertex ordering. What is unfortunate is that these examples actually do arise in practice because of the way vertices are ordered when they are delivered from modeling packages or generated procedurally.

Actually, the same types of problems can occur even if we don't average the vertex positions during vertex welding. However, using a simple rule such as "always weld the higher numbered vertex to the lower numbered vertex" solves the problem, provided that we don't average the vertex positions.

There are techniques to avoid these types of problems. For example, we might first search for groups of vertices within tolerance and then weld all such groups in a second pass. Or, we might disqualify a vertex from being welded a second time. Or, we might remember the original positions of the vertices that got welded and choose not to weld a vertex if any of these original positions are out of tolerance. All of these techniques are fraught with problems and we do not advise incurring the added complexity for a dubious payoff. The purpose of vertex welding is primarily to remove redundant vertices. Vertex welding is not intended to perform *mesh decimation*, that is, to drastically reduce the number of triangles and vertices while maintaining the overall shape of the mesh as much as possible. For decent mesh decimation, you must use a more advanced algorithm. (See Section 14.4.5 for more information.)

Another complication with vertex welding has to do with information that is stored at the vertex level, such as surface normals or texture mapping coordinates. When vertices are welded, any previous discontinuity is lost. We saw one example of this problem in Figure 14.8.

Finally, the straightforward implementation to weld all vertices is *very* slow. Models with even just a few thousand vertices and faces can take more than a few seconds or so to process on today's hardware. Searching for pairs of vertices to weld is an $O(n^2)$ operation. (If you are unfamiliar with big-Oh notation, $O(n^2)$ is known as *quadratic* running time. It means, in this case, that if we double the number of vertices, our algorithm could take *four times* as long — not twice as long, as might be expected. If we quadruple the number of vertices, our algorithm could take *sixteen* times as long. As the number of vertices increases, the time taken by our algorithm increases even more.) Replacing vertex references after a vertex is welded requires a pass through the triangle list. Even deleting a vertex requires a pass through the triangle list to repair the references to vertices numbered higher than the deleted vertex. Luckily, with a little thought, we can devise a much faster vertex welding algorithm. The triangle mesh class we will preview in Section 14.5 uses an algorithm that runs in expected linear time. (This means that the running time of our algorithm will be proportional to the number of vertices; if we quadruple the number of vertices, the time quadruples, but it doesn't increase by a factor of sixteen.) The source code for this reduction algorithm is available at `gamemath.com`.

14.4.3 Detaching Faces

Detaching a face refers to the act of duplicating vertices so that an edge is no longer shared. It is somewhat the opposite of vertex welding. Obviously, detaching faces creates topological discontinuities since the faces are no longer adjacent. This is usually our exact intention, to create a topological discontinuity where a geometric discontinuity (such as a corner or sharp edge) exists. Figure 14.13 shows two triangles being detached from one another. Although we have separated the edges of the two triangles to show that there are multiple edges and vertices, this is only for illustration. No vertices have moved, and the new vertices and edges are actually coincident.

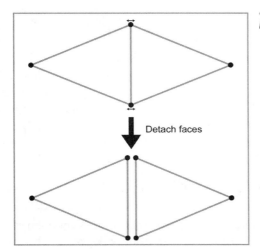

Figure 14.13: Detaching two triangles

In practice, we frequently detach *all* faces.

14.4.4 Edge Collapse

An *edge collapse* is a mesh operation that "collapses" an edge down to a single vertex. The opposite operation is known as a *vertex split*. This is shown in Figure 14.14. Notice that an edge collapse welds the two vertices of the edge into a single vertex, and the triangles that shared the edge (the shaded triangles in Figure 14.4) are removed. Edge collapse is often used in mesh decimation algorithms (which will be discussed in Section 14.4.5) because it reduces the number of triangles and vertices in the mesh.

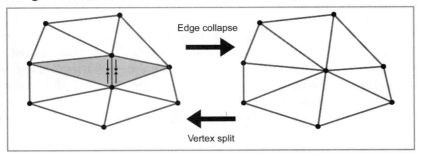

Figure 14.14: Edge collapse and vertex split

14.4.5 Mesh Decimation

Mesh decimation is the process of taking a mesh with a relatively high number of triangles and vertices and manipulating it into another mesh with fewer vertices and triangles. Hopefully, the basic shape of the mesh, including significant points of inflection, is retained as much as possible during this manipulation.

Hugues Hoppe has shown that it is possible to achieve good results using only edge collapse operations. The process of selecting which edges to collapse is usually a relatively slow one, depending on the complexity of the heuristic used. In [13], Hoppe gives advice for selecting the best sequence of edges to collapse.

While the selection of edges is slow, the actual collapse operation can be implemented efficiently. If we record the sequence of edge collapse operations as we decimate the mesh, we can "replay" them quickly to generate a triangle mesh in real time with any level of detail desired, give or take a few triangles. (We discuss LOD selection in Section 15.7.1.) Hoppe's paper describes how this process can be implemented in reverse by starting with a decimated mesh and applying vertex splits in order. A mesh stored using this technique is known as a *progressive mesh*.

14.5 A C++ Triangle Mesh Class

In this section, we present a C++ class to store an indexed triangle mesh. A common mistake made by beginners is to attempt to write one triangle mesh class that does *everything*. This is an exercise in frustration.

For fast rendering, the mesh must often be massaged into a very specific format, depending on the target platform. The mesh may need to be stored as a triangle strip. Or we may actually convert our mesh into a sequence of instructions to a specialized graphics processor. (This is the case on the PlayStation II, for example.) No matter what the platform, we usually want the data to be as small as possible for fast memory access and downloading to the video card. For fast collision detection, on the other hand, we may need precomputed surface normals or to have the data partitioned or stored in some sort of tree structure.

These specialized requirements can make general mesh manipulations, such as adding or deleting individual vertices or triangles, building up a triangle mesh procedurally, or welding vertices, extremely cumbersome. For that reason, we do not even attempt to make "the ultimate" triangle mesh class that does everything.

Class `EditTriMesh` is designed to make mesh manipulations easy, but it is not intended for doing anything else efficiently, such as rendering or collision detection. The data is not optimized in any way, although we do provide operations on the mesh that prepare it to be rendered. To save a tree (and to save you money), we have only listed the class definition. The implementation file is available to download at `gamemath.com`.

Class `EditTriMesh` is defined in EditTriMesh.h, which is listed below. We will discuss a few significant points about the interface after the listing.

Listing 14.3: EditTriMesh.h

```
/////////////////////////////////////////////////////////////////////////
//
// 3D Math Primer for Graphics and Game Development
//
// EditTriMesh.h - Declarations for class EditTriMesh
//
// Visit gamemath.com for the latest version of this file.
//
// For more details, see EditTriMesh.cpp
//
```

```
/////////////////////////////////////////////////////////////////////

#ifndef __EDITTRIMESH_H_INCLUDED__
#define __EDITTRIMESH_H_INCLUDED__

#ifndef __VECTOR3_H_INCLUDED__
    #include "Vector3.h"
#endif

class Matrix4×3;

/////////////////////////////////////////////////////////////////////
//
// class EditTriMesh
//
// Store an indexed triangle mesh in a very flexible format that makes
// editing and mesh manipulations easy (not optimized for rendering,
// collision detection, or anything else).
//
// This class supports texture mapping coordinates and vertex normals
//
/////////////////////////////////////////////////////////////////////

class EditTriMesh {
public:

// Local types

    // class Vertex represents the information we keep track of for
    // one vertex

    class Vertex {
    public:
        Vertex() { setDefaults(); }
        void   setDefaults();

        // 3D vertex position;

        Vector3      p;

        // Vertex-level texture mapping coordinates. Notice that
        // these may be invalid at various times. The "real" UVs
        // are in the triangles. For rendering, we often need UVs
        // at the vertex level. But for many other optimizations,
        // we may need to weld vertices for faces with different
        // UVs.

        float u, v;

        // vertex-level surface normal. Again, this is only
        // valid in certain circumstances

        Vector3       normal;

        // Utility "mark" variable, often handy

        int    mark;
    };

    // class Tri represents the information we keep track of
```

```
// for one triangle

class Tri {
public:
      Tri() { setDefaults(); }
      void  setDefaults();

      // Face vertices.

      struct Vert {
             int    index; // index into the vertex list
             float u,v;   // mapping coords
      };

      Vert   v[3];

      // Surface normal

      Vector3        normal;

      // Which part does this tri belong to?

      int    part;

      // Index into the material list

      int    material;

      // Utility "mark" variable, often handy

      int    mark;

      // Return true if the triangle is "degenerate" - it uses
      // the same vertex more than once

      bool   isDegenerate() const;

      // Return index of vertex (0..2), or -1, if we
      // don't use that vertex.

      int    findVertex(int vertexIndex) const;
};

// This is the information we store for a "material."
// In our case, we're only going to store a simple
// diffuse texture map. However, more complex properties
// are often associated with materials.

class Material {
public:
      Material() { setDefaults(); }
      void  setDefaults();

      char   diffuseTextureName[256];

      // Utility "mark" variable, often handy

      int    mark;
};
```

```
// This class contains options used to control
// optimization

class OptimationParameters {
public:
        OptimationParameters() { setDefaults(); }
        void   setDefaults();

        // A tolerance value which is used to
        // determine if two vertices are coincident.

        float  coincidentVertexTolerance;

        // Triangle angle tolerance. Vertices
        // are not welded if they are on an edge
        // and the angle between the normals of the
        // triangles on this edge are too
        // far apart. We store the cosine of this
        // value since that's what's actually used.
        // Use the functions to set it

        float  cosOfEdgeAngleTolerance;
        void   setEdgeAngleToleranceInDegrees(float degrees);
};

// Standard class object maintenance

        EditTriMesh();
        EditTriMesh(const EditTriMesh &x);
        ~EditTriMesh();

        // Operator = makes a copy of the mesh

        EditTriMesh &operator=(const EditTriMesh &src);

// Accessors to the mesh data:

        int    vertexCount() const { return vCount; }
        int    triCount() const { return tCount; }
        int    materialCount() const { return mCount; }

        Vertex          &vertex(int vertexIndex);
        const Vertex    &vertex(int vertexIndex) const;

        Tri             &tri(int triIndex);
        const Tri       &tri(int triIndex) const;

        Material        &material(int materialIndex);
        const Material  &material(int materialIndex) const;

// Basic mesh operations

        // Reset the mesh to empty state

        void   empty();

        // Set list counts. If the lists are grown, the new
        // entries will be properly defaulted. If the lists
```

```
                    // are shrunk, no check is made to ensure that a valid
                    // mesh remains.

                    void    setVertexCount(int vc);
                    void    setTriCount(int tc);
                    void    setMaterialCount(int mc);

                    // Add a triangle/vertex/material. The index of the newly
                    // added item is returned

                    int     addTri();
                    int     addTri(const Tri &t);
                    int     addVertex();
                    int     addVertex(const Vertex &v);
                    int     dupVertex(int srcVertexIndex);
                    int     addMaterial(const Material &m);

                    // Handy functions to reset all marks at once

                    void    markAllVertices(int mark);
                    void    markAllTris(int mark);
                    void    markAllMaterials(int mark);

                    // Deletion.

                    void    deleteVertex(int vertexIndex);
                    void    deleteTri(int triIndex);
                    void    deleteMaterial(int materialIndex);
                    void    deleteUnusedMaterials();
                    void    deleteMarkedTris(int mark);
                    void    deleteDegenerateTris();

                    // Detach all the faces from one another. This
                    // creates a new vertex list, with each vertex
                    // only used by one triangle. Simultaneously,
                    // unused vertices are removed.

                    void    detachAllFaces();

                    // Transform all the vertices

                    void    transformVertices(const Matrix4×3 &m);

            // Computations

                    // Compute triangle-level surface normals

                    void    computeOneTriNormal(int triIndex);
                    void    computeOneTriNormal(Tri &t);
                    void    computeTriNormals();

                    // Compute vertex level surface normals. This
                    // automatically computes the triangle level
                    // surface normals

                    void    computeVertexNormals();
```

```
// Optimization

    // Re-order the vertex list in the order that they
    // are used by the faces. This can improve cache
    // performace and vertex caching by increasing the
    // locality of reference. This function can also remove
    // unused vertices simultaneously.

    void   optimizeVertexOrder(bool removeUnusedVertices);

    // Sort triangles by material. This is VERY important
    // for efficient rendering.

    void   sortTrisByMaterial();

    // Weld coincident vertices

    void   weldVertices(const OptimationParameters &opt);

    // Ensure that the vertex UVs are correct, possibly
    // duplicating vertices if necessary.

    void   copyUvsIntoVertices();

    // Do all of the optimizations and prepare the model
    // for fast rendering under *most* rendering systems,
    // with proper lighting.

    void   optimizeForRendering();

// Import/Export S3D format

    bool   importS3d(const char *filename, char *returnErrMsg);
    bool   exportS3d(const char *filename, char *returnErrMsg);

// Debugging

    void   validityCheck();
    bool   validityCheck(char *returnErrMsg);

// Private representation

private:

    // The mesh lists

    int        vAlloc;
    int        vCount;
    Vertex     *vList;

    int        tAlloc;
    int        tCount;
    Tri        *tList;

    int        mCount;
    Material   *mList;
```

```
// Implementation details:

    void  construct();
};
```

```
//////////////////////////////////////////////////////////////////////
#endif // #ifndef __EDITTRIMESH_H_INCLUDED__
```

Most of the behavior of the class is (hopefully) obvious from the function prototypes and adjacent comments. Further comments on details of behavior and implementation are contained in the .cpp file (available for download at gamemath.com). Several items do warrant elaboration, however.

One important question involves how to actually access individual vertices, triangles, and materials. First of all, the class names for these items are contained within the EditTriMesh class namespace. The idea of having a single global class Vertex would be a problem, since there are so many different types of vertices used in different applications. Second, to access the lists, use the vertex(), tri(), and material() functions, which return a reference to the item you are accessing, just like an array. For example, to change the material on a particular face, you could use something like:

```
int i;
EditTriMesh mesh;
int newMaterialIndex;

mesh.tri(i).material = newMaterialIndex;
```

There are const and non-const functions of each accessor to preserve the logical "constness" of the mesh through which they are invoked. (You can't modify a const object.)

A word of warning: be careful when using references and pointers to items in the lists for more than a few statements. Avoid passing these pointers or references into function calls that manipulate the mesh, and avoid storing a reference or pointer across such a function call. The reason is that if the lists need to grow, they may need to be moved around in memory during the realloc call, and any pointer or reference would no longer be valid. For an example of a situation where naïve coding would have fallen into this pitfall, see the comments near the definition of EditTriMesh::dupVertex().

In the code in EditTriMesh.cpp, we have chosen to use these accessor functions whenever possible, even from inside the class in places where we should "know" that the index is in range and could access the list directly. (The purpose of the accessor functions is supposedly to check for array bounds errors.) However, we do often use a shortcut pointer to a triangle, vertex, etc., when accessing the same item multiple times in a row. This not only makes the code slightly easier to read, but it avoids calling the accessor repeatedly.

Another potentially confusing point is the duplication of texture mapping coordinates (the u and v members) in the triangles and vertices. The "official" copy of the texture mapping coordinates is always stored at the triangle level. The texture mapping coordinates in the vertices may be invalid at some points. The reason we allow this to happen is to make some operations easier. Most notably, when we compute vertex normals, we need to average the normals of *all* triangles adjacent to the vertex, regardless of any discontinuity in the texture mapping. (Other types of discontinuity may matter, though, like a sharp edge at a box corner.) So our vertex welding ignores mapping coordinates. The reason texture mapping coordinates are stored in the vertices at all is because most modern rendering hardware and APIs store the texture mapping coordinates at the vertex level. To copy the UVs from the triangles into the vertices, call `copyUvsInto-Vertices()`. This may create additional vertices if multiple triangles share the same vertex but have different texture mapping coordinates. All of these details are handled by the `optimizeForRendering()` function.

The `importS3D()` and `exportS3D()` functions load and save the mesh in the .S3D file format. S3D stands for "Simple 3D" and is a very simple text file format used for delivery of art assets at Terminal Reality. Visit `gamemath.com` for complete documentation on this file format. There you can also download tools which can be used to interface the S3D file format with modeling packages, such as 3D Studio Max, LightWave, and Maya. These are the same tools we use at Terminal Reality.

The `OptimizationParameters` helper class is used to control tolerances and other preferences for vertex welding.

Chapter 15

3D Math for Graphics

This chapter shows how 3D math is used for graphics. It is divided into ten main sections.

- Section 15.1 gives an overview of the graphics pipeline.
- Section 15.2 describes how to set the view parameters. The main concepts are:
  - How to specify the output window
  - The pixel aspect ratio
  - The view frustum
  - Field of view angles and zoom
- Section 15.3 returns to the subject of coordinate spaces. The main concepts are:
  - Modeling and world space
  - Camera space
  - Clip space
  - Screen space
- Section 15.4 covers lighting and fog. The main concepts are:
  - Math on colors
  - Light sources
  - The standard lighting equation
  - The specular component
  - The diffuse component
  - The ambient component
  - Light attenuation
  - Fog
  - Flat shading and Gouraud shading
- Section 15.5 describes the buffers used during rendering. The main concepts are:
  - The frame buffer and double buffering
  - The depth buffer
- Section 15.6 covers texture mapping.

- Section 15.7 covers geometry generation and delivery. The main concepts are:
  - ◆ Level of detail selection and procedural modeling
  - ◆ Delivery of geometry to the API
- Section 15.8 covers transformations and lighting. The main concepts are:
  - ◆ Transformation to clip space
  - ◆ Vertex lighting
- Section 15.9 covers backface culling and clipping.
- Section 15.10 covers rasterization.

In this chapter, we will discuss a number of mathematical issues that arise when creating 3D graphics on a computer. Of course, we cannot hope to cover a subject like computer graphics in any amount of detail in a single chapter. Entire books are written that merely survey the topic. This chapter will be somewhat like a condensed version of one of those books. Our aim is to survey the basic principles, touching a bit on theory and practice, with a particular focus on the math involved.

15.1 Graphics Pipeline Overview

In this section, we attempt to give an overview of the "typical" modern graphics pipeline. Of course, the number of different rendering strategies is equal to the number of graphics programmers. Everyone has his or her own preferences, tricks, and optimizations. Still, most rendering systems have a great deal in common.

We will attempt to describe the basic procedure for generating a single rendered image with basic lighting. We will not consider animation or techniques for global illumination, such as shadows or radiosity.

Another caveat is that this is the conceptual flow of data through the graphics pipeline. In practice, we may perform some tasks in parallel or out of sequence for performance reasons. For example, depending on the rendering API, we may transform and light all vertices before submitting triangles on to the next stage (clipping and culling), or we may transform and light vertices as triangles are submitted to the clipper. Or, it may be faster to defer lighting computations until after backface culling has been performed.

Another extremely important point that we will not discuss in detail is the distribution of work between the main CPU and specialized rendering hardware. Delegating tasks properly in order to maximize the amount of parallel processing is crucial for high performance rendering.

With these simplifications in mind, the following is a rough outline of the flow of data through the graphics pipeline.

- **Setting up the scene**. Before we can begin rendering, we must set several options that apply to the entire scene. For example, we need to set up the camera, or more specifically, pick a point of view in the scene to render it *from*, and choose where on the screen to render it *to*. We will discuss this process in Section 15.2. We also need to select lighting and fog options, which are discussed in Section 15.4, and prepare the *z-buffer*, which is discussed in Section 15.5.

- **Visibility determination**. Once we have a camera in place, we must decide which objects in the scene are visible. This is extremely important for real-time rendering, since we don't want to waste time rendering anything that isn't actually visible. We will survey a few high-level techniques and cover a number of trivial rejection tests in Chapter 16.

- **Setting object-level rendering states**. Once we know that an object is potentially visible, it's time to actually draw the object. Each object may have its own rendering options. We must install these options into the rendering context before rendering any primitives associated with the object. The most common property associated with an object is its *texture map*. We will discuss texture mapping in Section 15.6.

- **Geometry generation/delivery**. Next, the geometry is actually submitted to the rendering API. Typically the data is delivered in the form of triangles, either as individual triangles, or an indexed triangle mesh, triangle strip, etc., as discussed in Section 14.1. At this stage, we may also perform LOD (level of detail) selection or generate geometry procedurally. We discuss a number of issues related to delivering geometry to the rendering API in Section 15.7.

- **Transformation and lighting**. Once the rendering API has the geometry in some triangulated format, vertices of the triangles are transformed from modeling space into camera space and vertex-level lighting computations are performed. These processes are discussed in Section 15.8.

- **Backface culling and clipping**. Next, individual triangles that face away from the camera are removed ("culled"), and any portion of a triangle outside the view frustum is removed in a process known as *clipping*. Clipping may result in a polygon with more than three sides. We discuss culling and clipping in Section 15.9.

- **Projection to screen space**. Once we have a clipped polygon in 3D clip space, we then *project* the vertices of that polygon and map them to the 2D screen space coordinates of the output window. The math behind this operation is explained in Section 15.3.4.

- **Rasterization**. Once we have a clipped polygon in screen space, it is *rasterized*. *Rasterization* refers to the process of selecting which pixels on the screen should be drawn for a particular triangle and delivering the appropriate interpolated parameters (such as lighting and texture mapping coordinates) to the next stage for pixel shading. We will discuss this surprisingly complicated operation in Section 15.10.

- **Pixel shading**. Finally, at the last stage of the pipeline, we compute a color for the triangle, a process known as "shading." We then write that color to the screen, where it might need alpha blending and z-buffering. We will discuss this process in Section 15.10.

The following pseudocode describes the rendering pipeline. It is intended to be an overview, and there are many details which have been left out. Also, there are many variations that arise in practice due to differences between different rendering platforms or APIs.

Listing 15.1: Pseudocode for the graphics pipeline

```
// First, figure how to view the scene

setupTheCamera();

// Clear the zbuffer

clearZBuffer();

// Setup environmental lighting and fog

setGlobalLightingAndFog();

// Get a list of objects that are potentially visible

potentiallyVisibleObjectList = highLevelVisibilityDetermination(scene);

// Render everything we found to be potentially visible

for (all objects in potentiallyVisibleObjectList) {

        // Perform lower-level VSD using bounding volume test

        if (!object.isBoundingVolumeVisible()) continue;

        // Fetch or procedurally generate the geometry

        triMesh = object.getGeometry()

        // Clip and render the faces

        for (each triangle in the geometry) {

                // Transform the vertices to clip space, and perform
                // vertex-level lighting

                clipSpaceTriangle = transformAndLighting(triangle);

                // Is the triangle backfacing?

                if (clipSpaceTriangle.isBackFacing()) continue;

                // Clip the triangle to the view volume

                clippedTriangle = clipToViewVolume(clipSpaceTriangle);
                if (clippedTriangle.isEmpty()) continue;

                // Project the triangle onto screen space and rasterize

                clippedTriangle.projectToScreenSpace();
                for (each pixel in the triangle) {

                        // Interpolate color, zbuffer value,
                        // and texture mapping coords

                        // Perform zbuffering and alpha test
```

```
if (!zbufferTest()) continue;
if (!alphaTest()) continue;

// Shade the pixel.

color = shadePixel();

// Write to the frame buffer and zbuffer

writePixel(color, interpolatedZ);
        }
    }

}
```

15.2 Setting the View Parameters

Before we render a scene, we must pick a camera and a window. That is, we must decide where to render it *from* (the view position, orientation, and zoom) and where to render it *to* (the rectangle on the screen we want to render to). The output window is the simpler of the two, and so we will discuss it first.

15.2.1 Specifying the Output Window

We don't have to render our image to the entire screen. For example, in split-screen multiplayer games, each player is given a portion of the screen. The *output window* refers to the portion of the output device where our image will be rendered. This is shown in Figure 15.1.

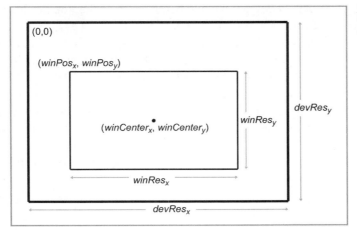

Figure 15.1: Specifying the output window

The position of the window is specified using the coordinates of the upper left-hand pixel, ($winPos_x$, $winPos_y$). The integers $winRes_x$ and $winRes_y$ are the dimensions of the window in *pixels*. Defining it this way, using the size of the window rather than the coordinates of the lower right-hand corner, avoids a number of sticky issues caused by integer pixel coordinates. We are also careful to distinguish between the size of the window in pixels and the physical size of the window, which we will discuss in the next section.

With that said, it is important to realize that we do not necessarily have to be rendering to the screen at all. We could be rendering into a buffer to be saved into a .TGA file or as a frame in an .AVI, or we may be rendering into a texture as a subprocess of the "main" render. For these reasons, the term "frame buffer" is often used to mean the area of memory holding the image that we are rendering.

15.2.2 Pixel Aspect Ratio

Regardless of whether we are rendering to the screen or an off-screen buffer, we must know the *aspect ratio* of the pixels. The pixel aspect ratio basically tells us the ratio of a pixel's height to its width. This ratio is often 1 (i.e., we have "square" pixels), but this is not always the case. The formula for computing the aspect ratio is given below:

Equation 15.1:
Computing the
pixel aspect

$$\frac{\text{pixPhys}_x}{\text{pixPhys}_y} = \frac{\text{devPhys}_x}{\text{devPhys}_y} \cdot \frac{\text{devRes}_y}{\text{devRes}_x}$$

pixPhys refers to the physical size of a pixel. Usually the units of measurement are not important and only the ratio matters. *devPhys* is the physical height and width of the device on which the image is displayed. This could be in inches, feet, picas, etc., since the actual dimensions may be unknown and only the ratio is important. For example, standard desktop monitors come in all different sizes, but the viewable area on most monitors has a ratio of 4:3 — the viewing area is 33 percent wider than it is tall. Another common ratio is 16:9 on high-definition televisions and DVDs. The integers *devRes$_x$* and *devRes$_y$* are the number of pixels in the *x* and *y* dimensions. For example, 640x480 means that *devRes$_x$* = 640 and *devRes$_y$* = 480.

As we mentioned, we often deal with square pixels and the aspect ratio is 1. For example, on a standard desktop monitor with a physical width:height ratio of 4:3, many common resolutions have square pixel ratios; 320x240, 640x480, 800x600, 1024x768, and 1600x1200 are all 4:3, resulting in square pixels.

Notice that nowhere in these calculations is the size or location of the window used. This makes sense; the location and size of our rendering window has no bearing on the physical proportions of a pixel. However, the size of the window *will* become important when we discuss field of view in Section 15.2.4, and the position is important when we map from camera space to screen space in Section 15.3.4.

15.2.3 The View Frustum

The *view frustum* is the volume of space that is visible to the camera. It is shaped like a pyramid with the tip snipped off. An example of a view frustum is shown below in Figure 15.2.

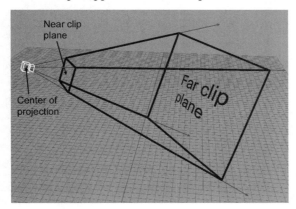

Figure 15.2: The 3D view frustum

The view frustum is bounded by six planes, known as the *clip planes*. The first four of the planes form the sides of the pyramid and are called the *top*, *left*, *bottom*, and *right* planes, for obvious reasons. They correspond to the sides of the output window. It is often desirable to prevent objects from getting too close to the camera. For this purpose, we have the *near clip plane*, which "chops off the tip" of the view frustum. We can also add a *far clip plane*, which limits the distance that the camera can "see." Although the number of objects that the camera can see probably increases with distance, far objects eventually get too small to render effectively and can safely be clipped entirely.

15.2.4 Field of View and Zoom

A camera has position and orientation, just like any other object in the world. However, it also has an additional property known as *field of view*. Another term you are probably more familiar with is *zoom*. Intuitively, you already know what it means to zoom *in* and zoom *out*. When you zoom in, the object you are looking at gets "bigger," and when you zoom out, the object gets "smaller." Of course, this is all very general. Let's see if we can be more precise.

The *field of view* is the angle that is intercepted by the view frustum. We actually need *two* angles: a horizontal field of view and a vertical field of view. Let's drop back to 2D briefly and consider just one of these angles. Figure 15.3 shows the view frustum from above, illustrating precisely the angle that the horizontal field of view measures. The labeling of the axes is illustrative of *camera space*, which will be discussed in Section 15.3.2.

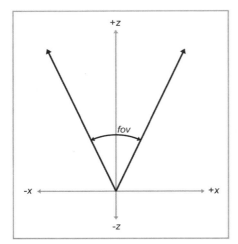

Figure 15.3: Horizontal field of view

Zoom measures the ratio of the apparent size of the object relative to a 90 degree field of view. So larger numbers zoom in, and smaller numbers zoom out. For example, a zoom of 2.0 means that the object will appear twice as big on screen as it would if we were using a 90 degree field of view. Zoom can be interpreted geometrically, as shown in Figure 15.4.

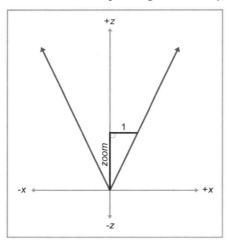

Figure 15.4: Geometric interpretation of zoom

Using some basic trig, we can derive the conversion between field of view and zoom, as shown below:

Equation 15.2:
Converting
between zoom
and field of view

$$zoom = \frac{1}{\tan{(fov/2)}}$$

$$fov = 2 \operatorname{atan}{(1/zoom)}$$

Field of view is a convenient measurement for us to use, but *zoom* is the number that a computer usually needs.

In 3D, we need two different zoom values, one for the horizontal and one for the vertical. Of course, we can choose any two arbitrary values, but if we do not maintain a proper relationship between the horizontal and vertical zoom, then the rendered image will appear stretched. (If you've ever watched a movie intended for the wide screen that was "squashed" to fit on a regular TV, then you've seen this effect.) In order to maintain proper proportions, the zoom values must be proportional to the physical dimensions of the output window:

$$\frac{\text{zoom}_x}{\text{zoom}_y} = \frac{\text{winPhys}_x}{\text{winPhys}_y}$$

Of course, you usually don't know the ratio of the *physical* dimensions of your output window, but you know the dimensions in *pixels*. Here's where the pixel aspect ratio comes in:

$$\begin{aligned}
\frac{\text{zoom}_x}{\text{zoom}_y} &= \frac{\text{winPhys}_x}{\text{winPhys}_y} \\[2mm]
&= \frac{\text{winRes}_x}{\text{winRes}_y} \cdot \frac{\text{pixPhys}_x}{\text{pixPhys}_y} \\[2mm]
&= \frac{\text{winRes}_x}{\text{winRes}_y} \cdot \frac{\text{devPhys}_x}{\text{devPhys}_y} \cdot \frac{\text{devRes}_y}{\text{devRes}_x}
\end{aligned}$$

In the above formula:

- **zoom** refers to the camera's zoom values.
- **winPhys** refers to the physical window size.
- **winRes** refers to the resolution of the window, in pixels.
- **pixPhys** refers to the physical dimensions of a pixel.
- **devPhys** refers to the physical dimensions of the output device. Remember that we usually don't know the exact size, but we usually know the proportions.
- **devRes** refers to the resolution (number of pixels) of the output device.

Many rendering packages allow you to specify the camera using only one field of view angle (or zoom value). When you do this, they automatically compute the other value for you, assuming you want uniform display proportions. For example, you may specify the horizontal field of view, and they compute the vertical field of view for you. Or, you specify the vertical, and they compute the horizontal. Or, you supply the field of view for the larger of the two angles, and they compute the smaller angle (or vice versa).

15.3 Coordinate Spaces

The next few sections discuss a few different coordinate spaces related to 3D viewing. Unfortunately, the terminology is not consistent in other literature on the subject, even though the concepts are the same. We will discuss the coordinate spaces in the order that they are encountered as geometry flows through the graphics pipeline.

15.3.1 Modeling and World Space

The geometry of an object is initially described using *object space*, which is a coordinate space local to the object being described (see Section 3.2.2). The information described usually consists of vertex positions and surface normals. Object space is also known as *modeling space* or *local space*.

From modeling space, the vertices are transformed into *world space* (see Section 3.2.1). The transformation from modeling space to world space is sometimes known as the *model transform*. Typically, lighting is specified using world space, although, as we will see in Section 15.8, it doesn't really matter what coordinate space is used to perform the lighting, provided that the geometry and the lights can be expressed in the same space.

15.3.2 Camera Space

From world space, vertices are transformed using the *view transform* into *camera space* (see Section 3.2.3), also known as *eye space*. Camera space is 3D coordinate space with the origin at the center of projection. One axis is parallel to the direction that the camera is facing (perpendicular to the projection plane), one axis is the intersection of the top and bottom clip planes, and the other axis is the intersection of the left and right clip planes. If we assume the perspective of the camera, one axis will be "horizontal" and one will be "vertical."

In a left-handed world, the most common convention is to point $+z$ in the direction that the camera is facing, with $+x$ and $+y$ pointing "right" and "up" (again, from the perspective of the camera). This is fairly intuitive, and it is shown in Figure 15.5. The typical right-handed convention is to have $-z$ point in the direction that the camera is facing. We will assume the left-handed conventions for the remainder of this chapter.

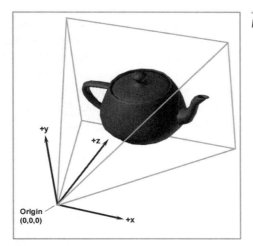

Figure 15.5: Camera space

15.3.3 Clip Space

From camera space, vertices are transformed once again into *clip space*, also known as the *canonical view volume space*. The matrix that transforms vertices from camera space into clip space is known as the *clip matrix*.

Until now, our vertex positions have been "pure" 3D vectors. That is, they only had three coordinates, or if they had a fourth coordinate, w, then w was always equal to 1. The clip matrix changes this and manipulates the vector, placing meaningful information into w in the process. The clip matrix serves two primary functions:

■ Prepare the vector for perspective projection, which will be done by division by w.

■ Scale x, y, and z so that they can be compared against w for clipping.

Let's examine each of these in detail. The first purpose of the clip matrix is to prepare the vector for perspective division by w. We discussed perspective division using w in detail in Section 9.4.4, so let's just review the key points.

Recall from Section 9.4.1 that a 4D homogenous vector is mapped to the corresponding physical 3D vector by dividing by w:

$$\begin{bmatrix} x \\ y \\ z \\ w \end{bmatrix} \implies \begin{bmatrix} x/w \\ y/w \\ z/w \end{bmatrix}$$

One goal of the clip matrix is to get the right value into w so that the proper projection occurs. In Section 9.4.6, we learned how to project onto a plane perpendicular to the z-axis and d units away from the origin. (The plane is of the form $z = d$.) The rectangular portion of the projection plane that is inside the view frustum gets mapped onto the screen. If we vary the distance d, we move the projection plane forward or backward. Inside a real camera, varying the distance from the focal point to the projection plane (known as the *focal distance*) causes the camera to zoom in or out. However, this does *not* occur with the projection plane in a computer. Why not? Inside a real camera, the image projection gets bigger as we increase the focal distance, and the film stays the same size. Inside a computer, the image projection also gets bigger as we increase the focal distance, but the "film" (that is, the rectangular portion of the projection plane that is inside the view frustum) will *also* get bigger as we increase the focal distance d. Because the film and projection increase by the same proportion, there is no change in the rendered image on the screen. Thus, in computer graphics, zoom is controlled completely by the shape of the view frustum, and the value of d is not really significant. So we can pick any value for d and always use that value. The most convenient value for us to use is 1.

If this was the only purpose of the clip matrix, to place the correct value into w, the clip matrix would simply be:

$$\begin{bmatrix} 1 & 0 & 0 & 0 \\ 0 & 1 & 0 & 0 \\ 0 & 0 & 1 & 1 \\ 0 & 0 & 0 & 0 \end{bmatrix}$$

Multiplying a vector of the form $[x, y, z, 1]$ by this matrix, and then performing the perspective divide, we get:

$$\begin{bmatrix} x & y & z & 1 \end{bmatrix} \begin{bmatrix} 1 & 0 & 0 & 0 \\ 0 & 1 & 0 & 0 \\ 0 & 0 & 1 & 1 \\ 0 & 0 & 0 & 0 \end{bmatrix} = \begin{bmatrix} x & y & z & z \end{bmatrix}$$

$$\Rightarrow \begin{bmatrix} x/z & y/z & 1 \end{bmatrix}$$

Now we know how to use a matrix to get the correct value into w. At this point, you may think that this seems like a lot of work for what basically amounts to dividing by z. You're right. The simpler "old school" way of doing things didn't involve w and divided by z. One reason for homogenous coordinates is that they can represent a wider range of camera specifications, including "exotic" projections like when the projection plane is not perpendicular to the direction of the camera. Another reason is that it makes z-clipping (to the near and far clipping planes) the same as x- and y-clipping. This similarity is exploited on rendering hardware. In general, the use of homogenous coordinates and 4×4 matrices makes things more compact, and (in some people's minds) more elegant. Regardless of whether or not using 4×4 matrices improves the process, it's the way most APIs want things delivered, so that's the way it works for better or worse.

The second goal of the clip matrix is to scale the x, y, and z components so that the six clip planes have a trivial form. Points are *outside* the view frustum planes according to the inequalities below:

Equation 15.3:
The six planes
of the view
frustum in clip
space

bottom	$y < -w$
top	$y > w$
left	$x < -w$
right	$x > w$
near	$z < -w$
far	$z > w$

So the points inside the view volume satisfy the inequalities:

$$
\begin{aligned}
-w &\le x \le w \\
-w &\le y \le w \\
-w &\le z \le w
\end{aligned}
$$

Any geometry that does not satisfy these equalities must be clipped to the view frustum. Clipping is discussed in Section 15.9.

To stretch things to put the top, left, right, and bottom clip planes in place, we scale the x and y values by the zoom values of the camera. We discussed how to compute these values in Section 15.2.4. For the near and far clip planes, the z coordinate is biased and scaled so that at the near clip plane, $z/w = -1$, and at the far clip plane, $z/w = 1$.

Let $zoom_x$ and $zoom_y$ be the horizontal and vertical zoom values, and let n and f be the distances to the near and far clipping planes. Then the following matrix scales x, y, and z appropriately, while simultaneously outputting the z coordinate into w:

Equation 15.4:
OpenGL-style
clip matrix

$$
\begin{bmatrix}
zoom_x & 0 & 0 & 0 \\
0 & zoom_y & 0 & 0 \\
0 & 0 & \frac{f+n}{f-n} & 1 \\
0 & 0 & \frac{2nf}{n-f} & 0
\end{bmatrix}
$$

By "OpenGL-style," we mean that z ranges from $-w \dots w$ from the near to far clip plane. (We don't mean that we are using column vectors.) Other APIs, (notably, DirectX) scale z from $0 \dots w$. In other words, a point in clip space is outside the clip plane if:

$$
\begin{aligned}
\text{near} \quad & z < 0 \\
\text{far} \quad & z > w
\end{aligned}
$$

with the points inside the view frustum satisfying the inequality:
$$0 \le z \le w$$

A slightly different clip matrix is used in this case:

Equation 15.5:
DirectX-style
clip matrix

$$
\begin{bmatrix}
zoom_x & 0 & 0 & 0 \\
0 & zoom_y & 0 & 0 \\
0 & 0 & \frac{f}{f-n} & 1 \\
0 & 0 & \frac{nf}{n-f} & 0
\end{bmatrix}
$$

15.3.4 Screen Space

Once we have clipped the geometry to the view frustum, it is projected into *screen space*, which corresponds to actual pixels on the display device. Remember that we are rendering into an output window that does not necessarily occupy the entire display device. However, we usually want our screen space coordinates to be specified using coordinates that are absolute to the rendering device.

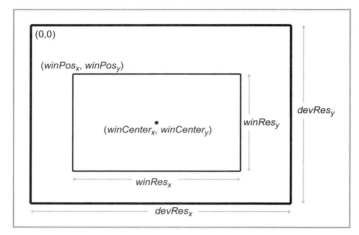

Figure 15.6: The output window in screen space

Screen space is a 2D space, of course. Thus, we must project the points from clip space to screen space to generate the correct 2D coordinates. We do this using the standard homogenous division by w. Then, the x and y coordinates must be scaled to map into the output window. This is summarized below:

Equation 15.6: Projecting and mapping to screen space

$$x_{\text{screen}} = \frac{x_{\text{clip}} \, \text{winRes}_x}{2 \cdot w_{\text{clip}}} + \text{winCenter}_x$$

$$y_{\text{screen}} = -\frac{y_{\text{clip}} \, \text{winRes}_y}{2 \cdot w_{\text{clip}}} + \text{winCenter}_y$$

Notice the negation of the y component, since $+y$ points *up* in clip space, and $+y$ points *down* the screen in screen space.

What about z_{screen} and w_{screen}? Since screen space is a 2D space, these don't really exist. However, we won't discard z_{clip} and w_{clip}, since they are useful for z-buffering and/or perspective correction.

15.4 Lighting and Fog

The idea of covering a topic as complex and rich as lighting in a subsection with a number like "15.4" is actually a bit absurd. We will not even begin to cover all the different lighting techniques that are available; entire volumes have been written on each of these topics. We will focus on the "standard" lighting model used by most rendering APIs, including OpenGL and DirectX. This lighting model, despite its limitations, has become the de facto standard.

The standard lighting model is a *local* lighting model — that is, when we are lighting one particular object, none of the *other* objects in the scene matter. Objects cannot cast shadows on each other. In fact, an object can't even cast a shadow on itself. Shadows are generated using *global* illumination models, which will not be discussed in this book.

15.4.1 Math on Colors

A color is usually represented inside a computer using the RGB color model, where RGB stands for red, green, blue. The precision of these components varies depending on the platform and rendering stage. We will consider the RGB values to range from 0…1 and will not be concerned with the number of bits used to represent the components.

In computer graphics, colors are frequently manipulated as mathematical entities. We will use the same notation for colors as we do for vectors, i.e., a lowercase roman letter in boldface, such as **c**. Usually the context will make it clear if a quantity is a color or vector.

We can think about colors as existing in a 3D unit cube of "color space," as shown in Figure 15.7. Unfortunately, this book is in black and white, but we've indicated the colors using text.

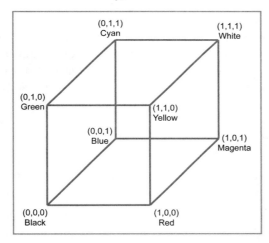

Figure 15.7: The color space cube

White and black are especially important colors, represented in RGB as (1,1,1) and (0,0,0), respectively. We use the special notation **1** and **0** to stand for these colors. All of the grays in between are on the "line" in color space from the black corner to the white corner.

Colors can be added, subtracted, and multiplied by a scalar. These operations are performed in the same way as they are for vectors. Two colors can also be component-wise multiplied. We will use the $\otimes$ symbol for this type of multiplication.

Sometimes the mathematical operations we perform on colors may result in one or more of the RGB values being outside the [0,1] range. (For example, when accumulating light, it is possible for the light to become too bright.) In this case, the color values are usually clamped in range. Depending on the situation, this clamping can occur after each intermediate operation, or it may be that we are able to allow the values to be out of range temporarily and then clamp the value at the end of a series of computations.

Clamping colors may result in a shift in hue if only one value is out of range. For example, the color (1,2,1), in theory, should be a brighter version of (.5,1,.5), which is a lime greenish color. By simply clamping the colors, however, the green hue is lost and we are left with white. A smarter solution would be to scale all of the components uniformly in order and the largest component by one. For example, in this case, the largest component is two, so we'd multiply by .5. Of course, avoiding out-of-range colors to begin with (for example, by adjusting the intensity of light so that the over-bright condition doesn't happen) is usually the best solution.

15.4.2 Light Sources

In order to render a scene, we must describe the lighting in the scene to the graphics API. This is simply a list of light sources. In this section, we discuss the most common types of light sources supported by most rendering APIs:

- Point lights
- Directional lights
- Spot lights
- Ambient light

A *point* light source represents light that emanates from a single point outwards in all directions. Point lights are also called *omni* or *spherical* lights. A point light has a position and color, which controls not only the hue of the light, but also its intensity. A point light may also have a falloff radius, which controls the size of the sphere that is illuminated by the light. Figure 15.8 shows how one popular modeling package, 3D Studio Max, represents point lights visually.

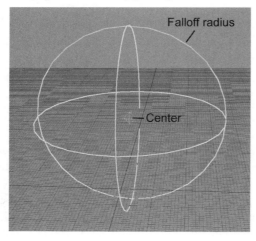

Figure 15.8: A point light

The intensity of the light normally decreases the farther away we are from the center of the light and is zero at the falloff distance. We will discuss attenuation in more detail in Section 15.4.7. Point lights can be used to represent many common light sources, such as light bulbs, lamps, fires, etc.

A *directional* light represents light emanating from a point in space sufficiently far away that all the rays of light involved in lighting the scene (or at least the object we are currently considering) are effectively pointing in the same direction. Directional lights do not have a position, nor do they attenuate. The sun is the most obvious example of a directional light. (We certainly wouldn't try to specify the actual position of the sun in world space in order to properly light the scene…)

A *spot* light is used to represent light from a specific source in a specific direction. These are used for lights such as flashlights, headlights, and of course, *spotlights*! A spotlight has a position and an orientation and, optionally, a falloff distance. The shape of the lit area is either a cone or pyramid.

A conical spotlight has a circular "bottom." The width of the cone is defined by a *falloff angle* (not to be confused with the falloff *distance*). In addition, there is an inner angle that measures the size of the *hotspot*. A conical spotlight is shown in Figure 15.9.

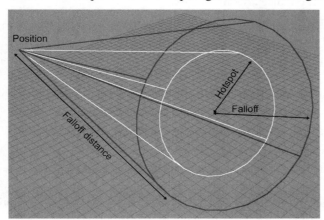

Figure 15.9: A conical spotlight

A rectangular spotlight forms a pyramid rather than a cone. Rectangular spotlights are especially interesting because they are used to project an image. For example, imagine walking in front of a movie screen while a movie is being shown. An image projected in this manner is known as a *projected light map*.

Finally, the *ambient* light for the scene is simply a constant color for the entire scene representing light that isn't coming from any of the other light sources. Without ambient light, objects that were in shadow would be *completely* black, since they are not lit directly by any one light source. In the real world, these objects are lit indirectly. Ambient lighting is a rudimentary way to account for this indirect lighting. We will discuss ambient light in more detail in Section 15.4.6.

15.4.3 The Standard Lighting Equation — Overview

The standard lighting model that we referred to in the introduction to Section 15.4 defines a *standard lighting equation* to compute a color value for a single pixel. An overview of the lighting equation is given by:

Equation 15.7:
Overview of
the standard
lighting
equation

$$\mathbf{c}_{lit} = \mathbf{c}_{spec} + \mathbf{c}_{diff} + \mathbf{c}_{amb}$$

where:

- c_{lit} is the resulting "lit" color value, as opposed to an "unlit" color value, which has full lighting intensity. Contrary to normal use of the verb *light*, in computer graphics lighting normally refers to the process of taking an unlit color, say, from a texture, and darkening it. As the lighting process is explained, this will become clear.
- c_{spec} is the *specular* contribution, discussed in Section 15.4.4.
- c_{diff} is the *diffuse* contribution, discussed in Section 15.4.5.
- c_{amb} is the *ambient* contribution, discussed in Section 15.4.6.

The appearance of an object depends primarily on four factors:

- The properties of the surface of the object itself. These properties are known as *material* properties.
- The location and orientation of the surface being lit. The orientation is usually described using a surface normal, a unit vector that is perpendicular to the surface.
- The properties of various lights that are shining on the object.
- The location of the viewer.

Each of the three components in the lighting equation takes into account a different combination of the above factors.

Next, we will dissect each component of the lighting equation separately. In Section 15.4.8, we will put the pieces together to derive the complete lighting equation.

15.4.4 The Specular Component

The specular component of the lighting equation models *direct* reflection of light from a light source to the eye. The important vectors are labeled in Figure 15.10.

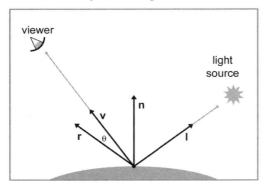

Figure 15.10: Phong model for specular reflection

The specular component is what gives surfaces a "shiny" appearance. Rougher surfaces do not exhibit a high degree of reflectivity, and so this component will not be very significant. The amount of specular lighting depends on the object, the lights, and the viewer.

- **n** is the surface normal.
- **v** points toward the viewer.

- **l** points toward the light source. For directional lights, **l** is constant.
- **r** is the "reflection" vector, the result of reflecting **l** about **n**.
- θ is the angle between **r** and **v**, given by **r·v**. This angle measures how *direct* the reflection is.

All vectors are unit vectors. As shown in Figure 15.11, **r** is given by 2(**n·l**)**n**–**l**:

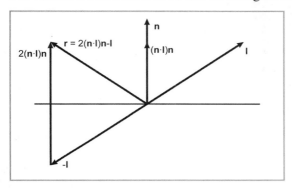

Figure 15.11: Constructing the reflection vector r

The following equation for the specular component is known as the *Phong* model for specular reflection:

Equation 15.8: Phong model for specular reflection

$$\mathbf{c}_{spec} = (\cos\theta)^{m_{gls}}\,\mathbf{s}_{spec}\otimes\mathbf{m}_{spec}$$
$$= (\mathbf{v}\cdot\mathbf{r})^{m_{gls}}\,\mathbf{s}_{spec}\otimes\mathbf{m}_{spec}$$

m_{gls} is the glossiness of the material, also known as the *Phong exponent*. This controls how wide the "hotspot" is; a smaller value results in a larger, more gradual falloff from the hotspot, and larger exponents result in a very tight hotspot with sharp falloff. (This hotspot is not to be confused with the hotspot of a spotlight.) Perfectly reflective surfaces, such as glass, will have a very high value for m_{gls} — only a perfectly reflected ray of light will enter the eye. Shiny surfaces that are not perfect reflectors, like the surface of an apple, might have lower values, resulting in a larger hotspot.

Another value related to the "shininess" of the material is $\mathbf{m}_{spec}$, which is the material's specular color. Usually, this is a grayscale value that is constant for the entire material. While m_{gls} controls the size of the hotspot, $\mathbf{m}_{spec}$ controls its intensity. Highly reflective surfaces will have a higher value for $\mathbf{m}_{spec}$, and more matte surfaces will have a lower value. If desired, a *gloss* map may be used to control the brightness of the reflections using a bitmap, much as a texture map controls the color of an object.

$\mathbf{s}_{spec}$ is the specular color of the light source, which controls the basic color and intensity of the light. For rectangular spotlights, this value may come from a projected light map. $\mathbf{s}_{spec}$ is often equal to the light's diffuse color, $\mathbf{s}_{diff}$.

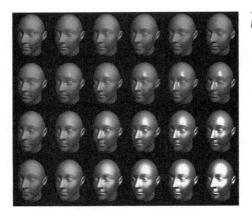

Figure 15.12: Different values for m_{gls} and $\mathbf{m}_{spec}$

Figure 15.12 shows how different values of m_{gls} and $\mathbf{m}_{spec}$ affect the appearance of an object with specular reflection. In the figure, the color $\mathbf{m}_{spec}$ goes from black on the leftmost column to white on the rightmost column. The exponent m_{gls} is very large on the top row, and it decreases with each subsequent row. Notice that the heads in the leftmost column all look the same; since the specular strength is zero, the specular exponent is irrelevant, and there is no specular contribution in any case. (The lighting comes from the diffuse and ambient components, which will be discussed in the next sections.)

If the distance to the viewer is large relative to the size of an object, then $\mathbf{v}$ may be computed once and then considered constant for an entire object. The same is true for a light source and the vector $\mathbf{l}$. (In fact, for directional lights, $\mathbf{l}$ is always constant.) However, since $\mathbf{n}$ is not constant, we must still compute $\mathbf{r}$, a computation which we would like to avoid if possible. The *Blinn model* does this by measuring a slightly different angle, as shown in Figure 15.13.

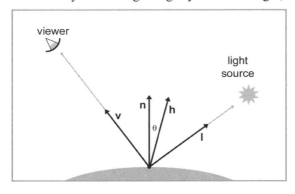

Figure 15.13: Blinn model for specular reflection

The Blinn model uses $\mathbf{h}$, the "halfway" vector between $\mathbf{v}$ and $\mathbf{l}$, which is computed by averaging $\mathbf{v}$ and $\mathbf{l}$ and then normalizing the result:

Equation 15.9:
The halfway
vector h, used in
the Blinn model

$$\mathbf{h} = \frac{\mathbf{v} + \mathbf{l}}{\|\mathbf{v} + \mathbf{l}\|}$$

The Blinn model is similar to the Phong model, only θ measures the angle between $\mathbf{n}$ and $\mathbf{h}$:

Equation 15.10:
The Blinn model
for specular
reflection

$$\begin{aligned} \mathbf{c}_{spec} &= (\cos \theta)^{m_{gls}} \mathbf{s}_{spec} \otimes \mathbf{m}_{spec} \\ &= (\mathbf{n} \cdot \mathbf{h})^{m_{gls}} \mathbf{s}_{spec} \otimes \mathbf{m}_{spec} \end{aligned}$$

This equation is usually easier to implement in hardware, especially if the viewer and light source are far enough away from the object to be considered a constant, since then $\mathbf{h}$ is a constant and only needs to be computed once. For a comparison of the Blinn and Phong specular models, see [7].

One slight detail that we have omitted is that $\cos \theta$ may be less than zero in either model. In this case, we usually clamp the specular contribution to $\mathbf{0}$.

15.4.5 The Diffuse Component

Like the specular component, the *diffuse* component also models light that strikes the object directly. However, whereas specular light accounts for light that reflects perfectly off the surface into the eye, diffuse light models reflections that are scattered in random directions due to the rough ("diffuse") nature of the object's surface. Figure 15.14 compares how rays of light reflect on a perfectly reflective surface and on a rough surface.

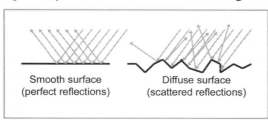

Smooth surface
(perfect reflections)

Diffuse surface
(scattered reflections)

Figure 15.14: Diffuse lighting models scattered reflections

Diffuse lighting does not depend on the location of the viewer because the reflections are scattered randomly. However, the position of the light source relative to the surface *is* important. If we imagine counting the photons of light that hit the surface of the object and have a chance of reflecting into the eye, a surface that is perpendicular to the rays of light receives more rays per unit area than a surface oriented at a more glancing angle. This is shown in Figure 15.15.

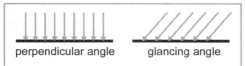

perpendicular angle   glancing angle

Figure 15.15: Surfaces more perpendicular to the light rays receive more light per unit area

Notice that in both cases, the perpendicular distance between the rays is the same. (Due to an optical illusion in the diagram, the rays on the right may *appear* to be farther apart, but if you look closely or measure them, they are not.) So, the perpendicular distance between the rays is the same, but notice that on the right side of Figure 15.15, they strike the object at points that are farther apart. Thus, the amount of light per unit area is smaller. The surface on the left receives nine light rays, and the surface on the right receives only six, even though the "area" of both surfaces is the same. This same phenomenon is responsible for the fact that the climate near the equator is warmer than near the poles. Since the earth is round, the light from the sun strikes the ground at a more direct angle near the equator.

Diffuse lighting obeys *Lambert's law*: the intensity of the reflected light is proportional to the cosine of the angle between the surface normal and the rays of light. We will compute this cosine using the dot product:

Equation 15.11:
Calculating
the diffuse
component
using Lambert's
law
$$\mathbf{c}_{diff} = (\mathbf{n} \cdot \mathbf{l})\mathbf{s}_{diff} \otimes \mathbf{m}_{diff}$$

$\mathbf{n}$ is the surface normal and $\mathbf{l}$ is a unit vector which points toward the light source, just as in the previous section. $\mathbf{m}_{diff}$ is the material's diffuse color. This is the value that most people think of when they think of the "color" of an object. The diffuse material color often comes from a texture map. $\mathbf{s}_{diff}$ is the diffuse color of the light source, and is often equal to the light's specular color, $\mathbf{s}_{spec}$.

As with specular lighting, we must prevent the dot product term from going negative by clamping it to zero. This prevents objects from being lit "from behind."

15.4.6 The Ambient Component

Specular and diffuse lighting both model light rays that travel directly from the light source to the surface of the object and are then reflected to the viewer. However, in the real world, light often bounces off of one or more intermediate objects before hitting an object and reflecting to the eye. This is why when you open the refrigerator door in the middle of the night, the entire kitchen will get a bit brighter, even though the refrigerator door (and your body) block most of the direct light.

To model these reflections, we can use *ambient* light. The ambient portion of the lighting equation depends on the properties of the material and a global ambient lighting value used for the entire scene. None of the light sources are involved in the computation. (In fact, a light source is not even necessary.) The following equation is used to compute the ambient component:
$$\mathbf{c}_{amb} = \mathbf{g}_{amb} \otimes \mathbf{m}_{amb}$$

$\mathbf{m}_{amb}$ is the material's "ambient color." This is almost always the same as the diffuse color, which is often defined using a texture map. $\mathbf{g}_{amb}$ is the global ambient light value for the entire scene.

15.4.7 Light Attenuation

Light *attenuates* with distance. That is, objects are illuminated less by a light as they move farther away from the light. In the real world, the intensity of a light is inversely proportional to the square of the distance between the light and the object:

Equation 15.12:
Real-world light attenuation is inversely proportional to the square of the distance

$$\frac{i_1}{i_2} = \frac{d_2{}^2}{d_1{}^2}$$

where i is the intensity of the light, and d is the distance.

In practice, Equation 15.12 can be unwieldy. Instead, a simpler model is used based on *falloff distances*. In Section 15.4.2, we mentioned that the falloff distance controls the distance beyond which the light has no effect. Normally, a simple linear interpolation formula is used such that the light gradually fades with the distance d:

$$i(d) = \begin{cases} 1 & \text{if } d \leq d_{min} \\ \frac{d_{max} - d}{d_{max} - d_{min}} & \text{if } d_{min} < d < d_{max} \\ 0 & \text{if } d \geq d_{max} \end{cases}$$

As you can see, there are actually *two* falloff distances. Within d_{min}, the light is at full intensity (1.0). As the distance goes from d_{min} to d_{max}, the intensity varies linearly from 1.0 down to 0.0. At d_{max} and beyond, the light intensity is 0.0. Basically, d_{min} controls the distance at which the light *begins* to falloff. d_{min} is frequently zero, which means that the light begins falling off immediately. d_{max} is the actual falloff distance — the distance where the light has fallen off completely.

Distance attenuation can be applied to point lights and spotlights — directional lights are not attenuated. An additional attenuation factor is used for spotlights. *Hotspot falloff* attenuates light as we move closer to the edge of the cone.

Once we have computed the intensity multiplier i, it is applied to the diffuse and specular components. Ambient light is not attenuated, obviously.

15.4.8 The Lighting Equation — Putting It All Together

We have discussed the individual components of the lighting equation in detail. Now it is time to give the complete lighting equation:

Equation 15.13:
The standard lighting equation for one light source

$$\begin{aligned} \mathbf{c}_{lit} &= \mathbf{c}_{spec} + \mathbf{c}_{diff} + \mathbf{c}_{amb} \\ &= i\left(max\left(\mathbf{n} \cdot \mathbf{h}, 0\right)^{m_{gls}} \mathbf{s}_{spec} \otimes \mathbf{m}_{spec} + max\left(\mathbf{n} \cdot \mathbf{l}, 0\right)\mathbf{s}_{diff} \otimes \mathbf{m}_{diff}\right) \\ &\quad + \mathbf{g}_{amb} \otimes \mathbf{m}_{amb} \end{aligned}$$

Specular   +   Diffuse   +   Ambient   =   Lit

Figure 15.16: The visual contribution of each of the components of the lighting equation

Figure 15.16 shows what each of the lighting components actually look like in isolation from the others. There are several interesting points to be noted:

- The ear is lit just as bright as the nose, even though it is actually in the shadow of the head. This is a consequence of using a local lighting model. For shadows, a more advanced technique must be used.

- In the first two images, without ambient light, the side of the head that is facing away from the light is completely black. In order to light the "back side" of objects, you must use ambient light. Or, you can place enough lights in your scene so that every surface is lit directly.

- With only ambient lighting, just the silhouette is visible. Lighting is an extremely powerful visual cue that makes the object appear "3D." The solution to this "cartoon" effect is, again, to place a sufficient number of lights in the scene so that every surface is lit directly.

Speaking of multiple lights, how do multiple light sources work with the lighting equation? We must sum up the lighting values for *all* the lights. If we let $\mathbf{s}_j$ represent the *j*th light source, where *j* goes from $1\ldots n$, *n* being the number of lights, then the lighting equation becomes:

Equation 15.14: The standard lighting equation for multiple lights

$$
\mathbf{c}_{lit} = \sum_{j=1}^{n} i_j \left(max\,(\mathbf{n} \cdot \mathbf{h}_j, 0)^{m_{gls}} \mathbf{s}_{j\,spec} \otimes \mathbf{m}_{spec} + max\,(\mathbf{n} \cdot \mathbf{l}_j, 0)\mathbf{s}_{j\,diff} \otimes \mathbf{m}_{diff} \right) + \mathbf{g}_{amb} \otimes \mathbf{m}_{amb}
$$

Of course, since there is only one global ambient light value for the scene, it is not summed per light source.

15.4.9 Fog

In the real world, rays of light are reflected and refracted by millions of tiny particles in the air. If the particles are numerous enough per unit volume, we can actually see them. Fog, haze, and smoke are examples of this phenomenon. In computer graphics, all of these types of effects are approximated using a technique known as *fogging*.

Imagine we are looking at an object in the distance. The air between the object and our eye is filled with particles (of moisture, smoke, etc.) that interfere with the direct transmission of light from the object to our eye. Some rays of light that were *not* necessarily bound for our eye originally may bounce off these particles and wind up heading toward us. This is how we actually "see" the particles in the air. The visual result is that the color of the object we are looking at appears to shift toward the color of the fog particles. The more particles that lie between us and the pixel we are rendering, the more pronounced this effect will be.

The *fog density* is an arbitrary number, from 0...1, which controls how "fogged out" the object is. A density of zero indicates that there is no fog effect. A density of one means the object is completely fogged out, and the color of the pixel should be the same as the fog color. Values in between are used to linearly interpolate between the color of the object and the fog color.

How do we compute this fog density? As we have mentioned, the more particles that lie between our eye and the object, the more pronounced the fogging effect will be. How do we know how many particles there are, and how do we convert this number into a fog density? Luckily, we don't have to know the actual number of particles. Instead, we use two heuristics to compute a value that behaves as if we were counting the number of particles. The number of particles depends on only two factors: the overall density of the fog in the scene and the distance from our eye to the object.

The distance from the eye to the object can easily be computed. Thus, all that remains is to derive some function of distance that takes the overall fog density into account and returns a fog value for a single pixel. How do we specify how "dense" the fog in the scene is? What sort of units should we use for this? Rather than actually specifying a real "density" value, we use a much simpler system. The overall density of the fog is controlled by two distances, d_{min} and d_{max}. If the distance of a pixel is less than d_{min}, then no fogging occurs, and the fog value is zero. As the distance increases to d_{max}, the fog value increases from zero to one. At d_{max} and beyond, the object is completely fogged out, and the fog value is one. The following formula describes this succinctly:

Equation 15.15:
Fog value
computation
using minimum
and maximum
fog distances

$$f(d) = \begin{cases} 0 & \text{if } d \leq d_{min} \\ \frac{d - d_{min}}{d_{max} - d_{min}} & \text{if } d_{min} < d < d_{max} \\ 1 & \text{if } d \geq d_{max} \end{cases}$$

Two important items to note:

- The assumption that the fog is uniformly distributed is usually, but not always, reasonable. For example, in the real world, fog is often thicker in low-lying areas. This cannot be modeled using a simple distance-based fog.

- The definition of *distance* may vary. Of course, true Euclidian distance may be used, in which case we have *spherical* fog. This involves the slow square root operation. One simplification is to use camera-space z as the distance, which gives us *linear* fog. Linear fog is faster, but it has the annoying side effect that the fog density for a point can change depending on the orientation of the camera, which would not happen in the real world.

Once we have a fog density value from 0...1, a pixel is fogged using the linear interpolation equation:

$$\mathbf{c}_{fogged} = \mathbf{c}_{lit} + f(\mathbf{g}_{fog} - \mathbf{c}_{lit})$$

Where:

- c_{lit} is the color of the surface after lighting computations have been performed.
- f is the fog density, usually computed using Equation 15.15.
- g_{fog} is the global fog color.
- c_{fogged} is the resulting lit and fogged color.

In order to use fog in our scene, we must communicate to the API the properties of our fog. This usually consists of three pieces of information:

- **Master fog switch**. If we wish to use fogging, we must enable it.
- **Fog color**. This is c_{fog} in the equations above.
- **Fog distances**. d_{min} and d_{max}.

15.4.10 Flat Shading and Gouraud Shading

If rendering speed were not a concern, we would apply the lighting and fog equations per pixel. (For lighting, this technique is known as *Phong shading* — not to be confused with the Phong model for specular reflection). Unfortunately, these computations often cannot be performed fast enough, and we must make a compromise and perform them less frequently. We have two options. We may either compute them per polygon or per vertex. These two techniques are known as *flat shading* and *Gouraud shading*, respectively.

When using flat shading, we will compute a single lighting value for the entire triangle. Usually, the "position" used in the computations is the centroid of the triangle, and the surface normal is the normal of the triangle. As you can see in Figure 15.17, when an object is lit using flat shading, the faceted nature of the object becomes painfully apparent, and any illusion of smoothness is lost.

Figure 15.17: A flat shaded teapot

Gouraud shading, also known as vertex shading or interpolated shading, is a trick whereby values for lighting, fog, etc., are computed at the vertex level. These values are then linearly interpolated across the face of the polygon. Figure 15.18 shows the same teapot, rendered using Gouraud shading.

Figure 15.18: A Gouraud shaded teapot

As you can see, Gouraud shading does a relatively good job at restoring the smooth nature of the object. When the values being approximated are basically linear across the triangle, then the linear interpolation used by Gouraud shading does a good job of approximating them. The problem is when the values are *not* linear, as in the case of specular highlights. Compare the specular highlights in the Gouraud shaded teapot with the highlights in a Phong (per-pixel) shaded teapot, shown in Figure 15.19. Notice how much smoother the highlights are. Except for the silhouette and areas of extreme geometric discontinuities, such as the handle and spout, the illusion of smoothness is very convincing. With Gouraud shading, the individual facets are detectable due to the specular highlights.

Figure 15.19: A Phong shaded teapot

The basic problem with interpolated shading is that no value in the middle of the triangle can be larger than the largest value at a vertex. So highlights can only occur at a vertex. Sufficient tessellation can overcome this problem.

Despite its limitations, Gouraud shading is still the most common type of shading used on today's hardware. One question that you should ask is how the lighting can be computed at the vertex level if any maps are used to control inputs to the lighting equation (most notably, a diffuse texture map). We will discuss this issue in Section 15.8.2.

15.5 Buffers

Rendering involves many *buffers*. In this context, a buffer is simply a rectangular region of memory that stores some sort of data per pixel. The most important buffers are the *frame buffer* and the *depth buffer*.

The *frame buffer* stores one color per pixel; it holds the rendered image. The color for a single pixel may be stored in a variety of formats; the variations are not significant for the current discussion. The frame buffer is normally located in video RAM. The video card is constantly reading this area of video RAM, converting the binary data into the appropriate signal to be sent to the CRT. A technique known as *double buffering* is used to prevent an image from being displayed before it is completely rendered. Under double buffering, there are actually two frame buffers. One frame buffer holds the image currently displayed on the monitor. The other frame buffer, the *off-screen* buffer, holds the image currently being rendered.

When we have finished rendering an image and are ready for it to be displayed, we "flip" the buffers. We can do this in one of two ways:

■ If we use *page flipping*, then we instruct the video hardware to begin reading from the buffer that was the off-screen buffer. We then swap the roles of the two buffers; the buffer that was being displayed now becomes the off-screen buffer.

■ We may *blit* (copy) the off-screen buffer over the display buffer.

Double buffering is shown in Figure 15.20.

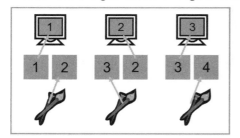

Figure 15.20: Double buffering

The second important buffer used for rendering is the *depth* buffer, also known as the *z-buffer*. Rather than storing a color at each pixel, the depth buffer stores a *depth* value per pixel. There are many variations in the specifics of exactly what value goes into the depth buffer, but the basic idea is that it is related to the distance from the camera. Often, the clip-space z coordinate is used as a depth value, which is why the depth buffer is also known as the z-buffer.

The depth buffer is used to determine which objects occlude which objects as follows. As we are rasterizing a triangle, we compute an interpolated depth value per pixel. Before rendering a pixel, we compare this depth value with the value already in the depth buffer for this pixel. If the new depth is farther from the camera than the value currently in the depth buffer, then the pixel is discarded. Otherwise, the pixel color is written to the frame buffer, and the depth buffer is updated with the new, closer depth value.

Before we can begin rendering an image, we must *clear* the depth buffer to some very far distance value (in clip space, this would be 1.0) so that the first pixels to be rendered will pass the depth buffer test. We don't normally double buffer the depth buffer like we do the frame buffer.

15.6 Texture Mapping

There is much more to the appearance of an object than its shape. Different objects are different colors and have unique patterns on their surface. One simple yet powerful way to capture these qualities is through *texture mapping*.

A *texture map* is a bitmap image that is applied to the surface of an object. Rather than controlling the color of an object per triangle or per vertex, with texture mapping we can control the color at a much finer level — per *textel*. (A textel is a single pixel from a texture map.)

Although you have almost certainly seen texture-mapped images before, let's look at an example to see just how powerful texture mapping is at conveying surface properties. Figure 15.21 shows a 3D model of a character, "Rayne," before and after texture mapping.

Figure 15.21: A 3D model before and after texture mapping

"Rayne" model by Chris DeSimone and Joe Wampole. Used by permission of Majesco.

So, a texture map is just a regular bitmap that is applied to the surface of a model. Exactly how does this work? Actually, there are many different ways in which we can "wrap" a texture map around a mesh. *Planar mapping* projects the texture linearly onto the mesh. *Spherical, cylindrical,* and *cubic* mapping are various methods of "wrapping" the texture around the object. The details of each of these techniques are not important to us at the moment, since modeling packages such as 3D Studio Max deal with these user interface issues. No matter how the map is placed by the artists, eventually each vertex is assigned *texture mapping coordinates*, which are nothing more than 2D Cartesian locations in the bitmap. Usually, we refer to these coordinates as u and v to avoid confusion with the many xs and ys involved in rendering. Texture mapping coordinates are usually normalized from 0...1 across the width and height of the texture. For example, Figure 15.22 shows one texture from the model in Figure 15.21.

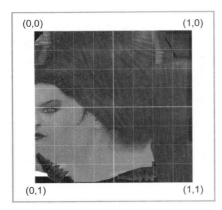

(0,0) (1,0)

(0,1) (1,1)

Figure 15.22: An example texture map

This texture map is used for Rayne's head. One single texture map goes all the way around one half of her head, from her nose to the middle of the back of her head. The artist has purposefully designed the texture so that it can be "wrapped" around the model. The other half of her head is mapped using the same texture, only it is mirrored for the other half.

Notice that the texture doesn't have to wrap "continuously" around the geometry in one piece. Since each triangle can be mapped independently, different areas of the texture may be mapped onto different portions of the model arbitrarily. For example, the "teeth" objects that you see in the corners of the texture map are just that; Rayne has fangs, which can be seen when she opens her mouth. Of course, if a "continuous" mapping is not used, the vertices will have to be duplicated at the texture "seams" if the texture mapping coordinates are stored at the vertex level. (They usually are.)

Notice that we have chosen to place the origin of texture mapping space in the upper left-hand coordinate, which mimics the way the texture is accessed in hardware. More "academic" literature places the origin in the lower left-hand coordinate.

As we have mentioned, each vertex is assigned a set of u,v coordinates in the texture map. In this way, the texture is "pinned down" to the surface of the mesh. To render a pixel from the middle of a triangle, we compute interpolated u,v mapping coordinates corresponding to the pixel (similar to Gouraud shading) and then fetch the textel at these u,v coordinates.

15.7 Geometry Generation/Delivery

Once we have determined what objects are visible (or at least *potentially* visible), we can generate or deliver the geometry for these objects to the graphics processor. Several tasks can be performed at this stage:

- Level of detail (LOD) selection.
- Procedural generation of geometry.
- Delivery of data to the graphics API.

15.7.1 LOD Selection and Procedural Modeling

We normally want to draw objects using the most number of triangles possible so that we can get the best visual appearance, but unfortunately, more triangles usually mean slower frame rate. We must strike a balance between visual appearance and acceptable frame rate. One way to improve both is to vary the *level of detail* (LOD) of the geometry, depending on the distance to the camera. The basic idea is that objects that are farther from the camera are smaller and can therefore be rendered with fewer triangles without sacrificing visual quality.

How do we obtain a mesh with fewer triangles? One easy way (from a programmer's perspective!) is for an artist to build one by hand. Then, the object's distance from the camera (or screen size — which works even when the zoom of the camera varies greatly) is used to select the appropriate LOD. The only problem with this technique is that there is a visible "pop" when the model switches from one LOD to the next, as the object moves closer or farther away from the camera. Of course, we hope to minimize this visual discontinuity — good meshes can help a great deal.

One way to avoid the "pop" associated with discrete LODs is to employ a *continuous* LOD. In this system, the number of different level of detail meshes are so many that they are effectively continuous; we can generate a mesh with almost any number of triangles we want. Progressive meshes are one such "mesh decimation" technique (see Section 14.4.5). It is important to note that there is overhead (possibly considerable) associated with generating a continuous LOD. If we use discrete LOD, then the mesh is already available and can be submitted for rendering immediately; all we have to do is decide which mesh to use. Thus, discrete LODs are used in practice most frequently, even if the actual meshes are generated procedurally using mesh decimation techniques.

Sometimes the geometry is not created by a human artist, but on-the-fly by the computer. This is known as *procedural modeling*. Fractal terrain is a good example of procedural modeling. Plants and "greenery" are other examples where procedural geometry gives good results. Sometimes LOD is employed within a procedural modeling algorithm, such that the geometry is generated only to a desired LOD. A complete discussion of procedural modeling is outside the scope of this book. One good resource is [5].

15.7.2 Delivery of Geometry to the API

Regardless of the source of the geometry data, it must at some point be delivered to the rendering API. (API stands for application programming interface — in this case, the software that we use to communicate with the rendering subsystem.) In this section, we will describe various formats used for geometry by modern APIs.

As we have mentioned previously, most modern APIs want the geometry delivered in some sort of triangle mesh format. The data may be individual triangles, an indexed triangle mesh, a triangle strip, or a triangle fan. (We discussed the various methods of representing triangle meshes in Section 14.1.) In all cases, the bulk of the data is usually contained in the *vertices*, and the data for the triangles is nothing more than appropriate linkage of vertices. In other words, the API usually doesn't need any extra data at the triangle level. Since we have already discussed different ways that the linkage of triangles can be represented, the remainder of this section is devoted to different methods for representing the vertex data.

APIs accept a number of different vertex formats, depending on what operations you want the API to do for you. (When we say that "the API" does some bit of work, we really mean "the graphics subsystem." Whether the work is done by the API in software or processed on dedicated rendering hardware is irrelevant to this discussion.)

Allow for a moment a gross oversimplification. The data in most of the common vertex formats can be put into one of three categories:

- **Position**. This describes the location of the vertex. This can be a 3D vector or a 2D screen space position with depth information. If a 3D vector is used, the position must be transformed into screen space using the current modeling and view transforms. Another advanced technique used in skeletal animation is known as *skinning*, where the position of a vertex is animated using one or more *bones*.

- **Lighting and fog**. For rendering, we usually assign a color to each vertex. This color is then interpolated across the surface of the triangle. We may specify this color ourselves, or we can let the API compute an appropriate lighting value. If the API does the lighting, then we usually must supply a surface normal per vertex. (For more on lighting computations, see Section 15.8.) In any case, a "color" is usually an RGB triple and an alpha value. If we specify the color directly, we may use a 32-bit ARGB value, with 8 bits for each component. Or, we may use a separate value for each component. If we are using hardware fogging, then a "fog density" value can also be associated with each vertex. Once again, we may specify this value manually, or we can let the API compute it for us. (For more on fogging, see Section 15.4.9.)

- **Texture mapping coordinates**. If we are using texture-mapped triangles, then each vertex must be assigned a set of mapping coordinates. In the simplest case, this is a 2D location into the texture map. We usually denote the coordinates (u, v). If we are using *multi-texturing*, then we will need one set of mapping coordinates per texture map. Optionally, we can generate one or more set of texture mapping coordinates procedurally (if we are projecting a light onto a surface, for example). Or, we may "procedurally" copy one set of mapping coordinates to another. In this case, we may not need to specify all (or any) of the mapping coordinates.

As mentioned before, this is a gross oversimplification, but it does cover the most common vertex formats used in practice. In short, there is no *one* single format that is used to submit vertex data. In fact, there are so many variations, DirectX has the notion of a *flexible vertex format* which allows you to "roll your own" vertex format, putting in whatever information you need in whatever order is most convenient for your application.

With all that in mind, let's give a few examples of C++ structs that would be used to deliver vertex data for a few of the most common vertex formats that arise in practice.

One of the most common vertex formats contains a 3D position, surface normal, and mapping coordinates. Most static texture-mapped meshes that we wish to be lit by the API use this vertex format.

```
// Untransformed, unlit vertex

struct RenderVertex {
    Vector3    p;    // position
    Vector3    n;    // normal
```

```
        float       u,v;  // texture mapping coordinates
};
```

Another common format, used for heads-up displays and other "2D" items, is a vertex with screen space coordinates and prelit vertices. Although the data is "2D," we often must supply some sort of depth information.

```
// Transformed and lit vertex

struct RenderVertexTL {
        Vector3     p;      // screen space position and depth
        float       w;      // 1/z
        unsigned    argb;   // prelit diffuse color (8 bits per component – 0xAARRGGBB)
        unsigned    spec;   // prelit specular color
        float       u,v;    // texture mapping coordinates
};
```

One final example is a vertex that is expressed in 3D, but does not need to be lit by the graphics API's lighting engine. This format is often useful for special effects such as explosions, flames, and self-illuminated objects, and for rendering "debugging objects" like bounding boxes, waypoints, markers, etc.

```
// Untransformed, lit vertex

struct RenderVertexL {
        Vector3     p;      // position
        unsigned    argb;   // prelit color (8 bits per component – 0xAARRGGBB)
        unsigned    spec;   // prelit specular color
        float       u,v;    // texture mapping coordinates
};
```

15.8 Transformation and Lighting

After mesh data has been submitted to the API, *transformation and lighting* occurs. (The abbreviation *T&L* is often used.) This stage of the pipeline actually refers to a wide range of vertex-level computations. Basically, any vertex-level computation can be performed during the T&L stage, but the most common operations are:

■ Object-space vertex positions are *transformed* into clip space.

■ Lighting values are computed using the current lighting settings and a vertex surface normal.

■ Vertex-level fog density is computed from the vertex position.

■ Texture mapping coordinates are generated procedurally.

■ In skeletal animation, skinning is performed to compute vertex positions.

Of course, depending on the rendering context and the type of data that was submitted, one or more of these operations may not apply.

Modern APIs allow complete flexibility in the T&L stage. Beginning with version 8, DirectX supports *vertex shaders*, which are essentially small programs that run on the graphics hardware. These microcode programs operate on a single vertex, accepting practically any number of inputs from the geometry delivery stage and producing any number of outputs to the clipper/rasterizer stage. Typical input values are those discussed in Section 15.7.2 — vertex positions and surface normals in modeling space, prelit vertex colors, texture mapping coordinates, etc. Possible outputs are transformed vertex positions (in camera space or clip space), lighting values for Gouraud shading, texture coordinates, fog density, etc. Often an input value is simply passed through the vertex shader and mapped to the appropriate output value (texture mapping coordinates or precomputed lighting values for example). Or, the vertex shader may perform calculations on the input values to generate entirely new output values, like transformed vertex positions, fog density, dynamic lighting, or procedurally generated texture mapping coordinates. (For more information, see *Direct3D ShaderX: Vertex and Pixel Shader Tips and Tricks* from Wordware Publishing.)

15.8.1 Transformation to Clip Space

The transformation from modeling to clip space occurs via matrix multiplication. Conceptually, the vertices undergo a sequence of transformations as follows:

- The *model transform* transforms from modeling space to world space.
- The *view transform* transforms from world space to camera space.
- The *clip matrix* is used to transform from camera space to clip space.

The matrix multiplications are as follows:

$$\mathbf{v}_{clip} = (\mathbf{v}_{model})(\mathbf{M}_{model \to world})(\mathbf{M}_{world \to camera})(\mathbf{M}_{camera \to clip})$$

If you've been following along from the beginning, you've probably already guessed that in practice, we don't actually perform three matrix multiplications. Under the hood, the matrices are usually concatenated so that the transformation of a single vertex doesn't actually take three vector-matrix multiplications. Depending on the design of the hardware and the implementation of the lighting (more on this later), we may be able to concatenate all matrices into one or two matrices. If we have low-level access to the T&L stage (i.e., a vertex shader), then we can control exactly how the transformation occurs. If not, then we must trust the API to make these optimizations.

15.8.2 Vertex Lighting

In Section 15.4, we described the theory behind surface illumination. At that time, we alluded to the fact that the ideal situation would be to use *Phong shading*, interpolating surface normals across the face of the triangle and applying the full lighting equation on a per-pixel basis. Unfortunately, in practice we are forced to use Gouraud shading, computing lighting at the vertex level and interpolating these results across the face of the triangle.

When lighting is computed at the vertex level, we can't use the lighting equation as given in Equation 15.14 directly. $\mathbf{m}_{diff}$ is usually not a vertex-level material property, since a texture map usually defines this value. In order to make Equation 15.14 more suitable for use in an interpolated lighting scheme, it must be manipulated to isolate $\mathbf{m}_{diff}$. As we do this, we will also make the very reasonable assumption that $\mathbf{m}_{amb}$ is equal to $\mathbf{m}_{diff}$.

Equation 15.16:
Rearranging the
standard lighting
equation to make
it more suitable
for vertex-level
lighting
computations

$$
\begin{aligned}
\mathbf{c}_{lit} \\
&= \sum_{j=1}^{n} i_j \left(max\,(\mathbf{n} \cdot \mathbf{h}_j, 0)^{m_{gls}} \mathbf{s}_{j\,spec} \otimes \mathbf{m}_{spec} + max\,(\mathbf{n} \cdot \mathbf{l}_j, 0) \mathbf{s}_{j\,diff} \otimes \mathbf{m}_{diff} \right) \\
&\quad + \mathbf{g}_{amb} \otimes \mathbf{m}_{amb} \\
&= \left(\sum_{j=1}^{n} i_j \left(max\,(\mathbf{n} \cdot \mathbf{h}_j, 0)^{m_{gls}} \mathbf{s}_{j\,spec} \right) \right) \otimes \mathbf{m}_{spec} \\
&\quad + \left(\sum_{j=1}^{n} i_j \left(max\,(\mathbf{n} \cdot \mathbf{l}_j, 0) \mathbf{s}_{j\,diff} \right) \right) \otimes \mathbf{m}_{diff} \\
&\quad + \mathbf{g}_{amb} \otimes \mathbf{m}_{diff} \\
&= \sum_{j=1}^{n} i_j \left(max\,(\mathbf{n} \cdot \mathbf{h}_j, 0)^{m_{gls}} \mathbf{s}_{j\,spec} \right) \otimes \mathbf{m}_{spec} \\
&\quad + \left(\mathbf{g}_{amb} + \sum_{j=1}^{n} i_j \left(max\,(\mathbf{n} \cdot \mathbf{l}_j, 0) \mathbf{s}_{j\,diff} \right) \right) \otimes \mathbf{m}_{diff}
\end{aligned}
$$

With the lighting equation in this format, we can see how to use interpolated lighting values computed at the vertex level. At each vertex, we will compute two values, $\mathbf{v}_{diff}$ and $\mathbf{v}_{spec}$. $\mathbf{v}_{diff}$ contains the ambient and diffuse terms in Equation 15.16, and $\mathbf{v}_{spec}$ contains the specular portion:

Equation 15.17:
Vertex-level
diffuse and
specular lighting
values

$$
\mathbf{v}_{diff} = \mathbf{g}_{amb} + \sum_{j=1}^{n} i_j \left(max\,(\mathbf{n} \cdot \mathbf{l}_j, 0) \mathbf{s}_{j\,diff} \right)
$$

$$
\mathbf{v}_{spec} = \sum_{j=1}^{n} i_j \left(max\,(\mathbf{n} \cdot \mathbf{h}_j, 0)^{m_{gls}} \mathbf{s}_{j\,spec} \right)
$$

Each of these values is computed per vertex, and interpolated across the face of the triangle. Then, per pixel, the lighting equation is applied:

Equation 15.18:
Shading pixels
using
interpolated
lighting values

$$
\mathbf{c}_{lit} = \mathbf{v}_{diff} \otimes \mathbf{m}_{diff} + \mathbf{v}_{spec} \otimes \mathbf{m}_{spec}
$$

As was mentioned earlier, $\mathbf{m}_{spec}$ is usually a constant color, but it also can be defined using a *gloss* map.

What coordinate space should be used for lighting computations? We *could* perform the lighting computations in world space. Vertex positions and normals would be transformed into world space, lighting would be performed, and then the vertex positions would be transformed into clip space. Or, we may transform the *lights* into modeling space and perform lighting computations in modeling space. Since there are usually fewer lights than there are vertices, this results in fewer overall vector-matrix multiplications. A third possibility is to perform the lighting computations in camera space. If you are not accessing the T&L pipeline directly through a vertex shader, then the API will make these decisions for you.

15.9 Backface Culling and Clipping

After vertices for a triangle have been transformed into clip space, we perform two important tests on the triangle. (The order in which we discuss these tests is not necessarily the order in which they will occur on a particular piece of hardware.)

15.9.1 Backface Culling

The first test is known as *backface culling*, and the purpose of the test is to reject triangles that don't face the camera. In standard closed meshes, we should never see a triangle from the back side, unless we are allowed to go "inside" the mesh. Removal of the backfacing triangles is not *necessary* — we could draw them and still generate a correct image, since they will be covered up by a closer (front-facing) triangle. However, we don't want to waste time drawing anything that isn't visible, so we usually want to cull backfaces, especially since, in theory, about half of the triangles will be backfacing!

In practice, less than half of the triangles can be culled, especially in static scenery, which in many cases is created without backfaces in the first place (one obvious example is a terrain system). Certainly, we may be able to eliminate some backfacing triangles (for example, on the backside of a hill), but in general most triangles will be frontfacing because we are usually above the ground. However, for dynamic objects that move around in the world freely, roughly half of the faces will be backfacing.

There are two tests we can use to detect a backfacing triangle. The first test we will discuss is a 3D test performed in clip space (or camera space) before clipping and projection. The basic idea is to see if the eye position is on the front side of the triangle's plane. This is shown in Figure 15.23, in which the backfacing triangles that could be culled are drawn in gray. Notice that backface culling doesn't depend on if a triangle is inside or outside the view frustum. In fact, it doesn't depend on the orientation of the camera at all; only the position of the camera relative to the triangle is relevant.

Figure 15.23: Backface culling in 3D

To perform a backface culling operation in 3D, we need the normal of the plane containing the triangle and a vector from the eye to the triangle (any point on the triangle will do — usually we just pick one vertex arbitrarily). If these two vectors point in basically the same direction (their dot product is greater than zero), then the triangle is backfacing.

One tempting optimization trick that doesn't work is to only use the z-component of the normal of the triangle in camera (or clip) space. It would seem that if the z value is positive, then the triangle faces away from the camera and could be culled. This would be a speed-up because we could avoid computing the rest of the normal and taking the dot product. Unfortunately, this trick doesn't work. An example of a case where it fails is circled in Figure 15.23.

The 3D backfacing culling test previously described was primarily used in the days of software rendering when the triangle normal could be precomputed and stored with the triangles. Today, the delivery of geometry to the hardware is a bottleneck, so any extraneous information is removed from the data stream. On modern graphics hardware, backface culling is performed based on clockwise or counterclockwise enumeration of vertices in screen space.

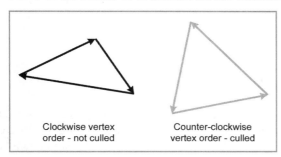

Clockwise vertex
order - not culled

Counter-clockwise
vertex order - culled

Figure 15.24: Backface culling of triangles with vertices enumerated counterclockwise in screen space

In this book, our convention is to order the vertices in a clockwise fashion around the triangle when viewed from the front side. Thus, we will normally remove any triangle whose vertices are ordered in a counterclockwise fashion on the screen. The API will let you control backface culling. You may want to turn backface culling off while rendering certain geometry. Or, if geometry has been reflected, you may need to invert the culling since reflection flips the vertex order around the faces.

15.9.2 Clipping

Even if a triangle is facing the camera, it may be partially or completely outside the view frustum and not visible. Before we can project the vertices onto screen space, we must ensure that they are completely inside the view frustum. This process is known as *clipping*. Since clipping is normally performed by the hardware, we will only describe the process with cursory detail.

The standard algorithm for clipping polygons is the *Sutherland-Hodgman* algorithm. This algorithm tackles the difficult problem of polygon clipping by breaking it down into a sequence of easy problems. The input polygon is clipped against one plane at a time.

To clip a polygon against one plane, we iterate around the polygon, clipping each edge against the plane in sequence. Each of the two vertices of the edge may be inside or outside the plane, so there are four cases. Each case may generate zero, one, or two output vertices, as shown in Figure 15.25.

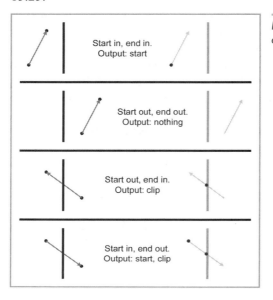

Figure 15.25: Clipping a single edge – the four cases

Figure 15.26 shows an example of how we can apply these rules to clip a polygon against the right clipping plane. Remember that the clipper outputs *vertices*, not edges. In Figure 15.26, the edges are drawn only for illustration. In particular, the final clip step appears to output two edges when actually only one vertex was output — the last edge is implicit to complete the polygon.

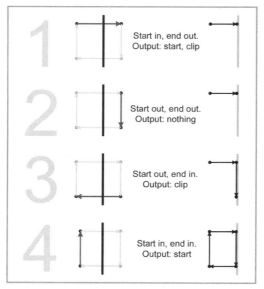

Figure 15.26: Clipping a polygon against the right clip plane

At the end of each stage, if there are fewer than three vertices remaining, then the polygon is rejected as being invisible. (Notice that it is impossible to output only one or two vertices. The number of vertices output by any one pass will either be zero or at least three.)

Some graphics hardware does not clip polygons to all six planes in 3D (or 4D). Instead, only the near clip is performed, and then 2D *scissoring* is used to clip to the window. We will discuss scissoring in the next section.

15.10 Rasterization

After clipping, the vertices are projected and mapped into the screen coordinates of the output window, according to Equation 15.6. Of course, these coordinates are *floating-point* coordinates, which are "continuous" (see Section 2.1). We typically render pixels, which are discrete. So how do we know which pixels actually get drawn? Devising an algorithm to answer this technique is surprising complicated. If we answer wrong, then gaps can appear in between triangles. If we are blending, then any overlap of adjacent triangles is noticeable. In other words, we must make sure that when we render a surface represented using triangles, every pixel is rendered *exactly once*. Luckily, the graphics hardware takes care of this for us and we don't have to sweat the details.

While we don't necessarily have to understand exactly how the graphics hardware decides *which* pixels to render for a given triangle, we *do* need to understand how it determines what to do with a single pixel. Conceptually, there are three basic steps.

- **Shade**. *Pixel shading* refers to the process of computing a color for a pixel. Usually, the pixel is first lit and then fogged. See Section 15.8 for details. The output of a pixel shader consists not only of an RGB color, but also an *alpha* value, which is often the "opacity" of the pixel, used for blending (see below).

- **Test**. The second step is to test the pixel for rejection. There are three tests that are usually performed. A *scissor test* rejects pixels that are outside the rendering window. (This test is not necessary if we clip to all of the planes of the view frustum.) The *depth test* rejects pixels using the depth buffer (see Section 15.5). The *alpha test* rejects pixels based on the alpha value of the pixel. All sorts of different alpha tests can be used, but the most common one is to reject pixels that are "too transparent." (We do not want such pixels writing into the depth buffer.)

- **Write**. If the pixel passes the depth and alpha tests, then the frame buffer and depth buffers are updated. The depth buffer is updated simply by replacing the old depth value with the new one. The frame buffer update is more complicated. If *blending* is not used, then the new pixel color replaces the old one. Otherwise, the new pixel color is blended with the old one, with the relative contributions of the old and new colors controlled by the alpha value. Other mathematical operations, such as addition, subtraction, and multiplication, are also often available, depending on the graphics hardware.

Chapter 16

Visibility Determination

This chapter covers visible surface determination. It is divided into six sections:

- Section 16.1 is on bounding volume tests. The main concepts are:
  - ◆ Testing against the view frustum
  - ◆ Testing for occlusion
- Section 16.2 introduces space partitioning techniques.
- Section 16.3 covers grid systems.
- Section 16.4 covers quadtrees and octrees.
- Section 16.5 covers BSP trees, both "old school" and "new school."
- Section 16.6 covers occlusion culling techiques. The main concepts are:
  - ◆ Potentially visible sets
  - ◆ Portals

Rendering a correct image requires *visible surface determination*, or VSD. The purpose of VSD is to figure out which triangles should be drawn in the final rendered image and, perhaps more importantly, which should not.

VSD occurs on several levels. In other words, some VSD techniques are able to reject one pixel, one triangle, one object, one room containing many objects, one floor containing many rooms, or an entire ten-story building. This section is concerned with all types of VSD above the triangle and pixel level. Pixel-level VSD is handled using the depth buffer, which we discussed in Section 15.5. Triangle-level VSD is accomplished during backface culling and clipping, which were covered in Section 15.9. This chapter is concerned with the higher level visibility determination, that is, determining which *objects* are potentially visible. Before diving into the algorithms that determine at a high level what might be visible, let's examine what might cause a single triangle or pixel to *not* be visible. There are two basic reasons this could happen:

- Any portion of a triangle outside the viewing frustum is not visible. (It is "off screen.") A triangle that is *partially* outside the viewing frustum is *clipped* to the viewing frustum, and the portion that lies within the frustum is processed further. A triangle that lies completely outside the viewing frustum is rejected and not processed further. In this case, the triangle is said to be *clipped out*.

■ A pixel may be obscured (or *occluded*) by another piece of geometry that is closer to the camera.

Our goal at this stage in the pipeline is to apply these two principles in order to pass as few objects as possible to the remaining stages. In other words, we begin with a working set of all the objects in the entire scene, and we wish to remove from consideration as many of those objects as possible, as quickly as possible. There are numerous techniques for doing this. The remainder of this chapter is devoted to a number of high- and mid-level VSD techniques.

16.1 Bounding Volume Tests

When we store the geometry of the world, we don't typically store one huge triangle mesh. Instead, the world is broken up into pieces. One very important reason for doing this is so we can move these pieces around dynamically. Even for static geometry, such as columns and walls, it can be beneficial for us to have our world divided up into a list of objects. In this way, we can perform batch operations on groups of triangles, rather than processing each triangle individually. The details of how the world should be divided into objects will vary depending on the application.

One of the most important benefits of breaking up our world into objects is so that during VSD we can reject entire objects at once using a *bounding volume* of the object. The bounding volume is usually a box (either axially aligned or oriented — see Section 12.4) or a sphere (see Section 12.3) because these objects have simple mathematical representations and are easy to manipulate. However, the bounding volume may itself be a triangle mesh. Of course, the bounding mesh should be much simpler than the geometry it bounds; otherwise, it is just as expensive to manipulate the bounding volume as it is to manipulate the geometry inside. Depending on the situation, it may be more important to have a tighter bounding volume or to have a bounding volume that is more easily manipulated and tested. Spheres are the most easily manipulated, but for many objects, spheres do not provide a very tight bounding volume. Arbitrary triangle mesh bounding volumes can provide the tightest bounding volume, but they are the toughest to manipulate. Boxes are the best compromise in many cases, having good worst-case performance as a tight bounding volume but also being easy to manipulate.

Whatever type of bounding volume is used, the basic idea is that if we can determine that the entire bounding volume is completely invisible, then all of the triangles are invisible as well and do not need to be considered individually. For all but the most trivial scenes, using bounding volumes for rejection is a great optimization compared to rendering every triangle in the scene. These types of "mid-level" VSD techniques are also relatively easy to implement.

Recall that there are two reasons that a triangle or pixel is not visible: it is off screen or it is occluded by closer geometry. We can apply these same principles to bounding volumes. If the bounding volume is completely off screen, then all of the triangles are off screen as well. If the entire bounding volume is occluded, then the triangles inside are occluded as well. Making the first determination is usually much easier than making the second determination — this will be a recurring theme in the pages to come.

The next subsection discusses how to determine if a bounding volume is invisible. Notice that if the bounding volume is invisible, then the triangles are invisible, but the converse is not necessarily true. It is possible for us to determine that the bounding volume is visible, when in fact none of the triangles inside are actually visible. So bounding volume tests either determine that the enclosed geometry is *definitely not* visible or is *potentially* visible. We usually can't tell conclusively that the geometry inside is definitely visible.

16.1.1 Testing Against the View Frustum

Testing a bounding box (either axially aligned or oriented) against the view frustum is relatively simple. The basic idea is to test the eight corner points of the box against the six clip planes. If all of the points are on the "outside" of one or more of the clip planes (for example, if they are above the top clip plane), then the box is obviously not visible and can be rejected. For example, in Figure 16.1, the box on the lower left can be rejected because it is completely outside the left clip plane.

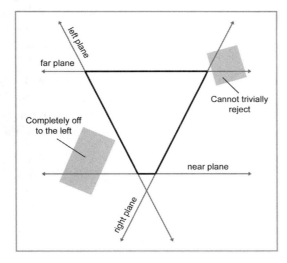

Figure 16.1: Testing a bounding box against the view frustum

Notice, however, that even though the box in the upper right is completely outside the view frustum, it is not outside any one clipping plane. These situations are more difficult to detect, but luckily they are also far less frequent. We will discuss how to handle these situations (and *if* we should even worry about them!) later in this section.

One of the easiest ways to determine if a box is completely outside a clip plane is to use the clip matrix (see Section 15.3.3). We transform the eight corner points into clip space and then check the points against each of the six planes. (Because of the nature of clip space, these tests are trivial — that's the whole purpose of having clip space!) A handy trick for keeping track of which points are outside which planes is to use a bitfield. This practice is known as *coding* the points. The basic idea is to compute, for a single point, an integer value, known as an *outcode*, that has certain bits turned on corresponding to the clip planes that the point is outside. For example, we might assign each clip plane to a bit, as shown in Figure 16.2.

Clip Plane	Point is outside if	Bit	Mask Value
Left	$x < -w$	0	0x01
Right	$x > w$	1	0x02
Bottom	$y < -w$	2	0x04
Top	$y > w$	3	0x08
Near	$z < -w$	4	0x10
Far	$z > w$	5	0x20

Figure 16.2: Outcodes use a simple bit encoding scheme to store the results of clip plane testing

Notice that we are using an OpenGL-style clip matrix here, which maps the near and far clip planes to z values from $-w$ to w, instead of 0 to w. A Direct3D-style clip matrix would be slightly different. Also, the assignment of planes to bits is arbitrary; it doesn't really matter which planes are matched up to which bits.

We compute an *outcode* for a particular point as follows. First, we start with zero, which assumes that the point is inside the viewing frustum. After transforming the point into clip space, we perform the six tests in the second column of Figure 16.2. If the point is outside a given plane, we turn on the corresponding bit. The following code snippet illustrates the concept, although it is *not* a good example of how to do this efficiently:

Listing 16.1: Computing an outcode for a point in clip space

```
// Compute an outcode for a point in clip space

int   computeOutCode(float x, float y, float z, float w) {

    // Start with an outcode of 0, assuming the point is in the frustum

    int   code = 0;

    // Check each of the six planes, and turn on the bit
    // if we detect the point is outside the plane

    if (x < -w) code |= 0x01; // left
    if (x >  w) code |= 0x02; // right
    if (y < -w) code |= 0x04; // bottom
    if (y >  w) code |= 0x08; // top
    if (z < -w) code |= 0x10; // near
    if (z >  w) code |= 0x20; // far
```

```
        // Return it

        return code;
}
```

The great thing about outcodes is that they can easily be manipulated using bit-wise AND and OR operations. If the logical AND of all of the outcodes for the eight vertices is nonzero, then the bounding volume is definitely off screen. Many platforms have a special instruction to compute the outcode for a point in clip space, performing all the work in Listing 16.1 in a single assembly instruction.

Also, if the logical OR of the outcode is zero, then all points are *inside* the view frustum, and we have a *trivial accept*. In this case, we know that none of the triangles inside the bounding volume will need to be clipped, and so we can bypass that stage of the pipeline. This can be a significant speed-up on many platforms. In practice, a minority of objects will need to be clipped, as most objects will either be completely inside the view frustum or completely outside.

As we mentioned earlier, the coding procedure does not reject all bounding boxes that are completely outside the view frustum; it only rejects those that are completely outside at least one plane. Some boxes will be outside the view frustum, but they will not be entirely on the outside of any given clip plane. For example, the bounding box in the upper right of Figure 16.1 crosses the right and far clip planes.

Fortunately, situations like this occur seldomly, although in 3D it can happen more frequently than in simplified diagrams in 2D. Still, in any given scene, there will usually only be a few pathological objects like this. We can deal with these cases by clipping the individual faces of the box to the view frustum, using the polygon clipping techniques we learned in Section 15.9. If all of the faces are clipped, then the bounding volume is not visible. If any face of the bounding volume is partially inside the view frustum, then the geometry inside is potentially visible.

The question becomes, should we even bother trying to detect these cases, or should we just render it? Clipping faces in software is relatively slow, and usually it must be done on the main CPU. Depending on the density of the geometry inside the bounding box, and the relative speed of the CPU and graphics processor, it may actually take less time to submit the geometry to be rendered, letting the API and graphics hardware deal with it, than it would be to figure out that it's not visible! Also, if we determine that the bounding volume *is* visible, we have wasted the time making this determination. Whether it is faster to be "smart" and handle these special cases in software, or to use the brute force of the graphics hardware, will depend on the platform and the application.

Testing a bounding sphere against the view frustum is not as easy as it might seem because the non-uniform scale applied for field-of-view makes the sphere become an ellipsoid when transformed into clip space. To circumvent this problem, we express the six planes of the view frustum in world space. Then, we test if the sphere is completely on the outside of these planes using techniques from Section 13.15. For more on testing spheres against the view frustum, see [16].

16.1.2 Testing for Occlusion

In general, it is very difficult to determine if a particular bounding volume is occluded by other geometry. One technique is to "render" the bounding volume, testing it against the z-buffer. We rasterize the faces of the bounding volume, but instead of actually rendering pixels, we merely check to see if any of the pixels are visible. This technique is called *z-checking*.

Z-checking is a great idea in theory. The problem is that z-checking requires direct access to the depth buffer. If we are hardware rendering, then this is troublesome. Different graphics cards may store the depth information in a proprietary format. The access is often very slow — about twice as slow as accessing main system RAM, or slower.

Some hardware is capable of performing z-checks for us. Even in this case, we still have a problem of pipelining. The graphics processor and main CPU usually work in parallel. For best performance, we must keep both processors as busy as possible; if either is idle for any period of time, then we are not getting the best performance. Whenever we need to perform a z-check, the hardware may be a bit backed up with previous requests. (Usually, this is a good thing, since it means that both processors are busy.) Unfortunately, we need the result of this test immediately so that we can decide whether or not to render what's inside the bounding volume. So we must wait for the graphics processor to catch up and finish rendering what has been submitted so far so it can perform our test and return the result. Meanwhile, the main CPU is idle. What's worse, we may wind up having to render what's inside the box anyway, in which case we have wasted this time trying to figure out if it's visible or not.

The bottom line is that on today's hardware, efficiently detecting if a bounding volume is occluded using *z*-checks requires extremely careful coordination between the graphics processor and main CPU if pipeline stalls are to be avoided. The test itself is relatively expensive, and it is difficult to even communicate the result efficiently.

Testing bounding volumes on an "ad hoc" basis to see if they are off screen is relatively easy. Whether or not a particular object is on screen or off screen only depends on the camera and that one object; the other objects are irrelevant. Unfortunately, occlusion testing for an object is inherently more complicated, because it *does* depend on the other objects in the scene. For this reason, efficient occlusion testing for real-time rendering requires a more high-level and systematic approach to VSD. We will discuss two such techniques in Section 16.6.

16.2 Space Partitioning Techniques

We have stated that bounding volume techniques in the previous section are "mid-level" VSD algorithms. In this section, we will discuss more "high-level" VSD algorithms, which can occlude even *larger* amounts of data at once. The basic idea is to not only divide the scene into objects, but to partition the 3D *space* of the world.

Before we begin, let's first establish why we even *need* higher level VSD algorithms. After all, using bounding volumes already enables us to render only a fraction of the triangles in the world. Unfortunately, in virtual worlds of any complexity, this is not good enough. The basic problem is that even though we don't render every object, we still have to *process* every object. That is, we still have to decide if it is visible or not. If there are many objects, then even making the determination *not* to render anything can be too slow. For example, let's say we have 10,000 objects in our scene. Depending on the speed of the main CPU and the memory architecture, we may not even be able to traverse a list of 10,000 items fast enough to maintain our desired frame rate!

In order to deal with scenes of this magnitude, we must take the idea of "group rejection" to the next level — we must be able to reject entire groups of objects at once. How many objects should be in a group? If there are too many objects per group, then a group may be too big and we may not be able to reject it often enough. If there are too few objects per group, then there will be too many groups, and we have only reduced the problem but not eliminated it. To solve this problem, we must use "groups of groups" and "groups of groups of groups." In other words, we must establish a hierarchy of objects.

For example, imagine one city block. There are many buildings in this city block. Each building has several floors. Each floor has several rooms. Each room has several objects. If we can reject an entire building at once, then we don't have to check each floor within the building. If we can reject an entire floor at once, then we don't have to check each room on that floor.

This type of hierarchy is a logical one: we know there is a hierarchy because we know about buildings and floors and rooms. However, it is difficult for a computer to deduce this type of logical hierarchy without a human's help.

Another way to establish a hierarchy is to use a geometric partitioning rather than a logical one. For example, we will partition the volume of 3D space using planes and boxes. Of course, it would be best if this partitioning was also sensitive to the organization of the scene, but as we will see, this is not strictly necessary. We will see that computers are better at this type of partitioning.

Whatever type of hierarchy is used, the idea is to determine what's visible in logarithmic time, rather than linear time. Without a hierarchy, if we double the number of objects, then the time needed to determine what's visible would double; this is linear time. Using a hierarchy, doubling the number of objects increases the time needed for VSD by a constant.

Just for illustration, let's say that we have two algorithms for VSD, one that runs in linear time and the other that runs in logarithmic time. Let's say that for a scene with 1,000 objects, it takes both algorithms 2ms to compute VSD. If we doubled that number to 2,000 objects, then a linear time VSD algorithm would take 4ms. A logarithmic one might take 3ms. Let's double it again to 4,000 objects. Now the linear time algorithm takes 8ms, compared to 4 for the logarithmic algorithm. When the number of objects gets very large, the logarithmic algorithm is orders of magnitude faster than the linear one. For example, a scene with 128,000 objects would take 256ms, which means we could not possibly render them faster than four frames per second. The logarithmic algorithm would take around 9ms, which is over 100Hz.

Of course, we are neglecting the time to actually *render* the scene, and these numbers are purely fictional, but you get the idea. Also, the time needed for VSD depends on many different factors, not just the number of objects. The algorithms in this section *do* have logarithmic characteristics, but the example above where doubling the number of objects always increased VSD time by the same amount was a bit oversimplified.

16.3 Grid Systems

One of the simplest ways to partition space is to use a 2D or 3D grid. 2D grids work well for more "outdoor" environments, and 3D grids are better suited to more "vertical" environments such as multistory buildings. Let's say we wish to store the city of Cartesia using a grid system. We might decide to use one grid square per city block, with the grid lines running down the center of the streets. Each building could be assigned to a grid square. (There may be more than one building in the same grid square, of course.) When it came time to render the scene, we could determine which grid squares were visible and then we would only need to render the buildings within those grid squares.

How would we know which grid squares are visible? One trick is to compute the axially aligned bounding box of the view frustum and then determine which grid squares intersect this bounding box. This is shown in Figure 16.3. Notice that no matter how big our city is, or how many objects are in it, the amount of time it takes to determine which grid cells to render is *constant*. This is even better than logarithmic time! (Unfortunately, as we will see later, grid systems do have their downsides.)

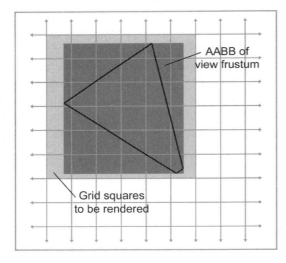

Figure 16.3: Using 2D grid system for visibility determination

AABB of view frustum

Grid squares to be rendered

You might have noticed that some of the grid squares labeled "Grid squares to be rendered" in Figure 16.3 are not actually inside the frustum. We can easily reject those using the bounding volume tests from Section 16.1.

So, a grid system gives us a very elegant way to cull the render set quickly. We know how to determine which grid cells are visible. All we have to do is go through each grid cell and render the objects in that cell. This works for static or dynamic geometry. Of course, each grid cell must contain a list of objects that are in that cell — a technique known as *pigeonholing*. If we have dynamic objects that move around in the world, then we must constantly maintain these lists, but usually this is not a problem. Using a linked list ensures that the storage for each grid cell is constant, regardless of the number of objects in the cell. Only the "head" link is stored in the cell, and the rest of the list data is contained in the objects themselves.

What do we do with objects that don't fit entirely within a single grid cell? Obviously, in any useful world, there will be a significant minority of objects that span grid lines. What do we do with these objects? If the objects are static, we may cut them on grid line boundaries so that this doesn't happen. This cutting would obviously happen in a preprocessing step. But what about dynamic objects? We probably can't afford the time to cut these objects up in real time.

One solution is to allow an object to be in more than one grid cell. Then we would need to keep track of *all* the grid cells that an object is in. This can be tricky and makes using linked lists impossible, since an item in a linked list can only be in one list at a time.

Another solution is to assign the object to the *nearest* grid cell. If all of our objects are smaller than one grid cell (a constraint that can be acceptable in many situations), then we just expand our list of potential visible grid cells slightly, taking into consideration that any objects in that grid cell may actually extend into the adjacent grid cells.

How big should we make our grid cells? This is a difficult decision. If we make our cells too small, then the overhead of processing the grid may be too high. Storage for the grid is quadratic in 2D and *cubic* in 3D, so memory may be a serious consideration. If we make them too big, then we may not be subdividing fine enough and we may not get good enough trivial rejection.

The basic problem with grid systems is that they are inflexible. The grid divides up space regularly, regardless of the complexity of the underlying geometry. Grid lines don't necessarily separate rooms from one another unless the walls happen to fall precisely on a grid boundary — something that rarely happens. The number of grid cells per square foot assigned to an airport runway is the same as the number of grid cells per square foot assigned to the airport terminal, even though the terminal obviously has far greater scene complexity and would benefit from finer subdivision. In the next few sections, we will learn some techniques that are more adaptable to the geometry of the scene.

16.4 Quadtrees and Octrees

We have seen that a simple grid system divides up space regularly, regardless of the complexity of the underlying geometry. Choosing one single grid size is difficult because it will always be too big for densely populated areas and too small for sparsely populated areas. In addition, dealing with objects that span multiple grid cells is difficult.

These problems can be avoided by subdividing space adaptively, that is, by making the subdivision only where it needs to be fine. In 2D, a *quadtree* is used. The 3D version is an *octree*. Both are *tree* structures consisting of a hierarchy of *nodes*. We will focus on quadtrees since they are easier to understand and make illustrations for. Octrees extend the idea into 3D in a straightforward manner.

In a quadtree, we begin with a single *root node* that covers the entire scene. This node is then divided into four non-overlapping child nodes. Each of these nodes is then further subdivided into four children, etc. This idea is shown in Figure 16.4:

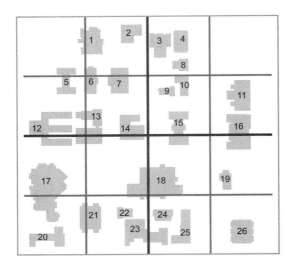

Figure 16.4: A quadtree

Quadtree diagrams can become confusing because each node overlaps and shares borders with its parent node. We have made the higher level boundary lines thicker.

Once we have subdivided space with our quadtree, we can then assign the objects of the world to nodes in the tree. Here's where the "tree" part of quadtree really comes in. To place an object in the quadtree, we start at the root node. If the object is wholly contained by one of the children, then we go down into that child. We continue drilling down the tree as long as the object is contained wholly by a child node or until we reach a leaf node. If an object spans either of the two separating planes, then we must stop our descent and assign the object to the node at that level. Figure 16.5 shows how the buildings would be inserted into the quadtree:

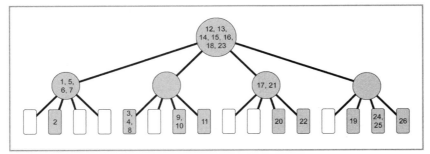

Figure 16.5: Assigning objects to a quadtree

In Figure 16.4, we subdivided evenly, down to the third level. In other words, we have a *complete* tree; all the leaf nodes are at the same level. However, this is not necessary. (We just did it to keep the example simple.) Sometimes one node may be sufficiently granular and does not require further subdivision. How do we know when a node is subdivided enough? Heuristics for making this decision vary, but generally we will not subdivide further if any of the following are true:

- The number of objects or triangles in the node is low enough that further subdivision would not be beneficial.

- The dimensions of the node itself are too small for further subdivision. Of course, there's no reason we *couldn't* subdivide a small node into even smaller pieces, but we may just want to prevent our nodes from going below a certain size.

- We have reached the maximum depth in our tree. For example, we may decide to only allow subdivision to the fifth level. Depending on how we represent our quadtree in memory, this may be necessary.

By only subdividing where necessary, quadtrees can be more adaptive to the underlying geometry. This is one of its advantages over simple grid systems. Figure 16.6 shows how the quadtree in our example might have been subdivided adaptively:

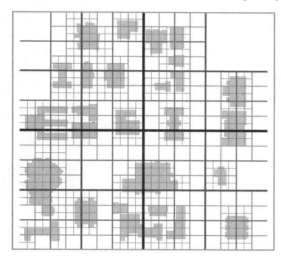

Figure 16.6: Adaptive subdivision using a quadtree

Another arbitrary simplification we have made so far is to always divide a node into four equal pieces. This is not strictly necessary, either. We can attempt to place the dividing planes within a node adaptively (choosing the location of the dividing planes so that roughly one-quarter of the geometry ends up in each quadrant, for example). This tends to result in a more balanced (and possibly smaller) tree, but tree construction is significantly complicated.

Once we have assigned objects to nodes in the quadtree, we have a powerful tool for locating objects within a certain radius of a given point, or for culling objects for rendering or collision detection. In each case, the basic idea is that if we can reject a node at one level, then all of its children (and their children, etc.) can be rejected at once. Let's look at an example. Imagine we wish to perform a ray intersection test with the world. A simple, recursive procedure will cull the set of objects under consideration rapidly. Listing 16.2 illustrates this:

Listing 16.2: Raytracing a quadtree

```
// Let's assume an object in our world has at least the following functionality

class Object {
public:

    // Perform raytrace operation and update minT if a
```

```
        // closer intersection is detected

        void   raytrace(Vector3 rayOrg, Vector3 rayDelta, float &minT);

        // Pointer to next object in the same quadtree node as me

        Object *next;
};

// An oversimplified class to store a quadtree node

class Node {
public:

        // Pointers to our children. Either we will have all four children,
        // or we are a leaf and all four pointers are NULL

        Node   *nw, *ne, *sw, *se;

        // To keep the examples simple, we are storing the
        // 2D bounds of the node here, even though we
        // could compute them during traversal.

        float  xMin, xMax;
        float  zMin, zMax;

        float  xCenter() const { return (xMin + xMax) * 0.5f; }
        float  zCenter() const { return (zMin + zMax) * 0.5f; }

        // Linked list of objects in this node

        Object *firstObject;
};

// We will need one global pointer to store the root

Node   *root;

// Recursive procedure to raytrace a quadtree. The value of mint is the
// parametric point of the closest intersection detected so far

void   Node::raytrace(Vector3 rayOrg, Vector3 rayDelta, float &minT) {

        // Check if the ray intersects my bounding box. Notice that this
        // takes into consideration the closest intersection already found
        // so far

        if (!rayIntersectsBoundingBox(rayOrg, rayDelta, minT)) {

                // Trivial reject me and all my descendants

                return;
        }

        // Raytrace all the objects in this node

        for (Object *objPtr = firstObject ; objPtr != NULL ; objPtr = objPtr->next) {
```

```
            // Raytrace the object.  minT is updated if a
            // closer intersection is found

            objPtr->rayTrace(rayOrg, rayDelta);
        }

        // Check if I'm a leaf, then terminate recursion

        if (nw == NULL) {
            return;
        }

        // Check which child the ray starts in.

        if (rayOrg.x < xCenter()) {
            if (rayOrg.z < zCenter()) {

                // Start in southwest child

                sw->rayTrace(rayOrg, rayDelta, minT);
                se->rayTrace(rayOrg, rayDelta, minT);
                nw->rayTrace(rayOrg, rayDelta, minT);
                ne->rayTrace(rayOrg, rayDelta, minT);

            } else {

                // Start in northwest child

                nw->rayTrace(rayOrg, rayDelta, minT);
                ne->rayTrace(rayOrg, rayDelta, minT);
                sw->rayTrace(rayOrg, rayDelta, minT);
                se->rayTrace(rayOrg, rayDelta, minT);


            }
        } else {
            if (rayOrg.z < zCenter()) {

                // Start in southeast child

                se->rayTrace(rayOrg, rayDelta, minT);
                sw->rayTrace(rayOrg, rayDelta, minT);
                ne->rayTrace(rayOrg, rayDelta, minT);
                nw->rayTrace(rayOrg, rayDelta, minT);

            } else {

                // Start in northeast child

                ne->rayTrace(rayOrg, rayDelta, minT);
                nw->rayTrace(rayOrg, rayDelta, minT);
                se->rayTrace(rayOrg, rayDelta, minT);
                sw->rayTrace(rayOrg, rayDelta, minT);


            }
        }
    }

// Function to raytrace the world.  Returns parametric point of intersection,
// or 1.0 if no intersection detected
```

```
float rayTraceWorld(Vector3 rayOrg, Vector3 rayDelta) {
    float minT = 1.0;
    root->rayTrace(rayOrg, rayDelta, minT);
    return minT;
}
```

Notice that at each level we recurse into our children in a different order, depending on which child contains the ray origin. The effect of this is that nodes are visited in the order that they are intersected by the ray. This is an important optimization. How? When we check if the ray intersects the bounding box of the node, we take into consideration the closest intersection found so far. In other words, the ray must not only intersect the node, but it must intersect the node earlier than the closest intersection already found. Thus, as soon as an intersection is detected, we can "chop off" the ray and only process nodes from that point forward if they intersect the "shortened" ray. (Imagine we are firing a gun at a wall six feet away, using a 500ft long ray to detect where the bullet will hit the world.) For maximum benefit, we must detect intersections as early as possible, and we must visit the nodes in the order that they are intersected by the ray.

As you have probably already guessed, quadtrees work best when we are able to push objects as far down the tree as possible, since that will allow for the best rejection. Unfortunately, objects near the center of nodes tend to get "stuck" higher up in the tree. Hopefully, this is a small percentage of the objects. If your objects are relatively large compared to the size of your world (which is the case in our example in Figure 16.4), then this percentage will be higher.

Loose quadtrees can be used to try to avoid this problem by using expanded nodes that overlap their neighbors, usually at the expense of having to process more nodes. We will not use loose quadtrees or octrees, but for further reading, see [25].

It is important to note that for static geometry we can avoid this problem entirely by slicing the geometry of the world on quadtree boundaries, and every piece of geometry will then be assigned to a leaf node. For dynamic objects, this is not possible, however.

16.5 BSP Trees

BSP stands for *binary space partition* tree. As you can probably tell by the name, a BSP is a tree structure where each node has *two* children. The children are separated by a dividing plane. In a quadtree or octree, the separating planes are always axially aligned. In a BSP, this is not necessary — we may use planes that are arbitrarily oriented. Of course, we *can* use axially aligned planes, and in fact, any quadtree or octree can be represented by a corresponding BSP. Of course, a BSP would likely take more data than a corresponding octree because there is a great deal of data that is implicit in an octree (such as the orientation of the planes) that must be stored explicitly in a BSP.

Figure 16.7: A 2D BSP tree

An example of a BSP is shown in Figure 16.7. The thicker lines represent planes that are higher in the tree. To better illustrate this tree structure, Figure 16.8 shows the same BSP with the nodes labeled alongside the actual tree structure.

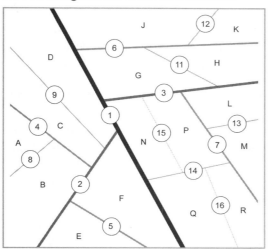
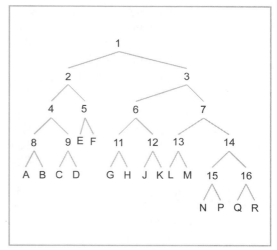

Figure 16.8: The hierarchy of a BSP tree

In this figure, we do not have a way to decide which child is which. In practice, we usually keep track of the "front" and "back" children of the dividing plane. The direction of the plane normal decides which is which.

We have chosen to label the interior nodes with numbers and the leaf nodes with letters, but it is important to understand that each node represents an area of space, even the interior nodes. Just like a quadtree, a node overlaps its parent and children. For example, node 1 (the root node) actually represents *all* of the space in the scene. In Figure 16.9, the space represented by node 7 has been shaded.

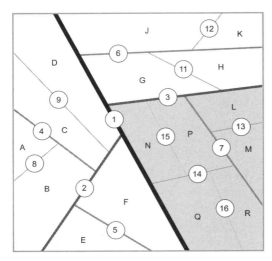

Figure 16.9: A BSP node represents a volume of space, not just a dividing plane

A BSP is used in much the same way that the trees were traversed in the previous section. We store objects in the BSP tree as far down in the tree as possible. To process objects in the tree, we begin at the root node and process all the objects in that node. Then we must decide if our area of interest (for rendering, collision detection, etc.) lies entirely on one side of the dividing plane or the other. If we are only interested in the volume of space on one side of the dividing plane, then we can reject the entire branch on the other side. If our area of interest spans the dividing plane, then both children need to be processed.

Using BPS trees once they have been constructed is relatively easy. The trick is deciding where to place the dividing planes. We have considerably more flexibility than we did with quadtrees or octrees.

16.5.1 "Old School" BSPs

One strategy for creating a BSP from a triangle mesh is to use the triangles themselves as dividing planes. Each node in the BSP tree contains one triangle. (We may also store a group of triangles at each node that all lie in the same plane, but we will not consider that technique here.) To build a BSP from a group of triangles, we pick a triangle to be the "root." This triangle defines the dividing plane for that node. We then separate the rest of the triangles into two batches. One batch lies entirely on the front side of the dividing plane, and the other batch lies entirely on the back side of the dividing plane. The same algorithm is then applied to each of these two batches recursively. What do we do with triangles that span the dividing plane? These triangles must be split along the dividing plane. Of course, this increases the number of triangles, and so these splits are to be avoided whenever possible. The trick to building a good BSP tree is to be smart when choosing the root triangle. We have two goals we wish to achieve when selecting a root triangle:

- We wish to minimize the number of split triangles.
- We wish to balance the tree as much as possible.

As it turns out, finding the optimal BSP is an extremely difficult problem. Merely selecting the best root triangle at each level doesn't guarantee the optimum BSP, since decisions made at one level can affect what will happen at lower levels. In order to find the absolute *best* BSP, we must basically try out every triangle as the root at every level. This requires *factorial* running time and is not feasible even for very small BSPs.

In practice, however, good results can be obtained simply by selecting the best root at each level. In fact, a reasonably good tree can be built much more quickly by selecting the root at *random*. This avoids poor worst-case performance, which does occur frequently in practice because the triangles are usually delivered in an order that has a great deal of structure.

16.5.2 Arbitrary Dividing Planes

The method of storing a triangle mesh described in the previous section can give good results for collision detection. However, it is not advisable for rendering. The reason is that we typically submit *batches* of triangles to the graphics hardware. This becomes difficult, if not impossible, when the world is broken down in a BSP to the triangle level. As we've seen before, there is a point of diminishing returns where it becomes faster to just submit something to be rendered than it is to figure out if it is visible or not. A better strategy for rendering is to use arbitrary planes (not necessarily those planes defined by the triangles themselves) and construct a BSP that divides the world down to the object level. During this process, static objects spanning the dividing plane can either be split or placed in the BSP at a higher level. Using this approach, we get the logarithmic culling power of the BSP, but we still are able to submit batches of triangles to the graphics hardware.

If we don't use the triangles as dividing planes, then what do we use? A full discussion is beyond the scope of this book, but one trick that works reasonably well in practice is as follows.

First, we generate a list of potential plane *normals*. (Basically, this is a list of planes, although in this case only the orientation of the plane matters, not the position, which is determined by the d value of the plane equation.) We will construct our BSP using only planes that have normals in this set. We can start with all the axially aligned planes and throw in all the 45 degree variations, etc. For many scenes, just this limited set of planes may be enough to work reasonably well. However, we can also give ourselves more options by constructing optimal oriented bounding boxes for all the objects in the world and adding in the normals of the faces of these bounding boxes. This will give us a good working set of planes that is in some way influenced by the actual geometry for which we are building a BSP.

When constructing our list of potential planes, we can throw out "duplicates." For example, if two normals are facing the exact opposite direction, then we only need one of them, since they will divide the world up in the same way; it usually doesn't matter which sides are considered the "front" and "back." We can also discard a normal if there is another normal in the list that points in *almost* exactly the same direction.

Once we have a working set of plane normals, we select a root plane: for each normal in our set of potential plane normals, we find the d value which "best" divides the world using that plane. Of course, there are an infinite number of d values we could choose, but we only need to check a small subset of them. For any given object, there is a certain point where the object is completely on the front side of the plane, but just touching the surface of the plane. There is another d value for which the object is on the back side of the plane, but just touching the plane. We can find these "event points" by scanning the vertices of the object and taking the dot product of the vertex position with the normal, resulting in a d value. The minimum and maximum d values are the event points. Luckily, these event points can be located in a preprocessing step before we begin building the BSP. Once they are computed, they will not change during the BSP generation process unless we chose to split an object on a dividing plane. To find the "best" d value for a particular normal, we will usually use some type of scoring heuristic — a number that is bigger when the choice of d value is "better" and smaller when the choice of d value is "worse." Obviously, splitting objects would lower the score, and balancing the tree would raise the score. Devising a scoring formula that balances these two goals is a bit of an art.

Scanning all event points for all potential normals, we find the plane (normal and d value) that has the best score. This is the plane that we use as our dividing plane. We divide the world into two groups using this plane, and then we recursively apply the procedure to the two groups. As we mentioned earlier, we can handle objects that span the dividing plane either by cutting the object along the dividing plane or storing it higher up in the BSP. If we split the object, then we will need to compute a new "event point" list for each half for each potential plane normal.

16.6 Occlusion Culling Techniques

Tree structures are effective at culling the data set in logarithmic time. However, using standard tree traversals, we only are able to cull nodes known to be out of the view frustum. We do not get any culling based on occlusion. In this section, we present two techniques that can be used to perform occlusion culling — potentially visible sets and portal rendering. Both techniques are usually used in conjunction with some sort of space partitioning technique, and the two can be used together.

In general, occlusion techniques work best in indoor environments where walls completely obscure the view of what is outside the room you are in.

16.6.1 Potentially Visible Sets

It is very difficult to determine which objects occlude which other objects at run time. However, there is a vast resource of processing power that we have available — preprocessing time. Instead of trying to determine which objects occlude which other objects in real time, why don't we try to do it offline in advance? We store the results of these tests for use in real time. This is the idea of *potentially visible sets*, or PVSs.

The basic idea is this. For each node in our world, we determine what could *potentially* be visible from anywhere in that node. By "node" we mean grid cell, quadtree node, or BSP node — whichever space partitioning system is used. By "what is visible" we could mean which other nodes are potentially visible and possibly even which objects are visible. The PVS for a node is the list of *all* other nodes or objects that are visible from *any* point within the node. We don't need to store the node itself (and the objects inside that node) in the PVS; those objects can be in the PVS implicitly.

How do we create the PVS for a node? Doing this efficiently is difficult. An offline process may take *hours* to determine the PVS for each node in the scene. As it turns out, creating a perfect PVS is very difficult because different objects are visible from different positions and orientations. One kludge that works in practice is to select various vantage points in the node, perhaps at regular intervals, and determine what is visible from those vantage points. How can we do this? One trick is to simply render the scene *without* the PVS. Instead of writing colors to the frame buffer, we can write object IDs, etc. Then we scan the frame buffer and figure out what is actually visible. This is a simple way to perform occlusion culling. It's slow, but it does work.

The system is not perfect because some node or object may be barely visible only from a very specific location, and we may never test quite near enough to that specific location. In practice, it works well enough. Other complications can arise, since not all vantage points within a node will be used for rendering — the space between the walls for example. BSP nodes may be infinite. Techniques for dealing with these complexities are outside the scope of this book.

16.6.2 Portal Techniques

Another technique for occlusion culling is to take advantage of the connectivity between "rooms." Examine Figure 16.10, which shows a floor plan of a typical apartment.

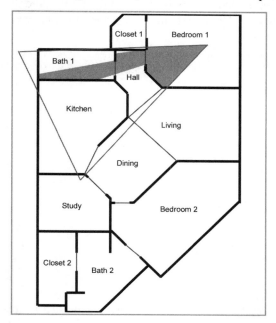

Figure 16.10: Apartment floor plan

Imagine that the viewer is standing in Bedroom 1 and looking out through the bedroom doorway. In Figure 16.10, the 3D view frustum has been outlined, and the area that is actually visible has been shaded. Notice that from this vantage point, the viewer can see Bedroom 1 (the room in which he or she is standing), the hallway, and a nearby bath. Notice that these rooms are visible *through the bedroom doorway*. Anything that is not visible through the doorway cannot be seen any other way. Figure 16.11 shows what the viewer would actually see.

Figure 16.11: The apartment viewed from the inside

In computer graphics, the doorways are known as *portals*. We have made the portals slightly visible in Figure 16.11. To take advantage of portal visibility, we must divide our world into volumes of space, known (not surprisingly) as *rooms*. We then make a *graph* out of the rooms. (If you don't remember what a graph is in computer science terms, the quick definition is that it's a set of *nodes* that are connected by *edges*.) In our graph, the nodes will represent the rooms, and the edges will be the portals (doorways). Figure 16.12 shows how we could turn the apartment from Figure 16.10 into a graph.

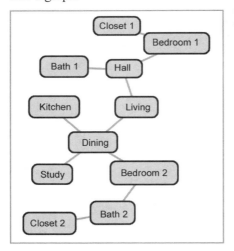

Figure 16.12: The apartment floor plan as a graph

Logically, a portal is an edge in the graph that connects two rooms. Geometrically, it is a polygon in 3D space that fits in between the rooms. When we store our world, we take special note of the 3D coordinates of the vertices of this polygon. Notice that some rooms have portals between them even though there isn't a real "door" in the apartment.

To render the scene using portal visibility, we first locate the room containing the viewpoint. Let's call this node V. Everything in V must be rendered. We then traverse the graph outward from V, rendering each node as it is visited, provided it is visible through the portals corresponding to the edges along the path to V. Likewise, we will only follow edges if the corresponding portal polygon is visible through the portals on the path so far. Let's see how this works for our earlier example.

We start by rendering node V, which in this case is Bedroom 1. We then examine the edges adjacent to V. In this case, there are two edges, one that leads into the hall and another that leads into the closet. Let's look at the doorway into the hall first. (We will use a depth-first graph traversal, so we will completely investigate the portion of the graph accessible through the hallway before returning to the closet. For now the closet is being "pushed onto the stack.") We take the polygon of the portal to the hall, clip it to the frustum and project it onto the screen, and take the 2D bounding box of the screen space coordinates. This is illustrated in Figure 16.13.

Figure 16.13: The bounding box of a portal polygon

For the rest of the traversal (except for the closet, which is still "on the stack"), anything that is to be rendered must fall inside this bounding box in screen space. On the other side of this edge is the hallway. We take the bounding volume of the hallway, project it onto screen space, and check if it overlaps the box of the doorway. Yes, it does, so we render the hall.

From the hall, there are two adjacent portals (not counting the one we came from). One goes into the living room, another into the bath. We project the portal polygon leading into the living room onto screen space. This projection does *not* overlap our bounding box for the doorway between Bedroom 1 and the hall. Thus, we do not follow the edge or traverse the graph into the living room.

Backing up to the hall, we check the doorway to the bath. That doorway *is* visible, and so we follow the edge to the bath node. This is shown in Figure 16.14.

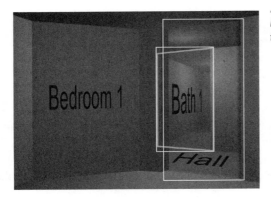

Figure 16.14: The second portal is visible through the first portal

Next we check the bounding volume of Bath 1. It is visible, and so we render the objects in Bath 1.

Since there are no edges adjacent to the bath, we are finished with that node, and we have also processed all edges adjacent to the hall. We now "pop the stack" all the way back up to return to the closet. (In so doing, we remove from consideration the portal into the hallway.) The portal polygon for the door into the closet is completely outside the view frustum. Thus, we do not follow the edge or traverse the graph into the closet node.

Our graph traversal is now complete, and we have rendered a correct scene. This is the basic idea behind portal visibility. Notice that we never even considered the living room, kitchen, dining room, or adjacent closet, even though those rooms are partially within the view frustum. Without occlusion culling, we would have had to render them.

There are several important items to note:

- Our example graph is a *tree*. In graph terms, this means that it does not contain *cycles*. Another way of saying this is that for any two nodes, there is only one path between the nodes. In other scenes, there may be some pairs of nodes for which there are multiple paths between them. Care must be taken to process these situations correctly.

- Visibility through multiple portals is *cumulative*. That is, if the path from a node to V traverses multiple edges (portals), then the node must be visible through *all* of the doorways. As we traverse an edge, we intersect the bounding box of the doorway with the bounding box of any previous doorway(s) to obtain the new screen space bounding box to be used for the remainder of the traversal in the branch.

- Portal visibility allows us to take advantage of doors that are closed. If a door is closed (and we can't see through it), then for purposes of visibility determination, the portal effectively does not exist, and we can ignore the corresponding edge in the graph. Thus, we can dynamically cull rooms on the other side of the door, depending on the current state of the door on any given frame.

Chapter 17
Afterword

You have reached the end of the book. Where do you go from here? Well, if you've stayed with us up to this point, then you probably understand enough to get started with some real code, and you're probably itching to put all this new knowledge to work, right? We've found that the best way to learn is by doing. So don't just sit there, start writing code!

Of course, it's sometimes hard to begin coding from scratch, and examples are always nice. Unfortunately, there was not room in this book for a complete working demo. However, on the companion web page, gamemath.com, we have prepared a small graphics demo using the methodologies and code samples from this book. Like the rest of our code, we have taken care to provide adequate comments and to *not* do anything "funky" that might cause you to get side-tracked from the meat of the material. Even if you want to write your own code from scratch, looking at this code may help you get some ideas.

As this book is an "introductory" book, you will undoubtedly want to expand in various directions. Of course, there are *many* books and online resources, many of which are listed at gamemath.com. However, the amount of information can be overwhelming. Therefore, we have picked a few books for suggested reading.

For a survey of graphic techniques, *Real-Time Rendering* [17] by Möller and Haines is a must-have. This book discusses graphics focusing on real-time rendering, updated to reflect issues for today's hardware. The "old school" standby, which is now a little dated but still a good reference, is *Computer Graphics: Principles and Practice* [8]. Another book that focuses on advanced graphics techniques is *Advanced Animation and Rendering Techniques* [23].

For a "toolkit" of graphics and geometry tricks and techniques, the entire *Graphics Gems* series is also an excellent choice. A newer series, *Game Programming Gems*, also has many tips by numerous contributors from the industry.

Appendix A

Math Review

This appendix presents a brief review of some key mathematical concepts. Other information can be found on the web page for this book, `gamemath.com`.

Summation Notation

Summation notation is a shorthand way to write a sum. Summation notation is like a mathematical `for` loop. Let's look at an example:

$$\sum_{i=1}^{6} a_i = a_1 + a_2 + a_3 + a_4 + a_5 + a_6$$

The variable *i* is known as the *index* variable. The expressions above and below the summation symbol tell us how many times to execute our "loop" and what values to use for *i* during each iteration. In this case, *i* will count from 1...6. To "execute" our loop, we iterate the index through all the values specified by the control conditions. For each iteration, we evaluate the expression on the right-hand side of the summation notation (substituting in the appropriate value for the index variable), and add this to our sum.

Summation notation is also known as *sigma* notation because that cool-looking symbol that looks like a Z is the uppercase version of the Greek letter sigma.

Angles, Degrees, and Radians

An angle measures an amount of rotation in the plane. Variables representing angles are often assigned to the Greek letter θ (theta, pronounced "THAY-tuh"). The most important units of measure used to specify angles are degrees (°) and radians (rad).

Degrees are an arbitrary unit convenient for us to use, where 360° represents a complete revolution.

Radians are a unit of measure based on the properties of a circle. When we specify the angle between two rays in radians, we are actually measuring the length of the intercepted arc of a unit circle, as shown in the following illustration:

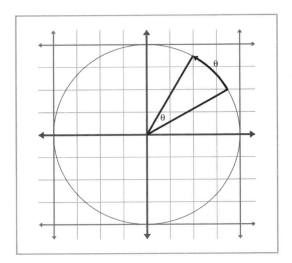

The circumference of a unit circle is 2π, with π approximately equal to 3.14159265359. Therefore, 2π radians represents a complete revolution.

Since $360° = 2\pi$ rad, $180° = \pi$ rad. To convert an angle from radians to degrees, we multiply by $180/\pi$ (57.29578) and to convert an angle from degrees to radians, we multiply by $\pi/180$ (0.01745329):

$$1 \text{ rad} = \left(\tfrac{180}{\pi}\right)° \approx 57.29578° \qquad 1° = \left(\tfrac{\pi}{180}\right) \text{ rad} \approx 0.01745329 \text{ rad}$$

The table on page 413 lists several angles in both degree and radian format.

In this book, specific angle measurements will usually be given in degrees, since degrees are easier for us to work with. In our code, however, we will typically store angles in radians, since the standard C functions accept angles in radians.

Trig Functions

In 2D, if we begin with a unit ray pointing toward $+x$, and then rotate this ray counterclockwise by an angle θ, we have drawn the angle in the *standard position*. This is illustrated on the following page:

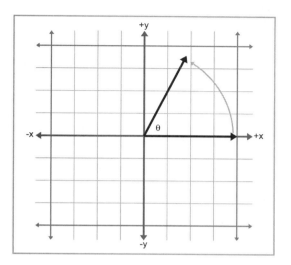

The values of x and y, the coordinates of the endpoint of the ray, have special properties, and are so significant mathematically that they have been assigned special functions, known as the cosine and sine of the angle:

$$x = \cos \theta$$
$$y = \sin \theta$$

You can easily remember which is which because they are in alphabetical order; x comes before y, and cos comes before sin.

We also define several other basic trig functions which are related to the sine and cosine of the angle, known as the *tangent*, *secant*, *cosecant*, and *cotangent*:

$$\tan \theta = \frac{\sin \theta}{\cos \theta}$$
$$\sec \theta = \frac{1}{\cos \theta}$$
$$\csc \theta = \frac{1}{\sin \theta}$$
$$\cot \theta = \frac{1}{\tan \theta} = \frac{\cos \theta}{\sin \theta}$$

If we form a right triangle using the rotated ray as the hypotenuse, we see that x and y give the lengths of the adjacent and opposite legs of the triangle, respectively. (Again, the terms *opposite* and *adjacent* are conveniently in alphabetical order.) Let the variables *hyp*, *adj*, and *opp* stand for the lengths of the hypotenuse, adjacent leg, and opposite leg, respectively:

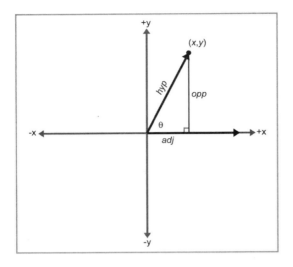

The primary trig functions are defined by the following ratios:

$$\cos \theta = \frac{adj}{hyp} \qquad \sec \theta = \frac{hyp}{adj}$$

$$\sin \theta = \frac{opp}{hyp} \qquad \csc \theta = \frac{hyp}{opp}$$

$$\tan \theta = \frac{opp}{adj} \qquad \cot \theta = \frac{adj}{opp}$$

Because of the properties of similar triangles, the above equations apply even when the hypotenuse is not of unit length. However, they do not apply when θ is obtuse, since we cannot form a right triangle with an obtuse interior angle. We can generalize by showing the angle in standard position and allowing the rotated ray to be of any length r and then expressing the ratios using x, y, and r:

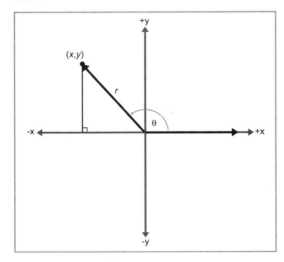

$$\cos \theta = \frac{x}{r} \qquad \sec \theta = \frac{r}{x}$$

$$\sin \theta = \frac{y}{r} \qquad \csc \theta = \frac{r}{y}$$

$$\tan \theta = \frac{y}{x} \qquad \cot \theta = \frac{x}{y}$$

The table below shows several different angles, expressed in degrees and radians, and the values of their principal trig functions:

$\theta°$	θ rad	$\cos\theta$	$\sin\theta$	$\tan\theta$	$\sec\theta$	$\csc\theta$	$\cot\theta$
0	0	1	0	0	1	undefined	undefined
30	$\frac{\pi}{6} \approx 0.5236$	$\frac{\sqrt{3}}{2}$	$\frac{1}{2}$	$\frac{\sqrt{3}}{3}$	$\frac{2\sqrt{3}}{3}$	2	$\sqrt{3}$
45	$\frac{\pi}{4} \approx 0.7854$	$\frac{\sqrt{2}}{2}$	$\frac{\sqrt{2}}{2}$	1	$\sqrt{2}$	$\sqrt{2}$	1
60	$\frac{\pi}{3} \approx 1.0472$	$\frac{1}{2}$	$\frac{\sqrt{3}}{2}$	$\sqrt{3}$	2	$\frac{2\sqrt{3}}{3}$	$\frac{\sqrt{3}}{3}$
90	$\frac{\pi}{2} \approx 1.5708$	0	1	undefined	undefined	1	0
120	$\frac{2\pi}{3} \approx 2.0944$	$-\frac{1}{2}$	$\frac{\sqrt{3}}{2}$	$-\sqrt{3}$	-2	$\frac{2\sqrt{3}}{3}$	$-\frac{\sqrt{3}}{3}$
135	$\frac{3\pi}{4} \approx 2.3562$	$-\frac{\sqrt{2}}{2}$	$\frac{\sqrt{2}}{2}$	-1	$-\sqrt{2}$	$\sqrt{2}$	-1
150	$\frac{5\pi}{6} \approx 2.6180$	$-\frac{\sqrt{3}}{2}$	$\frac{1}{2}$	$-\frac{\sqrt{3}}{3}$	$-\frac{2\sqrt{3}}{3}$	2	$-\sqrt{3}$
180	$\pi \approx 3.1416$	-1	0	0	-1	undefined	undefined
210	$\frac{7\pi}{6} \approx 3.6652$	$-\frac{\sqrt{3}}{2}$	$-\frac{1}{2}$	$\frac{\sqrt{3}}{3}$	$-\frac{2\sqrt{3}}{3}$	-2	$-\sqrt{3}$
225	$\frac{5\pi}{4} \approx 3.9270$	$-\frac{\sqrt{2}}{2}$	$-\frac{\sqrt{2}}{2}$	1	$-\sqrt{2}$	$-\sqrt{2}$	-1
240	$\frac{4\pi}{3} \approx 4.1888$	$-\frac{1}{2}$	$-\frac{\sqrt{3}}{2}$	$\sqrt{3}$	-2	$-\frac{2\sqrt{3}}{3}$	$-\frac{\sqrt{3}}{3}$
270	$\frac{3\pi}{2} \approx 4.7124$	0	-1	undefined	undefined	-1	0
300	$\frac{5\pi}{3} \approx 5.2360$	$\frac{1}{2}$	$-\frac{\sqrt{3}}{2}$	$-\sqrt{3}$	2	$-\frac{2\sqrt{3}}{3}$	$-\frac{\sqrt{3}}{3}$
315	$\frac{7\pi}{4} \approx 5.4978$	$\frac{\sqrt{2}}{2}$	$-\frac{\sqrt{2}}{2}$	-1	$\sqrt{2}$	$-\sqrt{2}$	-1
330	$\frac{11\pi}{6} \approx 5.7596$	$\frac{\sqrt{3}}{2}$	$-\frac{1}{2}$	$-\frac{\sqrt{3}}{3}$	$\frac{2\sqrt{3}}{3}$	-2	$-\sqrt{3}$
360	$2\pi \approx 6.2832$	1	0	0	1	undefined	undefined

Trig Identities

Pythagorean identities:

$$\sin^2\theta + \cos^2\theta = 1$$
$$1 + \tan^2 = \sec^2\theta$$
$$1 + \cot^2 = \csc^2\theta$$
$$\sin(-\theta) = -\sin\theta$$
$$\cos(-\theta) = \cos\theta$$
$$\tan(-\theta) = -\tan\theta$$
$$\sin\left(\frac{\pi}{2} - \theta\right) = \cos\theta$$
$$\cos\left(\frac{\pi}{2} - \theta\right) = \sin\theta$$
$$\tan\left(\frac{\pi}{2} - \theta\right) = \cot\theta$$

Sum and difference identities:

$$\sin(x + y) = \sin x \cos y + \cos x \sin y$$
$$\sin(x - y) = \sin x \cos y - \cos x \sin y$$
$$\cos(x + y) = \cos x \cos y - \sin x \sin y$$
$$\cos(x - y) = \cos x \cos y + \sin x \sin y$$
$$\tan(x + y) = \frac{\tan x + \tan y}{1 - \tan x \tan y}$$
$$\tan(x - y) = \frac{\tan x - \tan y}{1 + \tan x \tan y}$$

Double angle formulas:

$$\sin 2\theta = 2 \sin \theta \cos \theta$$
$$\cos 2\theta = \cos^2 \theta - \sin^2 \theta = 2 \cos^2 \theta - 1 = 1 - 2 \sin^2 \theta$$
$$\tan 2\theta = \frac{2 \tan \theta}{1 - \tan^2 \theta}$$

Law of Sines and Law of Cosines

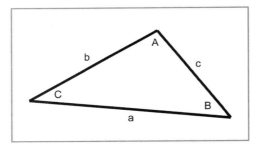

$$\frac{\sin A}{a} = \frac{\sin B}{b} = \frac{\sin C}{c}$$

$$a^2 = b^2 + c^2 - 2bc \cos A$$
$$b^2 = a^2 + c^2 - 2ac \cos B$$
$$c^2 = a^2 + b^2 - 2ab \cos C$$

Appendix B
References

[1] Arvo, James, "A Simple Method for Box-Sphere Intersection Testing," in *Graphics Gems*, Andrew S. Glassner (ed.), AP Professional, 1990.

[2] Badouel, Didier, "An Efficient Ray-Polygon Intersection," in *Graphics Gems*, Andrew S. Glassner (ed.), AP Professional, 1990.

[3] Dam, Erik B., Martin Koch, and Martin Lillholm, "Quaternions, Interpolation and Animation," Technical Report DIKU-TR-98/5, Department of Computer Science, University of Copenhagen, July 1998. `http://www.diku.dk/students/myth/quat.html`

[4] de Berg, M., M. van Kreveld, M. Overmars, and O. Schwarzkopf, *Computational Geometry — Algorithms and Applications*, Springer-Verlag, 1997.

[5] Ebert, David S., F. Kenton Musgrave, Darwyn Peachy, Ken Perlin, and Steven Worley, *Texturing and Modeling: A Procedural Approach*, second edition, AP Professional, 1998.

[6] Evans, F., S. Skiena, and A. Varshney, "Optimizing Triangle Strips for Fast Rendering," *Proceedings of the IEEE Visualization '96*, R. Yagel and G.M. Nielson (eds.), pp. 319-326, October 1996. `http://www.cs.sunysb.edu/~stripe/`

[7] Fisher, Frederick and Andrew Woo, "R·E versus N·H Specular Highlights," in *Graphics Gems IV*, Paul S. Heckbert (ed.), AP Professional, 1994.

[8] Foley, J.D., A. van Dam, S.K. Feiner, and J.H. Hughes, *Computer Graphics — Principles and Practice*, second edition, Addison-Wesley, 1990.

[9] Glassner, Andrew S., "Maintaining Winged-Edge Models," in *Graphics Gems II*, James Arvo (ed.), AP Professional, 1991.

[10] Glassner, Andrew S., "Building Vertex Normals from an Unstructured Polygon List," in *Graphics Gems IV*, Paul S. Heckbert (ed.), AP Professional, 1994.

[11] Goldman, Ronald, "Intersection of Three Planes," in *Graphics Gems*, Andrew S. Glassner (ed.), AP Professional, 1990.

[12] Goldman, Ronald, "Triangles," in *Graphics Gems*, Andrew S. Glassner (ed.), AP Professional, 1990.

[13] Hoppe, Hugues, "Progressive meshes," in *Computer Graphics (SIGGRAPH 1996 Proceedings)*, pp. 99-108. `http://research.microsoft.com/~hoppe/`

[14] Hoppe, Hugues, "Optimization of mesh locality for transparent vertex caching," in *Computer Graphics (SIGGRAPH 1999 Proceedings)*, pp. 269-276. `http://research.microsoft.com/~hoppe/`

[15] Hultquist, Jeff, "Intersection of a Ray with a Sphere," in *Graphics Gems*, Andrew S. Glassner (ed.), AP Professional, 1990.

[16] Lengyel, Eric, *Mathematics for 3D Game Programming and Computer Graphics*, Charles River Media, 2002.

[17] Möller, Tomas and Eric Haines, *Real-Time Rendering*, A K Peters, 1999.

[18] Mortenson, M.E., *Mathematics for Computer Graphics Applications*, second edition, Industrial Press, 1999.

[19] O'Rourke, Joseph, *Computational Geometry in C*, second edition, Cambridge University Press, 1994.

[20] Schorn, Peter and Fisher, Frederick, "Testing the Convexity of a Polygon," in *Graphics Gems IV*, Paul S. Heckbert (ed.), AP Professional, 1994.

[21] Shoemake, Ken, "Euler Angle Conversion," in *Graphics Gems IV*, Paul S. Heckbert (ed.), AP Professional, 1994.

[22] Shoemake, Ken, "Quaternions and 4×4 Matrices," in *Graphics Gems II*, James Arvo (ed.), AP Professional, 1991.

[23] Watt, Alan and Mark Watt, *Advanced Animation and Rendering Techniques*, ACM Press, 1992.

[24] Woo, Andrew, "Fast Ray-Box Intersection," in *Graphics Gems*, Andrew S. Glassner (ed.), AP Professional, 1990.

[25] Ulrich, Thatcher, "Loose Octrees," in *Game Programming Gems*, Mark DeLoura (ed.), Charles River Media, 2000.

Index

M

N

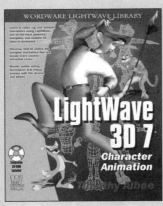

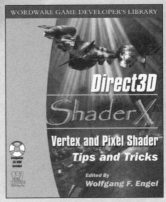

www.GameInstitute.com

A Superior Way to Learn Computer Game Development

The Game Institute provides a convenient, high-quality game development curriculum at a very affordable tuition. Our expert faculty has developed a series of courses designed to teach you fundamental and advanced game programming techniques so that you can design and develop your own computer games. Best of all, in our unique virtual classrooms you can interact with instructors and fellow students in ways that will ensure you get a firm grasp of the material. Whether you are a beginner or a game development professional, the Game Institute is the superior choice for your game development education.

Quality Courses at a Great Price

- ⬡ **Weekly Online Voice Lectures** delivered by your instructor with accompanying slides and other visuals.

- ⬡ **Downloadable Electronic Textbook** provides in-depth coverage of the entire curriculum with additional voice-overs from instructors.

- ⬡ **Student-Teacher Interaction** both live in weekly chat sessions and via message boards where you can post your questions and solutions to exercises.

- ⬡ **Downloadable Certificates** suitable for printing and framing indicate successful completion of your coursework.

- ⬡ **Source Code** and sample applications for study and integration into your own gaming projects.

"The leap in required knowledge from competent general-purpose coder to games coder has grown significantly. The Game Institute provides an enormous advantage with a focused curriculum and attention to detail."

—Tom Forsyth
Lead Developer
Muckyfoot Productions, Ltd.

3D Graphics Programming With Direct3D

Examines the premier 3D graphics programming API on the Microsoft Windows platform. Create a complete 3D game engine with animated characters, light maps, special effects, and more.

3D Graphics Programming With OpenGL

An excellent course for newcomers to 3D graphics programming. Also includes advanced topics like shadows, curved surfaces, environment mapping, particle systems, and more.

Advanced BSP/PVS/CSG Techniques

A strong understanding of spatial partitioning algorithms is important for 3D graphics programmers. Learn how to leverage the BSP tree data structure for fast visibility processing and collision detection as well as powerful CSG algorithms.

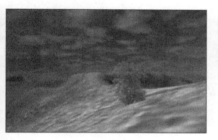

Real-Time 3D Terrain Rendering

Take your 3D engine into the great outdoors. This course takes a serious look at popular terrain generation and rendering algorithms including ROAM, Rottger, and Lindstrom.

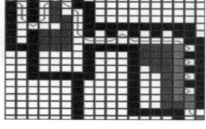

Path Finding Algorithms

Study the fundamental art of maneuver in 2D and 3D environments. Course covers the most popular academic algorithms in use today. Also includes an in-depth look at the venerable A*.

Network Game Programming With DirectPlay

Microsoft DirectPlay takes your games online quickly. Course includes coverage of basic networking, lobbies, matchmaking and session management.

MORE COURSES AVAILABLE AT

www.GameInstitute.com

nVSDK

developer.nvidia.com